Betrayed

STUDIES IN CANADIAN MILITARY HISTORY

The Canadian War Museum, Canada's national museum of military history, has a threefold mandate: to remember, to preserve, and to educate. It does so through an interlocking and mutually supporting combination of exhibitions, public programs, and electronic outreach. Military history, military historical scholarship, and the ways in which Canadians see and understand themselves have always been closely intertwined. Studies in Canadian Military History builds on a record of success in forging those links by regular and innovative contributions based on the best modern scholarship. Published by UBC Press in association with the Museum, the series especially encourages the work of new generations of scholars and the investigation of important gaps in the existing historiography, pursuits not always well served by traditional sources of academic support. The results produced feed immediately into future exhibitions, programs, and outreach efforts by the Canadian War Museum. It is a modest goal that they feed into a deeper understanding of our nation's common past as well.

1 John Griffith Armstrong, *The Halifax Explosion and the Royal Canadian Navy: Inquiry and Intrigue*
2 Andrew Richter, *Avoiding Armageddon: Canadian Military Strategy and Nuclear Weapons, 1950-63*
3 William Johnston, *A War of Patrols: Canadian Army Operations in Korea*
4 Julian Gwyn, *Frigates and Foremasts: The North American Squadron in Nova Scotia Waters, 1745-1815*
5 Jeffrey A. Keshen, *Saints, Sinners, and Soldiers: Canada's Second World War*
6 Desmond Morton, *Fight or Pay: Soldiers' Families in the Great War*
7 Douglas E. Delaney, *The Soldiers' General: Bert Hoffmeister at War*
8 Michael Whitby, ed., *Commanding Canadians: The Second World War Diaries of A.F.C. Layard*
9 Martin Auger, *Prisoners of the Home Front: German POWs and "Enemy Aliens" in Southern Quebec, 1940-46*
10 Tim Cook, *Clio's Warriors: Canadian Historians and the Writing of the World Wars*
11 Serge Marc Durflinger, *Fighting from Home: The Second World War in Verdun, Quebec*
12 Richard O. Mayne, *Betrayed: Scandal, Politics, and Canadian Naval Leadership*
13 P. Whitney Lackenbauer, *Battle Grounds: The Canadian Military and Aboriginal Lands*

Betrayed: Scandal, Politics, and Canadian Naval Leadership

Richard O. Mayne

UBCPress · Vancouver · Toronto

© UBC Press 2006

All rights reserved. No part of this publication may be reproduced, stored in a retrieval system, or transmitted, in any form or by any means, without prior written permission of the publisher, or, in Canada, in the case of photocopying or other reprographic copying, a licence from Access Copyright (Canadian Copyright Licensing Agency), www.accesscopyright.ca.

15 14 13 12 11 10 09 08 07 06   5 4 3 2 1

Printed in Canada on ancient-forest-free paper (100% post-consumer recycled) that is processed chlorine- and acid-free, with vegetable-based inks.

Library and Archives Canada Cataloguing in Publication

Mayne, Richard O. (Richard Oliver), 1971-
    Betrayed : scandal, politics, and Canadian naval leadership / Richard O. Mayne.

(Studies in Canadian military history, ISSN 1499-6251)
Includes bibliographical references and index.
ISBN 978-0-7748-1295-5 (bound); 978-0-7748-1296-2 (pbk.)

    1. Nelles, Percy Walker, 1892-1951 – Military leadership. 2. Admirals – Dismissal of – Canada – History – 20th century. 3. Canada. Royal Canadian Navy – Reserves – Political activity – History – 20th century. 4. Civil-military relations – Canada – History – 20th century. 5. World War, 1939-1945 – Naval operations, Canadian. I. Title. II. Series.

V64.C32N45 2006   359.3'3041097109044   C2006-903947-X

Canadä

UBC Press gratefully acknowledges the financial support for our publishing program of the Government of Canada through the Book Publishing Industry Development Program (BPIDP), and of the Canada Council for the Arts, and the British Columbia Arts Council.

This book has been published with the help of a grant from the Canadian Federation for the Humanities and Social Sciences, through the Aid to Scholarly Publications Programme, using funds provided by the Social Sciences and Humanities Research Council of Canada.

UBC Press
The University of British Columbia
2029 West Mall
Vancouver, BC V6T 1Z2
604-822-5959 / Fax: 604-822-6083
www.ubcpress.ca

To my Mom and Dad, for their love and support

Contents

Illustrations / ix

Acknowledgments / xi

Introduction: The Game and Its Players / 3

1 Confused Seas / 12

2 Equal Privileges for Greater Sacrifices / 42

3 The Strange Interpretation / 67

4 Trying to Keep Afloat / 93

5 Informers, Collaborators, and Promise Breakers / 120

6 A Loaded Investigation / 153

7 Covering Up the Conspiracy / 180

Afterword: Game's End and the Final Score / 208

Appendix A: Senior Appointments: Royal Canadian Navy, 1939-45 / 220

Appendix B: Naval Service Headquarters Organizational Charts / 225

Appendix C: Official and Unofficial Command Arrangements, 1942-43 / 227

Notes / 228

Bibliography / 261

Index / 267

Illustrations

8 Cross section of a corvette. DHH 84/8
13 Angus L. Macdonald, minister of national defence for naval services in William Lyon Mackenzie King's Cabinet. DHH 81/520/1000, BOX 148, FILE 29
14 Percy W. Nelles. YOUSEF KARSH PHOTOGRAPHER, LAC PA-206626
19 Q 052, the fairmile commanded by Lieutenant Commander Andrew Dyas MacLean for a short period in late 1941. DND O-1601
21 Type IXC U-boat surrendering to Canadian forces. DHH, RU (U-889)
23 Andrew MacLean dining onboard the Q 052 with one of his ship's officers. LAC PA-105646
25 The distinctive intertwined, straight, and wavy stripes of the Royal Canadian Naval Reserve, the Royal Canadian Navy, and the Royal Canadian Naval Volunteer Reserve. DHH 81/520/PHOTOGRAPHIC FILE, AND COURTESY CANADIAN MILITARY POLICE VIRTUAL MUSEUM
33 HMCS *Amherst*, Lieutenant Commander Louis Audette's ship. DHH 81/520/8000, BOX 179, FILE 11
34 J.J. Connolly and Captain Eric Brand, RN, on the last leg of their October 1942 trip to the Maritimes. H.H. BLACK PHOTOGRAPHER, LAC PA-105967
37 Ice-coated corvette. DHH 81/520/1000, BOX 142 FILE 4
44 Naval Board meeting for the first time, February 1942. LAC PA-180379
53 Andrew MacLean's last command, HMCS *Lynx*. DHH, RL (LYNX)
65 Algerine class minesweeper, HMCS *New Liskeard*. DHH 81/520/1000, BOX 141, FILE 27
69 The early 123 asdic. DHH 91/481
75 Commodore G.W.G. "Shrimp" Simpson, RN. F.R. KEMP PHOTOGRAPHER, LAC PA-161259
90 William Strange, 1944. DHH 81/520/1000, BOX 148, FILE 29
123 Rear Admiral George C. Jones. DHH, BIOG J (GC JONES)
126 The commanding officer of HMCS *Restigouche*, Commander H.N. Lay, explains the workings of his ship's .50 calibre anti-aircraft guns to the naval minister while Nelles looks on. LAC PA-104272
136 The depth charge, one of the corvette's primary weapons. DHH 81/520/1000, BOX 141, FILE 23
137 A gun crew operating a 4-inch gun, the corvette's primary weapon against surfaced submarines. DHH 81/520/1000, BOX 141, FILE 16

138 The .50-calibre gun used on Canadian corvettes. DHH 81/520/1000, BOX 141, FILE 16
139 The hedgehog projectile. LAC PA-112918
145 Vice Admiral Percy W. Nelles, RCN, stands back and watches manoeuvres from the bridge of the fairmile Q 069. DHH 2001/11, FILE 1
155 The crew's mess of a corvette reveals the confined conditions on board as the hammocks slung above crowd sailors who are cleaning up after a meal. DHH 81/520/1000, BOX 141, FILE 27
156 Sea conditions on the Atlantic. DHH 84/8
185 The boarding party from HMCS *Chilliwack* on 6 March 1944 alongside the battle-scarred U-744. DHH, 81/520/1000, BOX 155, FILE 15
204 Barry O'Brien's ship, HMCS *Snowberry*, providing escort for a convoy. DHH 81/520/8000, BOX 203, FILE 10
212 Vice Admiral George C. Jones, RCN, proceeds to sea with the naval minister, Angus L. Macdonald. DHH 81/520/1000, BOX 150, FILE 20

Acknowledgments

There are many people whose encouragement and support made this book possible. Perhaps it is best to start in the fall of 1996 when it all began. At that time I met Dr. Barry Gough, who became my thesis advisor and mentor at Wilfrid Laurier University. While this book has changed considerably from the original thesis, Barry's careful guidance and advice was instrumental in my development as a historian. Dr. David Monod and Terry Copp, also professors at Laurier, were an equally important part of this process, and for that they have my eternal thanks.

The book truly took form while I was writing a series of narratives on the politics of naval expansion for the Second World War Official History Naval Team at the Directorate of History and Heritage. Michael Whitby, my boss and friend, deserves the lion's share of the credit for my converting these narratives into a book. Mike was also an incredible sounding board for ideas, usually worked out at the local pub, as well as a source of constant encouragement. Bob Caldwell, a colleague at the directorate, requires special recognition for many insightful talks and advice. There was Master Corporal Justin Pike, who rendered invaluable assistance with the photographs for this book, and Warren Sinclair, whose ability to find missing and recatalogued files makes him an excellent naval archivist. Dr. Stephen Harris went well beyond the call of his duties as chief historian in reading and editing the manuscript not just once but three times. Like Steve, Dr. Richard Gimblett gave the manuscript a thorough "going over" and provided many useful suggestions. Other scholars who contributed in one way or another to the completion of this book include Dr. Allan English (my current PhD advisor at Queen's University), Jan Drent, Dr. Roger Sarty, Dr. W.A.B. Douglas, Dr. Marc Milner, Dr. Isabel Campbell, and Dr. Serge Bernier.

Aside from the historians, I would like to thank the directorate's librarian, Madeleine LaFleur-Lemire, for tracking down so many obscure references. Similarly, I am extremely grateful for the kindness, patience, and helpfulness of the staffs at Library and Archives Canada, Nova Scotia Archives and Records Management, Maritime Command Museum (Halifax, Nova Scotia), and the Queen's University Archives. The staffs at the international institutions I accessed, such as the National Archives (Kew, England), National Maritime Museum (Greenwich, England), and the National Archives (Washington, DC), were also impressive.

There were a number of veterans, or family members of veterans, who shared their experiences with me. Tony Griffin, a former RCNVR officer, maintained a lengthy correspondence and invited me into his home for fascinating talks on more than one occasion. The late John Band and St. Clair Balfour did the same, and their input, along with Tony's, shaped my understanding of life in the wartime reserves. Ed Connolly and J.M. Connolly greatly added to my knowledge of the executive assistant, John Joseph Connolly. So, too, did Gerald O'Brien, Kevin O'Brien Fehr, and Frances O'Brien, who provided me with insights on Barry O'Brien. Additionally, there was Charles W.J. Copelin, who shared information on his father. And finally, the late Debby Piers was kind enough to tell me, in a phone interview from his home in Nova Scotia, about his life at sea and in Londonderry.

There was, of course, a host of people who warrant the greatest credit because they lived with this book (and me, for that matter) almost on a day-to-day basis. Jamie Paxton, a long-time friend and fellow PhD candidate at Queen's, listened to much coffee shop talk on the book and offered particularly useful opinions. My mom, Helen; dad, Richard; brother, Michael; and sisters, Alyson and Susan, have always been a source of inspiration and have left me with the sense that anything is possible once one puts one's mind to it. But the greatest thanks must go to my wife, Tara. Having such a supportive spouse is the key to this book's completion – she not only kept me on track, but she also painstakingly listened to chapter after chapter as they were being written. No other man could consider himself so lucky.

Financially, this book has been published with the help of a grant from the Canadian Federation for the Humanities and Social Sciences, through the Aid to Scholarly Publications Programme, using funds provided by the Social Sciences and Humanities Research Council of Canada. I am grateful for this program and the assistance it provides to scholars. And finally, I would like to extend my appreciation to Canadian War Museum as well as the hard work of the editorial staff at the University of British Columbia Press, particularly Camilla Blakeley and Emily Andrew, for seeing this book through to publication, and to the anonymous readers whose suggestions for improvement were especially helpful.

Betrayed

Introduction: The Game and Its Players

On 14 January 1944, after almost ten years at the helm of the Royal Canadian Navy (RCN), Vice Admiral Percy Walker Nelles was replaced as the chief of the naval staff (CNS). With the public anxiously anticipating the invasion of Europe, Canadians had little reason to disbelieve the government's claim that the navy's top chief had given up his position in order to go to the United Kingdom to help plan and then supervise the RCN's participation in that historic event. It was all a pretence. Hidden in the overblown prose concocted by public relations professionals rested a cold hard truth: Nelles had, in fact, just been fired by the minister of national defence for naval services, Angus L. Macdonald. The victim of hidden agendas, Nelles was put out to pasture with a meaningless appointment, having lost a political game not knowing all the rules or, more importantly, most of the players.

History has not been kind to the admiral. With the notable exception of the official operational history of the RCN, *No Higher Purpose*, and the upcoming second volume, *A Blue Water Navy*, the consensus among naval historians is that Nelles was an unspectacular chief of the naval staff who "fell far too short in his failure to achieve the unachievable."[1] The task of managing the RCN's rapid expansion would have tested the mettle of the most skilled admiral from Canada's larger and more experienced Allies. Nevertheless, for most academics the Herculean tasks that faced Nelles did not excuse his poor performance as chief of the naval staff. In fact, one scholar even went as far as to claim that "Admiral Nelles removed or destroyed papers" in an attempt to hide his incompetence.[2] Such interpretations of Nelles are much too harsh and the charges of incompetence unjust.

Born into a middle-class Brantford, Ontario, family in 1892, Percy Nelles never seemed to have any doubt that his future was at sea. He joined the Fisheries Protection Service in 1908 at the age of sixteen, and when Wilfrid Laurier's Liberal government created the Canadian navy two years later it was a foregone conclusion that the young Nelles would be one of the first men to join. His career in that service was impressive, and his star rose quickly as a successful mixture of shore appointments, training courses, and postings on British warships put him on the fast track. Personally groomed by his predecessor, Commodore Walter Hose, RCN, Nelles was finally confirmed as CNS in July 1934.[3]

For the next half decade Nelles did well managing his tiny service while at the same time fighting for resources from a tight-fisted and Depression-riddled federal government. But nothing could have readied the CNS for the incredible rate at which the navy was going to expand during the Second World War. The RCN grew phenomenally and by war's end it would be some fifty times larger than in September 1939.[4] It was a chaotic time, but for many of those serving with Nelles during the earlier years there was little doubt that he was the right man for the job. As one flag officer later recalled,

> I would really like to enlarge on the importance of Admiral Nelles at the beginning of the war. He was a most excellent person to work for and we were all digging out for daylight about anything new that turned up, or anything new that had to be dealt with. If we needed his authority or his approval he could hoist in what it was one was saying at once – "Yes, carry on – sure, sure – make it so" was the way he used to put it, and off we went. This connected with all sorts of things from building ships to piers and jettys [sic], but I feel certain that any lesser man doubtful and unable to make up his mind, could have held up the works for months and months and we would not have got anywhere.[5]

Nelles was not an authoritarian leader. He avoided micromanaging the service and instead preferred to trust his officers, simply instructing them to "go to it chappie."[6] Such expressions capture his style quite nicely. A relatively small man with distinctive rounded glasses, Nelles' appearance never really matched his position as head of the navy. While capable of being curt with his subordinates when necessary, he seemed to depend on a relaxed leadership style, and for the most part it worked. The admiral's real problem was that he was – as one of his contemporaries so aptly put it – "a very fine, very straight fellow," and it was this lack of shrewdness and governmental acumen that left Nelles vulnerable to the politics of naval expansion.[7]

Historians have portrayed Nelles' removal as the dramatic conclusion to a fraught year in which many of the RCN's deficiencies were laid bare to the Canadian government. That the combination of rapid expansion and overtaxing operational commitments on the North Atlantic had created a situation where Canadian escorts were going to sea underequipped, and without the necessary training to effectively fight an antisubmarine war, is a well-established fact.[8] Rather, what needs to be re-examined is the widely held view that Macdonald fired Nelles because of these deficiencies. The true story is much more dramatic. A group of well-connected "hostilities only" reserve officers launched a concerted campaign against Nelles that gained momentum because it took place precisely at the moment when senior officers in the Royal Navy had particular reason to be concerned about the efficiency of the Canadian fleet.

The role of secondary figures – the so-called behind-the-scenes players – in shaping the history of the RCN has not received the attention in the literature that it deserves.[9] Nor has much work been done on the remarkable impact that the huge influx of reservists had on the wartime Canadian navy. This is not due to a lack of interest. Ever since this subfield of military history was resuscitated from obscurity in the mid-1980s, Canadian naval historians have busied themselves writing the much-needed, yet more generalized, accounts that have become its building blocks.[10] But exposing the individuals who were actually responsible for Nelles' removal requires a unique approach, one that looks beyond the ministers and admirals who normally stand as the most visible levels of the decision-making process. An investigation that digs much lower in the officer corps hierarchy is key to understanding the admiral's fate, as well as the politics of the navy's wartime expansion.

Senior officials often rely on subordinates to provide the data that allow them to make informed decisions. With that in mind, new methodological techniques propose that the only way to unravel the rationale behind certain decisions is to study the individuals who provide admirals and ministers with advice.[11] When it comes to analyzing Macdonald's decision to replace Nelles, therefore, this bottom-up approach suggests that the solution rests with an investigation not into the minister's motives but into the actions of the men who influenced him. Moreover, once this decision is traced to its lowest level in either the military hierarchy or governmental bureaucracy, this methodology can yield further results. But it does so only if one then follows the decision-making process upward to the minister.

The Nelles case clearly demonstrates the merit of this approach. In fact, only through this type of bottom-up examination does it become apparent how the chief of the naval staff fell victim to cells of complainers within the service who were willing to bypass normal channels so that their voices could be heard at the navy's highest political level. Beginning with a grassroots revolt in the spring of 1942, small networks of reserve lieutenants and lieutenant commanders grew into what one officer called "the underground movement" against Nelles.[12] Aside from being relatively junior, these officers were also members of the Royal Canadian Naval Volunteer Reserve (RCNVR). According to their own accounts, this put them at the disadvantage of occupying the bottom strata of the navy's hierarchy, and there was some truth to that view. Unlike the army or the air force, the RCN was divided into three categories of service: the RCNVR, whose members lacked professional marine experience; the Royal Canadian Naval Reserve (RCNR), which consisted of men with previous merchant marine experience; and the full-time permanent force, whose members had chosen the navy as a career. The true professionals came from the permanent force RCN, and the fact that the reserves were often treated as rank amateurs was something that many within these networks greatly resented. This rested at the heart of a larger battle of recognition, in which certain reserve networks demanded the same professional respect as was afforded to the regulars. The relations between the professional permanent force on the one hand and the civilians who volunteered to join the reserves for "hostilities only" on the other provide a unique look at questions of professionalism and social identity within the Canadian navy during one of the country's greatest emergencies. This story is particularly important because the conflicting assumptions and ambitions of these two groups had a tremendous impact on both naval and governmental policy.

The system of dividing the RCN into three branches was borrowed from the British model, yet the navy did have justification to distinguish its personnel in this fashion. Since wartime conditions would lead to a dramatic expansion in the force, the RCN needed a way to separate men who would be spending their lives in service from those who would not. In theory, this system would make the demobilization process easier and ensure that the career requirements of the regulars were not inhibited by the huge influx of reservists. There was much rationality to this thinking. The permanent force represented the core of the service, and the navy had no reason to unfairly lump the needs of those members' career development in with men who would return to the civilian professions once hostilities ended. Even the reservists remaining in the navy after 1945 would not be serving on a full-time basis. Instead, they readjusted to life as part-time sailors, which meant that they were only required to report for training to their local home unit on specified weeknights. Peacetime conditions make it obvious why it would be unfair to measure reservists on an equal footing with those serving each and every day in the regular force. During the war, reservists also served on a full-time basis, and that had the effect of blurring the distinction between them and the regulars. The need to get ships to sea forced the RCNRs and RCNVRs to perform the same tasks as the regulars, despite the difference in training. This is how one permanent force officer described the situation:

> Although courageous and colourful, [the Naval Reserve] was under-trained, poorly disciplined and, until late in the war not competent at its job. To my mind, the astonishing thing about it was that it functioned as well as it did, by trial and error and teamwork, inspired by the challenge of war ... The Canadian Army was more fortunate. It enjoyed a period of about three years in which to train and develop the form of discipline that it had inherited from the British. The result was a highly efficient force in which there was no significant difference between the permanent force professionals and the hostilities only volunteers. Had the navy had this good fortune, it would have done a much better job and much bad feeling and grief would have been avoided.[13]

Others in the permanent force expressed similar views, and it was this type of attitude that helped create the reserve networks that eventually toppled Nelles.

The men within these networks were bothered by their lack of standing within the navy. Having gone from being lawyers, journalists, and managers of industry, they suddenly found themselves in a "segregated" environment. Much of this segregation was based on the fact that RCNVR officers could be immediately identified by the wavy stripes on their sleeves, which distinguished them from their straight-stripe counterparts in the regular force. Moreover, the smaller escort ships – such as the corvettes, minesweepers, and fairmiles – were manned almost exclusively by the RCNVRs and RCNRs, which further isolated reservists from the regulars serving on the larger destroyers and fleet units. Putting "hostilities only" reservists on small escort ships that would be scrapped after the war made sense from a long-term operational point of view, but it had the effect of dividing the officer corps into two distinct communities. As former civilian professionals, some RCNVR officers found that the regulars would not listen to their advice (no matter what experience they had acquired at sea) simply because they were reservists. This treatment by the regulars led small groups of reserve officers with powerful social and political connections to develop networks that allowed them to circumvent normal military channels. Given that they were performing duties that were similar to the regulars, these men wanted the respect afforded to the professional navy, and they were ready to go directly to the minister's office to get it. In time, the desire for the reserves to be accepted as professionals developed into the political battle that pitted the minister's office against the navy's top brass.

It was not these reservists' willingness to buck the chain of command, but rather a crucial contact within the minister's office, that was the true source of their power. This contact was Macdonald's executive assistant, John Joseph Connolly, who, having become the linchpin between the minister and these networks, was the key player behind the admiral's downfall. At first glance, it might be difficult to accept that Macdonald's personal aide could have played such an important role. Connolly has often been treated as an errand runner, whose October 1943 investigation into the RCN's operational shortcomings managed to provide "the evidence Angus L. Macdonald was looking for" to relieve Nelles.[14] In reality, he was much more than just an assistant. He was also a watchdog responsible for protecting the minister's reputation, and to help with that task Connolly relied on these reserve networks to be his eyes and ears. Their purpose was to relay any problems within the fleet that could threaten the minister politically. It is in the study of Connolly's relationship with these networks where this book differs from other accounts, particularly since the availability of new sources makes it possible to finally identify how these reserve officers informed and influenced Connolly and how he, in turn, swayed the minister's decisions on their behalf.[15]

Over the past sixty years, the achievements and influence of this group of reserve officers in shaping the history of the RCN has remained largely undiscovered.

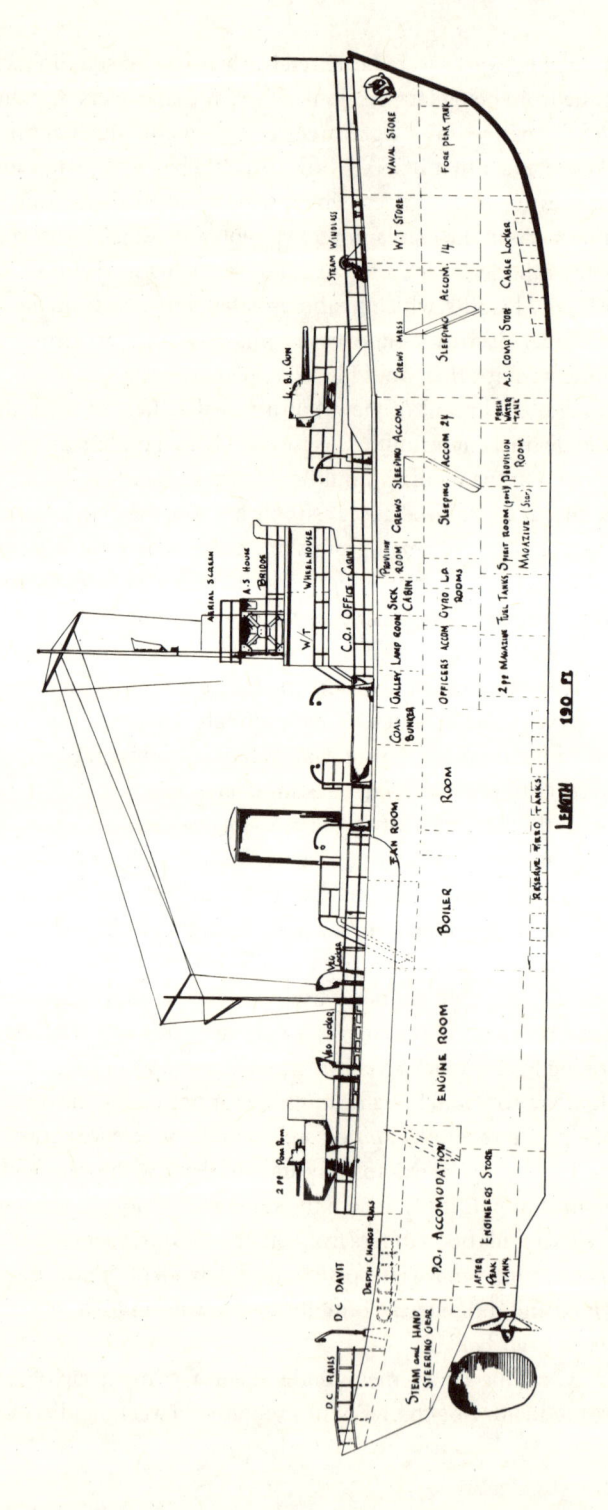

This cross section shows the anatomy of a corvette. Based on a civilian "whale-catcher," the corvette was a basic design that could be mass produced. Such numbers made it one of the most recognized antisubmarine platforms on the North Atlantic. DHH 84/8

One of the few scholars to uncover them was the navy's first official historian, Gilbert Norman Tucker. As his research notes make clear, Tucker did not consider a government-backed official history the proper forum to explore these reserve networks. Certainly, the fact that they came from influential Canadian families who enjoyed power in the public sphere gave good cause for concern, explaining why Tucker's team agreed that the "material is so contentious."[16] But that is precisely why a study of these networks is required. While enjoying social standing in their civilian life, these men were still relatively junior naval officers; yet by establishing links to the minister through the executive assistant, and exploiting their civilian status, they created power at a level in the military hierarchy where none was supposed to exist. Their activities were directly responsible for what was probably one of the worst breakdowns in the civil-military dialectic in the RCN's entire history.

In order to maintain discipline, military leaders rely on a strict chain of command that regulates the flow of information to their political masters. During the Second World War, the RCN was no different. Those serving either at sea or on shore reported to superiors who worked for the operational commanders on the coasts. In turn, these commanders would communicate with a group of senior officers at Naval Service Headquarters (NSHQ) in Ottawa who, by virtue of being members of the Naval Staff, were responsible for drafting policy. These policies were then sent to the Naval Board, where the RCN's highest-ranking officers would advise the minister on whether they should be accepted, rejected, or amended. However, by becoming a conduit for these networks, Connolly had endorsed an alternative chain of command, and that chain, it can be argued, caused Macdonald not only to lose faith in his top military advisor, but also to so shift his attitude toward the navy that it ultimately led to significant changes in Canadian naval policy.

Despite undermining Nelles' authority, a number of these networks truly believed that they were circumventing normal channels for the good of the service. The officers who believed that Naval Service Headquarters was not doing enough to modernize the RCN escort fleet had tried the chain of command, and in their opinion these efforts had proved fruitless. Totally convinced that their cause was just, these Canadian reservists had little compunction about going directly to the minister, a course of action they saw as the only option left. Nor did they stop there – a senior British flag officer and his staff were also persuaded to circumvent their own channels of communication. Playing a pivotal role in Nelles' firing, these foreign officers – who were members of Western Approaches Command (the British operational authority responsible for fighting the U-boat war in the Eastern Atlantic) – ignored the Admiralty (the British equivalent to Naval Service Headquarters) and instead turned to this particular network for results.[17] But while the modernization network was certainly one of the strongest cells within the RCN, it was by no means the only one. Other networks included a group that focused on the belief that the permanent force discriminated against reservists for their lack of experience, while another was convinced that morale was suffering because of prejudicial attitudes by the Royal Navy toward Canadians. There was, of course, overlap among these networks, with some members of one either supporting or rejecting the claims of others. And to top things off, a final set – consisting mostly of regular force officers – was able to take advantage of the chaos created by all the reserve cells to help their leader take over from Nelles as chief of the naval staff. This group was something of an anomaly: the product of a competitive permanent force community that encouraged officers to do whatever it took to advance their own careers. That mentality led to factionalism among the regulars, and as a result these particular officers, unlike the reservists, did not have a specific "cause" other than seeing Nelles replaced by their benefactor.

While the goals of the reserve networks varied considerably, there were commonalties among the groups themselves. Certainly the most pervasive characteristic was that they consisted of influential and educated professionals with strong links to Canada's social elite. Consequently, they were accustomed to a civilian environment in which problems were often discussed informally and in a more open and businesslike atmosphere. Placed in an unfamiliar organization structured on strict discipline, rules, and regulations, a few had trouble adjusting to the navy and chose to rely on personal connections to capture Connolly's attention. In some cases, these officers were Connolly's longstanding friends or had been fellow lawyers with him prior to his becoming an executive assistant, while in other cases his interest was peaked by prominent individuals currently serving in the reserves who knew exactly how to sway both politicians as well as their keepers. Despite having wildly divergent causes – with varying degrees of legitimacy – it is significant that all these networks employed the same methodology. With these groups bypassing normal channels by going directly to Macdonald, the Naval Staff began to lose credibility, particularly since the reserve networks exaggerated their specific complaints in the hopes that doing so would make it more likely that the minister would take notice. There was no way the professional head of the navy was going to survive after these groups consecutively hit Macdonald with issues that all had the same potential for public criticism and bad press. Using hyperbole may have helped capture the minister's attention, but this questionable tactic effectively politicized various operational deficiencies.

Thanks to these small yet vocal factions, Connolly and Macdonald took unsubstantiated claims seriously, such as the wild notion that the vast majority of naval reserve officers were on the verge of rebelling against the RCN's senior leadership. As ridiculous as the suggestion of mass mutiny might sound, both Connolly and Macdonald came to believe that the reserve navy was a powder keg of discontent.

Debatable rallying cries to the effect that the reserves deserved equal privileges with the regulars "for greater sacrifices" eventually received more than a sympathetic nod from Connolly and Macdonald.[18] In time, these words would translate into policy. That Macdonald accepted the advice of these networks over the senior staff clearly indicates that the minister and chief of the naval staff did not enjoy the type of healthy working relationship essential for the service to function effectively. Certainly there was little doubt that a communication gap existed between the two men when in November 1943 Macdonald accused Nelles of incompetence. Although Macdonald never revealed his sources of information, the minister charged that it was unacceptable that the chief of the naval staff had failed to tell him about issues affecting the navy's morale. Nelles flatly rejected this claim and countercharged that he had consistently tried to include Macdonald in the Naval Staff's proposed solutions. The chief of the naval staff was right, and explaining how the reserve networks managed to put the minister into a position in which the navy's top brass was falsely accused of withholding information is an essential part of this book.

The ability of the networks to manipulate the political process obviously spelled trouble for the unsuspecting chief of the naval staff. Under normal circumstances, the veracity of these grievances should have been filtered through the chain of command, but without that balancing influence both Connolly and Macdonald were flooded by unsubstantiated claims and allegations. While some were obviously accurate, others were not, and that gave Connolly a distorted interpretation of the navy and its problems. Trying to influence naval policy subsequently became a political game of survival, where unconfirmed criticisms were suddenly transformed into an artificial political crisis because of fears that they could cost the minister his Cabinet post if discovered by the public. These networks created a dysfunctional environment whereby Connolly engineered Nelles' removal as a political solution to protect the minister from potential scandal and embarrassment. The main purpose of this book, therefore, is to explore the role that these individuals and networks played in Nelles' downfall, and to clarify the impact they had on Canadian naval policy during the Second World War.

1
Confused Seas

When Vice Admiral Nelles stepped down as chief of the naval staff in early 1944, he had little reason to suspect that a quixotic reserve officer by the name of Andrew Dyas MacLean had played a large role in his downfall. The troublesome MacLean had been forced out of the navy himself in October 1942 and was now nothing more than a distant memory. Yet the network MacLean had established while in uniform had marked the beginning of Nelles' woes with the minister of national defence for naval services, Angus L. Macdonald. MacLean was frustrated that the permanent force never listened to his ideas because of their "discriminatory" attitude toward reserve officers, and was thus probably the first individual to establish channels of influence that effectively bypassed Nelles. Powerful political and public connections afforded MacLean the opportunity to open a direct dialogue with the minister, in which it was argued that reserve officers were tired of the regulars treating them as civilians in uniform and third-class citizens rather than equals. The fact that Connolly was asked to investigate not only their grievances but also charges that the senior chiefs were hiding a severe morale problem from Macdonald made MacLean and his followers a significant force in the navy's political landscape.

This embryonic campaign affected Connolly, who created another network with his friends in the naval reserves, whom he used as personal informants. This second network of reservists was not associated with MacLean, even though they were somewhat sympathetic to his cause. Their central complaint centred on the need to modernize the escort fleet. Morale among the reservists who manned the RCN's corvettes and minesweepers had plummeted, they argued, because their ships were not properly equipped to protect convoys and destroy U-boats.

The opinions of both these groups would eventually have tremendous consequences for Nelles. The reasons for their formation and their influence on Connolly and, ultimately, on Macdonald are crucial to our understanding of the Nelles case. No less important is whether the leaders of these networks were objective, disinterested men with legitimate grievances against the navy, or simply troublemakers whose motivation was based on hidden agendas and personal ambitions.

The leader of the first group of reservists was not an average officer. The nephew of John Bayne Maclean, the founder of *Maclean's* magazine, and the son of publishing magnate Hugh C. MacLean (the brothers could not agree on the proper spelling of their family's name), Andrew MacLean was a member of Canada's elite.[1]

Angus L. Macdonald, a former premier of Nova Scotia, was an experienced politician when he joined William Lyon Mackenzie King's Cabinet as the minister of national defence for naval services. Macdonald lost faith in his top advisor, Vice Admiral Percy W. Nelles, largely due to the efforts of small cliques of disgruntled reserve officers. DHH 81/520/1000, BOX 148, FILE 29

Being born to such a respected Toronto family afforded many opportunities. Certainly his education – Appleby College, Upper Canada College, and the University of Toronto – reflected his privileged roots. As a senior executive at Hugh C. MacLean Publishing, the young editor enjoyed status and influence within Toronto's business community. He also benefited from working as Prime Minister Richard Bennett's private secretary during the early 1930s, which naturally resulted in strong political ties to the Conservative Party of Canada.[2] Quite clearly, "Andy" MacLean was a powerful man whose opinions were both respected and followed, at least outside the Liberal Party of Canada.

MacLean also enjoyed power at the local naval reserve level during the interwar period. Having served with the Royal Navy during the First World War, MacLean advanced quickly after joining the RCNVR in 1927 and was given command of the

Perhaps one of the most recognized images of Percy W. Nelles, taken by renowned photographer Yousuf Karsh. For some he never looked the part of a chief of the naval staff, a conclusion that the naval minister also reached when he observed that Nelles did not have "the power, the personality [or] the respect of his officers." LAC PA-206626

local naval reserve division in Toronto, HMCS *York*, only three months later. MacLean had considerable independence at *York,* and that allowed him to run the unit more or less as he saw fit. Left largely on his own by his permanent force superiors, MacLean turned *York*'s wardroom into an elite gentleman's club where the sons of Toronto's rich and powerful would go for their military service. As one former officer recalled, York was seen "as an extension of the little big four private schools," which made it both "a very strange place, [and] very social."³ Other references to the little big four – Trinity, Ridley, St. Andrews, and Upper Canada College – or to the idea that York was a "University of Toronto/Rosedale/Royal [Canadian] Yacht Club, old boy net" reveal that education and status were used to exclude "unwanted elements" in a distinctive subcommunity that was operating outside the confines of regular naval life. For many it was a surreal and self-perpetuating environment: "The old Boy Net, particularly around Toronto, is an extraordinary thing. It's extraordinary anywhere, and it works because you wouldn't have been in it except for it."⁴

York was certainly not the only reserve division in which the wardroom served as an annex to the local yacht club or country club for the socially powerful and cosmopolitan elite. But it was probably the most exclusive reserve division within Canada. As the commanding officer of York, MacLean occupied the top slot in the unit's hierarchy. It was images of that status that were etched in his memory when he left the reserves in 1931 to devote all his time to serving Prime Minister Bennett. Things were much different when he was reactivated during the Second World War. Now MacLean faced an environment where neither his business, political, reserve, nor social status meant much to men who had spent their lives in the "real navy" – the regular RCN. They too had their own elitist attitudes, and it was the disparity between these two separate mentalities – one reserve, and the other permanent force – that would eventually collide with such force that it would cost Nelles his job.

The RCN had been neglected throughout the interwar years, and life in the tiny service had been tough.⁵ Despite low pay and limited opportunities for advancement, a cadre of loyal officers had nevertheless devoted themselves to a naval career. Beginning with their enrolment in the Royal Naval College of Canada, these men embarked on a long and arduous training process that eventually turned them into professional sailors. Having done so during such lean years only added to their sense of pride. In this community, officers earned advancement through a blend of sea time, staff positions, and years of service. Since the navy was small, competition among officers was often so fierce that they guarded both seniority and appointments with the utmost jealousy.

The onset of war in 1939 greatly disrupted this community, and it was hard for some regulars to take the reservists seriously. Most were fresh off civvy street, while others had been exposed to a maximum of two weeks' sea time during yearly pre-war training. Worse, volunteer reserve officers were easily identified by the intertwined gold braid ranks on their sleeves that differed from the straight stripes of their permanent force colleagues. Such distinctions apparently contributed to the sense of elitism among the regulars that, one former officer recalled, was based on a perception:

The majority [of reservists] knew nothing. There was great keenness and high-heartedness and so on, but absolute abysmal knowledge, lack of it, which bothered us like hell. [That] is one of the reasons why [we] straight stripers were so disliked, I expect, by the VRs. [From our perspective] we resented you, because you arrived there looking like naval officers with stripes on your sleeve, and it was patently obvious that you knew nothing about it ... This was bothersome to us who regarded ourselves as professionals; of course, we *were* professionals.[6]

Despite insufficient training and experience, reserve officers were often given ranks and positions of authority that it had taken the regulars years to achieve throughout the 1920s and 1930s. Undoubtedly, that was a difficult pill for some to swallow. Cutting corners for reserve officer training – while a necessary evil due to the emergency at sea – demeaned the profession.[7] The permanent force was glad to have the reserves but could not accept them as full members of the profession. Placing reservists like MacLean into this environment was bound to cause problems, since their first experience with regulars often led to bruised egos and injured pride.

What some described as their "favourite hobby" had suddenly become a full-time job; MacLean was not the only one who had difficulty bowing to the whims of men whose formal education had been obtained merely at the Royal Naval College of Canada.[8] One member of the group that complained about the state of the fleet's equipment, Lieutenant Commander Louis Audette, RCNVR, shed light on the problem: "As for many others, for me the transition from peaceable lawyer to belligerent sailor was not entirely smooth ... One of the contributory factors for these difficulties was the vast difference between my new leaders and my former leaders ... In civilian life, my leaders were basically men of education and of distinction. In the armed forces ... the leaders were men of almost no education."[9]

Unlike the permanent force's practice of using seniority as a measure of success, members of the particular reserve networks valued status as defined by educational standards and social standing. Mostly former lawyers, journalists, and businessmen, the individuals who followed MacLean (or, like Audette, who were concerned about the fleet's efficiency) possessed doubts about their permanent force superiors' ability to lead. As civilian professionals, they worried that the lack of university degrees among the regulars had, in Audette's words, left the navy "in the hands of a scantily educated and largely unimaginative group of officers who, nevertheless, clearly deemed themselves to be a very lofty elite."[10] That the regulars would not listen to reserve officers simply because they were reservists amounted to discrimination. This provided MacLean and his followers with all the justification they needed to take such matters directly to the minister. Ironically, their emphasis on education and status reveals that the motivation for bypassing Nelles and his officers was itself elitist. In its way, it was perhaps more insidious, for the disciples of this so-called crusade against the regulars consisted of a small yet socially and politically connected clique. Such networking had provided them with power and influence in their civilian lives, and they hoped to play some role in the military. That created a class of RCNVR officer aptly characterized by one reservist as the "undisciplined, free thinkers."[11]

There is little doubt that MacLean was cast from this mould. Certainly, his reactivation into the naval reserves during the summer of 1940 was a harbinger of things to come. MacLean, anxious to serve his country, and still on the list of retired officers liable for call-out in the event of hostilities, was bitterly disappointed when the navy did not contact him immediately on the outbreak of war in 1939. He broke regulations and applied to join the Royal Canadian Air Force, and when the navy ordered him to report for duty, he tried to use the Royal Canadian Air Force position as leverage. In what would become a common pattern in his dealings with the permanent force, MacLean overestimated his own importance to the service. Not surprisingly, snooty comments such as "the rank of Lieutenant Commander is not sufficiently attractive to induce me to resign my commission in the R.C.A.F." solicited stiff responses at headquarters, which included the possibility of charges, as well as the suggestion of "telling him to 'Go to Hell.'"[12] His impertinent demand to be made a commander prior to reactivation offended many staff officers. But Nelles believed that the simplest solution was to cancel the naval appointment and leave MacLean in the air force. There was no vindictiveness in the decision – the reality was that the navy could do without MacLean's services, and the chief of the naval staff was certainly not going to ignore regulations by negotiating with him. MacLean had been absent from active reserve duty for far too long. Making him a commander would have set a dangerous precedent and been grossly unfair to those who had served throughout the 1930s.

Nelles was in the right. But that was not how MacLean or his influential father, Hugh MacLean, interpreted events. Complaining to the postmaster general and MP for North York, W.P. Mulock, Hugh MacLean singled Nelles out and argued that the chief of the naval staff "bore a grudge" against his son because of a highly critical article that he had previously published on the navy. As Hugh MacLean wrote to Mulock, "It is a disgrace that the personal feelings of that Nelles (known on the Bermuda Station a few years ago as Lieut. 'Squirt' Nelles), should prevent him [Andrew MacLean] serving where he can be most effective."[13] Charges that his son was facing "persecution" from the RCN's highest-ranking officer were baseless and uninformed. No less a person than Nelles himself had originally insisted that MacLean be given a position in the navy at a time when others thought he was too old.[14] In fact, suggestions to Mulock that only a "mighty attractive offer" could entice MacLean from the Royal Canadian Air Force indicate that his father's influence peddling represented nothing more than an attempt to get his son what he wanted through political means.[15] The navy had little time for such tactics and made it clear that if MacLean were to serve in the RCN, it would be on their conditions, not his. As always, when pushing his luck too far, Andrew MacLean backed down and claimed that the entire affair was an unfortunate misunderstanding.

While this paved the way for his admission into the navy, MacLean's father was not finished with politicking. Placing his son's plight into a larger yet somewhat ambiguous context, Hugh MacLean wrote directly to naval minister Macdonald: "I'll be darned if I shall continue to stand idly by while the vicious treatment of volunteer officers continues on the present scale. I have faith in your ability to reform the Navy, and hope to see some evidence of apparent abuses rectified."[16] Exactly what this meant he did not explain, but the implications were all too clear. Unless his son was handled with care while serving in the navy, Hugh MacLean hinted that the family's media outlet and political connections would be used to make life extremely uncomfortable for Macdonald. That the minister understood the message was apparent from his conciliatory response. Acquiescing to such pressure was a grave mistake, as was his decision not to tell Nelles about this correspondence. This type of political intimidation gave Andrew MacLean a sense of power and fostered the belief that it was possible to operate above the chain of command. Like his father, he would rely on the ill-defined spectre of "abuses" toward the reserves as a means to gain access to the minister. MacLean's experience throughout his two years in the navy reveal that he was neither the victim of permanent force persecution nor the champion of repressed reservists. MacLean's campaign did not stem from a desire to right perceived injustices between the regulars and reserves but rather was a ploy to further his own naval ambitions.

The RCN gave MacLean every opportunity to prove his abilities. The evidence is overwhelming. After spending an unsuccessful year as a Canadian officer on loan to the Royal Navy, MacLean reported to Rear Admiral G.C. Jones, commanding officer Atlantic coast, for duty with the class of small and lightly armed submarine chasers known as fairmiles.[17] Despite word from the United Kingdom that MacLean was a renegade with a penchant for snubbing superiors, the RCN reassigned him to the Atlantic Command because of a desperate shortage of experienced officers. Accepting MacLean's claim that his First World War service on the motor launches had made him an expert, Jones gave him the title of senior officer fairmiles and a free hand in the training and administration of men and vessels. Despite the auspicious start, it was not long before the new senior officer started disobeying orders, proving that there was more truth than fiction in the tales that had dogged him from overseas.[18]

That MacLean's reputation had followed him back to Canada can be determined from instructions Captain E.R. Mainguy had provided prior to a commissioning ceremony for a number of fairmiles in Muskoka, Ontario. The orders were blunt. MacLean was merely accepting these vessels on Mainguy's authority as Captain (Destroyers) in Halifax; he was specifically told to speak neither with the public

The focus of Lieutenant Commander Andrew Dyas MacLean's passion, the 112-foot fairmiles were used for antisubmarine patrols in Canadian littoral waters. They contained a typical armament of 20 mm guns and depth charges with a crew of three officers and fourteen ratings. Pictured here is Q 052, which MacLean commanded for a short period in late 1941. DND O-1601

nor to the press at the ceremonies. Stressing that "some tact is desirable," Mainguy was obviously concerned whether MacLean could follow this mandate. Another officer was equally suspicious, scribbling a note on a draft of the order that MacLean's tact was "improbable."[19] The justification for this suspicion came two days later. MacLean could not keep his mouth shut, as a *Toronto Star* article reported: "The story of how these naval officers viewed their return to Canada as something to complain about comes from Lieut.-Com. Andrew MacLean."[20] Of course, MacLean claimed he had been misquoted. But he had obviously said something to make the journalist think that naval officers preferred to serve in the United Kingdom rather than under ineffective Canadian authorities.

Outraged by this innuendo, the director of technical division, Captain G.M. Hibbard, RCN, sent a terse memo to both Captain H.T.W. Grant, director of naval personnel (DNP), and the director of naval intelligence, Captain E. Brand. "Lt-Commander MacLean did not have any authority to act for the Department at this ceremony," Hibbard charged, in fact no duty other than "to stand by his vessel and take command." After a brief investigation, Brand discovered that too much information had been given to the press on the fairmiles and that these stories had generally been filed without the official censor's consultation. The source was almost always "due to LCdr MacLean."[21] That articles were appearing in the press without clearance was troubling, but the possibility that a Canadian naval officer was using the media for his own purposes was worse. Naval authorities feared that MacLean's attempt to drum up public support as a means to expedite the development of the fairmiles could cause problems for more important construction programs, such as the corvettes and minesweepers. And there was more. Having sailed to Toronto, MacLean was growing impatient with the time it was taking to complete the final additions to the fairmiles. He sent unauthorized signals to various manning depots at Halifax and Montreal requesting personnel for his ships, and the crews arrived too early, leaving the Toronto naval authorities scrambling to find accommodations. Nor was that all. MacLean disregarded sailing instructions throughout the journey down the St. Lawrence. Naval Service Headquarters finally caught up to MacLean in Halifax, at which point he was told that he had "incurred the displeasure of the Department."[22]

Barely three weeks had passed since MacLean had become senior officer fairmiles, and already many shared Grant's earlier assessment: "The Admiralty considered him unsuitable for a Naval Appointment. I am of the same opinion but there is as yet no conclusive proof."[23] While MacLean had made plenty of mistakes, Nelles gave him the benefit of the doubt. Belying the accusations, the chief of the naval staff chose not to release MacLean, trying instead to bring this troublesome officer into the fold through disciplinary procedures. While such leniency was typical of Nelles' leadership style, he had given MacLean too much credit. The reprimands had fallen on deaf ears. In fact, Naval Headquarters could do little to change MacLean's perception that he alone knew what was best for the fairmiles.

MacLean was infuriated that only four of the RCN's original fairmiles were operational by 1 February 1942.[24] Chalking this up as another example of the permanent force's inefficiency was all the justification needed to run the tiny flotilla his way. As the larger strategic picture clearly showed, his perceptions were misguided. The RCN was having trouble manning the last twenty corvettes from the 1940 shipbuilding program, which were desperately required in the North Atlantic. These transatlantic vessels were more valuable than ones built for coastal operations, and Naval Service Headquarters therefore instructed Jones to decommission all but four of the fairmiles temporarily so that their crews could be reassigned to corvettes and minesweepers.[25] The decision to man the corvettes was undoubtedly the right one, particularly since the RCN had incurred setbacks during the mid-ocean convoys SC 42 and SC 48 in September and October 1941. Moreover, the fairmiles would not be required until the spring because their assigned area, the St. Lawrence River, was still frozen over.[26] While Naval Service Headquarters had no obligation to explain this to MacLean, it nonetheless did so. But MacLean remained steadfast in his conviction that the regulars were a bunch of bunglers.

This close up of a Type IXC U-boat was the product of the U 889's surrender to Canadian forces at the end of the war. The Q 117 was one of several fairmiles that escorted the U 889 into St. John's. While providing invaluable work escorting inshore convoys, the RCN's fairmiles did not score any kills during the war. DHH, RU (U-889)

Lacking the ability to think strategically, MacLean cared only about his own small corner of the war and therefore greatly resented the attempt by higher authorities to strip it of its furnishings.[27]

At first MacLean's superiors were willing to ignore his myopic outlook, believing that his recalcitrance was based on a sense of duty to the fairmiles. Few doubted that MacLean was a fighter. In question over the winter of 1942 was whether he was directing his energy toward making the flotilla an effective fighting force or toward turning the fairmiles into his own personal empire. Although Jones had originally given him considerable leeway, MacLean never liked that most of his major initiatives had to pass through three levels of command (captain [D], commanding officer Atlantic coast, and finally Naval Service Headquarters) before a final decision was reached. Dealing with bureaucracies was nothing new to MacLean but he found the navy's administration particularly cumbersome. As frustrations grew, MacLean hatched a plot to use both his political connections and his media ties to gain more authority over the fairmiles.[28]

This came to a head when Macdonald faced questions in the House of Commons regarding the disposition of the fairmiles – precisely at the time when MacLean was complaining about the very same thing. The fact that these parliamentary inquiries had originated from the member for MacLean's home riding of Parkdale, Ontario, further suggests that the opening salvo had come from his political arsenal.[29] An anonymous editorial entitled "Fairmile Fuddle" published in

Boating Magazine (of which MacLean had been the editor), represented the second prong of MacLean's offensive. The piece disparaged the navy and contained details that only he would know. Comments that the top brass had attempted "to 'whitewash' the disgraceful handling of the Fairmile flotilla" were typical of a man who once admitted in his civilian life that he "was critical of those in public life [and] enjoyed writing editorials condemning those in high places."[30] The inclusion of secret details on the fairmiles constituted a serious breach of the Defence of Canada Regulations, and MacLean was fortunate that neither Macdonald nor his naval advisors were aware of the article. This was as far as his luck would carry him.

Changes on the East Coast throughout the spring of 1942 were occurring too quickly for MacLean to keep pace. With the opening of the Gulf to oceanic traffic fast approaching, Nelles informed the minister that the East Coast fairmiles would be divided into five flotillas of six ships each and based at Halifax, St. John's, Sydney, Botwood, and Gaspé.[31] MacLean was flabbergasted by this news, because this plan bore absolutely no resemblance to one he had submitted in September 1941. While arguing that Nelles' proposal was totally "impractical," he was dealt a second blow when Captain G.R. Miles, RCN, replaced Mainguy as the captain (D) in Halifax.[32] Unlike the genial and flexible Mainguy, Miles was the type of regular MacLean especially despised. A no-nonsense and temperamental man, Miles was a stickler for regulations and MacLean knew it. With the fate of his fairmile plans lying in the balance, the panic-stricken MacLean had no time to work around his new commander.

In early May 1942, MacLean approached Miles and suggested that the terms of reference as senior officer fairmiles were not sufficient. This was the first time that the two men had met, and Miles was struck by the duplicity of a request that seemed aggressive yet purposely unclear. Uncertain what he was being asked to do, the captain (D) told MacLean to put his proposals on paper – a move typical of Miles' caution. He was wise to be cautious, for MacLean's written response chronicled his ambition to turn Sydney, Nova Scotia, into an independent fairmile command that not only reported directly to Naval Service Headquarters in Ottawa but also had control over the St. Lawrence River. This plan was placing MacLean on a fast track to captain's rank, since these new responsibilities would have been comparable to the two rear admirals in charge of Halifax and St. John's. Having determined MacLean's true motivation, Miles was determined to stifle such arrogance. After telling Admiral Jones that he was going to take direct control of the flotilla, Miles then explained that such a course was necessary because "Lieutenant-Commander Maclean's efforts ... have produced almost no efficiency in the fairmiles under his charge." Remarkably, Miles displayed much restraint, since his final recommendation was not to get rid of MacLean, as expected, but to have him assume command of the depot ship, HMCS *Lynx*, along with one of the fairmile groups.[33]

Andrew MacLean (left) dining onboard the Q 052 with one of his ship's officers. It was MacLean's goal to turn the fairmiles into an independent command based out of Sydney, Nova Scotia, where they would be responsible for protecting the St. Lawrence River and gulf areas. LAC PA-105646

Following Miles' advice, Jones intended to abolish the position of senior officer fairmiles and replace it with a staff officer's appointment.[34] Effectively stripped of all duties, MacLean saw his world crashing down around him. Although he had picked a fight with the wrong officer, he was unwilling to concede defeat. In a last ditch effort, MacLean flooded captain (D)'s office with submissions on the fairmiles. Exactly what MacLean hoped to achieve with this letter-writing campaign is uncertain, but given the abrasive tone of these letters it was obvious that Miles' harsh words had not had the desired effect.[35] MacLean chose to rebel, and throughout May and June 1942 he tried to get other reservists to do the same. Claiming that his battle with Miles was yet another example of how regulars regarded reservists as the dregs of the navy, MacLean told his fairmile officers that they too would eventually bear the scars of permanent force discrimination. The only way to effect change, he preached to the small group of reservists who represented his core disciples, was to spread this gospel throughout the entire fleet. The results were disappointing. Typical of those who were not part of MacLean's campaign was the response of Lieutenant Commander A.G.S. Griffin, RCNVR: "MacLean had tried to enlist my support for his vendetta against the 'straight stripers' [but] ... all he ever got from me was boredom. Besides, I had a high regard for the RCN and the job they were doing in the face of such an enormous challenge."[36]

It is unlikely that MacLean ever had a substantial following, but such efforts were enough for his superiors to notice. Miles was fed up with this troublesome officer and submitted a performance report in mid-July that laid the basis for his dismissal:

> While holding the appointment of Senior Officer Fairmiles ... it became apparent that all was not well and steps were taken to correct matters[;] he failed to act on advice and neglected to carry out instructions given him. When called to account for his shortcomings, he deeply resented the criticism of his superiors, blamed this lack of co-operation for all his troubles, and attempted to spread this doctrine amongst the Fairmile officers ... It is difficult to suggest an appointment commensurate with his seniority in which he would be of real value to the service at the present time.

Providing a suitable epitaph for MacLean's naval ambitions, Jones endorsed Miles' appreciation by telling Naval Service Headquarters that "this officer is largely of nuisance value only."[37]

Sensing that his days were numbered, MacLean turned to an "old friend," who was also an Ontario Supreme Court justice, to arrange a private interview with Macdonald.[38] During this meeting, MacLean focused on his own feud with the permanent force, which, he argued, was "persecuting" him solely on the grounds that he was a reservist. Macdonald listened patiently. The minister was unprepared for what came next. MacLean had something to offer in exchange for a promise to block his removal from the navy. He was willing to expose a dangerous morale problem within the naval reserves, which the permanent force had purposely hidden from the minister. Macdonald was sceptical, believing that MacLean's offer to become an informant on reserve issues amounted to a bribe, but the allegations could not be ignored altogether.[39]

After returning to the East Coast, MacLean provided Macdonald with evidence: anonymous letters from reserve officers, who all complained about the way they had been treated by the regulars. The most compelling charge was that this "scandalous situation" was the product of "three distinct navies with different uniforms, regulations and pay, which is a source of confusion, friction and inefficiency which in time of war is inexcusable on any grounds. Among the volunteers, both RCNR and RCNVR there is much resentment that all the hard, dirty and dangerous jobs appear to be avoided by the officers of the Royal Canadian Navy, who are able to find themselves soft jobs in Ottawa or behind desks in the dockyards."[40]

For these particular reservists, the distinction between reserve and regular officers was not only "discriminatory," it also triggered the perception that the regulars could only be found in "safe shore postings" where "drinking ... pink gins" was reason enough to earn promotions and medals.[41] According to this view, the permanent force was unwilling to reward RCNVR officers although it was the reserves who were risking their lives against Germany's U-boats. "The sooner a move is made to bring the three branches together (RCN, RCNR, and RCNVR) with identical pay, rank markings (as now underway in the RN) and equity of service opportunity," one reservist claimed, "the better the Navy will be."[42] Simply put, the cornerstone of "segregation" rested in an officer's uniform, which, they argued, branded the RCNVR and RCNR with either wavy or intertwined braid on their sleeves. This allowed permanent force "straight stripers" to recognize reserve officers on sight and, the allegation went, to automatically assume the latter's lack of naval knowledge and incompetence. Worse yet, the regulars seemed to have more tolerance for the members of the merchant navy who, by virtue of this experience, were allowed to join the RCNR. They too were unfamiliar with military life, but unlike the RCNVR they at least had considerable sea time or even a master mariner's ticket. While the inequity that the distinctions caused were undoubtedly the main grievance of the officers who followed MacLean, it was by no means the only one.

One anonymous memo in particular listed the nine most common grouses offered by reserve officers. It clearly outlined how the navy could be reformed to alleviate the current friction. After repeating that the navy needed to abolish the distinctions between the three branches, the next four points dealt with officers being awarded various badges, pins, and clasps for achievements at sea. The sixth argued that all promotions should be based on merit without consideration for pre-war service, and that the promotion board should consist of an equal number of officers from the RCN, RCNR, and RCNVR. The remaining objections involved questions about which officers were entitled to serve ashore, commissioning from the lower deck, and the necessity for all officers to see their evaluation reports.[43] This list of demands was pivotal. At a broader level, it suggested that the RCN's caste system and feudal structure was foreign to the social norms of Canadian society and to the requirements and good health of a wartime "people's navy." Put

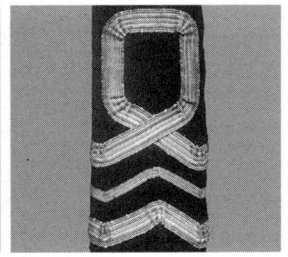

The root of much anxiety for Andrew MacLean and those who followed him: the distinctive intertwined, straight, and wavy stripes of the Royal Canadian Naval Reserve, the Royal Canadian Navy, and the Royal Canadian Naval Volunteer Reserve. DHH 81/520/
PHOTOGRAPHIC FILE AND CANADIAN MILITARY POLICE VIRTUAL MUSEUM

another way, having been overcome by culture shock, these particular reservists wanted the permanent force to adapt to the needs of the "citizen sailor."[44] In their view, the permanent force wielded too much power and their gripes signified an attempt to carve out some type of status within this hierarchy.

Whether these representations accurately depicted the permanent force and its established culture can be seriously questioned. Such suggestions nevertheless served MacLean well, as he tried to convince Macdonald that Connolly should investigate the charges. In fact, MacLean had already prepared the executive assistant, explaining that the "dissatisfaction is much more widespread and outspoken than I estimated and drastic action is essential at an early date if your Chief [Macdonald] is to maintain the respect which he now enjoys. The volunteers – the civilian sailors – look only to him for advice."[45] This reveals another reason why Macdonald was unwilling to disregard these complaints. Believing that MacLean was prone to overstatement, Connolly had already sought confirmation from reserve officers at Naval Service Headquarters. One officer wrote to Connolly, "you will remember that only a few days ago I stated that personnel wre [sic] being overlooked almost entirely and in a way that was creating a very unhappy and perhaps dangerous situation. The abuses must be corrected and the sooner the better."[46] Another reservist provided a similar message:

> The feeling that is developing between the permanent force officers and the volunteers is extremely serious and may before long assume really alarming proportions. There is of course a constant irritation by reason of the fact that RCN officers generally regard the volunteer as an interloper and a rank amateur (no matter what his proven abilities may be) – this is reflected in the unreasonable attitude exhibited by the RCN in refusing to permit any volunteer officers to hold important posts ... [which] is so grossly unfair as to seriously effect [sic] the morale of the whole volunteer organisation.[47]

Although these assertions corroborated MacLean's claims, they received a lukewarm response from Connolly, and the matter might have been left there had not MacLean and his supporters been willing to use political pressure to further their cause.[48] Mere days after Macdonald had received a warning from MacLean that "the rising discontent will soon be evident in the Press or in Parliament," six questions related to distinctions between the RCN, RCNR, and RCNVR were asked in the House of Commons. Neither Connolly nor Macdonald could afford to treat this as mere coincidence. A message had been sent and acted on – if Macdonald chose to ignore these complaints, he did so at his own peril.[49]

It was probably MacLean's personal connections that had the greatest impact on Macdonald. MacLean's former position as an editor was enough to make any politician anxious, but his strong ties to the official opposition and its current leader, R.B. Hanson, who was a personal friend, added most to Macdonald's apprehension.[50] Such links to the media and the Conservatives meant little to MacLean's naval bosses, however. To them he was simply a bad officer who repeatedly tried to bully superiors and consistently disregarded orders. Most of MacLean's seniors had tolerated his complaints and incessant bickering because the RCN had been desperately short of officers throughout the first half of the war. Almost two years later, the higher authorities had had enough, and from their perspective it would be easy to get rid of him.[51] This was a luxury that Macdonald did not share. MacLean's contacts and resources in the public sphere made him a political threat. Even if his evidence did not justify reforms, it was to be feared.

Connolly was not totally convinced of the accuracy of the reservists' claims. Nonetheless, it was troubling that all the memos had not only sent the same message but were also more balanced than MacLean's venom-filled submissions. Moreover, Connolly suspected that one of these anonymous informants was a Victoria Cross recipient from the First World War, Lieutenant Commander Roland Bourke, RCNVR.[52] This provided instant credibility to at least that officer's memo. Bourke was currently serving on the West Coast, and it worried the executive assistant that the gripes had spread right across the country. Connolly had now seen enough, and suggested to Macdonald that "some effort should be made to find a partial solution at least." In turn, Connolly told MacLean that Macdonald was sympathetic to the plight of the reservists and would address their concerns in the near future.[53] The executive assistant did not admit to MacLean that he had caught Macdonald's attention with the suggestion that the navy's top brass was hiding a problem from the minister. Yet while MacLean's allegations had led to a moment of pause, Macdonald also questioned his motives for attacking the senior staff.

MacLean's offer to act as the minister's personal informant on the East Coast was probably sincere. For example, in his political memoirs, MacLean had stated that any minister whose advisors were not providing information should have the power to "phone direct to [any] man that was able to give it accurately and quickly."[54] Nevertheless, Connolly and Macdonald were suspicious. Far too often MacLean seemed more interested in his own status and position. This they considered odd for someone who was portraying himself as the leader and martyr of this disaffected group. MacLean finally betrayed his own agenda when asking the minister to organize the fairmiles under a separate command:

> It is essential that the administration of Fairmiles be removed from Captain (D) Halifax (who has no use for the boats themselves or for the RCNVR) and set-up under a suitable and senior RCNVR officer. At present available in Canada there is no better officer than Lt. Cdr. MacLean who has served in such a capacity in England and in the Near East in both wars. Commander Hibbard of Captain D's staff here is entirely unsuitable and is largely responsible for the present confusion ... Sorry for the length

of this letter and for introducing my name in connection with the Fairmiles but let's start putting round pegs in round holes for a change. I did a good job on Fairmiles this winter and would be doing a better job if I had the right kind of gold rings on my sleeves. Why could not you suggest that I be sent for by NSHQ to discuss the whole Fairmile set-up?[55]

While such suggestions indicated that MacLean was preying on the insecurities of a relatively small number of reservists in what was possibly nothing more than a cover campaign to get what he wanted, Macdonald and Connolly were afraid to confront him. Using terms that would capture any politician's attention, MacLean also noted in the letter that "politically [the fairmiles] are dynamite and already it is common gossip in many yacht clubs that they are not being used to the best advantage by the Canadian navy." MacLean was essentially warning the minister that the campaign to fight permanent force discrimination would be made public unless his removal was blocked. Worse, as the summer progressed, MacLean's correspondence revealed that he was becoming more impulsive.[56]

Official assessments of MacLean's personality attest that Connolly and Macdonald had good reason to fear him. Their concern that he was both paranoid and narcissistic was well founded, especially since even those who knew him best thought he was a "very nice guy but very erratic."[57] Accordingly, Connolly had tremendous difficulty responding to MacLean's endless tirades that "the persecution of an officer by the most senior of the RCN [Nelles] demands drastic action by the Minister to ensure that it cannot effect [sic] other officers and the service as a whole."[58] Perhaps MacLean truly believed that his own situation and that of those who followed him were one and the same. Claims that Nelles was engaged in a juvenile vendetta were difficult to accept, and instead were chalked up to MacLean's egotism. The fact that a number of other reserve lieutenant commanders received excellent performance reports from their permanent force superiors further diminished his credibility. MacLean's own illustrations best show how his perception of events was skewed. In one instance, for example, MacLean told Connolly, "My leadership and technical knowledge is not desired here and I may have to return to England to find an outlet for my enthusiasm – and half the Fairmile officers and men will apply to come with me." In reality, the British would not have wanted him back, for as two Royal Navy admirals had previously reported, MacLean did not respond well to criticism and was prone to manipulate his surroundings for personal gain. In words reminiscent of Miles' assessment, one even argued that MacLean had "got into a comfortable habit of living and lost the art of sterling hard work." Yet another was so bothered by MacLean's disrespect that he rejoiced at having "helped to kick A.D. Maclean out of [the] RN."[59]

Ironically, had it not been for MacLean's erratic behaviour and political connections, navy minister Macdonald would probably have been willing to let him go without hesitation. But the minister simply could not ignore the anonymous memos that suggested there was some truth to MacLean's allegations. Macdonald's safest approach was to pacify MacLean. In the short term, this strategy worked, and MacLean found the minister's appeasing tone "most encouraging."[60] By this juncture, the question of MacLean's future in the naval reserves was being decided in the halls of the Naval Service Headquarters. That future was not expected to last much longer. Already the chief of naval personnel had recommended to both Macdonald and Nelles that, "if he is not willing to tender his resignation ... he should be discharged from the service."[61]

The minister was in a bind. While the navy would clearly be better off without MacLean, the very fact that he was in the service gave Macdonald ultimate leverage and control: MacLean could be charged under naval law if he went too far, privately or publicly, in his criticisms. Once freed from the bonds of military regulations, MacLean could wield his power in the public sphere in any manner he saw fit. On the other hand, if Macdonald overruled the Naval Staff's verdict, he would be risking his reputation with his chief naval advisors because it would show that any officers with public connections could intimidate him. In the end, the minister did the best he could in a difficult situation. First, it was decided that Connolly would travel to the East Coast and investigate the allegations. Second, the minister chose not to interfere when MacLean was asked to retire his commission in October 1942, and opted instead to deal with any possible political repercussions. And finally, Macdonald distanced himself from the Naval Staff's position, though never stating that his military advisors were wrong. As it turned out, this diplomatic solution worked, as MacLean agreed to retire his commission. Better yet, there was no reason at this time to punish the minister by taking the story either to the press or to Parliament. MacLean simply interpreted Macdonald's inability to help as an illustration of Nelles' and the Naval Staff's determination to get rid of him.[62] Unfortunately for Macdonald, these tactics worked only in the short term. A few weeks later, MacLean would return to haunt the minister with renewed threats to make public the complaints about the regular force's discrimination against the reserves.

Given MacLean's eccentric character, few were surprised that his association with the permanent force ended with such acrimony. Certainly, the fact that the navy promoted him to commander the day after his release left a bittersweet taste. They had approved the rank he demanded in 1940, knowing he would not be around to enjoy it. Although the Naval Staff was extending an olive branch for "long service," MacLean was unimpressed. He referred to the official press release on his retirement as his "obituary."[63] Perhaps the greatest irony was that Connolly left for the East Coast investigation on 20 October, which, as fate would have it, was the same day that MacLean's name was added to the navy's retired list.[64] One can question whether this was more than a mere coincidence, for MacLean's removal conveniently guaranteed that the quest to uncover the true situation between the regulars and reserves would no longer be marred by any personal ambitions.

Why Macdonald did not tell the chief of the naval staff about MacLean's complaints against the permanent force is a mystery. Nelles had never given the minister any reason not to trust him. Since the allegations had tarnished all the regulars with the same brush, perhaps Macdonald worried that it would be naïve to expect an honest appraisal from the highest-ranking permanent force officer of them all. It is also possible that Macdonald was simply unwilling to place too much faith in military men who, it could be assumed, either hid their own plans for the RCN or whitewashed problems to avoid any complications with their political masters. The task of investigating whether the reserves were on the verge of rebelling thus fell to Connolly.

This was a new role for the executive assistant. MacLean's interference had not only sparked the minister's curiosity but was also changing Connolly's responsibilities. Throughout the summer, the executive assistant's primary duty had been to protect the minister's reputation from the potential trouble MacLean's allegations could cause; that the minister emerged from the ordeal unscathed was a testament to Connolly's abilities as a protector. But with Connolly's investigation in the offing, he was now assuming the part of the minister's watchdog. It was the executive assistant's responsibility to observe the navy and discover whether Nelles and his staff were providing Macdonald with the information he needed. In a larger sense, this marked the beginning of a pattern whereby the minister would continually use Connolly rather than normal channels to unravel the truth behind these types of rumblings from the fleet. Macdonald's actions had bestowed power and influence on Connolly that went well beyond the norm for an executive assistant.

In many ways Connolly was well suited to this task. A compassionate and honest man, he was deeply concerned about the quality of life for the average sailor. With four diplomas hanging on his office wall – including a University of Notre Dame doctorate and a law degree from the University of Montreal – few could doubt his determination and intelligence. He also had a reputation for being naturally inquisitive, a quality that had earned the thirty-six-year-old lawyer a partnership at the firm of Clark, Macdonald, Connolly, Brocklesby, and Gorman – a particularly young age for such a position.[65] As far as Connolly was concerned, the only potential weakness in his investigation was that he might miss the nuances of naval life. After all, he had had no experience with the military prior to becoming the minister's assistant in the summer of 1941.

His solution was to have a naval officer accompany him to the Maritimes. However, choosing a suitable travelling companion presented a problem. He could not select a permanent force officer for fear that word of the trip would get back to Nelles. Likewise, it would be equally disastrous to take a reservist who was actually a MacLean sympathizer. Connolly's decision to ask Captain Eric Brand was undoubtedly the correct one. Information gathering was Brand's job. In his capacity as the director of naval intelligence and British naval attaché at Naval Service Headquarters, Brand regularly wrote classified reports to the Admiralty on Canadian officers, and that, Connolly assumed, ensured his impartiality.[66] Brand's working rapport with Connolly was excellent, and having become good friends since February 1942, the executive assistant knew he could count on the Naval Intelligence officer's discretion.[67]

Quipping that he wanted to show Connolly "how the poor lived," Brand met his obligation with much enthusiasm.[68] Despite having spent almost all of his time in Ottawa, it is likely that Connolly had at least some understanding of what was meant by "the poor." Certainly MacLean's account had painted a dreary picture of life in the fleet, and his campaign was not the only indication that there were morale problems at the RCN's Maritime bases. In fact, Macdonald had received information from "two very responsible citizens of Canada" in early June, suggesting that the "attitude of certain Naval Officers in the city, and their conduct" had turned Halifax into a hotbed of discontent. As the former premier of Nova Scotia – and hoping to return to that position after federal politics – Macdonald was troubled by reports that the citizenry were fed up with naval personnel drinking to "excess."[69] Likewise, similar accounts from the mayor of Shelbourne, Nova Scotia, indicated that Halifax was not the only place suffering problems.[70]

Macdonald found it difficult to accept the explanations from the commanding officer Atlantic coast, Rear Admiral Jones, who hinted that there was a small faction of reservists behaving in an unruly fashion.[71] Nor was Jones the only RCN officer to believe that the RCNVRs were causing problems, as another later charged that he "had never seen a Naval Officer drunk in a ship until 'those god-damn reserves' came into the service during the war."[72] It is extremely doubtful that they were the only ones drinking to excess, but it was clear that some naval personnel were unhappy. So was the minister, as he found himself answering opposition questions about the rowdiness in Halifax at the same time that MacLean first approached him.[73] Naturally, Connolly expected to see some evidence of this discontent, but instead was treated to another interpretation.

Responsible for the circumstances that led to the executive assistant's investigation, MacLean also indirectly had a hand in the formation of another group of reserve informants in the wartime naval port of St. John's, Newfoundland. Unlike MacLean and his followers, this new group was not actively attempting to bypass the chain of command but rather came to help Connolly because they were his friends and former legal colleagues. There was no clear leader among them, although the commanding officer of the corvette, HMCS *Amherst*, Louis Audette, undoubtedly held the most sway with the executive assistant. Not only had Audette and Connolly been friends since childhood but they had also shared the same adolescent dream of becoming lawyers. Audette was the best man when Connolly married Ida Jones, and Audette's older brother, J. deG. "Gap" Audette, immediately found room in the family law firm for the newlywed after he passed the Quebec bar in the early 1930s. Other men in this network also had well-established pre-war links to Connolly. The father of Lieutenant Barry O'Brien (serving on another corvette, *Trillium*), gold mine magnate John Ambrose O'Brien, had in 1933 given Connolly a big first break by making him the family's lawyer.[74] As trusted friends, Audette, O'Brien, and others in seagoing billets were well situated to provide the executive assistant with front-line observations on conditions in the fleet. It also helped that they were respected. Comments that Audette was an "excellent commanding officer," or that O'Brien "was a prince" were typical of those who served with them.[75] Nor were they the only ones Connolly would use as he cast a net over a wide range of positions that covered shore appointments as well.

Perhaps one of Connolly's greatest shore assets was Sub-Lieutenant J.S. Hodgson, RCNVR, who had followed Rear Admiral H.E. Reid from Ottawa to his new position as the flag officer Newfoundland force. A Rhodes scholar with a PhD from Oxford University, Hodgson had not only attended the vast majority of Naval Staff and Board meetings while Reid was the vice chief of the naval staff but had also drafted numerous "policy and plans" papers for the navy. Accordingly, he was one of the few reservists who could compare what was in the minds of the top brass in Ottawa with the realities that he was now witnessing in St. John's. There also was Hodgson's pre-war experience as an executive assistant with the Department of Labour, and that made him particularly valuable.[76] He too understood the importance of "insider information," a fact reflected in a letter to Connolly after the investigation:

> Glad you considered your trip a success. Being so much nearer to the ships makes it possible for one to feel "useful" without need of farsighted analysis. "Bubs" [Lieutenant J.C. Britton] has been asking about you, and asked to be remembered as did his colleague [Lieutenant J.H.] Kyle; also [Lieutenant Commander] Bob Keith, [Lieutenant] Charlie Donaldson – and all points west. Haven't seen Louis [Audette] since you left, but hope to ere long. If at any time, John, you may want some (non-secret but personal) information which is hard to get through official sources, let me help pls.[77]

This second network started with a small group of Connolly's friends, but as Hodgson's comments indicated, it already had the potential for growth after originating with an innocent visit to a single corvette.

With Brand in tow, one of Connolly's first stops in St. John's was to the *Amherst*. After getting a complete tour of the ship, Audette recorded their reaction as follows: "Eric Brand turned up one day with John Connolly, the Executive Assistant

A tour of Lieutenant Commander Louis Audette's ship, HMCS *Amherst*, gave J.J. Connolly his first taste of the equipment issues on Canadian corvettes in October 1942. Had it not been for a refit, this ship would have transported Connolly to Londonderry on a second equipment investigation one year later. DHH 81/520/8000, BOX 179, FILE 11

to the Navy Minister ... He had never seen a corvette, which is why he came down. I took them all around the ship. Back in the wardroom Eric sat down with a drink and said with a sparkle, 'It's been interesting, but I can't imagine how you get the bloody thing from A to B, or how you fight it.'"[78]

Their conversation in the wardroom did not stop there, and Connolly was interested in what Audette had to say. The message was blunt: MacLean's charge was flawed because the real issue for those serving at sea had nothing to do with permanent force discrimination against reserves; it was the inadequate equipment on their warships. Having just returned from escorting convoy ON 137 from Londonderry, Northern Ireland, Audette was unimpressed with Canadian equipment such as the SW2C radar, which in his words, "could not compare with the [British-built] 271 radar." This explained why Audette had taken such care to show Connolly his ship's equipment and argued that this matter needed investigation more urgently than did complaints about discrimination against reserves.[79] In time Connolly would do just that, and the issue of modernization of the RCN eventually contributed to Nelles' dismissal.

J.J. Connolly (far right) and Captain Eric Brand, RN (third from the right, front row), on the last leg of their October 1942 trip to the Maritimes. In this instance, they are pictured with officers and officials in Sydney, Nova Scotia, while HMCS *Lethbridge* rests impressively on the marine haul-out. H.H. BLACK PHOTOGRAPHER, LAC PA-105967

Despite Audette's efforts, an hour and a half on the *Amherst* was simply not enough time to explain a complicated issue like the RCN's modernization dilemma. As seagoing officers, Audette and O'Brien – as well as Connolly's other friends and colleagues – knew that inferior equipment on their ships made it more difficult to protect merchant ships and destroy U-boats. Unlike MacLean, these men were motivated by a desire to help a friend in his quest to see the welfare of the fleet improved. Connolly did not immediately recognize that they were telling him about a problem with the fleet unrelated to MacLean's complaints. And so, when it became obvious that Connolly was not following up on the equipment issue once back in Ottawa, they let the matter rest. They would help Connolly only when he asked for assistance. As far as the modernization question was concerned, that assistance was not required because Connolly did not yet understand its importance.

The desperate need for escorts had initiated the largest naval shipbuilding program in Canadian history. While the corvette and minesweeper hulls were coming off the slips in droves, these ships lacked the most up-to-date radar and sonar, as well as advanced weapon systems. At the time there was little the Naval Staff could do. During the first three years of the war, the Allies faced a situation in which a poorly equipped and trained escort was better than no escort at all. By October 1942, the effects of three years of expansion had finally caught up with the Canadian navy, which was starting to witness some of its worst setbacks of the war. Poor equipment was not the only factor contributing to these disasters – inadequate training, too few destroyers, and ineffective manning policies also played a part – but it was a significant concern. At the time Audette spoke with Connolly, however, the worst convoys had yet to materialize.[80] As a commanding officer, Audette certainly realized that the successes of the summer – Canadian escorts had participated in the destruction of four of the five U-boats sunk in the mid-Atlantic – would be short-lived. Convoy ON 127 may have acted as a harbinger of things to come, but convoy SC 107 left little doubt that the RCN was in trouble. Occurring as Connolly was returning to Ottawa, this convoy was the RCN's worst experience in over a year – 15 merchant ships were lost before it reached the United Kingdom.[81]

MacLean's complaints seem to have blinded the executive assistant to the significance of what Audette was trying to tell him. Worse, this was not Connolly's first warning about the problem. One of MacLean's own disciples had tried to do the same. Arguing that the corvettes were the workhorse of the escort fleet, this individual had charged that "officers and ratings of these vessels have been sent to sea frequently with defective engines, guns and with bad leaks and inadequate equipment."[82] When asked to comment on this report, another reserve officer was equally candid, telling both Connolly and Macdonald in mid-July, "Here again is a case of neglect on the part of RCN officers of one of the greatest opportunities of the service. There have been far too many cases of these ships being sent to sea improperly equipped." Since both these reservists were MacLean supporters, neither believed that the modernization issue should take precedence over the grievances about discrimination.[83] But that they had raised the equipment issue at all indicates that there was at least some crossover between the two reserve networks. Those other officers interested foremost in seeing the fleet modernized were not totally unsympathetic to MacLean's criticisms. They, too, had complaints about discrimination. Their concerns, however, were not with the permanent force but rather with the attitudes of some shore personnel, and in this they would be joined by some seagoing regulars.

Gruelling weather, the threat of U-boats, sleep deprivation, and even bad food all conspired to make life at sea a miserable experience. For the men who withstood the pressure, the sight of land should have represented a reprieve, complete with welcoming comrades, hot nourishment, and some "wets" to wash it all down before either retiring to a soft bed or a night on the town. Instead, what they saw and endured while ashore only added to their frustration; complaints circulated throughout the fleet that shore personnel displayed an annoying air of superiority over those serving at sea. With a tone reminiscent of MacLean's grievances, Lieutenant Commander James Lamb explained this "them and us" mindset in greater detail: "Pride kept us at sea, month after month, year after year; to leave and get a berth ashore was to yield, to surrender, to let the side down. Pride was one factor; resentment was the other. Resentment of the shore-orientated organization of the Canadian navy, which cast everyone in the little ships of the escort fleet, officers and men, in the role of poor relations of their counterparts in the big institutions ashore."[84] Although these complaints were similar to MacLean's, the network in St. John's argued that the reserve-discrimination interpretation was somewhat misleading, and they were right to say so.

Unlike those serving on the fairmiles, reservists on the corvettes operated closely with the destroyers and their permanent force crews. There was a sense of kinship between the vessels in Canadian mid-Atlantic groups, and this suggests that the discontent within the navy was not reserve against regular, but rather sea versus shore. While most members of Connolly's network agreed with this assessment, there was at least one dissenting opinion, as Audette let it be known after the war: "There was a bit of resentment from the seagoing towards the chairborne. However, not nearly as much as James B. Lamb suggests ... When you can't undress, you naturally envy the man who climbs nightly into the crisp sheets, and perhaps not alone. When you can't even take a shower, you equally envy the chap who can soak comfortably each day in his tub. However, I don't think that this mattered as much as many seem to think."[85]

Arguing that the equipment shortage was the most pressing problem in the navy, Audette may not have shared the same sensitivities as some of his colleagues. Nevertheless, the sea versus shore interpretation had some powerful supporters, including the new commanding officer Atlantic coast, Rear Admiral L.W. Murray, who wrote, "[I feel] bound to inform the Department that a feeling has been apparent for some time amongst the seagoing officers that ... it is easier to gain distinction and promotion in the RCN onshore, under the eye of higher authority, than at sea ... It is respectfully submitted that my remarks ... should not be considered as a criticism of the Promotion Board, but that they should be accepted as the earnest endeavour to bring these facts to the notice of the Department which was my sole intention in making them."[86]

Strangely, Naval Service Headquarters reprimanded Murray for having "definitely stuck his neck out" on what they considered a baseless issue, and instructed him "that such unfounded criticisms are not acceptable to the Department."[87] That Murray was censured for offering an opinion suggests that there was at least a kernel of truth to MacLean's claim that Naval Service Headquarters was uninterested in outside advice. On the other hand, the fact that Murray was a regular did little to support MacLean's assertion that the top brass in Ottawa only snubbed

This ice-coated corvette not only shows the uncomfortable conditions at sea but also identifies the danger of sailing in winter conditions. The added top-weight of the ice affected the ship's stability and had to be removed to prevent capsizing. DHH 81/520/1000, BOX 142 FILE 4

ideas from reservists. It did, however, reinforce the shore versus sea perception, particularly since Murray was angered that the Naval Staff, which was hundreds of miles away, was ignoring warnings from the man on the spot.[88]

Murray was not the only one who thought this way. Throughout the summer of 1942, rumours had circulated within the seagoing reserves that another respected permanent force officer, Commander J.D. "Chummy" Prentice, had been rebuffed for sending recommendations to the Naval Staff regarding the need to modernize the corvettes. Yet another version held that his reports had "been conveniently mislaid by NSHQ," suggesting that most of the reservists' anger was not directed at all shore officers but instead fixated on the ones in Ottawa.[89] In fact, those who had a chance to visit headquarters often found that the navy consisted of two separate worlds. Capturing this perception, one veteran remembered that "I only visited NSHQ twice during the whole war, and each time felt a wholly unreal atmosphere – disconnected from the sea, not just geographically but in spirit."[90]

Those on the coast had their own way of dealing with their frustration toward headquarters. Some tried to use humour, such as the officer who posted a fictional port order in St. John's that listed the RCN's enemies in the following order of priority: "(1) The German Reich (2) Naval Service Headquarters (3) Imperial Japan."[91] Others passed their observations directly on to the minister's executive assistant. Certainly, O'Brien had summed up the nuance of this problem in a poem he had written to Connolly about his experiences with convoy SC 100:

Bless them all, Bless them all,
The long and the short and the tall.
Bless all the Brass hats,
And the chairs where they sit.
Planning our Westomp and the rest of that shit ...
Bless them all, Bless them all,
The long and the short and the tall.
Bless old CinCWA and COMINCH too.
Bless old COAC and N-S-H-Q.
As we've waited all trip for this day,
To stalk these U-boats as prey.
It's then they combine, to spoil our good time,
By taking three escorts away.[92]

While O'Brien managed to blame almost every operational authority (including the British and Americans) in this acronymic outburst for mysteriously reassigning three corvettes from the convoy, Connolly knew better. O'Brien had wrongly assumed that the extra escorts were joining his group on a permanent basis, when in fact the top brass were reserving them for the planned invasion of North Africa. The executive assistant could not tell O'Brien that the minister had personally approved the decision for the RCN to commit seventeen ships to this operation. Nevertheless, such observations were not entirely lost on Connolly, who realized that his friends represented a valuable source of information for both himself and the minister.

Even before forming his own network of personal informants, Connolly had recognized the importance of consulting reserve officers who could provide pertinent details about sensitive matters. During the initial contact with MacLean, for example, Connolly had turned to Commander W.G. Shedden, RCNVR, for advice. Shedden was a good choice. Not only had he served at sea during the war, giving him insight about the complaints themselves, but because he had been

HMCS *York*'s executive officer in the late 1920s he was also able to assess MacLean's personality.[93] Similarly, only days before leaving for St. John's, Connolly had made arrangements for another one of his friends to join the navy so that he could provide the minister with information on the RCN's overseas recreation facilities. The sudden announcement that Walter Gilhooly was getting commissioned as a lieutenant commander and was to serve as the senior naval auxiliary service officer in the United Kingdom caught the Naval Staff off guard. A lawyer turned journalist in civilian life, Gilhooly was considered ideal for his current position as the head of the Directorate of Naval Information. Suspicion that the new special service appointment was politically motivated was correct. Covering his bases, Connolly had sent Gilhooly – as a trusted friend – to keep an eye on the situation overseas while checking the situation on the East Coast for himself.[94]

Connolly's predisposition for "insider" information and the network of informants he had created in the Maritimes assisted tremendously in the investigation. He believed that the men had "helped me a great deal in connection with my work here for the Minister."[95] In fact, Connolly's trip would otherwise have yielded disappointing results, especially because the vast majority of sailors in St. John's were unwilling to discuss sensitive matters with someone they considered an "outsider."[96] But the executive assistant was able to gain an appreciation of the state of morale from his friends, who naturally had few reservations about sharing their experiences. They had done so out of friendship and, unlike MacLean, had no motivation other than improving conditions for all sailors who were at sea. As highly educated civilian professionals, they too had experienced culture shock when first confronted by permanent force officers who treated them as rank amateurs. In their view, this was not the product of discrimination but was akin to hazing. Often a quick wit was all that was required to defuse such situations, as one unsuspecting permanent force officer discovered when he asked Audette, "'Why is it, just because you've taken a degree, or whatever you call it, in law, you go about referring to each other as my learned friend and my learned counsel, and my learned opponent.' The VR lawyer [Audette] replied, 'Oh, it's nothing, quite meaningless. It's like referring to you as a gallant officer.'"[97] By indicating that some reservists could dish out the insults as well as they received them, this network cast grave doubts on MacLean's interpretation.

While these officers had provided Connolly with an alternative explanation of the discontent on the East Coast, they did share some of MacLean's elitist attitudes. Rather than blaming the top brass, they found fault in the training system that produced those officers. As Audette later explained, the inability of the permanent force to understand problems in the fleet was the product of an education that stressed "the constant repetition of an act and on the observation of its performance by others." Audette then clarified his claim:

> It is too much an effort of memory and too little an effort of reasoning. The mental deficiencies engendered by this faulty system and by the inadequacy of the sum of his education are usually most apparent among those Officers holding very high rank or filling appointments which require them to consider subjects beyond the confines of strictly naval life ... I do not think that this absence of a more liberal education gives him a proper sense of broad social responsibility, nor does it prepare him to deal with problems beyond the scope of his technical Naval duties ... I do suggest that if the reserve officer was capable of doing what he did in so short a time, then the career officer could well afford to lengthen his period of training in order to receive a more liberal education; he would acquire thereby the intellectual development necessary to absorb all that he is receiving at present in the way of professional training and more.[98]

Apart from a fixation on education, there were few similarities between this network and MacLean's. Perhaps the message about the fleet's equipment would have had a greater impact on Connolly had the network employed some of MacLean's tactics, but that was not their style. Instead, Audette and those like him merely passed observations on to the executive assistant. By doing so they had raised the possibility that the apparent discontent was the product of a morale problem – not just with the reserves but with all those who were serving at sea. It was up to Connolly to determine whether these networks had legitimate grievances against either the permanent force or shore establishments like Naval Service Headquarters.

While their motivation for contacting both the minister and the executive assistant may have differed, the formation of these reserve networks marked the beginning of a process that would alter the balance of power at Naval Service Headquarters. That Macdonald was willing to consider the opinions of those who fell outside of the normal chain of command meant that the Naval Board no longer monopolized the flow of information. It did not matter that MacLean was driven by personal ambition; what was troubling was the implication that the minister's permanent force advisors were hiding things. Despite their altruistic intentions, Connolly's own network inadvertently sent the same message, because they too provided information that caught the executive assistant off guard. Whether intentional or not, both networks preyed on the minister's political insecurities, and by doing so they created a level of mistrust that made Macdonald suspicious of Nelles. The problem was that this information had come from men who, while enjoying rank and power in the public sphere, were relatively junior naval officers.

The minister did not understand that the birth of these networks also represented a clash of two separate communities in which a well-established permanent force hierarchy was being challenged by elitist elements within the naval reserves. The scholarly reservists had difficulty adapting to a world in which the so-called "ill-educated" regulars were the privileged ones and in which the reserves saw themselves as the dregs and second tier of the navy. Under the banner of creating a more equitable "people's navy" they cried out for justice. As MacLean's motivations reveal, what they truly wanted was to create power where none had existed before. As Macdonald was about to learn, these men were willing to use that power. Despite his best efforts, the minister's political manoeuvring had brought only a temporary reprieve from MacLean. Having returned to his editorial duties at Hugh C. MacLean Publishing, this former naval officer would try throughout November and December 1942 to persuade the minister of the need to reform the service. And one month later, he would show Macdonald exactly why reservists with media and political connections were a force to be feared.

2
Equal Privileges for Greater Sacrifices

Although Andrew MacLean's immediate departure from the navy went smoothly enough, it did not take long before he began pressuring the minister to institute drastic reforms. In his view, only Macdonald could fix the inequitable balance between the regulars and the reserves. Despite Macdonald's and Connolly's best efforts to placate the irksome editor, MacLean's correspondence throughout November and December 1942, threatening to go public with his complaints, indicated that his frustration was growing. The minister's attempts at appeasement ended in failure. By late January 1943, MacLean exacted a terrible revenge against the RCN's senior leadership by letting the public know that there was trouble brewing in the senior service. Something had to be done, he told Canadians, to stop the rising tide of discontent among reserve officers from spilling over into open revolt.

Not surprisingly, both the press and official opposition were fascinated by his warnings of mass insurrection among reserve officers. But as the scandal broke, the public was entranced with a confrontation that pitted the naval minister against one of the most prestigious families in Canada. Just as Macdonald had feared, MacLean was a powerful nemesis and a hazard to the reputation of the Liberal government. However, the cunning and experienced minister also proved a formidable opponent, and after much mudslinging both men emerged from their public battle bloodied and bruised.

Defeating MacLean, no matter what the cost, was a priority for Macdonald and Connolly. While doing so, they found themselves in the awkward position of having to determine whether there was any truth to the allegations. It was the minister's job to answer the cries about permanent force anti-reserve discrimination that were echoing across the country. It was also his responsibility to tell Canadians whether the navy required reforms that would guarantee the reserves better treatment and "equal privileges." The problem was that Macdonald still did not know if the reserve grouses were real or imagined and therefore could not make an informed decision on the need for change. His desire to separate fact from fiction became an essential element of his battle with MacLean. In the end, Macdonald learned that the veracity of the allegations did not really matter. At issue was the public's interpretation of these events. The negative publicity had threatened the minister's political career, and the fact that others in the fleet might follow MacLean's example made Macdonald feel vulnerable. It was this hypersensitivity to perceived problems within the navy that spelled trouble for the chief of the naval staff who, rightly or wrongly, was eventually held responsible for MacLean's attack. What that showed was that the perception of failure was just as dangerous to senior naval leaders, like Nelles, as an impression based on fact.

In early November, Connolly and Macdonald had received disturbing letters from both Hugh and Andrew MacLean. Firing a shot at the chief of the naval staff along with his top officers, Hugh MacLean told the minister he was upset that his son had "surrendered" to the "Nelles gang." While this indicated that the Toronto publisher blamed the navy's military leadership rather than Macdonald for his son's so-called shabby treatment, he still provided an ambiguous warning that "[Andrew's] story may now be told." Andrew MacLean's letter, sent on the following day, was more direct. It had become his personal mission to fight the inequity between the permanent force and reserves, which would include advocating the need for reform and "stirring up [the] Press and Opposition" if necessary.[1] Should the minister decide to co-operate, MacLean elaborated, it would not be necessary for Canadians to learn how the permanent force was excluding reservists from the navy's decision-making process, going so far as to erect enormous roadblocks that hindered them from assuming more senior appointments.

The aim of MacLean's proposals was to overcome this barrier through positive action – to place reservists on the promotion and honours boards (the organizations that selected the officers who would be promoted and receive medals) and to ensure that combat or suitable civilian experience replace simple longevity as criteria for advancement. Together, equal opportunity for promotion and a fairer distribution of medals and other honours would recognize the tremendous sacrifice reservists were making at sea. It would also justify their appointment to senior staff positions. Once a balance in command appointments had been achieved, MacLean continued, the time would then be right to disband the reserve branches so that everyone would belong to the same service. That would bring the Canadian military into balance because, unlike the army and Royal Canadian Air Force, "the navy is the only service that still makes a distinction between the permanent, the professional and the volunteer." A comparison between navies, MacLean claimed, showed that "the Royal Navy is more advanced than the RCN – for the RNVR on promotion to Lieutenant become RN (temp[orary]). The RN looks forward – not backward."[2] Finally, he argued, Macdonald needed to appoint RCNVR and RCNR officers to the Naval Board immediately, since it could be anticipated that the regulars would resist these suggested reforms. While Connolly and Macdonald were not dead-set against reform, the idea of bringing reservists to the Naval Board – just because they were reservists – was extreme, and both rejected it out of hand.[3]

There was good reason why Connolly and Macdonald could make this decision so quickly. The Naval Board's main purpose was to serve as the minister's advisory body, so reserve membership was not necessary in this functional organization.

Replacing the Naval Council, the newly formed Naval Board meets for the first time in February 1942. Macdonald is at the far end of the table. Nelles sits to the minister's right, followed by Rear Admiral H.E. Reid (vice chief of the naval staff), Captain H.T.W. Grant (chief of naval personnel), Lieutenant Commander R.A. Pennington (secretary of the Naval Board), Captain G.M. Hibbard (chief of naval equipment and supply), Engineering Captain G.L. Stephens (chief of naval engineering and construction), and finally Gordon Mills (deputy minister). LAC PA-180379

Moreover, while the naval secretary did not have any real authority or voting rights, he was an RCNVR officer who also served as a personnel representative on reserve issues when the regulars needed advice. According to another argument, reservists were wartime call-outs; that meant that the need for representation would suddenly evaporate once hostilities ended. And finally, giving in to MacLean's suggestion might cause more problems than it solved, as it would treat reservists as a special class who could potentially gain entitlements that the regulars in the fleet might not share.

Macdonald also had pragmatic reasons for not tinkering with the composition of his top advisory body, believing that the present set-up was "as big as a Board is workable." Political experience had taught him that executive committees tended to become less efficient as their membership grew: he deemed enlarging the Naval Board simply to satisfy a disgruntled editor "impractical."[4] That did not sit well with MacLean, who was unconvinced that there could ever be true justice for the reserves as long as they were denied a direct channel to the minister through the Naval Board. Connolly and Macdonald were not giving MacLean much feedback, making him more desperate and unpredictable and, therefore, more dangerous as well. Perhaps because of that, Macdonald – who had not yet seen conclusive proof to support MacLean's allegations – prepared minor concessions that would make it easier to promote reserve officers and allow them to share seniority with the RCN at sea, and to improve their general terms of service. Whether Macdonald truly believed such measures were required is uncertain, but it is clear that he was following his executive assistant's advice. Connolly had seen enough evidence to convince him that some minor changes would suffice to quell the apparent dissatisfaction.[5] In fact, these reforms had been in the works since the previous summer, but with MacLean threatening to go public, it was considered politically expedient to make these changes sooner rather than later. Knowing that change was in the offing, Connolly tried to cool things off by hinting to MacLean that he was influencing naval policy and that any additional suggestions he cared to submit would be carefully considered.

Connolly could not accurately gauge whether the majority of reservists felt as vehemently about these issues as MacLean did, but between the RCNVRs at Naval Service Headquarters and those he met during his October investigation, it was obvious that there was at least some substance to the larger allegations. On the other hand, Connolly had no way of knowing whether there was any truth to MacLean's prediction that the Naval Board would resist changes designed to improve conditions for the two branches of the reserves.[6] As a result, it would not be politically prudent to follow the hard-line approach with the Naval Board that MacLean was advocating, as the minister needed time to see how the situation would play out. Macdonald was in a bad situation. Particularly so since MacLean kept insinuating that he was going to go public unless someone got tough on the reserve discrimination question.

The key was to handle MacLean diplomatically. This was not an easy task – by this time the troublesome editor was flooding the minister's office with a steady flow of "recommendations" – but it was nonetheless one that Connolly did well. For example, in early December, MacLean sent a carefully crafted letter to the executive assistant:

No reply has yet been received to my letter of 13 October, addressed to the Minister of Naval Services, asking that certain ideas I submitted to the RCN be either used or released to me for disposal elsewhere. On November 3rd I wrote the Minister a personal letter suggesting that he appoint an Advisory Committee and the Naval Board be enlarged. I hope he was not offended. I do hope some measure of reform is to shortly be instituted. Enclosed is a copy of a letter sent to the Naval Secretary on November 26th ... for your information. I have not been well since leaving the Service

– the reaction, presumably, from three years of war with the enemy and from guarding my rear, ineffectually, against the RCN.[7]

The executive assistant's response to this letter was a brilliant illustration of political evasion. Through months of corresponding, Connolly and MacLean had developed their own unique language in which both men jockeyed for position without going so far as to corner the other. When MacLean let it be known that his ideas were either to be taken seriously or else "released to me for disposal elsewhere," Connolly understood what that meant: ignoring these recommendations meant they would next appear in a newspaper or on the leader of the official opposition's desk. Likewise, the executive assistant also realized that MacLean's references to his health – such as the phrase "I have not been well" – often served as a hint that he was on the verge of doing something that might strain his relationship with the minister. And it was for that reason that Connolly sent his own message: MacLean should know "that reform is always looked for by the Minister. If war problems were not so terribly pressing, I think conditions in the Service would be radically different than they are." In short, the executive assistant was telling MacLean that the minister was listening and patience was required. Providing yet another clue, Connolly then commented, "I am very sorry to hear that your health is not good, and I hope that it will improve quickly." This stood as a signal that he did not want MacLean to do anything rash.[8] In the short term, at least, MacLean got the inference. Such stalling tactics consequently allowed Macdonald the opportunity to discuss Connolly's reforms with the Naval Board.

That these reforms had come from the minister's office was evident when Jones, who had become vice chief of the naval staff a month earlier, tabled a recommendation designed to accelerate promotions for all trained officers below the rank of commander. "The Minister is prepared to consider the granting of additional seniority," Jones told his fellow board members, "to Lieutenants and Lieutenant Commanders ... who have proved themselves by meritorious war service to be exceptionally efficient Officers." Although this was applied equally to all three branches, RCNVR sub-lieutenants did receive preferential treatment. Instead of requiring a superior's recommendation before being advanced, as was still done with the RCN and RCNRs, this new naval order made their promotion to lieutenant automatic.[9] The opportunity to obtain "qualified status" represented another leap forward for reserve officers who, regardless of their seniority, were previously expected to yield control of a group of ships to their permanent force counterparts. Akin to modern-day affirmative action policies, this directive meant that regulars and "qualified" reservists at the same rank were considered equals who "shared seniority." Although an explanation was never offered to those serving at sea, a few reservists interpreted the policy as an attempt to level the playing field, which, of course, it was.[10] Nor was that all, as another reform included a proposed reorganization of the promotion board so that it could better cope with issues such as the preliminary selection of officers, the commissioning of officers from the lower deck, and the methods of and qualifications for promotion.[11] That other grievances from the summer were also discussed at this time – such as giving sailors service chevrons for sea service or clarifying the procedures governing "confidential reports on officers" – all provide compelling evidence that Macdonald had listened to Connolly. There was more to come.[12]

Although a reserve representative was not going to sit on the Naval Board, Macdonald and his advisors did reorganize the reserve divisions across Canada, placing them under the command of Captain Eustace Brock, RCNVR. This gave the reserves a degree of autonomy over their own affairs and addressed one of MacLean's central complaints that no RCNVR officer had been assigned a senior appointment. Given the title commanding officer reserve divisions, Brock's new position was "analogous to COAC [commanding officer Atlantic coast] or COPC [commanding officer Pacific coast]," meaning that he enjoyed status that was somewhat comparable to the rear admirals responsible for the East and West coasts.[13] Ironically, MacLean did not like Brock and therefore resented his enlarged stature, all the more so because the commanding officer reserve divisions would reside at the naval mansion in Rosedale, making him a close neighbour of Hugh MacLean.[14] But despite the occasional setback this type of interference had affected Connolly, and perhaps the strongest evidence that MacLean was influencing policy came when the Naval Board discussed the "fairmile situation."

The condition of the fairmiles only seemed to worsen after MacLean left. After much heated debate between the operational authorities, Naval Service Headquarters finally conceded that the administration of these vessels had created "certain problems which appear impossible of resolution under the present arrangements."[15] Placed under the chairmanship of Commander H.G. DeWolf, RCN, a seven-member Fairmile committee was struck in December to develop an operational plan for the flotillas. Just as MacLean had argued in July, their final report found that the fairmiles had serious deficiencies in training, equipment, maintenance, and manning, and that there was a "need for some form of central control." It was suggested that Naval Service Headquarters create a new position called captain (motor launches), which, while still under the authority of the Atlantic Command, would be given a semi-autonomous command in Halifax. This appointment was a scaled down version of the one MacLean had proposed seven months earlier, especially since the captain (motor launches) was "responsible direct to NSHQ for policy with regard to operation and training of ML's [motor launches]."[16]

Other reforms followed that, on the surface at least, vindicated many of MacLean's criticisms. However, it would have been dangerous for Macdonald to share the details of these changes with MacLean, as Connolly believed that such knowledge would only encourage further interference with naval policy. Suggestions were welcomed but Macdonald had no intention of giving MacLean an honorary seat on the Naval Board, and there was only so much intervention the minister could tolerate before putting his foot down, especially from someone as erratic as MacLean.

While MacLean was motivated by self-interest, those who believed in his crusade against the regulars represented an extreme manifestation of what some have called "sharp-end" grousing. In this, the ones "doing the fighting [in the war at sea] tend to vilify those at headquarters who are not, particularly when the latter's folly seems self-evident."[17] The problem was that such analysis was often based on empirical evidence drawn from their immediate surroundings, and that rarely provided those at the sharp end with enough hard data to support their sweeping statements. Simply put, sharp-end grousers were often fuelled by ignorance of the factors behind official decisions. Had MacLean's followers known that 43.8 percent of the RCN was serving on the ships, for example, compared to 44.7 percent for the RCNVR, it is unlikely they would have supported the allegation that headquarters was sending the latter to sea in place of the former. The reservists appeared to be the only ones fighting the war because collectively they accounted for 88.4 percent of the navy's total strength.[18] MacLean's belief that regulars did not go to sea was thus rooted in the preponderance of reservists in the navy as a whole. That most of the seagoing permanent force served exclusively on destroyers also added to this illusion. When viewed through this prism, MacLean's entire campaign for special privileges for the reserves because of their "greater sacrifices" at sea loses much of its lustre.

The same is true of MacLean's accusation that the regulars bestowed an undue proportion of promotions upon themselves. When broken down into branches, the January 1943 promotion list clearly identifies that only 3.1 percent of all regulars were advanced as compared to 10.5 and 4 percent for the RCNR and RCNVR respectively. The charge that the RCN had too many senior officers was equally misinformed, as a comparison with the British, American, and Australian navies shows not only that the Canadians had the lowest ratio of admirals but also that they were desperately short of flag officers: the RCN had been forced to scoop up large numbers of retired Royal Navy captains living in Canada at the start of the war to fill vacancies at Naval Service Headquarters.[19] Moreover, if these men are removed from the equation, as one officer was quick to point out, the numbers of "brass hats (Commander and above)" at headquarters in February 1943 were "RCN, 20 – RCNR, 2 – RCNVR, 18."[20]

Macdonald may have seen some value in having operational informants but these comparisons expose the dangers of listening to junior officers who – while knowing their small corner of the war well – were often incapable of understanding the big picture. The minister may not always have realized that their observations frequently represented only perceived injustices and not necessarily the realities of a situation. Distinguishing one from the other was not easy, and the only reason Macdonald knew the truth about promotions and the percentages of those serving at sea was because Connolly had researched the matter and said as much. Instead of sympathizing with MacLean, the minister was therefore "happy to say that in the forthcoming [promotion] list there is a very large representation of men who are now actually at sea or who have served at sea during the present war."[21] This did not satisfy MacLean, who argued that simply comparing the promotions allocated to each branch did not "give the important part of the picture." Switching his emphasis, he told the minister how a disproportionate number of senior officers were permanent force. That, according to his logic, was the true injustice. In modern parlance, MacLean then proposed a policy of "reverse discrimination," as he claimed that the only way to correct such inequities was to promote reserve lieutenants and lieutenant commanders directly to commanders and captains.

Ironically, it was a reserve officer at Naval Service Headquarters, Sub-Lieutenant William Pugsley, who first spotted the contraction with this recommendation. MacLean wanted all promotions based on merit, yet at the same time he was advocating a "mathematical" formula that guaranteed reservists special consideration. Pugsley explained further:

> Are not these men [the regulars], so fully trained, the obvious choices to have at Headquarters? ... No one has a keener appreciation ... of the two Naval Reserves, but I know that, in joining, they did not expect to "begin at the top," and in fact it has taken time to train them. Only now is this beginning to bear fruit, and during the past year, with the continued expansion of the Service, the "permanent force officers in the key posts" have become, to use an industrial analogy, less General Managers and more like Chairmen of Board of Directors, as more and more responsibility has been parceled out to the Reserve Officers now at last trained to receive it ... RCNVR officers had received little more than their compulsory fortnight's training each summer in peace time ... [meaning that] somewhat junior RCNVR officers ... still had to put in time learning much of what RCN officers already knew ... It would have been a catastrophe if representation within these three sub-divisions had been the criterion for promotion, instead of actual experience and qualification for the job.[22]

Connolly also found MacLean's rationale absurd. The top brass had years of pre-war experience, making it obvious that "officers and men who have spent their life in the study of Naval Science should be placed in the Higher Administrative Technical positions."[23] In other words, the regulars were the true professionals and deserved to be treated as such. Moreover, MacLean's prediction that the regulars would resist any reforms for the reserves seemed equally baseless. Perhaps the Naval Board would have objected had they known that Macdonald's concessions were linked to MacLean, but as it stood they offered little opposition. In fact, some board members thought that more should be done, one going as far as to argue that he would have made it "easier" for "exceptional" seagoing reserve officers to get qualified status.[24] The perception that the entire senior staff was a bunch of bigots was wrong and promoting more reserve commanders and captains simply to counter that belief was, in Connolly's view, totally unnecessary.

Macdonald agreed. His – or more precisely, Connolly's – reforms were designed to give the reserves better opportunity to advance alongside the permanent force, and he was not going to balance one perceived injustice with a policy that clearly discriminated against the other. He was wise not to do so, because some of the enacted reforms were soon causing more problems than they solved. For example, some RCNRs resented the policy of promoting RCNVR sub-lieutenants without a superior's recommendation, as was evident when the captain (D) in Halifax reported to the commanding officer Atlantic coast: "Under existing regulations situations are arising where Sub-Lieutenants are adversely reported on, only to be shortly promoted to Lieutenants. On the other hand, RCNR Sub-Lieutenants require recommendations before promotion can be effected ... with the consequent result that the RCNR officer feels he is discriminated against when compared to the RCNVR officer of equal seniority ... automatic promotion destroys what little initiative a poor officer may have [to improve] ... The results of such a situation are obvious and can only result in a lowering of the standards of efficiency."[25]

Nor could the minister ignore that Connolly had caught wind of reports indicating that seagoing regulars were equally demoralized over this particular promotion policy. Any reforms based solely on MacLean's charges were not only likely to create new splits between the reserves, but also among the permanent force members, who were bound to resent too much preferential treatment for the RCNR and RCNVR. Moreover, there was no end to the promotion quagmire, some even going as far as to claim that RCNVR officers got more favourable recommendations overseas because the British did not "want to hurt the feelings of Canada."[26] Clearly the promotion issue was a hydra, explaining why Macdonald tried to tell MacLean that it was "not an easy thing to settle to one's entire satisfaction."[27] But the minister could not get a reprieve from MacLean who, after recommending that all RCN advancements should be temporarily suspended, again warned that "the excessive number of RCN promotions have already been raised in the House and will be raised this session."[28] MacLean was unimpressed, and his stubborn refusal to accept the minister's arguments inched the two men even closer to what now seemed like an inevitable public confrontation.

MacLean's frustration soon got the better of him. Knowing nothing about the proposed restructuring of the fairmile flotilla, he told the minister in early January

1943 that he had written a manuscript for publication in *Boating Magazine* entitled "Fairmiles and Foul." To MacLean, it constituted "one of the most damning criticisms of the RCN that I ever expect to see [and] in the hands of the Opposition, [this article] will bring you many a sleepless night." In typical flamboyant style, MacLean then compared his situation to the famous persecution of a French officer after the Franco-Prussian war: "You have a Dreyfus case on your hands and most VR [RCNVR] officers know and feel that there is little chance that they be allowed to fight to the best of their ability."[29] Moreover, an editorial that MacLean had planned to publish alongside his article was also forwarded to the minister's office, indicating that MacLean planned to take the moral high ground in any future confrontation:

> As long as the Department of Naval Services insists upon maintaining a very definite line of demarcation ... it is becoming increasingly clear that the Naval Board should be enlarged to include able, independent officers from both volunteer branches of the Navy – the RCNR and the RCNVR. Perhaps it is unusual to use the phrase "taxation without representation" when referring to the unsympathetic control that half a dozen permanent force officers exercise over the 45,000 officers and men who have given up their civilian careers for the duration of hostilities; yet the term is apt.[30]

MacLean's goal was all too clear: he was trying to frighten the minister by conjuring up images of legal proceedings, parliamentary inquiries, and public scandal. By now, however, Macdonald was fed up with this type of intimidation and lashed back, "I shall have to defend the Service and myself with all the weapons at my command. I feel it only fair to tell you this frankly. When the manuscript is published, I shall have to make ... the best reply that I can."[31] And perhaps one of the most powerful weapons in that arsenal included MacLean's personnel file. The file was MacLean's Achilles heel and his defensive claims that it had been filled with fabricated evidence by the "Nelles group" revealed his fear of the contents. Showing that Macdonald had touched a nerve, MacLean responded, "The weapon nearest your hand is an attack upon the writer ... I hope you will not use it and I do not think you will."[32]

MacLean may not have liked the minister's rules of engagement, but he was unprepared to yield the upper hand. Conceding that personalities and credibility were now fair game, MacLean decided to give the minister a preview of what was in store by sending him a rough copy of the manuscript. Although determined to publish, MacLean offered one last chance. A public clash could still be avoided, he tried to persuade Macdonald, providing that the manuscript was shown to Nelles with instructions to "clean up this navy of yours."[33] Macdonald did just that but instead of telling the chief of the naval staff to clean house, he gave orders to mobilize. The irony of this situation is difficult to overlook. For half a year, Macdonald had entertained MacLean's criticisms of the top brass, but now he was trusting that these same men would protect him. As a result, when he handed over the manuscript with instructions to assess the damage it could cause the navy's reputation, the minister effectively cut the regulars loose in the hopes that they would devour one of his own informants.

Most saw MacLean as a "crank" and believed that he did not represent a significant threat. "I have maintained," the vice chief of the naval staff advised, "that the best way to deal with a small boy was to ignore him."[34] Likewise, the deputy judge advocate general, Commander Duncan MacTavish (who himself was an RCNVR officer), refused to accept that any "experienced journalist" would publish this article because it would expose him to various libel suits as well as possible prosecution under the Defence of Canada Regulations. Suspicious about the claim that this was a "rough draft," the deputy judge advocate general instead was "led to the conclusion that it has been set up for the sole purpose of sending it to the Minister with the view to endeavour to intimidate him or blackmail him." Supporting this conclusion was an incriminating letter from MacLean that Macdonald handed the chief of the naval staff, in which MacLean suggested he would destroy his manuscript if arrangements were made for an appointment in the Royal Navy. In the end, MacTavish's position was similar to the vice chief's, recommending as he did "that the wise course is to advise the Minister ... to take no such action whatsoever with respect to the article at this time." Clearly, they underestimated MacLean but it is difficult to understand what Macdonald expected from the Naval Staff. There was no way these officers could accurately predict whether the article was a threat because Macdonald had provided them only with selected snippets of his previous correspondence with MacLean. Without such knowledge they lacked context and therefore reasoned that in the unlikely event the letter was published, the navy could judge its response based on "the reception it receives from the public."[35]

Since his advisors could not provide the type of help he needed, and knowing that MacLean's attack was in the near offing, Macdonald went on a snap visit to St. John's. This trip, which included a day sail on a fairmile, allowed him to witness conditions on the East Coast for himself, and indicated that Macdonald was going to extreme lengths to prepare for the confrontation.[36] The minister was obviously anxious but by this juncture some officers at Naval Service Headquarters were equally worried. Only days earlier a staff officer was reminded of a grievous error that, if discovered by MacLean, would have resulted in much embarrassment for the navy. In mid-July 1942, an armed yacht was almost turned into scrap metal and spare parts because someone on the staff of commanding officer Atlantic coast misread a signal from Naval Service Headquarters to have it "de-stored" as "destroyed." In any event, the ship was no longer seaworthy, and its near dismantling would have been almost comical except for one thing – the vessel was MacLean's

Andrew MacLean's last command, HMCS *Lynx*, was nearly sent to the scrap yard when someone misread a message instructing that the ship was to be "de-stored" as "destroyed." Despite the close call, this armed yacht suffered from constant mechanical problems and was sold off to commercial interests after being paid off in the spring of 1943.
DHH, RL (LYNX)

last command, HMCS *Lynx*.[37] At that time, MacLean was unaware of these events, but as one former officer explained, the navy was now "terrified that he would learn of this faux pas and giving another example in his view, of the inefficiency of the Navy."[38] The presence of skeletons in the closets at Naval Service Headquarters made some staff officers rethink their lackadaisical attitude toward MacLean, and once the minister returned they were ready to tell him so.

Soon after landing in Ottawa, Macdonald had to be whisked away to Nova Scotia to be with his dying mother. Sadly, the day that Veronica Macdonald passed away was also the one in which the first reports of MacLean's allegations hit the newsstands.[39] "Fairmiles and Foul" was published during the first week of February 1943. It read like a declaration of war:

> There's enough about the conduct of the Navy in this issue to warrant a searching Parliamentary Enquiry ... and if this is still a democracy we shall have it soon and it is

long, long overdue. The honest, capable officers of the RCN – and there are a few – will welcome reform. The volunteer officers and men of the RCNR and RCNVR should enjoy, as one of our readers writes, "equal privileges for greater sacrifices." ... We have not told one-half of what might be told of abuses, of neglect that has brought injury to Canadians who go down to the sea in ships. It is up to every Member of Parliament to see to it that he forcefully represents those of his constituency that are serving in the Navy ... Today, we attack the administration of the Royal Canadian Navy and should be able to save hundreds of lives, millions of dollars and better assist our Allies.[40]

The rest of the article, which in fact took up almost the entire issue of *Boating Magazine*, summarized the way the navy had persecuted MacLean, how the permanent force discriminated against the RCNVR and RCNR, the manner in which the Naval Staff had bungled the administration of the fairmiles, and the reasons why the reserves deserved representation on the Naval Board.[41] The *Globe and Mail* knew a good story when it saw one, and its report was all that MacLean could have wanted as it claimed that "every member of the House of Commons and the Senate has a duty to delve into those accusations."[42] Other papers followed suit, and the opposition pounced on the alleged scandal. The Tories' G. Graydon, and the leader of the Co-operative Commonwealth Federation (CCF), M.J. Coldwell, tag-teamed the Liberals, as the latter asked whether Prime Minister William Lyon Mackenzie King would personally respond to these charges, while the former argued that MacLean's article was "sufficiently serious and urgent to warrant some comment being made by the government."[43] King could not respond to the allegations because he knew nothing about them, and that provided his political opponents with the sense that they were onto something big. Catching the politically astute King flat-footed suggested that the naval minister was purposely hiding some sort of scandal.

With Macdonald attending his mother's funeral, both the Conservatives and the CCF were willing to give the government some leeway. Parliamentary courtesies only extended so far, though, and neither opposition leader could ignore the mounting piles of letters from concerned relatives who wanted to know whether their sons and husbands were being exposed to the conditions that MacLean had described. Nor could the Liberals dodge the journalists, whose articles had made it clear that "a considerable section of the press in Canada is calling for some kind of inquiry with respect to it."[44] The role of defending the navy thus fell to the air force minister, Charles "Chubby" Power, who was filling in for Macdonald. Power had obviously been given some background information on MacLean, as he described his charges as the ramblings of "a disgruntled officer," but doing so without corroborating evidence only managed to stoke the fires. The air minister had gaffed, allowing Graydon to claim that the government could not simply whitewash an issue that "ought to be aired to see if there is anything in his charges."[45] The press was also quick to capitalize on the government's folly, running sensational headlines like "Tirade against Navy Held Purely Personal," and "Power Slams Navy Critic."[46] Things could hardly have gone better for MacLean, who enjoyed two solid weeks without so much as a word from Macdonald or the navy.

Better yet, MacLean had also thrown Naval Service Headquarters into a state of chaos and paranoia, as some officers within the Naval Information office were placed under suspicion for being MacLean sympathizers. Responsible for publicity and liaison duties with the press, Naval Information was a civil-military hybrid filled with former journalists and serving reserve officers working under a civilian director. That mixture had, at times, created some uneasiness among the permanent force, but in this instance the director of operations division, Captain Horatio Nelson Lay, RCN, wanted an explanation why this particular directorate had written an article for MacLean's issue of *Boating Magazine*. Naturally, it was a positive piece on the navy, but it gave MacLean the valuable opportunity to make highly critical editorial comments on the navy's "official" position. This was an unfair exercise, since it allowed him to blast holes in what had purposely been designed as an over-optimistic propaganda item. The whole episode was strange, and Captain Nelson Lay – who had "strongly advised against it when it was first written" – wanted to repair the damage it had done through a rebuttal article that would be planted "by someone outside the naval service and published in an opposition magazine."[47] Deemed too excessive, that idea was dropped, but the Naval Staff was willing to explore the possibility that MacLean had "spies" within the directorate. The Naval Information officer, H.C. Howard, was therefore ordered to prepare a special report on the directorate's activities throughout January and February 1943. Given the volume of their work, combined with the fact that Naval Information had just undergone a major reorganization, it was decided that providing MacLean with this article had been a simple oversight.[48]

MacLean had brought substantial political pressure to bear on the minister. This was where he had blundered. So long as MacLean's criticisms had been behind the scenes, Macdonald had reason to doubt whether the Naval Board was telling him everything he needed to know. Now, though the doubts might remain, the minister had to defend the service, and that required him to shield his officers publicly from MacLean's more outrageous statements. Allegations that the Naval Board members were "jackasses" and that Naval Service Headquarters was both "the root of all evil" as well as a "lunatic asylum run by the inmates" could not go unanswered, particularly when the "inmates" served as Macdonald's military advisors.[49] Officers at Naval Service Headquarters, however, were also guilty of exaggeration. One of them claimed that MacLean had "a make-up similar to Hitler" and that he had attacked the navy "with the cunning of a German General,"[50] while another captured the mood by rewriting the lyrics to the song "Bonnie Dundee":

> To an unlistening country through "Boating" he spoke,
> The Navy is stupid – promotions a joke
> So all of you failures who love to raise cain,
> Come follow the teachings of Andy Maclean.
> If reforms they are needed, and that's as may be,
> There is no use reviling the top of the tree,
> We must build, not destroy, or our effort is vain,
> So away with disgruntled old Andy Maclean.
> ... Then, away with this moaner and all of his flock,
> We must fight in the War for the round of the clock.
> The weaklings must go and the strong men remain
> So we haven't got time for old Andy Maclean.[51]

Few doubted that some measure of reforms was required, but these lyrics echoed the sentiment at Naval Service Headquarters, which was that it would not be in the service's best interest if the public interpreted the future changes as coming from MacLean's threats.

With emotions running high in both camps, some did not think that the navy could wait for the minister to return. For example, the new fairmile staff officer, Lieutenant Commander R.M. Powell, RCNVR, wrote to Lay that "the constant harping on inefficiency etc. at Naval Service Headquarters is, I believe, detrimental to National morale and McLean should be disciplined." Lay agreed. Before passing this memo on to the chief of the naval staff, he jotted down his own recommendation: the navy needed to institute immediate "proceedings" against the publishers of *Boating Magazine*.[52] Nor was Lay alone, as MacTavish observed that the navy could easily prosecute MacLean under Article 39 of the Defence of Canada Regulations. Nelles was unwilling to do that without approval, and his focus was on preparing for Macdonald's anticipated defence in the House of Commons. Accordingly, he instructed various staff officers to produce suitable responses.[53]

It is uncertain why MacLean was never prosecuted – if it was believed that a trial would only succeed in giving him additional publicity, that advice was never put in writing. His defence would rest on the veracity of the allegations, in which case Canadians might interpret a favourable verdict as a ruling on the navy's efficiency; this was a risk the senior staff could not take. Certainly Nelles did not pull any punches in his briefing, telling the minister that the navy was experiencing "growing pains." Likewise, the executive assistant had drawn a similar conclusion. "No claim to perfection should be made, the Naval Service in three years of war grew phenomenally, mistakes have been made," Connolly told Macdonald; but more upbeat than the chief of the naval staff, he continued, "generally speaking, the Service has profited from the experience which it has gained thus far."[54] In fact, all the candidate responses prepared for the minister admitted that the navy had its fair share of problems, and some even believed that MacLean's criticisms were worthy of additional study once they had been "tabulated [and] drained of their personal venom."[55] Nelles was willing to go further to explore these "reserve issues," but only after MacLean had been defeated. This was the primary goal, and it was suggested that the minister should open his remarks to the House along the following lines: "On several occasions during the last session of this House, I listened to some fairly critical remarks about the other two Services, and I remember wondering when it would be the Navy's turn to come in for some strong but well-meant censure. That time has now apparently arrived ... [but] is so full of bitterness, almost of malice, that I seriously doubt if it was intended to be constructive at all."[56]

The best way to defeat MacLean was to go on the offensive and show the public that his motivation for attacking the navy was not based on a noble crusade to reform the service. It was instead a petty vendetta. Nelles thought so too and also recommended that Macdonald emphasize how MacLean was "found temperamentally unsuited to naval warfare ... and retirement was therefore considered (mandatory)."[57] It was Harry DeWolf who, after reading Nelles' submission, best summarized the navy's suggested strategy: "I consider it merely the story of Lt. Com. MacLean's failure to make good in the RCNVR, and as such makes him the goat – not the RCN as intended."[58]

These submissions were composed with the utmost care and professionalism, and Macdonald required little time to prepare after returning from Nova Scotia. Their hard work represented a consolidated effort by both regulars and reservists. That numerous RCNVR officers at Naval Service Headquarters had rallied behind Nelles and his staff further indicated that MacLean's allegations were exaggerated. Accordingly, suggestions from men like Powell, MacTavish, and again Pugsley – who thought that MacLean's campaign was nothing more than the sad tale of a man who "didn't get what he himself wanted" – led Connolly to believe that the splits witnessed at Naval Service Headquarters the previous summer had now healed. That MacLean's attack contributed to this process was evident when Pugsley observed, "We're fighting the enemy, not ourselves."[59] Likewise, MacLean's disciples had been willing to support the campaign providing it were discreet, but his attempt to bring reserve issues to a boil in a stew of public acrimony was simply too much, and his previous support soon evaporated. Similarly, the minister's staff's accomplishments were impressive and their devotion infectious. MacLean's article drove the Naval Board members back into the minister's confidence, and with their help Macdonald was able to protect himself and the navy with the skill, style, and cunning of the experienced politician he was.[60]

Addressing the House of Commons on 17 February 1943, Macdonald shielded the navy's reputation while at the same time portraying MacLean as a narcissistic man who had engineered a methodical attack on the RCN in order to justify his own personal failure as an officer. Macdonald had little choice but to discredit MacLean. MacLean had timed the publication of his article so that it would correspond with the opening of Parliament, a moment when the government was extremely vulnerable to public criticism regarding Canada's war record. For example, as one historian has observed, Mackenzie King's "government was under siege" when the new session in the House of Commons began on 1 February 1943. Their handling of Canada's military effort was less than stellar and the public was not happy, leading the minister of national defence, Colonel J.L. Ralston, to exclaim: "If the war ended now we would have to hang our heads in shame."[61] Macdonald was defending a navy that had suffered a recent string of failures at sea, and the last thing he needed was for the press and opposition to champion MacLean's cause.

Given that Mackenzie King's Liberals had survived much worse, it might be difficult to understand why Macdonald feared MacLean so much. After all, the minister's naval advisors had done an excellent job of showing how they were "simply" dealing with "a retired RCNVR officer with a grouch."[62] From their perspective that may have been obvious, but as a politician Macdonald could not ignore MacLean's connections to the official opposition and the media, as well as his ties to the business community in Toronto. MacLean's political arsenal was impressive, and that made him a considerable threat to both the navy's and, perhaps more seriously, the government's reputation. It gave Macdonald good reason for concern. While events such as the conscription crisis of 1942 suggest that the Liberals could weather just about any political storm, Mackenzie King was extremely susceptible to issues that endangered the party's position.[63] Convincing the press and Parliament that MacLean had orchestrated the entire campaign for his own purposes was a shrewd but necessary tactic.

Few understood why a man of MacLean's civic stature would risk his reputation by attacking the navy unless his concerns were legitimate. But with the assistance of the Naval Staff Macdonald had given the public an alternative theory:

> He has criticized the ability and the judgement of others; he cannot blame us if we look now at his own talents and his own training ... I pass on now to what is perhaps the most significant comment I have to make. I have looked over all files relating to Commander MacLean and to his service, both in Canada and in England. He has sneered at and belittled the Canadian navy so violently and so openly; he has lauded the British navy so highly – and quite properly lauded it – that I expected to find in his records something to indicate that he stood very high indeed in the opinion of

officials of the great British navy. But what did I actually find? I found that his standing in British naval circles was exactly the opposite of high. The reports by his senior Canadian officers are not very flattering, but one of them at least is absolutely fulsome when compared with the reports by officers of the royal navy.[64]

Macdonald's counterattack was powerful but in some measure it was a façade. Quite simply, the minister had already decided that changes incorporating some of MacLean's recommendations were necessary. Precisely because of that, the forthcoming reforms could not be mentioned: there could be no link between them and the troublesome editor. Instead, Macdonald chose to discredit the suggestions that would not be implemented, such as board representation for the reserves.

Unfortunately for the minister, his response in the House of Commons on this matter was weak, as he argued that the Naval Board already had a reservist within its membership. Whether Macdonald's logic was flawed can be questioned but the opposition struck where it could, remarking that this man was merely a secretary and thus had no power. In hindsight, Macdonald might have been well advised to listen to Connolly, who had observed that the Naval Board was not created as "a parliament" to represent all those who served. "To suggest that a man without naval experience would be a completely satisfactory member of this board," he explained further, "is, I think, incorrect."[65] The present Naval Board was composed of men with twenty-five or more years of service, and it could be assumed that they had accumulated knowledge and skill that no reservist could match. This also shows that Connolly agreed with the permanent force's perspective, arguing that MacLean and his followers wanted equality in an organization that was designed to protect democracy not practice it.

Flawed as it was, Macdonald's approach nevertheless had the desired effect. The substance of MacLean's argument was deflected and the minister survived the battle in the House. The press and the opposition soon lost interest in the matter, and even that master of parliamentary tactics, Prime Minister King, had to acknowledge that Macdonald had made a good presentation.[66] The triumph was more than just a victory for the navy. It also showed that the minister and Connolly were capable of working both efficiently and effectively with Nelles and his subordinates in a time of extreme crisis. Unfortunately – like his reprieve from MacLean – the minister's rejuvenated enthusiasm for his senior staff was short lived.

As the inspector of contract built ships – a position connected with the construction of the fairmiles – Commander G.L. Roome, RCN, was one of the few officers who realized that the "MacLean threat" was not over. "The answer by the minister to the House on 17 February, although a proper and concise reply to the article itself," Roome cautioned Connolly, "is not satisfactory to the tone of [the] entire article." Wanting to ensure that the executive assistant understood the score,

Roome then emphasized that MacLean "has obviously sabotaged the war effort by trying to spread discontent. He has probably done so in some of the young Officers already and more probably in the minds of parents of the younger RCNVR officers." Given that MacLean had attracted followers within the fleet, Roome worried the renegade editor was so well organized that he had the potential to do the same with the public. He therefore suggested that the only way to silence MacLean was to hit him with a media blitz in his hometown of Toronto.[67] Although Macdonald's decision not to follow this advice can be questioned, solid evidence soon emerged that neither MacLean nor his father were conceding defeat. In two separate letters, Hugh MacLean berated the minister and his "Permanent Staff's tactics," which had apparently "opened a door, which we plan to make full use of in due course."[68] Both Connolly and Macdonald suspected that Andrew MacLean would launch a second offensive, and they were right: in April 1943, he again used *Boating Magazine* to respond to the minister's speech. This time, however, his attack focused on the minister and powerful new allies were enlisted to discredit Macdonald.

Since his original beef had been with the RCN's top brass, MacLean had purposely avoided any direct commentary on Macdonald's performance as minister. Macdonald's comments in the House of Commons changed all that, and now MacLean turned on his new target. He told Canadians how "every accusation of maladministration, of abuses and inefficiencies in the administration of the Royal Canadian Navy ... was brought to the attention of the Minister of National Defence for Naval Services many months before publication. We did not wish to wash the Navy's dirty linen in public, but men are dying while Ottawa fuddles." That Macdonald knew about the allegations prior to the confrontation not only hurt his credibility with the public, but also with his naval advisors, who were now aware that their political master had not given them the full story. Worse yet, the April issue was filled with submissions, apparently from reserve officers and their relatives, who all supported the allegations. "Hang on to your temper Mr. Editor, and don't let the dirty tactics of the Navy Minister worry you," wrote a serving officer of the RCNVR, "there's a thousand officers and men who know you did a fine and courageous job." To strengthen the impression that MacLean had influential allies, two additional letters by "anonymous Members of Parliament" appeared within the editorial section. If accurate, they are verification that the opposition wanted MacLean to continue pressuring the navy. One MP lent his support to the crusade:

> I have read with considerable pleasure your article "Fairmiles and Foul" and must congratulate you both on this and the Editorial Comment, as it is about time somebody exposed this RCN racket. I have a very substantial file collected from various officers who come in here with their tales of woe and some of the stories they have

told me are really scandalous. I have had many questions asked in the House and when Session closed last year, and many more on the list, which I have no doubt will be answered in due course during the coming Session. A naval officer of some considerable standing informed me that the [minister's] answers were damn lies.[69]

Such letters from the opposition further illustrated why the Liberals saw MacLean as a potential threat. Macdonald knew he was in trouble, as it was likely there would be a second battle in the House of Commons. His reaction to MacLean's new offence therefore differed greatly from that of his senior officers, suggesting that he had adjusted course and was once again sailing them all into a sea of confusion and mistrust.

Unlike Macdonald, the Naval Staff were confident that MacLean had been defeated: while the "outside" editorials were troubling, simply reprinting old arguments was not likely to produce the same type of sensationalism in the press. They were right. After thanking Canada's national newspapers for their assistance in bringing the navy's deficiencies to the public's attention, MacLean reported that he intended to use the present issue of *Boating Magazine* to address how the minister had "neglected to comment on the broad issues involved." This much was true, and MacLean could have capitalized on that weakness had he explained the larger implications of his charges. Instead, he could not resist the temptation to "correct the record" by fixating on the "specifics" of the minister's speech. This obsession with technicalities was MacLean's undoing; nothing new had been introduced, and without continuity his counterattack was ineffectual. He had made other mistakes too. Although probably an attempt at atonement, MacLean admitted that he was "guilty of careless writing" and that "the last promotion list (January 1943) was an agreeable surprise." Following such concessions with statements such as "some appalling promotions [within the RCNVR] have been made" was unwise, as it gave the impression that there was no way to satisfy him.[70] Put simply, more reservists had been advanced yet MacLean now complained about those who were promoted.

Tired of the incessant interference and complaints, the Naval Staff had had enough.[71] By early May, Nelles was ready to put his foot down; no longer wanting to subject staff officers to such harassment he gave orders "to cease this futile correspondence." As far as the chief of the naval staff was concerned, this marked the end of MacLean's association with the navy, especially since all future letters would be ignored.[72] It was easy for Nelles to do so. His business was running the navy, and now that MacLean had been publicly discredited, he could get back to that job without interruption. Macdonald did not share that luxury.

There were some subtle yet highly significant changes in Macdonald's behaviour that imply MacLean's relentless public campaign had finally led to a fundamental shift in his attitude toward both the navy and Nelles. First, the frequency of

Macdonald's attendance at Naval Board meetings skyrocketed after the publication of MacLean's second article in April. Between February 1942 – when the Naval Board was first created – and April 1943, Macdonald missed 51 percent of all meetings. Immediately after the publication until he resigned as minister in April 1945, his absentee rate fell to less than 1 percent.[73] Second, in his postwar memoir, Lay recounted how Macdonald believed in spring of 1943 that "because of his lack of sea time, Nelles was not the right person to remain as CNS [chief of the naval staff]."[74] MacLean's article had told Canadians that their admirals' "lack of sea experience" explained why the senior staff had lost touch with the realities on the coast. At the time, Macdonald thought that the slanderous nature of this statement had left MacLean vulnerable to a possible libel suit but a month later it seems he changed his mind.[75] It would take another four months before other problems in the navy, such as the training and equipment deficiencies, captured Macdonald's full attention, so MacLean's allegations were the only controversial issue facing Macdonald in April 1943 that might explain why he became more active at meetings and questioned Nelles' position as chief of the naval staff.

The minister's reaction might seem odd, as it was obvious MacLean's campaign was grinding to a halt after his second article had fallen flat. From Macdonald's perspective, however, MacLean's constant reappearance was disturbing. He could never be certain that the scandal was truly over as long as MacLean had the power, wealth, and connections to regroup and stir up trouble at a later date. Events would prove the minister's instincts correct. Another reason Macdonald continued to fear MacLean was that he seemed to have captured public opinion to an even greater extent than had originally been estimated. In fact, after returning from Toronto, an officer at Naval Service Headquarters reported that the article "was the subject of conversation everywhere."[76] Connolly agreed, confiding to his diary that "whole VR and NR [RCNVR and RCNR] is definitely and unmistakably against the RCN. Whole country is with the VR's."[77] Such a bold admission indicated that the executive assistant was re-evaluating the situation. MacLean's attack had united Macdonald and his advisors but perhaps, Connolly now worried, the minister had aligned himself with the wrong side. This raised the disturbing possibility that Nelles had either lied or was completely out of touch with the realities at sea. Neither option was attractive, and all Macdonald could do at this juncture was keep a close eye on his naval chief. The more so because publicly reversing his position at this time would have been politically disastrous. Even MacLean realized that it was too late for compromise. He told the executive assistant that "it is obvious to anyone reading the Minister's speech and my articles that one of us is very much in ignorance of what actually has transpired."[78] Three months of battling MacLean had taken its toll on the minister, and he was still no closer to understanding whether there was a grave morale problem with the naval reserves or not.

Nor would he ever get an answer because the whole issue depended on the personal perceptions and experiences of the individual reserve officers. It is possible to find accounts in which reserve officers serving at the same place and at the same time give a wide range of interpretations on their regular force superiors.[79] It would take considerable time, energy, and investigation for Macdonald to determine whether the sharp-end grouser's perception of the regulars actually spoke for the majority of reservists. In some respects, however, that no longer mattered. Whether real or imagined, MacLean's campaign had proven that the navy's perceived troubles could be just as dangerous to the minister's political career as a situation based on fact. The contention that Macdonald had ignored serious problems was attractive political fodder for the minister's opponents, and as time would soon prove, it was a perceived weakness that the opposition would try to exploit.

After an unsuccessful attempt to contact the prime minister, MacLean once again appealed to the press to take up his cause.[80] Most newspapers had lost interest and refused, but in late May 1943 the *Quebec Chronicle-Telegraph* covered a speech MacLean gave to a local naval veteran's association meeting.[81] This gave the Conservatives an excuse to launch another attack on Macdonald in early June. This three-day assault on the navy was well planned, and its goal was to explore MacLean's claim that the minister was uninterested in naval affairs. On the first day, a number of questions were asked that attempted to clarify whether it was the minister or the Naval Board that was truly running the navy. It was clear that the Conservatives were baiting Macdonald, as he deeply resented the implication that he was not an active participant in the decision-making process at Naval Service Headquarters. It was at this time that MacLean's charges were once again used as evidence.

Accusing Macdonald of relying too heavily on the advice of his Naval Board during the February debate, the leader of the Conservative Party, R.B. Hanson, asked

> whether the minister ever investigated this matter himself because, after all, where there is smoke there may be fire and there is a good deal of smoke around Commander MacLean. I know him extremely well, and he thinks he has a real grievance against the permanent force officers of the navy. I do not know anything about the matter myself, but I suggest that the minister's reply does not indicate that he himself made any investigation. We ought to know just what the position is with reference to the complaint of this man, who is certainly not a fool by any means. He is certainly a man who is actuated by high patriotic motives. He wanted to help ... Did the minister himself ever make any investigation of his complaint?[82]

Other Conservatives – worried that the debate would once again centre on MacLean's motives for attacking the navy – tried to focus their criticism on the question of board representation for the reserves. This was a subject that had substance and could not be muddled by fruitless rhetoric over the nature of MacLean's character. As in February, Macdonald defended his naval advisors, repeating his view that reserve representation was not required. But Conservative member (and future prime minister) John Diefenbaker pressed home the attack, informing Macdonald that he had personally been contacted by a number of RCNVR officers, at least ten of whom had expressed the same desire to have special representation for the reserves at Naval Service Headquarters.[83] This was a disturbing revelation for Macdonald, as it further confirmed that MacLean was not acting alone – he did have at least some followers who were willing to take their discrimination complaints to the opposition, particularly since Diefenbaker felt obliged to "secure information on this subject and thus be able to reassure these RCNVR officers." Diefenbaker continued, "they feel that they are deserving of greater representation on the Naval Board than they have had heretofore. Has the minister given consideration to increasing this representation?" Since Macdonald had admitted on the previous day that the Naval Board was merely an advisory body, Diefenbaker suggested the appointment of an RCNVR officer to represent the reserves would pay "great dividends in the way of morale, and it certainly would do no harm in connection to policy." Diefenbaker's argument was logical, so Macdonald found it difficult to counter. Sensing that he was on shaky ground, Macdonald finally conceded that he would "bear it very carefully and fully in mind."[84]

Despite the minister's weak performance against Diefenbaker, the battle was finally over as this represented the last exchange in the House of Commons over MacLean's charges. Of course, at the time there was no way for Macdonald to know that. As far as he was concerned, MacLean was an ongoing concern, and because of that Macdonald lived in continuous fear that the renegade editor might strike again. The executive assistant felt the same way, particularly since MacLean had discovered that the navy had enacted various policies based on his proposed reforms: "The Minister must be well aware that everything that I have fought for while Senior Officer Fairmiles has now been put into effect ... It is a pity to see a man of his high calibre jeopardize his political future to support the persecution of one that has only offended his advisors ... the Minister is entitled to know the truth of what goes on in his own department."[85]

Such a discovery had vindicated MacLean in his tirade against the navy. The problem was that after two failed attempts to do battle with the navy, no one would listen. Embittered over his failure, MacLean probed the service throughout 1943 for any newsworthy item that could lead to a renewed attack. Indeed, he had almost stumbled on potential scandal when he observed in the April edition of *Boating Magazine* that "a chain is only as strong as its weakest link and the administration of the Fairmiles leaves so much to be desired that it may be assumed that the rest

An overhead shot of the *Algerine* class minesweeper, HMCS *New Liskeard*. Although not as famous as the corvettes, the minesweepers nevertheless played an equally important role as antisubmarine escorts and were largely manned by the RCNR and RCNVR. DHH 81/520/1000, BOX 141, FILE 27

[of the fleet] is none too well managed."[86] The conditions on the corvettes and minesweepers would soon become a key issue at Naval Service Headquarters, and Connolly later considered it lucky that MacLean never acted on this hunch.[87] This new "crisis" had been lurking in the shadows, and like the complaints that the regulars discriminated against the reserves, it too was brought to the minister's attention through reserve officers using backdoor channels. Macdonald had survived one scandal only to be led into another. Perhaps MacLean's greatest legacy was therefore that he made Macdonald extremely sensitive to any problem within the navy that threatened to become political. By doing so, MacLean gave reservists the necessary credibility to influence the minister.

Macdonald had spent an entire year trying to discover whether MacLean's allegations were the manifestation of real problems in the service or the exaggerated half-truths of a man with a personal agenda. With the gift of hindsight, the latter seems more likely: the minister's attempt to deal with these issues only left MacLean confused and agitated. In the end, Macdonald learned that reality did not matter – perceived problems were just as dangerous to his career as factual situations, and that had ramifications for his relationship with Nelles. At no time did the chief of the naval staff resist the minister's reforms, and Nelles' hard work during the early stages of the confrontation ensured that Macdonald was prepared for MacLean. Such efforts indicate that Macdonald could count on Nelles, and that the two men were capable of working extremely well together in a crisis. Unfortunately for Nelles, this partnership was based on a poor foundation.

The Naval Board enjoyed the minister's confidence not because he believed it was right but because he needed its support to defeat MacLean's public campaign. When Macdonald received further evidence that Canadians had been swayed by MacLean's arguments, his insecurities got the better of him and he again started to doubt the chief of the naval staff. Clearly, MacLean's public attacks exposed Macdonald's vulnerability and heightened his sensitivity to any issue that threatened to become political. MacLean had brought tremendous political pressure to bear on Macdonald, and it was not an experience that either he or Connolly cared to repeat. This explains why Macdonald would overreact when another officer – who also claimed to be acting on behalf of disgruntled reservists – would tell him that there were grave morale problems on the fleet's corvettes and minesweepers. Since it was determined that this new scandal had the potential to dwarf the MacLean affair, Macdonald lost what little faith he had left in his top admiral, and that marked the beginning of the end for Nelles.

3
The Strange Interpretation

The Royal Canadian Navy suffered from political interference. That, at least, was the expert opinion of Commodore G.W.G. Simpson, RN, the senior British officer in charge of the port of Londonderry, Northern Ireland, who oversaw all RCN escorts arriving from their transatlantic voyages. Simpson understood the Canadians serving at sea and sympathized with them. To his mind, their political woes had been triggered by "a lack of cohesion and direction from the professional top due to a percentage of officers in the intermediate and lower ranks, with political axes to grind, (but with limited experience and knowledge) causing disruption by playing the political game."[1] While MacLean's campaign was the epitome of political interference, Simpson's recollections centred on a small group of reserve commanding officers who tried to use political connections to get modern equipment for the RCN's corvettes and minesweepers. As commodore (D) Londonderry, Simpson was disturbed by the attitude expressed by some of his countrymen, who treated the Canadians as amateurs. In his view, Canadians would never get the chance to prove their true abilities as long as the gear on RCN ships was substandard. At first, he did what any responsible officer would do: he tried to communicate his concerns through regular channels. When that failed to produce results, he took advantage of a visit by the assistant naval information officer at Naval Service Headquarters, Lieutenant Commander William Strange, RCNVR, hoping that this reservist would convey the complaints on to whatever authority was in a position to help best.

Simpson had unknowingly tapped into Connolly's network of reserve informants. As one of Connolly's friends, Strange passed on the message that seagoing officers were on the verge of rebelling over the equipment situation. By doing so, he began a process that eventually led Commodore Simpson to bypass chains of command in the Royal Navy and RCN so that he could communicate problems directly to the Canadian naval minister. Simply put, while the MacLean scandal had left Macdonald vulnerable, Strange's interference had opened the floodgates at Naval Service Headquarters and perhaps sealed Nelles' fate by turning a perceived morale problem with an operational deficiency on the North Atlantic into a political crisis in Ottawa.[2]

A string of critical memos throughout the spring of 1943 hinted at dissatisfaction within the escort fleet. The first of these – written in May by captain (D) Newfoundland, Captain J.M. Rowland, RN, to the flag officer Newfoundland, Rear

Admiral H.E. Reid – offered a highly technical account that chronicled the RCN's inability to get type 123D asdics as well as 271 Mark IV radars, and how this affected its efficiency at sea. Reid, on the other hand, cut to the heart of the issue in plain words to the Naval Staff in Ottawa when he observed in a covering letter how "Canadian escorts thus are at a great disadvantage compared with RN escorts [because] they are placed in the unacceptable position of having to fight a modern war with outmoded instruments."[3] Exactly one month later, the commanding officer of HMCS *Restigouche*, Lieutenant Commander Desmond Piers, RCN, covered much of the same ground in a report to Rowland. Having spent over five years at sea, Piers was finally being posted ashore. His report was intended to share his experience senior officers, including the observation that "it is a blunt statement of fact that RCN ships are out dated in the matter of A/S [antisubmarine] equipment by 12 to 18 months, compared to RN ships."[4] But it was Lieutenant Commander James George, a reservist serving as the historical records officer in London, who graphically captured the impact that this deficiency was having on Canadian officers while in Londonderry. After visiting "one or two ships in all Groups" and having "met all Commanding Officers" George wrote to his superiors in mid-June that "the failure to equip these ships with modern material is keenly felt by all their Officers and widely discussed, and is tending to discourage them."[5]

In itself, the similarities between these accounts indicate that the discontent was widespread. Beyond that, the fact that the reports paralleled the RCN's convoy route – having come from an operational commander in St. John's, a seagoing captain, and a concerned officer visiting Londonderry – further suggests the dissatisfaction crisscrossed the Atlantic with a steady regularity.

Memos from other shore-based authorities told a similar tale. Discovered during postwar research, the memos explain why a historian working on the first official history wanted to record that "in 1942-43 a wave of protest swept in from many Commanding Officers of Canadian ships who did not see why ... Canadian ships should, in equipment, fall so far behind the Royal Navy escorts."[6] The chief naval historian, Gilbert Tucker, cut this passage from the manuscript. Other postwar historians have made use of these reports to illustrate how a number of officers, both regular and reserve, were desperately trying to tell Naval Service Headquarters about the RCN's technological backwardness or "equipment crisis."[7] Given the tone of the critical memos, it is easy to see why historians have drawn the conclusion that the lack of modern equipment caused a serious morale problem in the fleet.[8]

Without much evidence from the commanding officers themselves, however, there is little to support the conclusion that the majority was bitter. Instead, postwar interviews suggest that – while they may have wanted better weapons and sensors – seagoing officers were focused on winning the war, and so made the most of the equipment they had on board. Likewise, had they wanted to do so,

The 123 asdic was essential to locating submerged U-boats. It was an earlier type that would eventually be replaced by the superior 144 sets. The wheel under the compass on the right would turn the sonar dome under the ship. The mechanism on the left would trace out an image from the sonar's beam. DHH 91/481

commanding officers had ample opportunity to voice their displeasure through their monthly "Report of Proceedings." With the exception of the occasional perfunctory comment, the reports do not even hint at the possibility that the fleet was rife with discontent over the state of equipment.[9] There is no doubt that the RCN's equipment lagged far behind the Royal Navy in the spring of 1943, but perhaps historians have overestimated the extent of the acrimony. Instead there is strong evidence that a small and vocal fringe element of seagoing RCNVR officers with pre-war political connections was willing to use unconventional means to get what it wanted. Like MacLean, these officers contacted the minister directly.

Convinced that the top brass had ignored warnings about equipment, they tried to persuade others of a grave and potentially explosive morale problem within the navy. Having adopted one of MacLean's tactics, these particular reservists realized that the minister was more likely to listen if they exaggerated the extent of the dissatisfaction. And that was the problem. The substance of their argument was a real concern in the RCN but their attempts to convince the minister that Naval Service Headquarters' ignorance was at the root of both the shortage and the discontent constituted unwarranted political interference. In reality, naval officers in Ottawa had listened. The Naval Staff had been busy finding solutions to this problem months before the critical reports arrived, though most seagoing commanders did not know this. Consequently, a perception formed among some seagoing elements that Naval Service Headquarters was simply uninterested in the critical reports and in the claim that the RCN needed upgrading. That this was their perception was not the fault of Naval Service Headquarters – the responsibility of briefing the fleet fell to another authority.

On closer examination, headquarters had actively considered both Rowland's memo and Piers' reports (of which more will be said in Chapter 5). The Atlantic Command was told exactly how the Naval Staff was working on the situation and that they could expect to see improvements with the RCN's equipment in the near future.[10] As a result, it was the downward flow of information at this operational level where the chain of command broke down. Perhaps Naval Service Headquarters could have done more to ensure that the ships at sea knew they were working on the issue, but naval regulations made it clear that it was up to commanding officer Atlantic coast and flag officer Newfoundland to brief their respective commands on what Ottawa was doing. In other words, the flow of information was not from Naval Service Headquarters to individual vessels, but rather from Naval Service Headquarters to the operational commands, to the captain (D), and finally to the senior officers of escort groups or a ship's captain. And that explains why the politically connected reserve commanding officers – despite having a legitimate concern over modernization – were crossing the line by going directly to the minister. Moreover, this complex situation would have dire consequences for Naval Service Headquarters, as the very formation of this particular network of reservists was the product of the faulty assumption that the Naval Staff did not care about the fleet's upgrading.

After long convoys, Canadian commanding officers in Londonderry had a tendency to come together for "bull sessions" in local pubs or wardrooms "where the 'shop talk' never ended" because others were not encouraged to "frolic with them."[11] The therapeutic process of sharing trials and tribulations at sea, which invariably included some type of commentary on issues such as equipment, was a means to relieve stress. Few had the opportunity to lodge complaints outside the confines of North Atlantic life, although one of those who did found it a richly rewarding experience. "While in Ottawa I got a great many legitimate beefs off my chest," this officer wrote to one of his seagoing brethren in December 1942, concluding with "beefs which all of us have but rarely have the opportunity of voicing. All of which was good for the soul."[12] For most, this type of grumbling was kept among themselves, which was why George entitled his report, "Summarizing RCN wardroom technical grouses." The same was true for Piers, whose observations spoke not only for permanent force officers, "but also those experienced Reserve Officers who now command the vast majority of HMC ships and who are diffident about forwarding their opinions to Naval Service Headquarters."[13] Given the nature of that comment, Piers obviously did not know about the small group of RCNVR officers who had found another avenue through which to make equipment a priority at Naval Service Headquarters.

Being responsible naval officers, Rowland, Piers, and George all filed their reports through normal channels. For a group of well-connected seagoing reservists, that particular route was too slow and cumbersome. At least one member of the Naval Staff knew that various seagoing reserve officers were taking their concerns directly to Macdonald. For example, in a postwar interview this officer revealed that "our officers would come back, somewhat naturally, complaining about their lack of modern equipment and that they were very open about this. They used to go see the Minister behind Nelles' back, and that sort of thing, and say that we hadn't got certain equipment."[14] Perhaps the most compelling indication that it was reserve officers who were bypassing Nelles and the Naval Board came from Macdonald. "A lot of the RCNVR officers who come back from sea call in to see me and they talk quite frankly," Macdonald admitted in June 1943, "[and] I always encourage them to do that."[15] Unlike MacLean's campaign, there is little to suggest that these particular reserve commanding officers were an organized group who hatched plots to undermine the hegemony of the regular officer. Instead, each had his own political connection, and the decision to contact the minister was probably an individual and personal choice.

Nor was that the only difference between them and MacLean. Some had already challenged MacLean's fixation on issues that pitted reservists against regulars with claims that there was friction between seagoing types and those on shore, but these new officers had thrown yet another interpretation into the mix. In late April 1943, former corvette captain Lieutenant Commander W.E.S. Briggs, RCNR, warned his superior that trouble was brewing in Londonderry. Similar to the other critical reports, he too suggested that the RCN was lagging behind the Royal Navy in modernizing. According to Briggs, this was not the only problem, as "rightly or wrongly, the average Canadian officer resents the reaction he gathers when dealing with the RN. The feeling that he is being looked upon as a 'ruddy colonial.'"[16]

Briggs' report is the only one that made a direct correlation between Royal Navy attitudes and the RCN's modernization problem. In his view, the British mocked the Canadians because they were not sinking U-boats, and that inefficiency was linked to the RCN's lack of equipment. Undoubtedly, discussing delicate subjects such as British discrimination against Canadians caused Briggs some discomfort, yet he emphasized that equipment parity with the Royal Navy was the key to improving the RCN's reputation. Nor was he the only one who had heard Royal Navy officers making derogatory comments about the Canadians.

Spring 1943 proved a pivotal moment in the battle of the Atlantic. Intensive training, modernization, special intelligence (ULTRA), and hard-earned experience had turned the Germans from hunters into prey. For those who equated success with the destruction of the enemy, that victory was reserved almost exclusively for the Royal Navy. Canadian warships played an active and important role in the U-boat war throughout this period, escorting a number of convoys "in a safe and timely manner," yet their kill ratio was unspectacular. Aside from HMCS *Drumheller*'s shared destruction of U-456, in which she was credited with one-third of a kill, the RCN's tally remained unchanged for another six months.[17] British authorities responsible for the battle of the Atlantic at Western Approaches Command Headquarters in Liverpool, England, were unimpressed, the more so because Canadian-escorted convoys were often interpreted as chaotic adventures.[18] Things probably would have been different, certain Western Approaches officers believed, had their Commonwealth partner swallowed its nationalistic ambitions and sailed with the more experienced British groups. According to the commanding officer of HMCS *Summerside*, F.O. Gerity, RCNR, that view of his countrymen was widespread, he having heard it "expressed at Western Approaches Tactical Courses in Liverpool and Londonderry as well as by high-ups in the Western Approaches Organization."[19] Even a British officer serving at Naval Service Headquarters thought his colleagues were being excessively snobbish, observing that "it was only after repeated letters to people in the Admiralty that I was finally able to stop the attitude which could be described as 'On your way back from Washington, put your head in the [Canadian] Nursery and see how the kids are getting on.'"[20] A senior American officer in Londonderry was equally unimpressed and believed that the Admiralty treated the RCN like a wayward adolescent instead of as a mature partner in the western alliance. "British officers as a class think the Canadians very ineffective," he told his superiors in Washington, and "in all the time I was there I did not hear one single word in their favour."[21] Naturally, there were many in the Royal Navy who admired the RCN and appreciated the sacrifices they were making at sea, but there was much negativity nonetheless, and that was bound to rub the officers of Canada's wartime reserve navy the wrong way.

The Royal Navy "air of superiority" was nothing new for the regulars. They had seen it all during the interwar years when the young, small, and inexperienced RCN had little choice but to send its officers to the United Kingdom for much of their training and sea experience.[22] Still in the process of developing its own infrastructure and identity, the RCN needed the parent service, and so it was only natural that they followed the ways of their guardians. The Royal Navy was, after all, one of the most experienced navies in the world. More often than not, the Canadians were grateful to the imperial mother, and stories of Canadian officers returning from the United Kingdom sporting new English accents, posh attitudes, and a hankie up the sleeve (a tradition in the Royal Navy) were not uncommon. Lacking these experiences, reservists often found it difficult to identify with the parent service and instead preferred the company of their North American cousins in the United States Navy. The huge influx of reservists and the birth of what MacLean had labelled the "people's navy" were largely responsible for this shift in the Canadian service's relationship with the Royal Navy. That they were fresh from Canadian society, trained by the permanent force RCN, and operated from HMC ships in Canadian groups, made the RCNVR a truly national institution.[23] Canadians were unimpressed by British quips that the acronym RCN stood for the "Royal Collision Navy" or the "Royal Colonial Navy." In fact, for the politically connected RCNVR officers, it proved a good reason to contact the minister. While they believed the Royal Navy discriminated against the RCN because of the latter's inexperience, these men were not really angry with the British or their so-called elitist attitudes. After all, that mentality was merely a symptom of the larger sickness. Illequipped escort vessels was the true cancer, and it was one that only the treatment centre at NSHQ could cure. Since little help appeared to be forthcoming from that quarter – and perception here was all-important – they turned to the minister. The fact that he, too, seemed distracted and indifferent, at least in the beginning, reinforced their sense that the senior Naval Staff was delinquent: had Nelles been doing his job, surely the minister would have known, and cared.

Part of the problem was a lack of communication resulting from a truncated organizational structure that did not serve Canadian interests well. Convoy cycles in the spring of 1943 gave Canadian warships a sixteen-day layover period in the United Kingdom as compared to four days in St. John's, but there was no Canadian shore authority or support staff in spite of the time RCN commanders were spending at Londonderry. Responsibility for the port's administration was shared between the British commodore (D) and the American commander of Task Group (CTG) 24.7. Although the Canadians technically fell under the USN's jurisdiction, this dual control of the base was confusing and Canadian issues and concerns thus often received insufficient attention. The disbanding of CTG 24.7 and the American withdrawal from Londonderry helped to alleviate growing tensions at the base, as did a British reorganization that saw Simpson take over as the commodore (D), but in the short term such moves had still not established a clear chain of command for the Canadians.[24]

Likewise the understaffed and neglected offices of the captain commanding Canadian ships in London – the main RCN authority overseas – were unable to pay much attention to the base at Londonderry. The inability to approach a senior officer for advice or, conversely, to listen to criticisms, had left Canadian seagoing officers with the perception that they were "nobody's baby" in Londonderry.[25] Such gaps in the chain of command shook some officers' faith in the navy's leadership, and it seemed only natural that those with political connections would use them. Their chances to do so were few and far between, and while Macdonald may not have immediately understood the equipment deficiencies, the reservists did find a British officer who was sympathetic to their cause.

"Shrimp" Simpson was unhappy with what he saw when he became the commodore (D) in Londonderry on 26 April 1943. Generally regarded as a stickler for efficiency who went about his business like "a ball of fire," Simpson razed the old administration and created his own organization out of its ashes.[26] Operations, training, and maintenance received the bulk of his attention as he hand-picked a team of administrators to handle the mundane and time-consuming tasks of port management and barracks routine.[27] While he was willing to farm out these administrative duties to trusted officers, the operational side of the command was entirely Simpson's preserve. This mixture of delegation and authoritative control was the key to his success, and Simpson's radical approach led one senior Royal Navy officer to the conclusion that "Londonderry under the new Commodore has changed out of recognition."[28] A unified command structure allowed Simpson to achieve miracles at the base, but the American withdrawal also meant that he inherited the thorny issue of what to do with the Canadians.

It had been the Royal Navy's practice to respect American jurisdiction over the operational and administrative control of the RCN while in Londonderry as a means to avoid turf wars. Unfortunately this created a perception among the Canadians "that the RN authorities were not particularly interested in their welfare."[29] Now that these RCN crews were his responsibility, Simpson wanted their trust. Certainly the convoy escort conferences initiated by his predecessor – which permitted discussion of tactics and technical developments between seagoing officers and the commodore[30] – were a good start, but Simpson knew that he had to develop his own initiatives in order to make a breakthrough with the leery Canadians. Accessibility was the key. Some characterized his solution as an open-door policy, but instead of waiting for captains to come to his office with their comments, Simpson went down to their ships. He also announced his intention to sail

Without a Canadian operational authority in the port, Commodore G.W.G. "Shrimp" Simpson, RN, became the de facto father of the RCN escort groups that Debby Piers had called "nobody's baby" in Londonderry. A down-to-earth and likable British officer, Simpson's popularity among the Canadians was legendary. F.R.. KEMP PHOTOGRAPHER, LAC PA-161259

with every Canadian group while training near Londonderry "at least every second trip and, if possible, more frequently."[31] Nor was that all. In an attempt to formalize the new relationship with his Canadian captains, Simpson invited the top Canadian administrative officer in London to Londonderry for a three-day conference on command arrangements at the base.

Like Simpson, Commander Fred Price, RCNVR, was new to his appointment. Having become the captain commanding Canadian ships only three days before Simpson took over as commodore (D), he too was in the process of rebuilding a shattered command.[32] Price was filling the billet only temporarily and merely maintaining the regular liaison routine with the Admiralty until his successor arrived. Most of the time, Price and his staff busied themselves keeping abreast of any Admiralty policy that might be of interest to Naval Service Headquarters or, conversely, giving the British information on the RCN. By doing so, the captain commanding Canadian ships' main duty was to prepare the way for "direct signalled negotiations" between Naval Service Headquarters in Ottawa and the Admiralty.[33] This was the level at which the RCN's equipment situation was discussed with the British, and all information on the subject should have been filtered through the respective chains that led either to Naval Service Headquarters in the Canadian case or the Admiralty for the British.

Beyond that, Price's responsibilities toward Londonderry were ambiguous, providing Simpson with an opportunity. Interest in creating a Canadian captain (D) Londonderry was circulating around the base, yet that was something the commodore wanted to avoid because it would lead to a situation of dual control as had existed with the Americans. Even picking a senior RCN or RCNVR officer as an assistant to his chief of staff was not encouraged, for fear that "a separate unofficial Canadian organisation would materialise" from commanders reporting to this officer rather than the appropriate Royal Navy authority. Price agreed, telling Naval Service Headquarters that "with the personality of Commodore Simpson, it is very doubtful whether the appointment of a Senior Canadian officer is desirable." In exchange for a unified command, the responsibility for looking after the RCN in Londonderry unofficially fell to Simpson. And the orphans of the Eastern Atlantic were grateful to have such a caring father figure waiting for them after each crossing.[34]

Simpson's tender nurturing produced an instant reaction from the Canadians. "I find that a different atmosphere," a pleasantly surprised Price told his superiors in Ottawa, "is even now prevailing [in Londonderry]," barely a month after Simpson's arrival.[35] Price was right. The commodore was characterized as a "man of the people" and the "anti-thesis of the 'stuffy' [Royal Navy] type" who showed absolutely "no sense of superiority," which was exactly what the citizen sailors of Canada's wartime reserve navy wanted and, for that matter, needed.[36] Simpson's tendency to break with tradition – including taboos such as occasionally messing with the ranks while commanding the 10th Submarine Flotilla – made him somewhat of an anomaly in the Royal Navy.[37] Simpson's ability to mix sociably while maintaining a command presence made him a virtual legend among his Canadian subordinates.[38] His popularity was infectious, as most Canadians both admired and trusted him, but that faith came with a price. Taking care of the RCN in Londonderry meant that the commodore had to deal with the modernization complaints. The state of equipment in the RCN was a legitimate concern, and he was pleased to help those who filed their complaints through normal channels. But he was not impressed with the Canadian reservists who were "playing the political game" by circumventing normal military channels.[39] Simpson probably learned of the networks as a result of his practice of socializing in the wardrooms of RCN corvettes, where the members of these networks were more willing to open up and confide in the commodore when the liquor was flowing freely. In Simpson's view, it was not the substance of their argument that was wrong but their method of going to the minister that was distasteful.

There was, after all, a clearly defined Canadian chain of command through which these complaints were to be filed. Starting with the individual commanding officer, recommendations to improve efficiency would be given to the senior officer of an escort group, who then wrote a report to either the captain (D) in Halifax or St. John's (depending on the command to which the ship belonged). In turn, these officers were responsible to the commanding officer Atlantic coast (in Halifax) or the flag officer Newfoundland (in St. John's) who, if they believed it was warranted, would pass word on to Naval Service Headquarters. For the politically connected reservists, it was evident that this chain had broken down, and most suspected that the break was somewhere in Ottawa. As future events would prove, that assumption was in error, but again perception was the key.

In time, Simpson would become more sympathetic to these particular officers – so much so that he would use their pull in the minister's office to communicate concerns to Macdonald – but his initial criticism of them was well founded. Service discipline depended on the chain of command, and that chain would lose all relevance if officers enjoyed the privilege of bypassing their immediate superior. Simpson defined such activities as "political interference" and, according to him, it was a scourge that all services had to avoid. Senior officers regularly possessed knowledge that juniors did not have, and dealing with so many problems at the same time often made it difficult, if not impossible, for commanders to keep the fleet informed of their remedies. For Simpson, juniors only made things worse when they took matters into their own hands, particularly since they had little idea of what their seniors were actually doing.[40] But that was exactly what this small group of reserve officers had done when they sidestepped the top brass in Ottawa, and whether it was intentional or not, Simpson's future actions would only encourage this type of behaviour.

Usually the same rules applied to flag officers like Simpson but his accessibility gave the complainers an opportunity that they certainly were not going to pass up. Like their seagoing brethren who followed the chain of command, they believed

Simpson was a blessing. More than seeing him as a mentor, this network of reservists instead saw a potential leader and champion for their cause. As Simpson later recalled, for example,

> the vast body of [Canadian] officers ... comprised Volunteer Reservists. I found them in general completely loyal to me, but, due to brief training in sea discipline, [they] were natural and outspoken in criticism, and loyalty to the service was not sufficiently inculcated to prevent disloyal though sincere comment. Finding in me an RN Officer, they would pour out their woes, which were often weighty ... They were highly intelligent Canadian civilians in a seafaring role, with initiative and determination to win the war; they were frank, sincere and sometimes rather angry ... My point is that, due to inherent sea discipline, the RCN and RCNR officer got on with the job with little comment. The Volunteer Reserve officer, finding me a Senior beyond the arm of home politics, said exactly what he thought, and you will appreciate that if I was to help him in his troubles (whatever they might be) I must needs listen and endeavour to be to individual officers their guide, philosopher and friend.[41]

The commodore did not understand at this time that the loudest complaints had come from a fringe element who thought that morale was extremely bad, and as a result Simpson's sweeping generalization about RCNVR officers being undisciplined and unhappy was not really just. Like the RCN and RCNR, a vast preponderance of RCNVR officers also "got on with the job with little comment."

In fairness, Simpson was probably influenced by the conviction of this group as well as their claim that there was a link between poor morale in the RCN and modernization, and their passion could have easily been misconstrued as a plea from the majority. Once this seed was planted into the commodore's psyche, all further comments – no matter how minor, harmless, or inconsequential – by any Canadian officer, even in passing, would only serve to reinforce the perception that there was mass discontent. While various sources suggest that the fringe element of reservists obsessing about morale and modernization consisted of only a handful of officers, determining this group's actual size is virtually impossible. Ethically questionable attempts to circumvent channels by contacting the minister meant that they were not in the habit of revealing their identities.

What these particular reserve officers were doing in Londonderry, however, was neither nefarious nor a breach of regulations. After all, Simpson had encouraged them to speak freely. Perhaps their only offence was to exaggerate the level of discontent over the equipment gap between the Royal Navy and the RCN. Simpson would have been derelict in his duty had he not taken some form of action over the modernization concerns, especially since the Canadians had been denied their own captain (D) in Londonderry. The commodore was aware that he was caught up in a battle of recognition, whereby some reservists wanted both Canadian shore-based regulars and British officers in general to afford them the same respect that others were receiving for being "professional" sailors.[42] The problem was that as a British officer Simpson did not fall within any Canadian chain of command, and that greatly hindered his ability to help them. Instead, Simpson's closest link to Naval Service Headquarters was through Price, but the captain commanding Canadian ships was dealing with many issues, one of which, ironically, was how to improve channels of communication so that he could start getting prompt responses from Ottawa.

Simpson was acting in good faith when he tried to get word through to Naval Service Headquarters that the RCN's seagoing fleet was unhappy with the equipment on their ships. In fact, as the senior operational authority in Londonderry, the commodore (D) was just doing his job. The RCN's technical backwardness was a problem, and lacking any tangible evidence that senior Canadian officers were taking corrective action, it was assumed it was a problem that Naval Service Headquarters knew little about. In reality (and as will be seen in Chapter 5), the naval brass in Ottawa were well aware of the equipment gap and were actively attacking the problem. Without that knowledge, however, Simpson also began to question whether information was getting through to Ottawa. He knew that Canadian officers, such as Piers, Briggs, and George, were using normal channels to report the equipment situation to their superiors. The commodore also had a chain of command through which to pass on observations about the Canadians. This consisted of his immediate superior, the commander in chief Western Approaches (the British counterpart to Canada's North West Atlantic Command), who would then have reported to the Admiralty in London (the British counterpart to Naval Service Headquarters in Ottawa). After that, it was up to the Admiralty to either communicate these concerns on to the captain commanding Canadian ships or, conversely, directly to Naval Service Headquarters. The mistaken assumption that Naval Service Headquarters was still not reacting to the equipment situation suggested that attempts to get word through to Ottawa via the Admiralty had also met with disappointing results. At this juncture, Simpson was simply displaying the characteristic of a good officer – the Canadians under his command had a problem, and he let his superiors know as much.

There was good reason why Simpson was so desperate to make contact with Ottawa in the spring of 1943. Londonderry was filled with extra equipment that could easily be fitted on RCN escorts during their layovers, creating a frustrating situation for Simpson. Canadian commanders wanted the equipment that was lying in warehouses in Londonderry, but without financial authorization from Naval Service Headquarters Simpson was powerless to act. According to his understanding of RCN modernization policy, Londonderry had first to secure permission from Naval Service Headquarters before adding new equipment, but the ships slated for this gear often had to go back to sea before Ottawa responded. In time, word of this situation spread across the Atlantic. As the captain (D) in St. John's, for example, Rowland had reported that valuable refit opportunities were being missed because of "the question of who is to pay."[43] Simpson had become commodore (D) only three days before Rowland wrote this memo, so it is unlikely that it reflected any personal communication between the two men. Future attempts to get word through to Naval Service Headquarters were nonetheless the product of Simpson's brainstorming, and although he never specifically asked anyone to go directly to the minister's office, that was exactly where these initiatives would lead.

It should not be surprising that Simpson and Rowland did establish a private correspondence after the former took over as commodore (D). Not only were they both Royal Navy officers, but also, with the exception of being on separate sides of the Atlantic, their respective responsibilities were almost identical. The practicality of a dialogue allowing them to share experiences was obvious. And it was through this exchange of information that Rowland told Simpson about a British officer who "made disparaging remarks about Canadians" by describing them as "colonials," "barbarians," and "cannibals," as well noting that they were "a race apart."[44] Simpson already knew about the problem because reserve officers in Londonderry had told him so. This he considered grossly unfair. In his view, no navy – including the Royal Navy – could compete with the "intelligence" and "enthusiasm" of the average Canadian sailor.[45] The reasons behind the perceived inequity were explained to Rowland by Piers, who, like Briggs, observed that "Commodore Londonderry and his Staff realize that Canadian personnel are not getting the chance they deserve, due to the lack of the latest equipment." Further references to Simpson strongly suggest that he played some type of role in shaping Pier's report, but remarks by other senior officers at Western Approaches indicate that the commodore was not the only one trying to access the Canadian chain of command. Their aim, like Simpson's, was to change the apparent lack of cohesion with the financial aspects of the RCN's modernization policy.[46]

Comments in reports filed by the Allied Anti-Submarine Survey Board identify another factor that further explains Simpson's interest in Naval Service Headquarters' perception of the RCN's modernization situation. Established in March 1943 under the chairmanship of Rear Admiral J.L. Kauffman, USN, the Allied Anti-Submarine Survey Board toured bases in the United States, Great Britain, and Canada in an attempt to standardize antisubmarine training, tactics, and doctrine between the three major allies.[47] While in Londonderry, "the necessity for better equipment was fully discussed" because officers there wanted to bring "pressure to bear on the Canadians on the question of maintenance."[48] Likewise, the Allied Anti-Submarine Survey Board had encountered a similar mentality the previous week when it met with the commander in chief Western Approaches, Admiral Max Horton, RN, and his staff in Liverpool.

With escort forces stretched to the limit on the North Atlantic, Western Approaches had learned that the Canadians wanted to withdraw entire groups for modernization. Horton disagreed with that proposed policy, going as far as sending a message to his Canadian counterpart, the commander in chief Canadian North West Atlantic (formerly the commanding officer Atlantic Command), Rear Admiral Murray, stating that he needed the RCN to maintain a high commitment on the North Atlantic.[49] Horton was asking much from the RCN, wanting them to both expedite the modernization process while at the same time keeping as many ships at sea as possible. Although such demands were unrealistic, the question of the RCN's technical backwardness loomed so heavily in Horton's mind that he personally asked Kauffman to approach Murray's chief of staff (Operations) about this issue when the Board arrived in Halifax.[50] Given that these events took place prior to Simpson's arrival in Londonderry, it appears that the commodore (D) was merely a more vocal advocate of a larger Western Approaches campaign to get the Canadians to modernize. Although there is no direct evidence linking Simpson's actions to his new boss, an incident in early June strongly suggests that Horton supported the commodore's attempt to get Naval Service Headquarters to take the modernization issue more seriously.

Wanting to familiarize himself with the Western Approaches organization, Murray travelled to England for a week of consultations with Horton and his staff.[51] Overall, Murray found this trip "helpful" but was caught off guard after a formal dinner when "Max Horton gathered up all his captains (D) and the Commodore from Derry [Simpson] and I found myself the butt of everybody complaining, 'Why weren't our ships better equipped.'"[52] Although Simpson was at the forefront of this conversation, a letter from the Allied Anti-Submarine Survey Board's secretary, Lieutenant Commander M.A. McMullen, RN, leaves little doubt that it was Horton who most wanted Murray to take the modernization question up with Naval Service Headquarters in Ottawa. "With regard to Canada," McMullen observed, "Admiral Horton has apparently expressed his views personally, and in no uncertain terms, to Admiral Murray."[53] Although he enjoyed the support of his superior and colleagues, any hope that Simpson may have drawn from this incident was soon dashed because over the next few weeks there was little evidence that Naval Service Headquarters had responded to the concerns. This did not sit well with the commodore who, while worrying about growing signs of a recent string of discipline infractions committed by Canadian personnel in Londonderry, became more frustrated.

Equipment was apparently not the only issue that was making the Canadians unhappy. With no military recreational facilities of their own, RCN personnel were left to roam the streets of Londonderry, which, having been described as one of "the grimmest ports from a sailor's point of view," offered little in the way of amenities and entertainment.[54] A drastic increase in petty crime committed by RCN personnel worried Simpson, especially since the local newspaper, *The Derry Standard*, was filled with accounts characterizing the Canadians as "intoxicated hooligans" who were "worse than the Americans." There was only so much the commodore could do to help. He had asked Price to seek Naval Service Headquarters' permission to make RCN personnel members of the "Lion and Eagle" (a social club for the Royal Navy and United States Navy) and stressed the absolute necessity of getting a Canadian special services officer appointed to the Londonderry staff. Like the equipment issue, such measures required Naval Service Headquarters' approval, and that permission had still not arrived, adding to Simpson's frustration.[55]

Little has been written on the issue of the welfare of Canadian sailors, but preliminary research indicates that potential discipline problems and poor morale in the fleet had more to do with inadequate special service support facilities ashore than with equipment shortages at sea. Historians such as Bob Caldwell have shown how the navy's inability to harness the power of groups, such as the YMCA and Knights of Columbus, to provide sailors with entertainment led to discipline problems in Halifax.[56] But while Caldwell's study focused exclusively on that port, it is clear that St. John's and Londonderry experienced similar situations in which bored sailors got into serious trouble. In fact, according to the account of one RCNVR officer, Simpson had uncharacteristically waited until his Canadian commanding officers were on leave to call a meeting "to discuss [the RCN's] behaviour ashore ... Simpson led off with a sneering attack on the Canadian Navy, and for two hours all the officers vied with each other in horror stories concerning the Canadian Navy."[57] Unlike equipment, which was very much an "officer issue," the problems with special service support and the impact it had on the lower ranks requires much more study, the more so since it is probably the root cause for the apparent discontent in the RCN. Nevertheless, while equipment was his top priority by far, Simpson argued that both the "welfare" and modernization issues were conspiring to wipe out RCN morale. From his perspective, the Canadian headquarters had turned a blind eye and he was losing faith in the Canadian chain of command, telling a reservist that he had "briefed more senior RCN officers in the matter, without result."[58] Fortunately for Simpson, events unfolding on the East Coast of Canada finally created an opportunity to sound the alarm bells in the halls of Naval Service Headquarters.

At the same time that Horton and Simpson were busy unloading their equipment concerns on Murray, word of the welfare grouses was finally spilling into St. John's. Troubled by reports from several commanding officers that Canadian sailors in Londonderry were prone to "leave-breaking, drunkenness and clashes with local authorities," Reid immediately wrote to Naval Service Headquarters warning that the lack of recreation facilities at that port represented a serious "handicap to morale."[59] Rowland, who was visiting Halifax when Murray returned from overseas, corroborated these allegations by observing that the commander in chief Canadian North West Atlantic was composing a similar report. Murray was also concerned at the possibility that morale problems in Londonderry were reaching crisis proportions and believed that further investigation was required.[60] As a response he sent his chief of staff, Captain R.E.S. Bidwell, RCN, on "a rapid visit to the UK." Realizing that something was wrong overseas, Reid's chief of staff, Captain F.L. Houghton, RCN, thought it advisable that the Newfoundland command do the same.[61] He was also encouraged by the fact that there was an experienced investigator from Ottawa currently in St. John's, who was ideally suited to explore the welfare issue on his behalf.

There was good reason why Houghton had so much faith in this officer. During his former appointment as the director of plans at Naval Service Headquarters, Houghton had been involved with the creation of the Directorate of Naval Information. While recruiting for this directorate – which was responsible for publicity and liaison duties with the national press – Houghton spotted a rising star in the Canadian Broadcasting Corporation named William Strange. Recognizing talent when he saw it, Houghton offered Strange, who also had experience as a freelance journalist with the *Toronto Star*, an immediate position in the RCNVR at the rank of lieutenant commander. One and a half years later he had proven Houghton's instincts correct. Strange was now second in command of the directorate with the title of assistant naval information officer.[62] Such credentials, it was believed, made Strange the perfect investigator, and after wrapping up an inspection of the St. John's naval information set-up he was asked by Houghton to "gather some information on the welfare question" in Londonderry.[63] Strange was due back in Ottawa, but since this request had come from "a great friend," he could hardly say no.[64] Moreover, he saw it as a unique opportunity to "secure material" for the directorate on the war at sea and life in Londonderry, so a message was sent to Naval Service Headquarters on 24 June asking permission for Strange to go overseas.[65] "Oddly propelled" into a role that he "had certainly not asked for," Strange was sent on a journey that would lead directly to Simpson.[66] Houghton had asked him to investigate the condition of special service support in Londonderry, but those who wanted the state of the fleet's equipment to become an issue at headquarters soon hijacked Strange's agenda.

There is an undeniable sense that some officers in St. John's were troubled by the fact that the Naval Staff did not seem to understand the gravity of the equipment situation; those officers saw a unique opportunity with Strange. As an officer from Ottawa, Strange represented another conduit through which that message could be relayed to headquarters, especially if he were given the opportunity to see conditions overseas with his own eyes. Using Strange as a courier was merely the last in a string of attempts to get word through to Ottawa. The officers in St. John's believed they had done everything in their power to enlighten the Naval Staff and they told Strange as much. Like Simpson, Strange also became convinced that the breakdown in Canadian channels was occurring in Ottawa rather than with the Halifax or St. John's commands. And it was that belief that seemed to justify unorthodox attempts to prod Naval Service Headquarters out of its apparent indifference.

Critics of the Canadian headquarters both then and now have been quick to point out that it took the Naval Staff too long to respond to all the critical memos. On the surface, at least, this argument has merit as the Naval Staff's response times to these reports averaged about six weeks. In reality, Ottawa's administration was no slower than either of the operational commands.[67] Nevertheless, there were those in St. John's who went out of their way to explain to Strange that Ottawa did not seem to care, and that was the interpretation he carried over to Londonderry. More to the point, there is little doubt that Strange was being driven by officers in St. John's, particularly since someone had made specific arrangements for him to travel with Commander Peter Gretton, RN, whose ship, the destroyer HMS *Duncan*, was part of the escort for convoy SC 135. There were other convoys that had left earlier in the week, but according to Strange his anonymous benefactor had specifically selected Gretton – who had taken over the *Duncan* from Rowland in 1942 – because he "had very high reputation ... and it was felt that I could learn a certain amount."[68] Anxious to do just that, Strange approached Gretton while they were at sea and asked for his impression regarding the relative efficiency of the RCN as compared to the Royal Navy.

Timid at the start – suggesting that he had little foreknowledge about the investigation – Gretton became more frank throughout their conversation, going as far as to state that he preferred to sail without Canadian ships in his group. Moreover, even when the RCN did score kills, it was assumed that the victory was the product of "lucky occasions." This was not a reflection on Canadian sailors, whom Gretton considered "as good as those of the Royal Navy." Like Simpson and the critical memos, he too emphasized that "given better equipment and more training ... they would be able to give an excellent account of themselves," and by doing so was simply reciting chapter and verse of what had obviously become Western Approaches' gospel on the Canadians. Having been forewarned about certain British attitudes, Strange initially chalked Gretton's comments down as "prejudice." By the end of their discussion, however, Gretton had convinced Strange "albeit reluctantly, to revise my first impression ... HMC Ships were, almost without exception, inadequately equipped to fight submarines."[69]

Herein lies a major problem with Strange's investigation. Few could question Gretton's integrity and skill. He was, after all, one of the best U-boat hunters on the North Atlantic. Yet according to one staff officer at St. John's, Strange was looking to prove an hypothesis he had formed even before leaving port.[70] Although there is no evidence that officers in St. John's had collaborated with their counterparts in Londonderry to get Strange overseas, this impromptu investigation was marked by a number of odd coincidences that suggest Rowland may have had an undue influence over the naval information officer. Whether Strange was merely a patsy for some other authority remains a mystery, but he was certainly not an impartial observer by the time he reached Londonderry. Of course, there was nothing wrong with his conclusions on the unsatisfactory state of equipment within the RCN; it was the inference that Naval Service Headquarters did not care about the situation that made Strange susceptible to the extreme interpretations circulating throughout Londonderry.

On arriving in Londonderry on 12 July, Strange was immediately taken by Gretton to Simpson. Bombarded with a mixture of sincere commentary and damning documentation that exposed a darker side of the navy and its leadership, Strange was presented with evidence that was "even more disturbing than had been my conversation with Commander Gretton." Simpson's message was blunt: there was a perception that the Naval Staff was fiddling instead of addressing the burning desire of the fleet for up-to-date equipment. To support that allegation, he then provided Strange with specific examples. The ahead-throwing projectile weapon (hedgehog) and gyroscopic compasses were essential pieces of equipment yet there was no evidence that the Canadian Naval Staff was attempting to acquire them for the RCN. Likewise, signals from Londonderry to Naval Service Headquarters indicating that the equipment was available were either ignored or solicited inconclusive responses, providing proof-positive "that 'the proper channels' had proved totally ineffective." Worse yet, it also meant "apathy and ignorance seemed to be going hand in hand" back in Ottawa.[71]

Strange did not know what the commodore expected him to do. Houghton's request to reconnoitre the "welfare question" was still within Strange's province, but highly technical issues like equipment were well beyond the jurisdiction of a naval information officer. "He [Simpson] stated that he was aware of this," Strange later explained, "but felt that the matter to be of such paramount importance that he wished to lose no opportunity of expressing himself on the subject to any officer from Naval Service Headquarters occupying a position of responsibility."[72] Moreover, according to Simpson the welfare question and equipment issues were so closely linked that it was impossible to understand one fully without exploring the other. (While equipment was probably discussed within the lower ranks, their morale problems were more closely linked to the lack of recreational and support facilities in Londonderry, St. John's, and Halifax. The need for more special service support was not only the ratings' primary grouse but also a totally separate issue from their superiors' concern over equipment.) He nevertheless pleaded with

Strange to "convey his views to whatever authority I might think appropriate from the view point of effectiveness," and it is clear that this objective was met, as Strange had already decided that "the Minister should be informed of this conversation."[73]

It remains unclear whether this was the route that Simpson intended Strange to take. On the one hand, the naval information officer did have various avenues through which to get this message to Macdonald, but there is little evidence he ever told Simpson as much. And so it is possible that the commodore was merely encouraging Strange to bypass the arteries of the intermediate levels of naval bureaucracy, rather than the heart of the decision-making process, which rested with the admirals on the Naval Board. On the other hand, Strange did send a highly suggestive letter to the commodore once he returned to Ottawa. "I do not feel free to say very much in a letter," he immediately advised Simpson after having spoken to the minister, "but would like you to know that the matter was taken up in the manner I intended, and very definite action is under way."

Even before Strange left Londonderry, the commodore's actions strongly indicate that he knew something "unorthodox" was transpiring.[74] Simpson made plans for Strange to meet the fleet engineering officer, Captain R.R. Shorto, RN, and also prepared the ground for a complete tour of the base. First, however, the commodore had to deal with the fact that Strange had lost almost a week in St. John's waiting for Gretton's group and was slated to return to Canada in only four days. This was not nearly enough time for the thorough investigation Simpson envisioned, so he sent a message to Naval Service Headquarters indicating that Strange would be delayed "due to a shortage of service accommodation." With three separate convoys sailing between this time and Strange's eventual departure, the explanation was less than honest but it served its purpose well as Naval Service Headquarters responded that he could stay until suitable passage was arranged.[75]

No longer concerned with time constraints, Strange met Shorto, whose comments were similar to Simpson's although more technical and detailed. He too emphasized the importance of acquiring both hedgehog and gyroscopic compasses, which, in combination with 271 radar, were said to increase the efficiency of the basic corvette design "some 60 to 75 times." Unlike the commodore, however, Shorto also made some rather frank and disturbing comments, noting that he believed "the men at sea were placed at so great a disadvantage by what he [Shorto] implied must be the failure of NSHQ to grasp the situation ... [which] was not only damaging to present morale but might become explosive." In fact, describing the conversation in full, Strange later told Connolly, "there is considerable dissatisfaction in certain ships. Commander Shorto personally feels a time may come when this feeling, at present only partially pent up, will come out into the open with consequences which cannot be foretold, but might be serious. He stated that there were certain [Canadian] officers, whose names he did not give, who were determined to take some form of drastic step to secure action in this matter of equipment. I did not press inquiry in this direction."[76]

The implication was that the navy was facing a possible mutiny, and that naturally caught Strange's attention. With Simpson and Shorto's assistance, he found ample evidence to support such claims at the base. No matter how powerful and conclusive it was, however, accepting that evidence is problematic because of the unmistakable impression that Simpson was directing Strange so that he visited the right people as well as specific ships.

Accusing the commodore of manufacturing confirmation for the equipment allegations would be unjust. He was, after all, responding to perceived grouses among Canadian officers. That the worst of those complaints – most notably that the RCNVR was about to openly rebel over equipment – had come from the exaggerated interpretations of politically connected reserve officers pardons the hyperbole of Simpson's account. Despite his altruistic motives his methodology was flawed, and even Strange found it curious that "a good deal of 'evidence' had been gratuitously handed to me." As a shore officer with absolutely no sea experience, Strange had few ideas how to proceed with the investigation, so he did require a certain degree of guidance. More often than not, that direction came from British officers on the commodore's staff. Consequently, comments from the antisubmarine officer, Lieutenant Commander A.M. Lee, RNVR, regarding the "pleasure I had in getting all the moans off my chest," were indicative of a frustrated command rather than seagoing personnel on the verge of mutiny.[77] Even when Strange did get the chance to speak with Canadians, the process was tainted. It was the small group of politically connected reservists who had the greatest impact on Simpson, so it was logical that he, in turn, sent Strange to them. This probably explains why Strange, who visited only three pre-selected corvettes, was able to extrapolate that there was "very serious dissatisfaction" among all commanding officers. Unfortunately, aside from further confirming the existence of this network, neither Simpson nor Strange ever provided the names of these officers or the ships on which they served.[78]

It was during these discussions that Strange also learned that Canadian reserve officers were equally demoralized by certain Royal Navy attitudes toward the RCN. This he found odd. Everything Strange saw suggested that the British were doing their best to help the Canadians. Nevertheless, despite Shorto's assertion that Naval Service Headquarters was responsible for the modernization mess, these reservists laid the blame squarely on the Royal Navy who, it was assumed, kept "all the best things [equipment] for themselves."[79] This was an important observation because it indicated that Canadian officers were not nearly so hostile toward Naval Service Headquarters as either the staff officers in Londonderry or St. John's implied. Like Briggs' report, such perceptions suggested it was actually British arrogance that inflamed the Canadian dissatisfaction over equipment. Strange never made that link, so he did not get what Lieutenant Commander F.O. Gerity, RCNR – a former corvette captain who replaced Briggs at the Tactical School – meant when he observed how British scuttlebutt held that the RCN would "be given operations of comparative safety and simplicity" because of its litany of substandard performances. Ignoring the larger implications, Strange remained fixated only on Gerity's equipment theme, which he considered "the view point of the hard-thinking sea-going officer of the modern school."[80]

Twenty days had passed since Strange first set foot in Londonderry, and he was anxious to get back to Ottawa. Simpson had finally found an officer from headquarters who was willing to make a difference, especially since Strange later admitted that "what had started out as being none of my business had gradually become the one business by which I was obsessed."[81] Whether intentional or not, chiselling a complicated issue like modernization down to manageable proportions for an impressionable officer like Strange, while also moulding him into the ideal envoy, was dangerous. Lacking formal technical training and knowledge, Strange was incapable of providing measured criticism. As such, he not only accepted that Naval Service Headquarters was to blame for the situation, but also assumed the facts and figures he was given were correct simply because higher-ranking authorities had told him so. In some measure, it is difficult to fault Strange for exceeding his mandate. Simpson had exerted pressure on him to do so. In fact, while Simpson had already taught the naval information officer much about conditions in the RCN, he was not finished with Strange's education. The one thing Strange had not done was sail with a Canadian group. Rounding out what was already a well-orchestrated investigation, Simpson informed Commander K.L. Adams, RCN – the commanding officer of HMCS *Assiniboine* and commander of Group C1 – that he was to take a special guest back to Newfoundland while escorting convoy ON 195.[82]

Somewhere between Londonderry and St. John's, Strange unloaded the remarkable events of the past three weeks on Adams. It was nothing new to the destroyer captain. With the exception of the guided tour, Adams "funny enough got the same treatment from the Commodore of Londonderry, Shrimp Simpson about the failure of Canadian ships to meet the high standard in equipment ... So Bill [Strange] and I had a talk about it and he stirred me up further."[83] During their discussion, Adams repeated a commonly held British view that RCN corvettes were "'chiefly along for the ride.' Under attack ... one would wish the RCN corvettes luck, but they would probably be more useful as rescue ships than anything else."[84] Strange attributed this comment to Adams' interpretation of the RCN, and perhaps this regular force commander did believe that his own navy was incompetent. Yet a more probable explanation is that, like Gerity, Adams' views reflected Canadian sensitivities to Royal Navy attitudes. Adams was undoubtedly influenced by Simpson, but an incident of Royal Navy superiority the previous March also had an impact: after a refit at the Gladstone Docks in Liverpool, British officers "planted in my mind the fact that Canadian ships got better equipment in the UK. And I wasn't allowed to forget it by the senior officers ashore."[85] In isolation, such comments were nothing more than harmless observations. Perhaps some Royal Navy officers did make cruel jokes or engaged in petty name calling, but the majority were simply stating out loud what was plainly obvious whenever Canadian and British ships were tied up alongside one another.[86] Some Canadians were overly sensitive to such remarks, and a small minority of reserve officers tried to make a difference the only way they knew how – with their political connections. For permanent force officers like Adams, effecting change had but one route, and that was the chain of command. None of this mattered to Strange, who was prepared to go directly to the top.

While Strange's duties at Naval Service Headquarters often gave him the opportunity to speak with the minister, Connolly was the link to Macdonald. Describing the executive assistant as "a personal friend of mine," Strange had happily reconnoitred other issues on Connolly's behalf in the past and was therefore a member of Connolly's personal network of informants.[87] Strange knew his investigation would interest Connolly. Containing details such as Shorto's claim that some Canadian officers were on the verge of taking drastic action to secure equipment, the memo describing the investigation shocked Connolly, whose initial reaction was, "The minister knows nothing of this." Macdonald's response was similar. In Strange's words, the minister telephoned directly to state that "he had read the memorandum, which had caused him deep concern. He asked me to give the most definite assurance of the truth and accuracy of statements."[88] It had been Strange's goal to get Macdonald's attention in the most graphic way possible, and clearly that aim had been achieved. The minister would in the not so distant future send Connolly on a comprehensive investigation to St. John's, Londonderry, and London to verify Strange's account. And according to Connolly, that investigation led to "the greatest upheaval in Naval Service Headquarters organization," not to mention that it would cost Nelles his job.[89]

Strange never regretted the role he played in either bringing the equipment situation to the attention of Connolly and Macdonald or, ultimately, in Nelles' dismissal. Justifying the decision after the war, he remarked, "I felt, and still feel, that in such circumstances, the only action worth taking at all is the one you know *positively* will be effective. The proper channels would have to be by-passed. It was quite clear that they did not work." Moreover, he took full responsibility for having "triggered off the whole thing."[90] It is interesting that Strange asked the minister for a promotion to commander, much as MacLean had done, as a reward for blowing the whistle on a deficiency in the fleet.[91] Without more evidence it is impossible to say whether Strange was also motivated by personal ambition, at least in part.

After blowing the whistle on the RCN's equipment situation, William Strange (second from left) wrote to Connolly asking whether the minister would help with his promotion from lieutenant commander to commander. This photograph from 1944 not only shows that his efforts were successful but also captures the future Mrs. Strange seated at the far right. DHH 81/520/1000, BOX 148, FILE 29

While Strange was more than willing to accept responsibility for his role in Nelles' downfall, the question of whether Simpson shared accountability is difficult to answer. Simpson had no idea that he was about to tap into the executive assistant's network of informants. Other aspects of Strange's background led Simpson to conclude that the naval information officer could be trusted. Strange – who was born in Corozal, British Honduras, and did not immigrate to Canada until 1929 – believed that he "became Simpson's confidant" because he had been a member of the Royal Navy during the First World War. Both men had attended the Royal Navy training establishment at Dartmouth in 1915, and some of Strange's former classmates were now Simpson's seniors.[92] The Royal Navy connection might have built trust, but there is little doubt that Simpson had picked Strange for a specific reason.

By his own admission, Simpson had approached other Canadians in the hope that they would raise the equipment issue in Ottawa. Permanent force officers had not produced the desired result. As trained professionals, these men were unwilling to circumvent normal channels, so Simpson tried to convince Strange that "since I was a 'hostilities only' reserve officer, I had no career to risk, even if I were to take extreme measures."[93] This did not mean that Simpson wanted Strange to go so far up the chain of command as to contact the minister. He did know that this was a possibility, however, especially since the commodore's experiences had shown that certain Canadian reservists were willing to take chances that the regulars were not. In fact, during a postwar correspondence with another member of Connolly's network, Louis Audette, Simpson tried to take the moral high ground and chastised the reservists who had gone to the minister with their problems:

> Since I have said that in 1943 to 1945 there was political interference within the RCN, I will now confirm it. As I see it, in a democracy it is the duty of the elected representative to investigate, check and recheck every aspect of the office to which he is appointed or the Government Department in general. His means of doing this is surely to tackle the man at the top. If the man at the top does not know the answers, they get another one, but what must be avoided is to side-track a top man and listen to uniformed [sic] junior criticism, formulate opinions and act on immature prejudices, because such action undermines the citadel of authority. The service is disrupted.[94]

With tongue in cheek, Audette charged Simpson with being "guilty of exactly the same offence," and there were good grounds for him to say so.[95] Strange – a relatively junior officer with no technical knowledge – tried to right perceived injustices based on the prejudices of concerned British officers by taking the matter directly to the minister, and that, according to Simpson's own definition, was the epitome of political interference. Even if Strange's contacting the minister came as a surprise to Simpson, there is powerful evidence that he was happy with the result.

In Simpson's view, the punishment for officers who were guilty of political interference was that they "should be ruthlessly removed" from the navy. It was clear, however, that he was pleased with the outcome of Strange's actions, recording after the war that Connolly's upcoming investigation was "the reverse of disruptive and gave me help and assurance for which I will always be grateful." In reality, the improvement with the RCN's equipment was not the product of Connolly's investigation but the fruit of various policies enacted by the Naval Staff in late 1942 and early 1943. Simpson's assumption that Naval Service Headquarters was not doing anything to address the RCN's modernization shortfall was totally incorrect. Nevertheless, the impression that Ottawa did not care was passed on to the minister because Simpson's guided tour had led Strange to the unmistakable conclusion that the RCN's equipment deficiencies were "an almost nightmarish example of how a military Headquarters can become so remote from the realities as actually to stultify its own raison d'être. They were living in cloud cuckooland, while sailors were dying. There is a lesson here."[96]

The real lesson was the excellent illustration of the dangers of political interference provided by Strange's investigation. The naval information officer had breached what Simpson had called "the citadel of authority" with uninformed "junior criticisms." Strange's so-called evidence had come from a group of British officers and Canadian reservists in Londonderry who did not have a complete picture of the troubles Naval Service Headquarters faced when trying to modernize the RCN. This network's rather naïve interpretation that the RCN's troubles at sea could be traced to one single issue – equipment – was itself seriously flawed. This is not to imply that equipment was not a problem – the RCN was behind the Royal Navy in modernizing its escorts – but this constituted what could be more accurately described as an "equipment gap" rather than a "crisis."[97] From a Canadian operational perspective, it was no more, nor no less, important than many of the other deficiencies that were plaguing the RCN. Put another way, the Naval Staff was trying to rectify a great number of problems caused by the navy's unparalleled expansion, and equipment was merely a part of this kaleidoscope. Once solutions to those problems had been implemented and were producing miraculous results, the Naval Staff faced a hostile minister who believed his senior naval advisors were incompetent.

Employing the same methodology as MacLean and his followers, a group of politically connected seagoing reserve officers had played a significant role in bringing the modernization issue to Macdonald's attention. Since the substance of their arguments represented a legitimate deficiency in the RCN, these particular reservists had found a powerful advocate when Simpson took over in Londonderry. Believing that their views spoke for the majority, the commodore (D) was convinced that there was a grave morale problem among Canadian sailors because they lacked modern equipment. His initial attempts to get word about this situation through to Naval Service Headquarters through normal channels represented the actions of a good senior officer. Simpson nevertheless seems to have come to understand the value of bypassing the chain of command in certain extreme cases like modernization. No doubt reacting to this group's exaggerated interpretation of the dissatisfaction and probably motivated by an altruistic desire to help all the Canadians under his command, Simpson's experiences with Strange produced results. The minister's executive assistant was now coming to Londonderry, and when he did so Simpson began to slide down a path from being a responsible officer to becoming one of those who used "political interference" to further the modernization cause. As a result, even though the top brass in Ottawa had been working hard on solving the modernization shortfall, Strange's investigation had made the minister nervous; it suggested that an apathetic headquarters was either unaware of the fleet's equipment problems or worse, had conspired to keep the problem secret. Neither was true, of course. It is only through a thorough examination of the Naval Staff's policies – as well as Nelles' attempt to solicit Macdonald's help in implementing them – that the extent of the damage caused by interference from Strange, and ultimately Simpson, can truly be understood.

4
Trying to Keep Afloat

Strange's memo warning the minister that the escort fleet was woefully ill equipped to hunt U-boats contained two assumptions that cast Nelles in a negative light. The first was that Naval Service Headquarters was doing nothing to correct this deficiency; the second – and perhaps most damaging for Nelles' relationship with his political master – was that the chief of the naval staff and his officers had conspired to hide the truth. Macdonald was certainly convinced by those assumptions, to the extent that he would accuse those same men of negligence, claiming that they never once discussed the fleet's modernization with him and had lost all track of the fleet's needs. In reality, the chief of the naval staff and his officers had heard the complaints from the operational commanders on the East Coast, and they had been actively attacking this problem since early 1942; by the spring of 1943 they had a comprehensive plan that would create more opportunities and facilities for RCN ships to receive modern equipment. It was a massive effort that taxed the navy's resources and required much co-operation between various government organizations. This strategy would eventually achieve miraculous results, as a large proportion of the fleet was upgraded in less than a year. Although Macdonald later claimed that Strange's memo in the summer of 1943 was his first hint of trouble, an examination of these efforts clearly indicates that Nelles and his staff had not only already devised a comprehensive plan for the fleet's modernization by this time but also made numerous attempts to solicit the minister's support in implementing their solution.

Laden with essential war materials and produce, the allied merchant fleet constituted Great Britain's lifeline to North America. Lacking sufficient escorts during the early years of the Battle of the Atlantic, these vessels were easy pickings for the skilled commanders of Germany's U-boat arm. To meet that threat, the western alliance did the best it could in a difficult situation. The key to countering relentless U-boat attacks was not only to organize the merchant ships into convoys, but also to provide them with as many escorts as possible. Fighting a defensive campaign to ensure "the safe and timely arrival of convoys," the British and Canadian navies had little choice but to focus on quantity rather than quality. After initiating massive naval shipbuilding programs, both the RCN and Royal Navy rushed these poorly equipped escorts, and their haphazardly trained crews, to sea so that they could plug the gaping holes in convoy defences. This strategy gave the British much-needed time, and by the winter of 1941-42 they took action to improve the quality of their escort forces. Although it would take almost another year to complete this process – a time period in which Royal Navy-escorted convoys also suffered heavy losses – the British eventually created an extremely efficient hunting machine that swooped down on the U-boats with a powerful vengeance.[1]

Comparatively speaking, things had not gone so well for the Canadians. Their fleet was trying to fight the offensive convoy battles of spring 1943 with ships that clearly belonged in the previous year's defensive campaign.[2] Having switched doctrinal tactics and emphasis from protecting convoys to destroying the enemy, the Royal Navy was taking the war to the U-boats, and in doing so had left the struggling Canadians in their wake. Modernization and training were two important factors that had changed the nature of the Atlantic war, and without mastering this winning formula the RCN could not participate in the stunning U-boat kills that turned the tide of battle. For some officers at Western Approaches, like Simpson, that inability to sink U-boats was directly linked to Naval Service Headquarters' failure to modernize in 1942. Others were even more specific, believing that the Canadian Naval Board had blundered when it decided to wait for the shipyards to finish its frigate program instead of re-equipping the current fleet of corvettes. The late arrival of the frigates – a twin-screw antisubmarine platform that was vastly superior to the corvette design – only seemed to confirm that conclusion. In reality, the RCN did not have nearly as much latitude in making their modernization decisions as the Londonderry officers had ascribed to them. Well before Simpson took over as commodore (D), the RCN was led to the conclusion that the Royal Navy could not provide much material assistance in the Canadians' attempts to upgrade the fleet.

For reasons largely beyond the control of the Naval Board, wholesale modernization of the RCN was next to impossible in 1942. The British had done so by taking ships off operations and sending them to the shipyards, but that was something the Canadians could not do. In the process of a fifty-fold expansion, the RCN had barely enough ships to maintain both its commitment to the mid-Atlantic convoys and its own requirement to protect Canadian inshore waters.[3] The United States Navy, while gallantly bearing the brunt of the Pacific theatre almost on its own, had not lived up to many of its Atlantic obligations, leaving it to the Canadians to take up the slack. To meet these expanded responsibilities the RCN therefore needed to keep as much of its fleet operational as possible. Put simply, the Canadians could not modernize while at the same time maintaining its existing level of commitment on the North Atlantic run; in the end it was decided that their promises to a starving British ally was the RCN's first priority.

Whether that choice was based on benevolent motivations is debatable. With Canadian industry lacking the required manufacturing experience, the British (and later the Americans) were the only reliable source for much of the navy's high-tech gear.[4] According to senior RCN officers, there was continuous pressure throughout 1942 "being applied by Admiralty on the Canadian Naval Board to send more ships to sea," making it unlikely that the British would part with large quantities of their equipment just so the RCN could stay home and modernize. And so, despite Simpson's efforts a year later when he took over in Londonderry, the Admiralty had given Naval Service Headquarters the distinct impression that there was simply not enough gear to equip both navies, and what was available from British industry quite naturally went to the Royal Navy first. When the Naval Staff announced in March 1942 that they, too, were exploring the possibility of modernizing, Canadian requests for conversion gear to upgrade the fleet's asdic, as well as other minor equipment advances, solicited inconclusive responses or at best vague promises from the British.[5] Intentionally or not, the Naval Staff got the hint: the British were in no position to help the Canadians at this juncture, and that left the top brass with few options.

The decision to modernize was not easy to make. Originally, the Naval Staff was uncertain whether it should focus on providing the frigates under construction with newer equipment or on trying to modernize some seventy operational corvettes.[6] Given the RCN's operational commitments, the chances of accomplishing the latter in 1942 seemed remote, yet the Naval Staff obviously believed that the RCN would eventually get its chance to modernize the corvettes sometime during the following year.[7] In preparation for that day, they took preliminary steps so that the navy would be ready. Requests for Canadian-supplied gyroscopic compasses and radar continued, and – while fearful that the Admiralty could not accommodate such a large appeal – equipment orders for the much-sought-after British hedgehog (ahead-throwing explosive projectiles) were nonetheless placed at the end of the summer of 1942. Likewise, acquiring British 271 radar and 144 asdic sets in the near future seemed improbable, but the Naval Staff still authorized adjustments to the corvettes' bridges so that they would eventually be able to accommodate that gear. And with that, the Canadian modernization program for the RCN's corvettes, which was given a target completion date of July 1944, was launched.[8]

While the questions of where and when they would acquire the equipment remained, the Naval Staff realized in 1942 that there was another potential problem. British shipyards were already overtaxed with the Royal Navy's demands, which meant that the task of fitting this gear onto RCN ships would become the responsibility of the Canadian shipbuilding industry. Their inexperience with this type of work troubled some staff members, who feared that full modernization was simply "beyond the capabilities of Canadian Shipyards with their present commitments." Confidence was low, and banking on East Coast shipyards to perform the required work was too great a gamble.[9] After pointing out that it was not their intention to "discourage Canadian inventive genius," the Naval Board got the minister to approve a policy that would "accelerate the speed with which these alterations would and could be undertaken by the Admiralty on our behalf."[10] To do that, they wanted to give the British the authority to add equipment onto Canadian warships without the necessity of asking Naval Service Headquarters for permission. Until the RCN got the chance to implement its own modernization plans, making it easier for the British to perform piecemeal alterations was better than doing nothing at all. In time, that would prove a vital disconnect. Simply put, Naval Service Headquarters was anxious for any equipment the Royal Navy could spare, as well as any space in British yards so that the equipment could be fitted onto RCN ships. This was odd given that Simpson would eventually claim Londonderry had plenty of both in May 1943. Unfortunately, the fact that Londonderry could do much more than it was already doing was not passed on to Naval Service Headquarters because of a breakdown in communication between Londonderry and the Admiralty. Instead, naval officers in Ottawa knew only what the Admiralty had told them in the spring of 1943: that their current level of assistance was unlikely to be exceeded. Additionally, over the winter of 1942-43 Western Approaches officers were arguing that training rather than modernization represented the RCN's greatest hurdle, though they eventually made the RCN's equipment dilemma a priority once Simpson took over in Londonderry.

The RCN's training deficiencies have been well covered in other naval histories, so a brief summary will suffice here to explain how the issue reflected on the fleet's efficiency.[11] After a string of disastrous RCN convoys during the fall of 1942, the British asked the Canadian government to transfer control of its mid-ocean groups to the Royal Navy. In part, this was to help the British rearrange convoy routes so as to get more petroleum to the United Kingdom, thereby alleviating that nation's oil crisis. This request came as an embarrassment to the Canadian navy, however, as the transfer also stood as an example of its failure at sea. The Royal Navy felt that the RCN was inefficient, and the only way to correct that problem was to reassign their ships to new convoy routes under British control so that they could receive better training.[12] Unless the Naval Staff could come up with something better, there was little else the top brass could do other than recommending that Naval Service Headquarters "should place no obstacle in the way of the one proposed."[13] Worse, even if the Naval Staff had openly challenged the British proposal the results of the December convoy ONS 154, which had lost a staggering fourteen vessels and was perhaps the RCN's worst disaster, would have rendered this case moot.[14] For the nationalistic members of the Naval Staff, it was a difficult pill to swallow, but that disaster had left little doubt that their navy was in trouble and needed whatever remedy the British were willing to administer.[15]

No one was more disappointed with that conclusion than the chief of the naval staff. Some may have found that odd. Earlier decisions by Nelles, such as his recommending the transfer of seventeen RCN corvettes to the Royal Navy for *Operation Torch* (the November 1942 North Africa landings), had earned him a reputation as something of a "yes man" to the Admiralty.[16] But Nelles' reaction to this latest request left little doubt that he was not as much of an Anglophile as some believed. Certainly that was a lesson impressed upon a Royal Navy officer at Naval Service Headquarters who, after discovering that the proposed transfer "caused a powerful flap" among his fellow staff members, went to see Nelles only to be told to "keep the hell out of it."[17] While this officer was just trying to help, the navy's chief was probably venting his frustration at a member of the Royal Navy who was in the wrong place at the wrong time. Nelles was tired of British interference and told the minister as much, indicating that the transfer was "the third, but most serious, attempt on the part of the Admiralty to get operational control of our ships."[18]

Nelles' contention that the British oil crisis and Canadian training deficiencies were part of a deliberate Royal Navy plan to usurp control of the RCN was a little far-fetched and conspiratorial, but it painted the chief of the naval staff as a nationalistic leader who was proud of his service. Despite being a good ally and having helped the Royal Navy whenever needed, the RCN was being criticized by the British; and perhaps because of that, Nelles saw them as the ungrateful benefactor. Transferring the main portion of the RCN (forty-three corvettes and seven destroyers) to the other side of the Atlantic was too much for the chief of the naval staff. He worried about augmenting the Western Local Escort Force, which consisted of ships protecting Canadian littoral waters. Nor did he like the implication that the RCN was incapable of handling its own affairs, which explains why he told Macdonald that the British planning stage for oil convoys had been handled poorly. The RCN's top admiral was obviously irritated with the Admiralty, but he did not have sufficient grounds to block the transfer. After speaking with Captain J.M. Mansfield, RN, chief of staff to the commander in chief Western Approaches, who had been sent to Washington and then Ottawa to sell the Admiralty's new convoy arrangements, Nelles was given a better appreciation of what the Royal Navy wanted the RCN to do.

Nelles passed that interpretation on to Macdonald in early January 1943. Suggesting that he had originally jumped to the wrong conclusion, the chief of the naval staff noted that Mansfield had explained how the new convoy cycles were meant to improve the efficiency of "*all* escort forces" and "not only the Canadians as originally thought."[19] Moreover, indicating that Mansfield had done a good job of selling the transfer, Nelles then told the minister,

> From the training aspect the UK facilities ought to be better than ours and our ships based on UK ports will undoubtedly benefit according. The UK to Gibraltar convoys have less mileage and the weather is better than the North Atlantic. On the other

hand, the ships will have the same or greater submarine menace, plus that from enemy air forces. Thus it may become a hotter spot. In the meantime Canadian naval training facilities will continue to be developed in future, as in the past, just as quickly as possible. The same conditions apply to our repair facilities.[20]

That the RCN would face a greater threat from the Luftwaffe on the North Africa routes was undoubtedly true, but claiming that those routes offered a greater challenge than the North Atlantic was a stretch. Although Nelles had both downplayed the threat and avoided the question of the RCN's inefficiency, it was the Admiralty and not the chief of the naval staff who was guilty of sugar-coating the transfer. Such observations came from Mansfield and therefore reflected the Admiralty's fear that the Canadian senior staff might torpedo the proposal because of its hypersensitivity to criticism of the RCN.[21] Emphasizing that the RCN was helping the British with their oil crisis was far more likely to get the Canadians to accept the transfer than telling them that they were inefficient.

First fixating on training and then on equipment in the spring of 1943, Western Approaches was desperate to improve the relative efficiency of the RCN. Wanting to do so without offending the Canadians, Mansfield had led both Nelles and Macdonald to the conclusion that training was a secondary factor of the transfer. And it was that British interpretation, delivered with kid gloves, that Macdonald gave to the prime minister when Cabinet was debating whether to accept the transfer.[22] It is uncertain if Macdonald ever understood the wider implication of the transfer, but it is clear that the chief of the naval staff was not mincing words; he told the minister that they would "lose operational control of RCN forces," which required "this intensive training for a period of four months ... and further that, as and when Canadian groups are considered to be 100% efficient, they will be interchanged with other groups."[23] Nor was he the only one to impress this on the minister, who recorded how his "talk with Commodore Mansfield" had indicated that Canadian escorts on the North Africa run "will get better training here than in North Atlantic as Groups. Admiralty will take over the NA [North Atlantic] work."[24]

Unlike Mansfield, Nelles would inform Macdonald that training was not the only area where the RCN needed improvement. Although the British were stressing training at this time, Nelles ensured that the importance of the modernization issue was also conveyed to Macdonald: "In the matter of equipment, we cannot say the RCN are equipped as well as those of the RN because they are not. This is especially so in the matter of RDF and certain wireless equipment – (the 'Air Asdic'). The most modern equipment is simply not available, it is being installed as quickly as it does become available."[25]

By addressing this issue, the navy's chief was not telling the minister anything new. Not only had one of MacLean's informants raised its importance in July 1942 but Connolly had also been introduced to the same equipment grouses during his October 1942 investigation in the Maritimes.[26] Aside from these sources, however, the chief of the naval staff and his officers had discussed various aspects of the RCN's modernization in Macdonald's presence on numerous occasions. In fact, considering some of the more blatant examples, it is hard to understand how the minister would later claim that his naval advisors had never done so. For example, when the Naval Staff first started investigating the modernization question in March 1942, Nelles asked the minister to approve proposed changes that would make it easier for the Equipment Division to assess and acquire new gear from the United Kingdom.[27] Likewise, after seeking permission to send the Admiralty a signal requesting the first fifty hedgehog sets for the RCN, the minister was further told that "the Naval Board agreed that it is essential to adopt proven modern A/S [antisubmarine] attack devices." Macdonald's approval of this requisition meant he understood there was a need for up-to-date equipment, as did the warning to the Naval Board on 8 September 1942 that, "the minister directed that every possible effort be made to foresee commitments for the next fiscal year ... provision should be made ... for new anti-submarine devices which cannot now be foreseen."[28]

In fairness to Macdonald, little information on the modernization issue was passed on to him for another three months. Although the minister's attention was firmly fixed on the reforms Connolly was designing to answer MacLean's allegations during this time frame, the chief of the naval staff could undoubtedly have done a better job of involving his boss in the modernization issue between October and December 1942. Nonetheless, Nelles was certainly not mincing his words when he let the minister know in January 1943 that the RCN was having problems upgrading because "the most modern equipment is simply not available."[29] Moreover, the chief of the naval staff also briefed Macdonald on the difficulties Naval Service Headquarters was having in its efforts to use a corvette, HMCS *Saskatoon*, as a prototype to test East Coast refit facilities and their ability to handle a full Canadian modernization program. He further told Macdonald how this plan was experiencing delays due to the Admiralty's inability to deliver the promised equipment in a timely manner. So much so that Naval Service Headquarters had to substitute another corvette, HMCS *Edmundston*, for this experiment, since the *Saskatoon* had been out of service for far too long.[30] Delays in providing this equipment had left Ottawa disappointed with the Admiralty, as did the final results of the transfer, which was at best only partially carried out. The same operational requirement on the North Atlantic that ensured the RCN could not modernize in 1942 was ironically preventing the British from reassigning all the Canadian groups to the new convoy routes for retraining. Most remained on the North Atlantic protecting convoys, which allowed Royal Navy and United States Navy forces in hunter-killer groups to prosecute targets at will.[31]

Unlike the Royal Navy's fixation on training – although that too would receive attention at Naval Service Headquarters – the major question throughout the first half of 1943 was how to best continue with the immediate modernization of the RCN's current corvette fleet. Correcting this problem was a daunting, almost insurmountable, task that required the fullest level of co-operation between the top brass on the one side and the minister on the other. Before describing the Naval Staff's plan, as well as Macdonald's involvement in that process, a point of clarification is required. The so-called "equipment crisis of 1943" – a term first used by serving naval historians in the late 1940s to characterize the RCN's inability to modernize – has caused much confusion in the historical record.[32] Getting the equipment needed to modernize a corvette, which arguably consisted of gyroscopic compasses, type 144 asdic (SONAR), 271 Mark IV radar, and finally hedgehog, was undoubtedly a problem for Naval Service Headquarters. In what more accurately constituted an "equipment gap" between the RCN and Royal Navy, the Naval Staff had received indications that the flow of this gear from Britain and the United States would increase throughout 1943.[33] This left them to deal with the real crisis, one that both Naval Service Headquarters and the East Coast command considered the biggest problem facing the RCN – something they called the "refit situation."

Refits came in many forms. Some were routine and consisted of periodic maintenance work required to keep escorts seaworthy and operational. Others, such as fitting modern equipment, were more extensive and eventually required the lengthening of a corvette's fo'c'sle (forecastle). There were also the endless emergency repairs to damage from weather or enemy action. All this activity placed a tremendous burden on the East Coast shipyards and refit facilities, especially since merchant ships also required similar attention. And that represented the heart of the refit crisis, which was a separate issue, albeit related to the RCN's equipment gap. Correcting one depended on rectifying the other, and the requests to the Admiralty over the summer of 1942 were an attempt to close the equipment gap. While that problem remained, however, Naval Service Headquarters realized that further attempts to procure British and American equipment would be more or less meaningless if Canadian industry lacked the facilities, space, or required personnel to complete such an extensive modernization program. Without the ability to install the equipment – a function of the repair facilities – merely acquiring new weapons and sensors was placing the proverbial cart before the horse.[34] While the effort to secure as much equipment as possible would continue, resolving the refit crisis had become Naval Service Headquarters' first priority; and from that point on the navy's modernization was explained to the minister in this context.

Captain Lay was one of the first officers in Ottawa to claim that the East Coast refit situation was reaching crisis proportions. Disappointed with the time it took to finally get the *Edmundston* into a Canadian yard – work did not start on her until 5 January 1943 – the director of Operations Division argued that Naval Service Headquarters could no longer afford the luxury of testing the abilities of the East Coast shipyards. In his opinion, the Naval Staff had little choice but to take "more control" of the situation by developing a "clear cut [refit] policy." While not specifically blaming the commanding officer Atlantic coast, Lay felt that the time had come for Naval Service Headquarters to "consider fairly definite directions should be given to the Commands in respect to refits which should lay down the intervals between refits for the various classes."[35] And that began a process whereby Naval Service Headquarters would wrestle control of refits, which until this time rested with the commanding officer Atlantic coast, away from the operational authorities.

After providing an update on the progress of the *Edmundston* to the 15 February Naval Staff meeting, the chief of naval engineering and construction, Rear Admiral G.L. Stephens, RCN, tabled a signal from the naval officer in charge, Halifax. As a member of the Naval Board, Stephens did not generally attend Naval Staff meetings, but in this instance he thought it important to discuss this signal's estimate that "approximately 30 Corvettes could be taken in hand for the conversion on the East Coast during the next 12 months." Considering that forecast "rather optimistic," Stephens then told the Naval Staff that there were fifty-seven RCN corvettes – exactly three-quarters of the navy's total – that required extensive modernization. Lay shared Stephens' pessimism and was happy that his fellow staff members agreed with the plan to re-equip "at the earliest opportunity." Egged on by that backing, Lay clearly believed that extraordinary situations called for extraordinary solutions, and so advocated that the RCN withdraw entire groups at a time for modernization.[36]

Without adequate refit facilities or a steady supply of equipment, taking entire groups off operations for modernization – an idea that the Naval Staff would revisit at a later date – was simply not feasible in February 1943. The more so because few believed that the Canadian ship industry could handle an entire group at the same time. Yet doing nothing more than studying the hotly debated question of whether the East Coast shipyards could handle the staggered year-long modernization of thirty corvettes seemed equally irresponsible. There were, after all, twenty-seven corvettes that still had not even been allocated to a refit facility. The Naval Staff did what was logical given that a majority of the fleet had been transferred to the Royal Navy's control. Constituting a short-term solution, a single request was immediately sent to the Admiralty asking them to fully modernize as many Canadian escorts as their shipyards could take.[37] It received a lukewarm response from the Royal Navy, which stated that British refit facilities were also under a tremendous strain from their own requirements. They would, however, in good faith investigate the possibility of taking six RCN corvettes in hand, one at a time.[38] This, at least, represented a start, and Naval Service Headquarters was hopeful that the Royal Navy would modernize these ships and perhaps more.

While asking the British for help was the major component of their short-term remedy, other activities indicated that Ottawa was doing whatever it could to get as much modern equipment on the escorts as possible. Certainly, Naval Order 2587 did away with much of the administrative red tape that had slowed the piecemeal modernization of the RCN in United Kingdom ports. Promulgated on 27 February, that important order – which Simpson knew nothing about and of which more will be said later – gave all British refit facilities express permission to fit individual pieces of equipment "as occasion arise without prior reference for approval to Naval Service Headquarters."[39] Moreover, the Naval Staff also explored the possibility of whether American yards were capable of modernizing Canadian ships with comparable equipment. Despite much hesitation and reluctance, that source of assistance also promised relief, as US authorities eventually decided that they could take nine Royal Navy corvettes, which were on loan to the RCN, for upgrading in American yards under existing lend-lease agreements. These initial steps were the best the Naval Staff could muster at this time, and so on 25 February Nelles gave Macdonald a thorough appraisal of the situation:

> In view of the expected intensification of U-boat warfare, NSHQ considers it essential to have forecastles extended, bridges improved and all desirable modifications to armament on RCN Corvettes carried out as soon as possible. It is hoped that of the 59 RCN Corvettes [which included two RN corvettes that were serving alongside the RCN] in which this still remains to be done, 30 will be completed in Canadian East Coast ports during 1943. NSHQ has asked Admiralty to take as many as possible in hand in the UK and is relying on having the original 10 Flower Class Corvettes, which were built in Canada and manned by RCN crews, taken in hand in USA ports under Lease Lend.[40]

There was a good reason why Nelles made this pitch to Macdonald. Whether refits were done in Canadian, British, or American ports, the RCN would have to pay for each piece of equipment and the associated costs of installing it. Since justifying additional expenditures was ultimately the minister's responsibility, Nelles did not want Macdonald to look unprepared if the prime minister ever asked why the navy was spending more money than had been allocated in the budget. Moreover, it was C.D. Howe's Department of Munitions and Supply that had the actual purchasing power, and that meant Macdonald might have to defend the navy's request if that department refused to make the acquisitions.

Naval Order 2587 constituted a radical departure from the navy's financial policy. Each year it was the Naval Board's responsibility to keep its equipment acquisitions within the stated money allocations as defined by the naval budget. Now, however, while that responsibility remained, the Naval Board had effectively handed control over those particular acquisitions, and over the installation costs, to the operational authorities and ship industries both in and outside of Canada. It was a nerve-wracking experiment, the more so because Stephens was unable to provide firm estimates on the actual cost of modernizing in this fashion. Worse yet, these acquisitions would be made without Munitions and Supply's approval, and that represented a serious breach of governmental protocol. Given the anticipated increase in efficiency that modernization would bring, the top brass was willing to take the gamble but not without first securing the minister's permission. A memo was sent to Macdonald asking for "financial approval for the work on all ships," and having signed that request on 9 March 1943, the minister gave Nelles a blank cheque to modernize both the remaining corvettes as well as the minesweepers that still required upgrading.[41]

It is unclear whether the minister understood the full implications of the Naval Board's request – given that he would later claim they had hidden the problem from him – but he certainly had a good idea what his advisors were asking him to do. On 24 February, the day before Nelles had said that modernization was "essential," Macdonald wrote to the prime minister complaining that "as it is today, so far as the Department of Naval Services is concerned, outside the actual operation of ships, the Department is completely bereft of any real power. It cannot buy as much as five cents worth of material without the approval of either the Department of Munitions and Supply, or the Department of Finance, or both."[42] Moreover, it is odd that on the same day he gave his naval advisors the financial authority to proceed, Macdonald had attended a War Cabinet Committee meeting at which King – disappointed with excessive departmental spending – warned all his ministers "to keep a restraint on expenditures."[43] Nelles had left little doubt about why and for what reason the money was being used. In fact, only six days later the Naval Board elaborated further, telling Macdonald that he could anticipate additional unexpected costs before the fleet was fully modernized. "From time to time during the next 12 months," the vice chief of the naval staff stated clearly in Macdonald's presence, "it can be foreseen that similar development of scientific equipment which have not been foreseen in preparing estimates will arise." Impressing the importance of the modernization program, it was also stressed "that items such as this should as merited take priority over other expenditures or developments which are not as essential in A/S warfare."[44] Such statements clearly indicate that the Naval Board was involving the minister in the modernization process, and there was more yet to come.

In August 1942, Naval Service Headquarters had asked its operational commands to compile complete lists of the types of equipment on each and every escort. Despite repeated requests over the next seven months, the Mid-Ocean Escort Force's situation remained unreported, yet the statistics from the Western Local Escort Force and Halifax Force told a grim tale.[45] Out of thirty-four ships, only 25 percent had had their fo'c'sles extended; less than 1 percent of their asdics had been converted to 123D; 59 percent were still relying on unstable magnetic (rather than gyroscopic) compasses; and 75 percent were without 271 radar.[46] These figures were worse than anticipated, and they indicated that many of the modernization estimates at Naval Service Headquarters were too optimistic.[47] This did not sit well with the Naval Staff who, after receiving additional warnings from the Atlantic Command, would argue that full modernization required a radical solution.[48] The commanding officer Atlantic coast, Rear Admiral Murray, had little faith in either the British or American ability to help, and on 27 March he told Ottawa as much:

> We cannot expect to obtain much assistance from that source in the future. It behooves us to make the fullest possible use of the plants and machinery available to us in the Canadian Maritime Provinces, and in Newfoundland. At the moment, the Battle of the Atlantic and Anti-Submarine Warfare is placed in the order of importance to the Allied Cause as A-1. The refitting and the retention of our escort craft in a state of seagoing and fighting efficiency is, therefore, of the first importance compared with any part of Canada's war effort.[49]

Murray knew exactly what he was asking Naval Service Headquarters to do. The expansion of the East Coast shipyards was a massive undertaking that would require up to 1,500 more workers, new facilities, and exorbitant financial backing as well as co-ordination between other governmental departments. In fact, it was such an enormous request that Murray even suggested that, in order for the expansion to work, "it may be necessary to decide that the manufacture of tanks or of aeroplanes in the numbers now being turned out should be sacrificed in order to keep our escort vessels at sea."[50]

Murray's request did not come as a surprise to many at Naval Service Headquarters. Lay, in particular, was extremely worried about what he had seen and heard during an earlier visit to the East Coast. Besides having recently told Nelles that "the question of refitting of HMC Ships is, at present time, an extremely serious one," the director of Operations Division was also receiving personal updates from his old friend Roger Bidwell who, while serving as the chief of staff in Halifax, observed that "our facilities are strained to the cracking point."[51] Perhaps representing the greatest crisis that Naval Service Headquarters had yet faced, Lay argued that the refit situation was such "a grave issue" that it required immediate action. On 22 March, he passed his recommendation on to Nelles that "there should be formed, at once, at Naval Service Headquarters, a special committee to co-ordinate refits, repairs and alterations to HMC Ships."[52] By proposing a centralized organization, Lay was making a bold statement: jurisdiction for refits had to be taken away from the Atlantic Command as only Naval Service Headquarters was capable of providing the leadership and direction to prevent the system from collapsing.

The Naval Board first focused on the navy's East Coast refit and repair yards at its 1 February 1943 meeting. Troubled that the "inadequacy of repair facilities" had put the Atlantic Command's refit program "20 to 30% behind schedule," and realizing that more ships would become operational over the ensuing year, the Naval Board was led to the conclusion that "considerable expansion of existing facilities and those planned is essential." In what would become their long-term solution to the refit crisis, it was decided that the only way to accommodate the new ships as well as maintain refits for the current fleet was to expand the RCN's outports in Gaspé, Quebec, as well as Shelburne and Sydney, Nova Scotia. Fully aware that the RCN's primary facility, HMC Dockyard in Halifax, was already overburdened with emergency and running repairs, this extremely ambitious plan would require large sums of money and a substantial construction effort, but it was the only plan they believed was guaranteed to work.[53] That it was going to be such a massive effort meant it would require Macdonald's assistance, and although he missed this initial Naval Board meeting, he was given an update at the next one.[54]

The real problem was that no one knew if the proposed expansion was even possible. There were simply too many uncertainties, particularly when it came to the question of whether the Department of Munitions and Supply as well as the Department of Labour would spare the necessary workers for enlarging the naval facilities. Nor was that all: the idea of expanding or building more civilian yards was still being considered another long-term option. Manpower shortages were endemic throughout Canada's wartime industry, and the attempt to squeeze 1,500 tradesmen from a pool of labour that was quickly drying up was bound to meet resistance. It was feared that the Maritime yards were nearing their breaking point and that any further expansion would result in the collapse of the entire system.[55] While the majority of staff officers believed the RCN's refit situation was urgent, no one within that consensus was willing to make hasty or irrational decisions. Without knowing whether the private yards were capable of such expansion, the risk was simply too great. Further study was required, and Ottawa therefore decided to follow a recommendation that originated from the East Coast command:

> [It is] strongly recommended that Messrs. The Halifax Shipyards Limited should be requested to consent to an invitation being extended to Mr. John Paterson, their Dartmouth Shipyards Superintendent, to make a survey of the Ship Repair facilities of the Maritimes with a view to deciding to what extent they are capable of expansion and what additional labour, etc. is required ... I feel [Mr. Paterson] would be of infinite value in enabling the Department to reach a decision as to whether or not the resources of the Ship Repair Yards in the Maritimes and elsewhere on the East Coast

of Canada can be made sufficient for the maintenance of the whole of the Fleet without having to send ships to Ports of the United States of America or to the United Kingdom for refit.[56]

Such precautions seemed like a good idea, so the deputy minister, Gordon Mills, wrote to Munitions and Supply on Macdonald's behalf requesting they send Paterson on the proposed investigation. Moreover, if it were determined that the expansion was possible, he further warned that in addition to the 1,500 workers for the shipyards in Nova Scotia, the Naval Service might also need another 500 for yards in New Brunswick.[57]

Instead of selecting one man to conduct the investigation, the Department of Munitions and Supply let Controller of Ship Repairs and Salvage D.B. Carswell chair a five-member committee whose mandate was to investigate the manpower shortage on the East Coast. This committee, which first met on 29 April, represented an important first step to understanding the navy's shipyard requirements. Since it was assumed the situation was desperate, the committee was instructed to work quickly, yet such a comprehensive investigation naturally took time to complete.[58] That made some naval officers nervous. While no one wanted to overwhelm the system, there was growing concern that the refit situation would only get worse the longer the Naval Board waited. Consequently, a British request to improve the facilities at the naval base in St. John's – although modest in comparison to the larger expansion plan – was an opportunity that the RCN could not pass up.

During a visit to Ottawa, the head of the British Admiralty delegation, Admiral Percy Noble, RN, attended the 18 March Naval Board meeting, where he announced that the British, Newfoundland, and Canadian governments were considering the "improvement" of the "facilities for maintenance and running repairs of escorts" in St. John's. One of the purposes of his trip was to discuss how the new facilities would be used. This allowed the chief of Naval Engineering and Construction to make a pitch that Noble found difficult to refuse. Arguing that the "refit schedule for the RCN will completely require all ship repair facilities in the Maritimes and Newfoundland," Stephens wanted the new amenities to cater primarily to Canadian escorts. That meant St. John's would handle the vast majority of the RCN's running repairs, and by doing so would clear much-needed room in other Maritime shipyards for long-term work, such as modernization. With the RCN clearly in dire straits, Noble was sympathetic to Stephens' plea, the more so because the Canadian government was willing to finance some of the construction costs and would be responsible for building the facilities.[59]

As the minister was briefed on the manpower shortage, the Naval board also emphasized the importance of the refit situation as it outlined the plan to expand the base at St. John's. After all, it was Macdonald who would have to get Cabinet to authorize the monies for the Canadian contribution to the base. The minister clearly understood the scope of the project, explaining to his Cabinet colleagues that "in addition, the new programme of expansion made necessary by the increased use of the base would require some $7,000,000 which would bring the total cost to approximately $16,000,000." Given that the costs of expanding just three of the RCN's outports had hit $5,416,982 and was expected to climb much higher, that sum must have made the minister nervous.[60] Yet the fact that King's cost-conscious government approved the money for the base at St. John's suggests that the minister had done a good job of selling the proposal.[61] Even before he attended the meeting with Noble, Macdonald was actively trying to find private shipyards to meet the RCN's needs. The Naval Board recognized how "the minister, on his last trip to Newfoundland, had informed Bowater's that the Naval Service would explore the possibilities of repairing and refitting HMC Ships in their plant."[62] For that reason it could be assumed Macdonald knew what the chief of the naval staff was talking about when he explained,

> British Admiralty Delegation has advised Admiralty that by next winter the shortage of repair facilities for Merchant Ships and Warships on the east coast of Canada and Newfoundland will be critical ... US Ports cannot be counted upon in view of the rapidly increasing number of US Escort vessels. A combined British, Canadian and US Committee should therefore meet to examine the problem. The urgency of proceeding immediately with the further development of St. John's, Newfoundland, as a base for running repairs for escorts and for emergency repairs for Merchant Ships is emphasized.[63]

In no uncertain terms, Nelles had once again informed the minister that the refit situation was serious, especially since it was now attracting the attention of Canada's principal allies.

Largely as the result of Noble's visit, Britain's high commissioner in Ottawa dispatched a letter to Canadian Undersecretary of State for External Affairs Norman Robertson, calling for the formation of a combined Canadian, British, and American committee to study the problems associated with repairs and maintenance in the Maritimes. Although Noble had explained that Canadian resources were being taxed to the limit, the British still warned Robertson that the refit and repair situation "will have become acute unless urgent steps are taken now to remedy the deficiencies."[64] The sense of urgency was passed on to Macdonald at the 19 April Naval Board meeting, where his advisors strongly recommended that the navy support the creation of what was later called the Combined Committee on Ship Repair Problems. Macdonald did so. Beyond that, however, the Naval Board also asked him to impress the committee's importance on the Department of Munitions and Supply, which, despite being the lead agency of the Canadian delegation, had not yet responded to the British proposal.[65] The Naval Board was asking too much from Macdonald, who was reluctant to prod a senior statesman like C.D. Howe. The Naval Board backed down, but once the Allied Anti-Submarine Survey Board (the Survey Board, for short) toured Canada and Newfoundland, the minister's advisors would state in no uncertain terms that successfully resolving the RCN's refit crisis depended in large part on the willingness of the Department of Munitions and Supply to help.

After trips to both the United Kingdom and United States, the Survey Board continued with its mandate to standardize antisubmarine training, tactics, and doctrine by visiting with senior RCN officers in Ottawa on 7-8 May.[66] During these meetings the Canadians were extremely candid, leaving little doubt that they considered the refit situation the RCN's biggest problem. Undoubtedly making a pitch for their planned expansion, the RCN officers made it clear that with the current size and organizational structure of Canadian shipyards "there would never be sufficient repair facilities and that in this respect, the position could never be really satisfactory."[67] Moreover, they were equally concerned that the already overburdened shipyards would be under additional "strain imposed on repair facilities by the converting of long fo'c'sle and fitting gyros et cetera to some seventy corvettes." Yet the navy's efforts to improve this situation were frustrated by the control of privately operated yards and dry docks being "in civilian hands" and resting with Carswell, the controller of ship repair and salvage at Munitions and Supply.

Although the formation of Carswell's manpower investigation represented a good start, Canadian naval officers were quick to tell the Survey Board that the navy did not have the authority to act unilaterally. Naval Service Headquarters did enjoy jurisdiction over naval dockyards and outports, but the civilian shipyards belonged to Munitions and Supply, and their respective workforces were the responsibility of the Department of Labour. That the selection of those workers was the responsibility of yet another branch of the latter department (National Select Services) clearly indicated that the navy would have to make a case for devoting so much of the country's resources to the proposed expansion of the shipyards. Unwilling to embarrass their minister, the Canadian officers stopped just short of telling the Survey Board what they had tried to explain to Macdonald two weeks earlier: nothing could properly be done without Munitions and Supply, and yet that department did not seem to understand the navy's refit crisis. However, the Survey Board members would witness the situation first-hand when they travelled to Halifax and St. John's, and perhaps because of that Nelles specifically asked them to write a report that should contain "a full and frank criticism of existing conditions upon the completion of their tour."[68] If the chief of the naval staff wanted to use the Survey Board as a means to pressure Macdonald to approach Howe, he received exactly what he needed and more.

On 18 May, the Survey Board fulfilled its promise to Nelles by submitting a report that assessed the state of operations, training, and maintenance on the East Coast. Although there was room for improvement, the Survey Board determined that much progress had been made in the former two fields, and as such it was the latter issue that received the most attention. "In general the facilities available at Halifax and St. John's for the maintenance and repair of escort vessels have passed the saturation point," they reported to Nelles, continuing with "the proportion of escort vessels undergoing or awaiting repair or refit is unacceptably high." The Naval Board had suspected, and the Survey Board also concluded, that the manpower situation was unsatisfactory. Lacking both trained executives and experienced workers, they found the smaller Maritime yards particularly "inefficient," and that was placing an unacceptable strain on the already overworked naval dockyard and outports.[69] But while such observations reinforced what Nelles had already told the minister, it was their final recommendations that supported the chief of the naval staff's contention that the refit situation had reached crisis proportions.

Effectively tripling the RCN's original manpower estimates, the Survey Board argued that the beleaguered Maritime yards would require 6,000 additional workers to meet the navy's needs. While the Survey Board had not recommended the building of more shipyards as the Naval Board was considering, the magnitude of their other suggestions, such as the proposal to give escort priority over merchant ships, was staggering. Cutting or curtailing the current construction program of frigates – something that Naval Service Headquarters was unwilling to do at this time – was another radical solution for what the Survey Board clearly considered a serious problem. This indicated that there was more than one possible solution to this complex issue, and the Naval Board had the job of explaining those options to Macdonald. Fortunately, Naval Service Headquarters was in the process of implementing a new staff organization that was not only capable of digesting the Survey Board's conclusions for ministerial consumption, but also was deliberately designed "for the purpose of establishing the standards of fighting efficiency of RCN ships and maintaining them."[70]

Like the ships at sea, Naval Service Headquarters had been under so much strain from the service's rapid expansion that it nearly broke down on several occasions. Realizing that band-aid solutions could no longer sustain a headquarters that was clearly bleeding to death, Nelles looked for curative treatments to end a sickly cycle where the staff was continually being tossed from one administrative crisis into another. One of these solutions was to create the Directorate of Organization in November 1942. Under the chairmanship of Captain Edmund Johnstone, RCN, that directorate's mandate was to find ways to keep the staff system working.[71] The other solution was to make Rear Admiral George Jones the vice chief of the naval staff in the fall of 1942 so that he could take charge of what would become one of the largest reorganizations at Naval Service Headquarters during the entire war. At the time, this was one of Nelles' greatest decisions, though it would come back to haunt him the following year, as the careerist vice chief had designs on Nelles' job. Quite simply, the new vice chief was arguably the best bureaucratic officer in the service, and had it not been for his appointment, the secretary of the Naval Board, Captain R.A. Pennington, RCNVR, was convinced that "the whole organization would have collapsed."[72]

Under Jones' close supervision, both Johnstone and Pennington discovered that the members of the Naval Staff and Naval Board were getting bogged down because they were micromanaging the navy and creating impossible workloads. That pressure was unhealthy for the men who collectively represented the navy's brain-centre. The key to stopping the haemorrhaging, according to Johnstone and Pennington, was to decentralize the Naval Staff by giving more discretionary power to the various directorates.[73] This new organization was to consist of seven directorates whose activities would be co-ordinated through the creation of a new staff appointment known as the assistant chief of the naval staff.[74]

Perhaps the most important of these directorates (as far as modernization was concerned) was the newly created Directorate of Warfare and Training. Divided into four sections that focused on fighting efficiency, tactical analysis, training, and scientific research, this directorate should have been formed much earlier than the spring of 1943.[75] The service's incredible expansion, in combination with its hefty operational commitments, had forced Ottawa to send most of its antisubmarine warfare experts where they were needed most, and for the first three years of the war that was on the East Coast. Now that more technical officers had been trained, the Naval Staff was in a position to balance the deficiency at headquarters.

A considerable readjustment to the original reorganization, this bold leap was indicative of Naval Service Headquarters' desire to improve conditions in the fleet. In fact, after it took effect on 1 June, Nelles argued that the two most important aspects of the reorganization were the creation of the assistant chief (Creery) to "unify staff activities," and the director of warfare and training who "would establish and maintain fighting efficiency."[76] He was right. The refit crisis was one of the first items raised by the newly reconstituted Naval Staff, and for the next two months devising an active and engaging policy to combat that deficiency was its primary purpose.[77]

The greatest impact of the new organization was that it convinced the Naval Staff that the refit crisis was even worse than they had originally suspected. While their long-term plan to expand existing naval facilities continued, the earlier suggestion that the RCN pressure the government into building more private shipyards, while not ruled out in its entirely, was put on hold. This idea was placed on the back burner not because it was unpopular but because more immediate action was required. In fact, from the moment he became chief of the naval staff, Nelles had advocated building warships in Canada, giving his political masters a prophetic warning in May 1938 that "the more shp [sic] building the Naval Service can give to Canadian firms in peace the better fitted these firms will be when emergency arises."[78] Ironically, had the government followed his advice at the time, the RCN's refit crisis may not have been as grim, and Nelles might have kept his job until he decided to retire.

Nelles' attempt to involve Macdonald in the Naval Staff's more immediate solution for the refit crisis is the strongest illustration of how weak the minister's case – that Nelles had hidden the modernization problem from him – actually was. Macdonald's direct involvement in this new initiative began at the 21 June Naval Board meeting. At that time the minister and his advisors discussed a memo written by Stephens regarding "certain alleged conditions which are said to exist in HMC Dockyard, Halifax." Unlike the general observations contained in an earlier report, this memo focused exclusively on a direct comparison between Stephens' own trip and the opinions of the Survey Board after they had visited the navy's refit facilities in Halifax. Given that there were some discrepancies between Stephens' and the Survey Board's interpretations, the Naval Board asked Macdonald to approach C.D. Howe with the aim of discovering whether the Department of Munitions and Supply would conduct "an independent survey" into the conditions at HMC Dockyard "in the interest of improvement of efficiency."[79] While that was undoubtedly the main goal of the Naval Board, there appears to have been a hidden design behind the request as well.

The Naval Staff's efforts to tackle the refit crisis had always been plagued by the fact that the power and responsibility to correct the problem rested almost exclusively with the Department of Munitions and Supply and the Department of Labour. Without their assistance, the navy's options were limited, and that was extremely frustrating for the Naval Staff. Take, for example, the Survey Board's recommendation that the refitting and repairing of escort vessels should be given priority over merchant ships. For their part, the navy had not only wholeheartedly agreed with that suggestion, but also furthered it by making the powerful argument that there "is no use building new merchant ships or repairing old ones if Escort vessels are not available for their protection at sea." While a number of naval officers had "stressed again the desirability of naval authorities having a greater say on the matter of priorities," the simple fact of the matter was that decisions such as these were not theirs to make. Worse yet, the lines of communication between Munitions and Supply and the naval service could be, at times, extremely poor.[80] Given this situation, it is easy to see what Macdonald's naval advisors were trying to do at the 21 June Naval Board meeting. Senior naval officers were not allowed to approach Howe on their own, but this proposed investigation seemed to be a good way to get Munitions and Supply involved. At the very least, it was imperative for them to be made aware of the navy's situation, and that was something that only Macdonald could achieve.

Perhaps the Naval Board was being somewhat crafty with the minister, but they had little choice. Macdonald had shown some reluctance to confront Howe on similar issues in the past, making it likely that he would reject a direct request from his naval advisors that Munitions and Supply do something about the refit crisis. Given Howe's seniority in King's Cabinet, it is hard to fault Macdonald for his reluctant attitude, the more so because any request from the navy for help could easily be reinterpreted as an accusation that the refit crisis was Munitions and Supply's fault. Aware of these political sensitivities, the Naval Board was careful when it broached this subject with Macdonald, but there were aspects of the proposed investigation where they needed him to take a firm stand. For example, if Munitions and Supply was to understand the navy's predicament, it was essential that their key official – the controller of ship repairs and salvage – be assigned to the investigation. While the Naval Board was willing to let Munitions and Supply choose the second candidate, they told Macdonald that Howe should select a "qualified businessman or administrator not connected with shipping ... to work with Mr. Carswell."[81]

Unfortunately for the Naval Board, Macdonald's letter to Howe, which rather politely inferred that improving the refit situation was mostly the responsibility of Munitions and Supply, did not produce all the intended results. Howe agreed to make Carswell available for the investigation and also recommended John Rannie, the superintendent of United Shipyards, as the second examiner. But his response left little doubt that he either ignored or possibly missed the subtleties of the navy's message, as Howe stated that Carswell and Rannie "would make a good team for *your* purpose." Despite Howe's apparent naïveté, there can be little doubt that Macdonald understood the significance of what was transpiring, especially since his letter clearly stated that the navy had recently encountered serious criticism for the efficiency of the ship repair organization.[82]

Macdonald, who was referring to the Survey Board's final conclusions, had met with that body before it left Ottawa for Halifax and St. John's on 10 May.[83] It is important to note that the naval minister recognized the Survey Board's criticisms of the repair organization because it indicates that he acknowledged the seriousness of the problem. Moreover, it was Macdonald, rather than the Naval Board, who insisted on handling the details for Carswell and Rannie's investigation, such as approving the expenses. The minister not only personally authorized the investigation but also issued direct orders to the chief of naval engineering and construction "that every facility available is to be afforded Mr. Carswell and Mr. Rannie in order that this survey may be executed thoroughly."[84] The Naval Board was encouraged by the active role that Macdonald was playing in the establishment of

Carswell and Rannie's investigation but disappointed that Munitions and Supply was not taking more responsibility for the refit situation. Even the navy's own plans to expand the outports would require some assistance from Munitions and Supply. Time was running out, leading at least one staff member to argue that "the expansion programme as planned represents the immediate wartime needs and must be considered as a minimum requirement. It is, therefore, recommended that it be proceeded with at once."[85] Nelles and his officers made what was undoubtedly their most deliberate effort to impress the minister with the seriousness of the refit situation, and they also presented another way to deal with it.

Given that the expansion of the navy's outports would take time, and working on the premise that Munitions and Supply would not build additional private shipyards, the new staff organization at Naval Service Headquarters came up with what could be considered a mid-term solution for the refit crisis. Based on a recommendation by the chief engineer, this idea involved a proposed reorganization of HMC Dockyard. This was something the navy could do on its own, and it was hoped that by making the Dockyard organization more efficient, it would be possible to squeeze a maximum number of refits out of the existing facilities. According to Stephens, there was much room for improvement. In his view, the Dockyard was not a single entity, but rather consisted of a number of shops and facilities. There was no centralized authority to control their activities, and that often led to delays, which was "not the fault of any individual, but a fundamental defect in the present organization itself."[86] His idea was therefore to create a "captain superintendent" who would be responsible directly to Naval Service Headquarters for co-ordinating all the work done at the Dockyard.

Nelles was intrigued and so instructed Johnstone's Directorate of Organization to investigate the possibility of restructuring the navy's refit organization on the East Coast. Johnstone was a good choice. Not only was his directorate designed to investigate reorganizations, but he had also personally played a central role in developing the RCN's long-term plan of expanding the RCN's outports.[87] He was well-acquainted with the refit crisis, and his report, completed 18 June, contained such radical and unorthodox recommendations that it prompted Nelles to establish a staff group to assess the merits of its conclusions. That the staff group's suggestions went even further afield than did the director of organization's report troubled Stephens, who wanted the chief of the naval staff to chair a special meeting to discuss all "the diversities of opinion" before the matter was again brought to the minister's attention.[88] Nelles disagreed. The refit crisis was too important, and in the chief of the naval staff's opinion, Macdonald needed to hear all the alternatives before any decision was reached. When viewed in the context of the minister's future charges of incompetence, that set the stage for a crucial Naval Board meeting where he was told – in no uncertain terms – that the navy was in trouble.

Johnstone's report and the staff group's appraisal were the central items of the 27 July Naval Board meeting. Both left little doubt that the navy was facing a terrible crisis. Certainly, the director of organization had captured this mood in the opening paragraph of his report, observing that the refit situation was "so urgent and of such vital importance that time does not permit of a full investigation of all factors contributing to it. It is considered essential that the broad lines on which improvement is to be effected must be established immediately and that steps be taken at once to effect a radical change in the existing conditions."[89] Johnstone's plans were more extensive than the changes that Stephens had proposed, since he suggested that the navy's East Coast yards should be totally reorganized "as a whole to facilitate repairs and refits of RCN ships."[90] Instead of appointing a captain superintendent as the chief engineer had advised, the director of organization wanted to create a director of dockyards who would have "point-men" at the RCN's refit and repair bases at Halifax, Sydney, and Shelburne while operating from Naval Service Headquarters. The establishment of such an organization would be an enormous undertaking, but according to Johnstone it was "the most fruitful angle from which this major problem can be attacked." There was more. Although responsibility for refits was traditionally assigned to the commander in chief Canadian North West Atlantic, Johnstone believed Ottawa should play a more active role in designing and implementing the fleet's refit schedule, just as Nelson Lay had argued in February 1943. Johnstone's message was all too clear: the only way to correct the refit crisis was for Naval Service Headquarters to take total control of the situation by both co-ordinating and directly managing almost every aspect of the navy's East Coast repair and refit set-up.

Johnstone's justification for these changes was equally revealing, and it is worth quoting in full, particularly since it would come back to haunt Macdonald some six months later:

Many Corvettes have completed two or more years service and it is therefore reasonable to suppose that increasing numbers of them will require major hull repairs and long refits which, in many cases, are overdue. The responsibility for this situation rests, theoretically, with the Commander-in-Chief [Murray], who is charged with the responsibility for making arrangements for the periodic checking and refit of HMCS [sic] Ships to ensure preservation of the hulls and maintain the fighting efficiency of the Fleet, in accordance with Chapter XXVIII of KR and AI. Nevertheless, Naval Service Headquarters cannot unload the whole of this responsibility for the present state of affairs onto the Commander-in-Chief. Naval Service Headquarters has in the past either tacitly, or by definite instruction, approved of the delays in refit. It is considered to be of the utmost importance that this situation should be corrected as rapidly as possible, and that in the last analysis this can only be done by clear direction from Naval Service Headquarters ... the problem which has to be dealt with is vital, immediate, and of the greatest urgency. Failure to grapple with it at once is inexcusable in view of the first importance of the Battle of the Atlantic.[91]

Such dire warnings should have produced some type of reaction from the minister; strangely they did not. Beyond that, however, Johnstone also hinted that the navy had to approach both the Department of Labour and the Department of Munitions and Supply for assistance. Like the private shipyards, the Dockyard was equally handicapped by a shortage of labour. Correcting that deficiency was outside of the navy's sphere of influence, so all Johnstone could do was comment on the impact that it was having on the refit situation. The same was true for another problem at the Dockyard, which was that newly constructed ships would arrive from private yards "with long lists of items still to be completed."[92] This work unnecessarily tied up much-needed space at the Dockyard, yet with the private yards belonging to Munitions and Supply, there was little the navy could do about that situation either.

Whereas Johnstone tiptoed around the issue of prodding other governmental departments into action, the staff group's conclusions were more direct. Wanting to obtain as many outside views as possible, Nelles had circulated Johnstone's report to a number of sources well before the Naval Board meeting. Generally, it received widespread support, and even Murray, while probably resenting the implication that his command had fumbled, agreed with its sweeping recommendations. As far as the staff group was concerned, Johnstone had not gone the distance, and they said as much in their appraisal:

4   The three main requirements are:
    (1) Yards (a) Civilian (b) Naval;
    (2) Labour;
    (3) Equipment and Material.
5   With the exception of (1)(b), all of the above are under the control of Civilian Departments of the Government.
6   Co-ordination of the highest order is, therefore, necessary of the relevant planning by Naval and civilian authorities responsible for these matters and, unless the machinery for such co-ordination exists, no Naval organization responsible for repair and refit of warships can possibly function efficiently, and disruption of operational programmes will be inevitable.[93]

This observation cut to the heart of the matter: whether Macdonald liked it or not, the only solution for the refit crisis was an interdepartmental approach.

To facilitate that end, the staff group proposed a committee that would consist of the director of warship construction, chief of naval engineering and construction, the future director of naval dockyards, the minister of labour, and the director of ship repairs. Much to Macdonald's chagrin, the staff group then suggested that the chairman of this committee should be none other than the minister of munitions and supply. Considering Macdonald's reluctance to approach Howe in the past, it is uncertain whether the staff group was trying to persuade the minister as much as they were defiantly baiting him. Given that Howe was the only one who could clear "obstacles such as shortage of labour, equipment, material, etc.,"[94] the former was more likely the case. The more so because embarrassing the naval minister would not help solve a condition that "can no longer be tolerated if the right balance between protection of sea borne trade, and the means of protection, the Navy, is to be maintained."[95] Despite the strength of that argument, Macdonald remained unmoved. And so, while a drastically scaled-down version of Johnstone's reorganization was given the green light, the staff group's "recommendations were considered as too far reaching, for the present, though ultimately some attention would likely be given to establishment of a co-ordinating authority."[96]

No one was more disappointed with that outcome than Murray, who reiterated to Naval Service Headquarters that "it is assumed, however, that the Naval Staff fully realizes that this change in organization cannot, in itself, provide a rapid cure for the evils which cause delay in the repair of ships." Like the staff group, Murray was advocating radical changes, ones that included

1. [An] increase in skilled labour to be made available to Naval Dockyards and civil repair yards in the Maritime area.
2. Removal from all yards in the Maritime Area of calls on their labour and equipment for any other purpose than ship repairs.
3. Priority in these yards for Naval work over merchant ship repairs.
4. A building up of the management of the civil yards to provide an organization and supervision which will allow them to work at the fullest efficiency.[97]

In his opinion as an operational commander, that was what was required to bring about an "immediate improvement," and by making such far-reaching recommendations, Murray, like the staff group, was just doing his job. Undoubtedly, he was right; a comparison between his recommendations and those of the staff group clearly indicated that the great minds in Halifax and Ottawa thought alike. The key to a quick resolution to the refit situation was to get other government departments involved. Despite their pleas for Macdonald to follow this advice, however, there was little the Naval Board could do once the minister had made up his mind. In fairness, not everyone at Naval Service Headquarters agreed that such drastic measures and policies were required, and they said as much in front of the minister. Though representing a minority opinion, these particular naval officers were relieved when Macdonald accepted a watered-down version of the proposals.

The Naval Board had done its duty. Macdonald was given options, he had received guidance on their respective merits, and that allowed him to select a course of action. Much to the Naval Board's disappointment, the minister remained unconvinced and was still unwilling to stand up for the navy by pushing other government departments into action. He was nonetheless prepared to approve some changes to the internal workings of the navy's administration. Representing a mixture of Stephens' advice and Johnstone's report, the navy's refit facilities would be reorganized and placed under the authority of a "Commodore Superintendent at Halifax" whose mandate was "arranging and carrying through all refits, alterations and repairs throughout the East Coast."[98] Although not as extensive as Johnstone had wanted, the reorganization still represented a significant upheaval of the existing refit structure, as he recalled in a postwar interview: "It became evident that some drastic action should be taken to improve the situation with regard to the repair of our ships and to re-equipping of them ... The whole East Coast organization was turned around in order to make this appointment possible and Commander Hibbard was appointed the First Commodore Superintendent with full charge under CNES [Chief Naval Equipment and Supply] of all repair and equipping of all ships on the East Coast."[99] The new Naval Staff had proven its worth. A mere three weeks after it had been established on 1 June, the restructured Naval Staff had discussed, investigated, and come up with a solution to the RCN's gravest problem. It was a shining, bordering on brilliant, example of staff work, particularly since the planned East Coast refit organization would be up and running two months ahead of schedule.[100] Unfortunately, while the refit situation was the RCN's greatest impediment to modernization, it was by no means the only one.

Spotting unfamiliar equipment on Royal Navy escorts was often the RCN's first indication that the British had developed a new weapon or sensor. This was the result of poor technical liaison with the Admiralty, which was another important factor that hindered Naval Service Headquarters' ability to modernize. The heart of this problem was that Canadian industry was capable of manufacturing British equipment, but to do so they needed plans, blueprints, and prototypes of the technologies being developed by the Admiralty. Those essential components were slow in coming, and it was recognized that much of the delay could have been avoided had Ottawa sent officers with technical experience to the United Kingdom so as "to keep touch with the development of new equipment and methods from their inception."[101]

Criticisms that Naval Service Headquarters was slow to implement those plans were not entirely baseless.[102] However, the overseas office was not the only Canadian establishment crying out for more technical officers. Naval Service Headquarters needed to staff its own positions for the new organization, while some in Newfoundland were upset that the commanding officer Atlantic coast continued to siphon technical officers to Halifax. The gift of hindsight suggests that the Naval Staff should have recruited and trained more technical officers earlier in the war, and in that regard they had suffered from short-sightedness.

As with the overall modernization question, Nelles was insulted when Macdonald accused him of failing to solicit his support to solve the problem of technical liaison. By late November 1943 the naval chief fired back at the minister, "Time and again at Naval Council, and afterwards at Naval Board, I have heard the Chief of Naval Engineering and Construction inform you that we could not get on with the work 'because we have no plans' – no plans of forthcoming ships, no plans of Asdic modifications, no plans from Admiralty of any kind until they are dragged out of them some six months or longer after they are in use in UK."[103]

Perhaps Nelles was being a little tough on the Admiralty, but he was certainly telling the truth about having previously raised this issue with Macdonald. Naval Board minutes make clear that the chief of the naval staff had done so as early as 15 June 1942.[104] While the Naval Board had not given this issue the same sense of urgency as they had done with the refit situation, they had at least made the minister aware of it. Yet less than three weeks after the crucial 27 July 1943 Naval Board meeting, Strange's report arrived on Macdonald's desk, and from that moment the minister's relationship with Nelles was never the same. As a result, the next chapter focuses on why Macdonald failed to appreciate what his advisors had told him over the year and why he so willingly accepted Strange's account. Considering what the officers on the Naval Staff and board had achieved, the majority of charges of incompetence emanating from Strange's report were unjustified.

Excessive operational commitments, in combination with the fact that the British did not have much equipment to spare, made the RCN's modernization next to impossible throughout 1942. Nevertheless, that summer the Naval Staff decided that modernization was not only necessary, but also that "if the operational use of the ships was not to be curtailed, that it would require approximately two years to finish the conversion."[105] Based on that estimate, the RCN had done better than they originally predicted. In May 1944, two months prior to that initial deadline, Macdonald accepted that the "modernization crisis" was over.[106] Since he had already been fired, Nelles was not in Ottawa to enjoy what should have been his finest hour. Overcoming the refit crisis was one of the greatest challenges that Nelles faced during his tenure as chief of the naval staff. Under his direction, Naval Service Headquarters had risen to that challenge by reorganizing the Naval Staff and developing a three-pronged plan that included a short-term solution of asking for British assistance and improving technical liaison with the Admiralty, a mid-term rearrangement of the existing East Coast refit structure, and a long-term proposal to expand the navy's outport facilities. While Macdonald did not seem particularly interested in these matters, Nelles had still taken particular care to keep the minister informed. And for that reason the justification for firing Nelles does not hold up to scrutiny. Largely because of Nelles' efforts, Macdonald had been an active participant in Naval Service Headquarters' solutions for the refit crisis but he did not seem to understand the significance of what Nelles had said. Explaining why the minister missed the message requires a thorough investigation of its own.

5
Informers, Collaborators, and Promise Breakers

Troubles with both the Admiralty and the Department of Munitions and Supply in August 1943 led to serious setbacks for Naval Service Headquarters' refit plans, but these so-called "promise breakers" were by no means Nelles' biggest problem. Given that his boss was a Cabinet member, Nelles had to vie with the plethora of governmental issues and meetings that monopolized much of Macdonald's time; and in view of that hectic schedule, getting the minister to take an active interest in questions like the refit situation was never easy. What Nelles did not always realize, however, was that throughout the first half of 1943, he was competing for Macdonald's attention against various outside influences such as MacLean and his followers, Simpson, his officers in Londonderry, and some Canadian commanding officers, as well as the executive assistant's own reserve network. Nor were they the only ones working behind Nelles' back. Naval Service Headquarters also had its collaborators, such as the vice chief of the naval staff, George Jones, who conspired with selected regulars to undermine the minister's confidence in Nelles. Although each of these groups operated independently of the other, they were all trying simultaneously to influence the minister, and that is the key to understanding how Macdonald missed Nelles' message on the refit situation. By politicizing their particular grouses and agendas, each of these people and groups exploited the minister's vulnerabilities and distracted him from the issues that mattered most to Nelles and the navy.

When MacLean made good on his threat to publish his grievances, Macdonald and Connolly had little choice but to busy themselves with the task of defending the navy. Both Parliament and the press were feasting on the fleshy parts of the reserve discrimination allegations, and as the reputation of the navy was hanging in the balance defeating MacLean was a priority.[1] Beyond that, MacLean's assault eventually included an attack on Macdonald's performance as minister, implying that he had never taken an active interest in the navy and had failed to supervise his own department. Although the examples used to illustrate Macdonald's negligence can be questioned, there was much truth to this view. Even before the refit crisis, Macdonald had shown little interest in the navy and its growing pains. Nelles' early warnings about modernization and the refit crisis should have caught Macdonald's attention, but tragically the minister was so firmly fixed on disproving MacLean's campaign that he hardly noticed. And so, in perhaps one of the greatest ironies of them all, MacLean contributed to one of the faults he was criticizing by distracting a minister whom he claimed was too easily distractible.

The allegation that Macdonald was indifferent to the navy's problems had touched a nerve. For example, only days after winning the first bout with MacLean in February 1943, Macdonald complained to King that as a Cabinet minister he had to attend a number of committees that continually diverted his attention from naval affairs. Besides Naval Board meetings, Macdonald was expected to sit in the House of Commons when it was in session, attend War Cabinet and Defence Council meetings, and hold sessions with his departmental deputies. A number of other "irregular" meetings also required his attention, and Macdonald calculated that on average "nearly six hours a day ... are spent in conferences or assemblies of one sort or another." He simply had too many commitments, and Naval Board meetings were often the first sacrificed when the minister was pressed for time.[2]

Nor did his responsibilities end there. His concentration was also required on larger governmental matters that often involved divisive, complex, and controversial issues such as conscription, manpower, or even the fortunes of the Liberal Party. For that reason both he and Minister of National Defence for Air Charles Gavin "Chubby" Power tried to persuade Prime Minister King to reorganize Cabinet. Running one of the national defence ministries was an enormous undertaking, which, their argument went, meant the defence ministers should be released from extraneous duties to allow them to supervise their respective departments.[3] King flatly refused. He was willing to entertain the idea of assigning special "assistants" to help with their workloads but curtailing any type of ministerial responsibility in a time of crisis was clearly unacceptable.[4] While not necessarily excusing Macdonald's lack of interest in the navy, the Canadian parliamentary system was at least in part responsible for his aloofness. It was asking quite a bit to expect anyone to keep on top of all the issues confronting the minister's office on a daily basis. Worse, larger governmental policy was always given top priority, explaining why Macdonald showed up to only half the Naval Board's meetings prior to the troubles with MacLean. The minister naturally felt vulnerable, and that sensitivity – in combination with the chaos created by MacLean's campaign – exposed a weakness that Nelles' rivals at Naval Service Headquarters were willing to exploit.

Macdonald and the Naval Staff had shown much solidarity in their collective efforts to defeat MacLean. In reality, though, Ottawa's naval leadership was built on a foundation peppered with cracks and fissures that, once exposed to destabilizing influences like MacLean's interference, threatened to turn Nelles' world upside down. In spite of MacLean's charges, the factionalism at Naval Service Headquarters had little to do with the so-called discrimination between permanent force and reserve officers but was the product of certain animosities among the regulars. Such acrimony among the top brass was not new; it was based on long-standing feuds that had plagued the RCN for at least two decades. The clash of personalities was only one factor that contributed to the development of these rivalries. Perhaps more important, the RCN's top brass had grown up in a pre-war community that rewarded individualism and by doing so encouraged what today would be called excessive careerism.

In this cutthroat environment every single day of seniority (time in rank) was prized and interpreted as potentially the difference between a plum job and eventual promotion or a stagnant career. Such a state of affairs had a tremendous impact on morale, and at least one individual complained that the infighting among RCN officers "will eventually undermine naval discipline to such a stage that a complete abolition [of the service] will be a saving grace."[5] While representing an extreme interpretation, this type of criticism reflected a naval community where "everyone knows everybody's business and relations." Chronic attempts to gain seniority over peers caused much bitterness within the RCN's officers' corps, and that collective mentality was responsible for one of the most intense and hate-filled rivalries in Canadian naval history – that between George Jones and Leonard Murray.[6]

By the late 1930s, it was obvious that Jones and Murray were jockeying for position in an unofficial leadership race to be crowned as Nelles' eventual successor. While both men were aggressive career manipulators, Jones was more efficient and ruthless. That had not always been the case. Longing for the innocence of his youth, Jones had argued that his early years at the Royal Naval College of Canada were the "healthiest" and "happiest" part of his life. Others agreed; one of his former classmates found Jones "always bright and sometimes brilliant ... His laugh was infectious and his smile a dream," while seven years later another recalled that "during his time at the College, Lieutenant Jones infused much admiration into our hearts. It is quite evident that this admiration had anything but died." The RCN's top admiral at the time, Walter Hose, was equally impressed, finding that Jones was "tactful, good tempered, and very cheerful ... A fine character."[7] He had been a likable and hard-working man whose only appreciable flaw was a "shyness" at mixed social functions – he either left prematurely or simply "disappeared for most of the time."[8] Despite these accolades and achievements, the young Lieutenant Jones discovered that he was falling behind his colleagues in a service where merit alone was not enough to guarantee advancement. Since they were getting promoted through a combination of manipulating naval regulations and influence peddling with superiors, he decided to do the same.[9]

Jones was often described as a "tyrant" or "a sort of cold figure," and "never one to be polite if he could avoid it," so most found it hard to get along with him when he became a senior officer. A common joke of the day was, "Isn't it wonderful? [Jones] spoke to me this morning. He told me to get the hell out of his way." Such tales about Jones' temperament were nothing new to those who had served with him before, and even the Naval Information Department was forced to admit in a press release that "Jones is credited with a sharp 'bark' but an unbounded enthusiasm for his men modifies his 'bite.'"[10] There were, of course, worse tales, which all indicate that years of competing with his contemporaries had transformed Jones into something of an ogre. But while he may not have been generally well liked, his approach certainly worked. Nelles was impressed. And in the end, for a man like Jones who was so desperately reaching for the top, that was all that mattered.[11]

Rear Admiral George C. Jones' use of the telescope under his arm illustrates his infamous temper. One witness, Angus G. Boulton, had a vivid memory of the admiral dealing with an able seaman who was "probably ten-minutes over leave or something [by] waving his telescope about and the poor bugger standing behind the table there, shaking in his boots and old GC Jones would weigh him off in no uncertain manner" (interview by Hal Lawrence, DHH, Biog B). DHH, BIOG J (GC JONES)

Despite trailing throughout most of the 1920s and 1930s, Jones' combination of hard work and career manipulation paid off, as he slowly eked out a lead over Murray. Interpreted as a confirmation that Nelles preferred him, Jones was promoted to captain on 1 August 1938 while Murray was confirmed in the same rank on the next day.[12] This pattern would continue, and Jones maintained his single day of seniority when he and Murray were promoted to rear admirals in December 1941.[13] Nelles was clearly grooming Jones to eventually take over, and the chief of the naval staff naturally expected that to happen whenever he decided to retire. Jones had other ideas. His plan was to expedite Nelles' departure, and that meant the chief of the naval staff had offered his own Judas the seat next to him at the Naval Board's table. As the new vice chief of the naval staff, Jones was one step away from achieving his ultimate goal; forging connections that afforded him the opportunity and confidence to strike at his benefactor, he initiated a behind-the-scenes campaign that whittled away at Nelles' weakening base of political support.

There was a reason Jones did not want to wait to become the Navy's top chief. He had suffered a heart attack in March 1942 while serving as the commanding officer Atlantic coast, and he swore the only witness to secrecy because he was "anxious only to finish out the war in harness."[14] For a man whose health was secondary to his sense of duty, Vice Chief Jones was literally working himself to death, and there was no guarantee that he would live long enough to replace Nelles. His superior administrative abilities and unparalleled work ethic attracted a small group of officers – the so-called "Jones men" – who were fiercely loyal to him.[15] Others had an affinity for Murray, and that had the effect of dividing many of the RCN's captains and commanders into two opposing camps. Not surprisingly, these entourages tended to follow their particular champion from posting to posting, and there were a number of "Jones men" at Naval Service Headquarters when the vice chief of the naval staff made his move for the top.

There was good reason why Jones believed he could undermine Nelles' position with the minister. He had lived in the same Halifax neighbourhood as Macdonald in the 1920s, and it was reputed that besides being one of his bosses at headquarters Macdonald was an old and trusted friend.[16] And aside from Jones' own connections, some of his followers possessed equally important political ties. While he undoubtedly appreciated Nelson Lay's hard work as the director of Operations Division, the vice chief was aware that this confirmed "Jones man" was the prime minister's nephew. Indicating that not all his "men" were regulars, Jones was also drawn to a well-connected reservist named Commander J.P. Connolly. Commander Connolly was unrelated to the minister's executive assistant, but Jones' friendship with that officer did help strengthen his own bond with Macdonald. After all, Commander Connolly and the minister had not only served together as lieutenants in the Canadian Expeditionary Force during the First World War, but also had been fellow law students at Dalhousie University and close friends in Halifax throughout the 1920s and '30s.[17] Recognizing good contacts when he saw them, the vice chief made the effort to befriend the other Connolly too. His efforts paid off, as the executive assistant later recorded that Jones was a "young, energetic type of man who will bring great credit to the service. I have been working with him ... and like him very much."[18]

The size of his network often made it difficult for Jones to conceal its activities, so there were officers at headquarters who realized that the vice chief was relying on his "political pull to reach the top."[19] With a front-row seat in Ottawa, the director of trade, Eric Brand, provided a better description of the drama that was unfolding before his eyes, going as far as defining the "skids under Nelles party" as "undoubtedly a movement against him [Nelles], an underground movement. Frankly I think Jones was very much in it. He was a great politician ... He never did anything without thinking how it was going to affect him and although I have no real evidence I'm pretty sure that he had quite a hand in that Nelles business. Quite a hand – just quiet remarks you know [to the minister]."[20] In time, word of these political machinations reached even the West Coast, where Rear Admiral Victor Brodeur called Jones' careerist tactics "gangsterism."[21]

Testimony from Lay makes it clear that Nelles first learned the vice chief had designs on his position as chief of the naval staff some time in March 1943. During that month, Lay went to see Nelles to find out why a much-desired appointment on the East Coast was being blocked.[22] When he did so, Nelles accused Lay of betraying his trust. A little confused by the accusation, Lay proclaimed his innocence, telling Nelles that he had reported his displeasure with the fleet's training only to the vice chief of the naval staff. Putting the pieces together, Lay came to his conclusion: "I imagine that Jones and Angus Macdonald had been discussing the matter and that this is the reason that Nelles felt that I had been telling Angus Macdonald all the shortcomings of the training establishment."[23] Although later admitting that the minister did in fact call on him "to discuss problems about the navy as a whole," Lay always maintained that he was uncomfortable with these conversations.[24] Perhaps that was true, but he had little difficulty passing criticisms on to his uncle, the prime minister. For example, King recorded in his diary, "Macdonald told him [Nelson Lay] that he had not been able to go into some of these matters and had to rely on the Chief of Naval Staff ... Nelson had been on the right track ... The whole Department has proceeded on the basis of expansion rather than adequate training."[25]

It is highly suggestive that a "Jones man" like Lay was stressing the exact same training issues to the prime minister that the vice chief of the naval staff was pushing on Macdonald. Put another way, while Jones was busy shaking the minister's confidence in the chief of the naval staff, Lay was sending King the same message, who observed in his diary that "I rather share his [Lay's] opinion of Nelles as not being any means a man large enough for the task in hand."[26]

The commanding officer of HMCS *Restigouche*, Commander H.N. Lay (far left) explains the workings of his ship's .50 calibre anti-aircraft guns to the naval minister while Nelles looks on. Lay, who happened to be the nephew of Prime Minister William Lyon Mackenzie King, was not only a confirmed "Jones man" but also during his tenure as the director of the Operations Division was accused of bringing sensitive matters to the minister's attention without Nelles' knowledge. LAC PA-104272

Jones was a shrewd administrator who knew how to work with politicians and felt comfortable in their world. Approaching the prime minister was simply too dangerous, and perhaps because of that, Lay was pressured to do so in his stead. That was wise. For King, there were two sides to Jones' enigmatic personality. When it came to dealing with politicians he was "a very pleasant fellow," but his attitude toward naval personnel was described as being "much more a disciplinarian than is really necessary ... I saw several evidences of his quick temper which discloses anything but a fine nature." From that the prime minister had drawn the significant conclusion that "Jones is a type which should be dismissed from the service."[27] Moreover, Nelles was now aware that Jones was undercutting him, leading to some unusual antics at Naval Service Headquarters. During a private conversation with another officer, for example, Nelles sneaked over to his adjoining door with the vice chief of the naval staff's office and abruptly opened it. Unable to hear Nelles' footsteps through the keyhole, the unsuspecting Jones fell into the room. Undoubtedly, Nelles' realization that the vice chief was going to the minister had changed their relationship, and there is evidence that Jones was cut out of the chief of the naval staff's inner circle.[28] But while Nelles was willing to tolerate some underhandedness in a career-driven service, attempts to contact the prime minister would probably have been too much even for Nelles.

For whatever reason, the chief of the naval staff did not see Jones as a significant threat during the spring of 1943. At first glance, that might seem odd, considering how MacLean's campaign had shaken the minister's confidence in his top advisor. With the exception of the refit crisis, things did not seem nearly so dark to Nelles. After all, Murray was in the process of establishing the country's first theatre command, the majority of the mid-ocean groups had stayed on the North Atlantic, and by most accounts the RCN's training problems were on the mend. And as far as Nelles was concerned, MacLean was licking his wounds in Toronto after being so soundly thrashed in the House of Commons. Nelles did not know – and Jones did – that Macdonald was vulnerable after MacLean's second critical article. It was an opportunity the vice chief of the naval staff simply could not pass up.

In defence of Jones going directly to the minister, it is important to note that the vice chief may have felt obligated to report problems that Nelles was apparently glossing over. In fact, Jones had once scolded an officer for refusing to bypass a superior, stating "it was his duty to represent this fact to a higher authority however distasteful this course might be."[29] Nevertheless, the timing of this meddling is difficult to overlook. Jones was feeding Macdonald information at a pivotal moment that seemed to have no other purpose than to pit the minister against Nelles. The vice chief of the naval staff would provide contradictory messages to both men, emphasizing training to Macdonald while telling Nelles that the refit situation was "probably the most serious problem with which we are faced at the moment."[30]

Jones' criticisms of MacLean are also suspect. Commander Connolly proved a valuable contact through which Jones could access various reserve networks. This reservist was much like MacLean, as he had, on numerous occasions, got himself into trouble for disobeying permanent force superiors. He, too, tried to gain more power for his own personal empire in the Special Services directorate, and he was censured for not seeking approval for many of his initiatives. It should not be surprising, therefore, that when MacLean had tried to get Macdonald to promote more RCNVR officers to flag rank, he placed Commander Connolly after himself at the top of the list. But this was no accident, as the two men were often in close contact and agreed on the need to reform the reserves.[31] Unlike MacLean, however, Commander Connolly had powerful patrons such as Jones and Macdonald to protect him, explaining why one former reserve officer argued, "a bigger wind bag and politician than Joe Connolly never existed."[32] Of course, that association does not necessary indicate that Commander Connolly was feeding Jones with intelligence on MacLean, but that relentless campaign was certainly taking its toll on Nelles' relationship with the minister. Ironically, MacLean's activities saved Nelles from Jones' meddling. Although Macdonald had considered replacing Nelles, the minister could not do so at the height of the battle over MacLean's allegations without the press and Parliament interpreting such a move as an admission that the renegade editor was right. The vice chief of the naval staff had to wait before he got another crack at Nelles over the modernization complaints.

The MacLean affair was delicate as well as embarrassing, and neither the executive assistant, Connolly, nor Macdonald cared to repeat the experience. Both men were thus extremely susceptible to any issues that threatened to become political. MacLean taught the minister a powerful lesson: ignoring criticisms from sources outside of Naval Service Headquarters was dangerous, and if Macdonald did so again it was at his own peril. The minister would not make the same mistake twice, and that mentality helped clear the path for Strange and the overseas officers. Avoiding MacLean's mistakes, they were both patient and willing to work behind the scenes to avoid embarrassing the minister, and their timing was impeccable. Macdonald had just survived the MacLean affair only to have Strange immediately lead him into an issue that threatened to become a new scandal.

With its warnings about possible mass insurrection among reserve officers, and implying that modernization was a political pitfall, Strange's nine-page report devastated Macdonald. It should not be surprising, therefore, that the minister reacted as he did. Just as with MacLean's attempt in 1942, Strange's graphic depiction was an attention-grabber that was designed to get the minister to institute immediate corrective action.[33] This certainly must have made the minister uncomfortable. Once again a former journalist was telling him that there was a problem within the navy, and perhaps because of that Macdonald reassured Strange that, no matter what might happen next, he would be protected from any retaliation from "the navy." But Strange was not afraid – after all, he had a career with the Canadian Broadcasting Corporation waiting for him if need be.[34]

MacLean's connections to the press had exacted a heavy personal toll on the minister, and whether intentionally or not Strange had made Macdonald extremely nervous by stating "that I was quite prepared to resign my commission should this become necessary or convenient from anybody's point of view; but that, in that event, I would continue to press for the necessary reform of our equipment situation 'from outside.'" All Macdonald needed to do was substitute the phrase "reserve discrimination" for "equipment," and the pronouncement was a carbon copy of what MacLean had said in the months before. This explains why the minister stressed to the naval information officer that resigning his commission "would be unnecessary"; this time Macdonald would act more decisively, and the modernization question would receive his undivided consideration.[35]

Although Strange had switched the focus from MacLean's discrimination complaints to the issue of modernization, both of these informants had indicated that something was wrong with the navy. Worse yet, John Connolly would later learn that Strange was not the first officer to report on the RCN's equipment gap. That there had been other critical memos warning Naval Service Headquarters about this deficiency was troubling, and it reinforced Strange's claim that Ottawa was generally apathetic toward the fleet's needs. Seeing no reason to disbelieve these reports, Connolly adopted this interpretation of the navy's top advisors. "One of the things that is wrong at N.S.H.Q.," he eventually told Macdonald, "is that the urgency for these needs for the boys who are on the ocean and exposed to the highly equipped submarines, are not as much in the minds of the great planners here, as they should be." Nor was that all. The critical memos had also shown that the Naval Staff had known about this problem for some time which, in the executive assistant's opinion, meant they had "not fought for the [equipment] requirements" because "the mid-ocean ships are not thought about as important enough."[36]

Connolly never found all the critical memos, but there is little doubt that the authors of the ones he did find would have been disappointed that he used them as evidence against Naval Service Headquarters. Unlike Strange or the Londonderry officers, these men had gone through the chain of command to report a condition they believed was affecting the fleet's efficiency. This was their duty. Whether intentional or not, some of these reports, along with Strange's account, created a perception that Naval Service Headquarters was filled with uncaring senior staff officers who had all but ignored pleas from the fleet. As with MacLean's allegations, the perception arose among officers who may have known their particular corner of the war well but lacked an understanding of the larger issues impinging on the RCN's ability to modernize. The executive assistant's inability to comprehend that element of sharp-end grousing – which it should be remembered is a term used by those doing the fighting to describe any complaint against the top brass – would play a pivotal role in Nelles' fate. Perceptions that Naval Service Headquarters ignored warnings from the fleet simply did not reflect the reality.

Once Connolly presented the critical memos to Macdonald some months later, the minister would charge Nelles with incompetence because these important documents "went the rounds at NSHQ" but were never passed on to him.[37] By making this argument, the minister showed how sharp-end opinions could lead to misunderstandings and eventual disaster when in the wrong hands and used for political purposes. Macdonald's argument was weak. Only one month before the critical memos began to arrive at Naval Service Headquarters, the minister had told Nelles not to burden him with the "finer details" of the navy's affairs because he was too busy. That led to a Naval Board discussion where Pennington, having cited how the chief of naval equipment and supply had an incredible 1,682 files cross his desk during a one-month period, observed that "the Minister and Members are dealing with far too much detail." In order to avoid clouding the "big picture," Pennington then suggested that Macdonald should only be consulted once a policy had been clarified and was ready for discussion. Macdonald agreed, and by doing so had sent a clear message: flooding him with extraneous correspondence was strictly discouraged.[38] The minister's own instructions ensured that the critical memos would never have reached his office.

The task of filtering complaints from the fleet began at a much lower level in the Naval Service Headquarters hierarchy, and there was good reason why this was necessary. Whether it was modernization, training, reserve discrimination, or some other issue, the authors of the complaints usually regarded their particular gripe as the most serious problem facing the RCN. Naturally, there was nothing wrong with that, providing they filed their criticism through the chain of command. A key element to maintaining naval discipline, that chain was an essential part of the process, as it allowed Naval Service Headquarters to separate the truly important gripes from those that were less so. In fact, without the authority to control the flow of information to the minister, the Naval Board not only lost credibility but also its very source of power and legitimacy.

Strange's actions were dangerous for that reason. His information had come from officers in St. John's and Londonderry who had little understanding of what Naval Service Headquarters was up against with the refit situation, and the minister was therefore treated to a somewhat jaded interpretation of the modernization issue. That this was done behind his back denied Nelles the opportunity to explain how the issue was linked to the refit deficiencies currently being discussed with the minister. Lacking that important connection, Macdonald erroneously saw the fleet's modernization as an altogether separate deficiency. Worse, he believed the Naval Board had never raised the issue with him. While Strange's bypassing the top brass represented the greatest threat to Naval Service Headquarters' "citadel of authority," putting responsibility for this situation squarely on the naval information officer's shoulders would be unfair. After all, a small number of permanent force officers had advance knowledge that Strange planned to go directly to the minister. Their decision not to intercede indicates that there were others among the regulars besides Jones and his officers whose loyalty to Nelles was questionable.

It is uncertain whether Frank Houghton had any prior knowledge of what was going to happen in Londonderry when he originally asked Strange to look into the "welfare question." There is little doubt, however, about what the Newfoundland chief of staff knew when Strange returned to St. John's five weeks later. At a meeting in Houghton's office on 9 August, Strange gave a complete briefing on everything the Londonderry officers had said and done during his impromptu investigation. None of it came as a surprise to Houghton, and instead of defending Naval Service Headquarters, he chose to stoke the fire. Fully aware that the minister's office was the naval information officer's next stop, Houghton told Strange about the tremendous difficulties the St. John's command had experienced in getting word through to Naval Service Headquarters about the equipment situation. This "completely unofficial conversation" would have significant ramifications for Nelles, as it convinced Strange "that everything possible had been done through the proper channels ... nothing was happening." And with a nod of approval, Houghton had bestowed his blessing on Strange's plan to contact the minister.[39]

Houghton's failure to warn Nelles about these events was disloyal, but unlike Jones it does not appear that he was motivated by a desire to see the naval chief ousted. Instead, Houghton belonged to the category of senior shore officers in both St. John's and Londonderry who, having heard the incessant complaints from the small but vocal element within the reserves, were frustrated by the perception that Naval Service Headquarters was not listening to their pleas for more modern equipment. As with these other sharp-end grousers, Houghton lacked a complete understanding of the larger issues that affected the RCN's ability to modernize. Private letters between Houghton and Murray's chief of staff in Halifax, Captain R.E.S. Bidwell, not only bear this out but stand as yet another powerful illustration of how staff officers in the larger Atlantic Command grasped what their counterparts in St. John's did not. The refit situation was at the centre of the RCN's problems, and Naval Service Headquarters was doing something about it. The importance of this point cannot be overstated. By focusing on individual pieces of equipment, the critical memos from St. John's and Londonderry missed the big picture and were, in actuality, fixating on the effect rather than the cause of the navy's technical backwardness. This is not surprising, because neither Londonderry nor St. John's were part of the Canadian refit structure. Accordingly, the officers at these operational bases were in the best position to see the equipment deficiencies first-hand, but had little knowledge that the refit crisis was at the root of the RCN's troubles. Without that understanding, the officers in St. John's never made the link between Naval Service Headquarters' aggressive policies over the refit situation and modernization. Certainly, Bidwell had tried to explain these larger implications to Houghton in late spring 1943. "Our arrangements and dispositions are being completely wrecked by the refitting situation," he told his friend, and while "everything possible is being done" to correct it, the effect was still much the same. Bidwell continued, "We [in Halifax] are down to our shoe-string ourselves, thanks to this blasted refitting difficulty." That meant little to Houghton, explaining why he found the whole refit situation far too complicated.[40]

Houghton was not the only regular who knew what Strange was about to do. After boarding the *Assiniboine* for his return trip to Canada, the naval information officer had asked Commander Ken Adams to read the memorandum he had prepared for the minister. Adams did so, and having been "stirred" by its contents, he agreed to let Strange help him write a second report that would be filed through normal channels.[41] It is obvious that Adams, like Houghton, was actively assisting Strange. Less certain is whether these two regular force officers were aware of the naval information officer's ties to the executive assistant.

Despite their friendship, no evidence has yet surfaced that Strange ever told Houghton he was serving as one of Connolly's informants. Adams' name, on the other hand, figured prominently in letters between the naval information officer and the executive assistant well before equipment became an issue with Macdonald.[42] It is difficult to prove with any degree of certainty that Adams had spied for Connolly's network in the past. That being said, it is equally clear that Adams (who himself had been a reservist at one time in the interwar period) was prone to such behaviour, as even Jones found him "difficult to assess as he always achieves results by methods that are slightly unorthodox."[43] Strange knew that as permanent force officers both Houghton and Adams were risking their careers by helping, and perhaps because of that he tried to mitigate their involvement. "After thinking over all the circumstances, I have come to the conclusion that it would be wise not to write to Captain Houghton," Strange advised Connolly. "I am telephoning my reasons for this, and I think you will agree that they are good." Likewise, Strange downplayed Adams' usefulness by warning the executive assistant that this officer's experience on the North Atlantic was "limited to five or six trips across." In reality, he wanted these regulars to decide their own level of involvement, telling Adams,

> I know that it is asking a lot to suggest that you be as frank with him as you were with me ... [but Connolly] is fully in my confidence over the battle that I am trying to wage for the man at sea, and is not only entirely sympathetic with the cause but is capable of furthering it considerably. I do hope you will therefore overcome your natural service reserve with him ... and I feel that here is a golden opportunity for you to rub the Ministerial nose (even through proxy) in those things that need putting right. I am hoping most sincerely that you will let him have the information that is required to get action. At any rate this letter is evidence that I kept my promise to you, that I am doing my level best to get the proper action, and have made some real progress in that direction. So far, very much to my surprise, I have not been shot.[44]

Strange may have felt under the gun but he was also aware that his status as an RCNVR gave him liberties that the regulars did not share; and nowhere was that more evident than in a comparison between his memorandum and Adams' report.

While Strange's account was a scathing indictment, Adams' report was typical of any officer criticizing the actions of a superior, as he dutifully observed that his submission was "intended to draw attention to the matter of equipment."[45] Strange, without the need to include the formalities of addressing superiors, was able to produce a much more blunt and outspoken document. The difference between these two reports helps explain why Strange was more successful than his RCN counterparts in venting the navy's deficiencies. Although his was tame in comparison to Strange's submission, Adams was still convinced that his criticisms to Naval Service Headquarters had put his "fat in the fire." This belief fuelled his suspicion that an unwanted posting to Ottawa had come about because Nelles had decided that "if you're going to complain, you'll be put in charge of fixing it." Unlike the reservists, who had civilian jobs to return to once the war ended, the navy was the RCN officer's livelihood, and mistakes could irreparably damage, or even end, careers. According to the reserve networks, this careerist mentality created a perception of the regulars as men who – fearing that it might cost them their jobs – preferred to duck for cover rather than tell the minister about problems in the navy; according to Strange "the whole atmosphere stifled initiative."[46]

Their willingness to rock the proverbial boat was not the only reason these reservists were able to capture the minister's attention. Unlike the Naval Board, which always discussed serious topics with the minister in a professional manner, reserve officers such as MacLean and Strange were prone to use flamboyant and exaggerated prose to get their point across. Macdonald was particularly susceptible to this tactic. A few years in the trenches with the army during the First World War were hardly the type of experience that could help with his responsibilities as the civilian head of the navy. Unfamiliar with naval terminology, his understanding of both the service as well as the finer points of antisubmarine warfare was extremely weak.[47] Macdonald's simplistic description of asdic as "a type of radio you get echo from hull of submarine" and Nelles' frequently simplified definitions for his political master clearly indicate that the minister had difficulty following the navy's lexicon.[48] And that sheds light on how Macdonald could sit at Naval Board meetings where the refit and modernization issues were discussed without realizing their true significance.

This important point requires some elaboration. What the minister (and even some modern naval historians) did not realize was that the officers on the Naval Board considered the installation of equipment as a function of the repair infrastructure. When they discussed improving the RCN's repair facilities, they were, in fact, addressing aspects of the navy's modernization. That was not made clear to the minister until November 1943, at which time Nelles explained that "the fitting of equipment which is required to keep our ships to the highest possible fighting efficiency ... divides into production and supply; distribution and finally installation, which is a repair problem."[49] Without understanding the navy's vocabulary, therefore, it was difficult for the minister to make the link between the "repair problem" and modernization. Perhaps Nelles gave Macdonald too much credit and should have taken better care to define the naval jargon used in the memos and discussions on the refit situation. Ultimately, it was up to Macdonald to ask for clarification. Instead of doing so, it appears that he tried to hide his ignorance at Naval Board meetings by pretending to appreciate what was being said.

Of course, the Naval Board did emphasize the importance of the refit situation to Macdonald in layman's terms at times. Certainly, when given a copy of Johnstone's report in late July, the minister should have had little difficulty digesting statements such as "the problem which has to be dealt with is vital, immediate, and of the greatest urgency," or "failure to grapple with it at once is inexcusable."[50] The real problem was that Macdonald never bothered to read Johnstone's report and thus had little idea that the Naval Board was asking him to approve their plans to combat the refit situation.[51] Moreover, this report would have provided some much-needed balance to Strange's ostentatious memo, which not only presented evidence with reckless abandon but also failed to place the problems in a larger operational context.

As with MacLean, Strange's colourful use of adjectives and metaphors was the source of his power. As in his past experience as a writer for the Canadian Broadcasting Corporation, the key to Strange's success rested in the ability to frame complaints in terms of the political damage they could potentially cause Macdonald. Possessing an excellent understanding of Canadian politics, men like Strange and MacLean knew how to work the bureaucracy and influence politicians. They played on the minister's fears, and it was this insecurity that ultimately led to changes in policy. Moreover, they appreciated the role that Connolly played as the minister's executive assistant, which was why Strange included some of the extravagant statements made by the officers in Londonderry. Aware that there were a great number of issues that embroiled the minister's attention on a day-to-day basis, Strange "politicized" the equipment issue with the hope that Connolly would put it on the top of Macdonald's list of priorities. This was the minister's Achilles heel and Strange knew it. He later justified his tactics: "There is a certain invulnerability about the 'high brass' in any Service. Ministers, however, are not invulnerable. They cannot ignore serious political considerations. The threat of serious trouble in the fleet, which I had heard voiced, and which commonsense would show must obviously exist in the circumstances I described, was not one which any politician could ignore. Apart from this, Mr. Macdonald would immediately appreciate the broader implications of the whole matter."[52]

Although he had successfully captured Macdonald's attention, Strange's methodology also cast further suspicion on the top brass and turned an operational deficiency into an artificial political crisis. Unlike MacLean, Strange's timing was perfect because he happened to strike at a moment when the Canadian political climate made the minister feel particularly vulnerable.

On 4 August the ranks of the Ontario Liberals were decimated by a provincial election, and that left some of their federal counterparts panic-stricken. Worse yet, in the federal by-elections held five days later, all four Liberal incumbents were defeated. The results of these elections caused much concern among many members of the government.[53] Believing that he was sitting on a possible scandal that could potentially bring the whole Liberal house down, the minister wanted to get to the bottom of the discontent in the navy.[54] On 21 August he ordered Nelles to furnish him with a report as soon as one "can be made available" regarding the "completeness of our Anti-submarine equipment as compared to similar equipment to UK vessels on the North Atlantic." Macdonald's order was delivered two days after he had received Strange's memo, but he gave no indication that his request was the product of outside influences. And so Nelles let the staff handle the details. Packaging their memos together on 1 September, Nelles sent them to the minister with the comment, "I think this covers the situation."[55]

The memos in the report did just that, and it is uncertain why Macdonald believed the Naval Staff would keep statistical equipment data on each warship for a foreign navy like those in the Royal Navy. In fact, Macdonald was lucky to get information on his own service. Despite constant prompting, it had taken both East Coast commands almost a year to respond to Ottawa's August 1942 request for detailed information on the equipment types on all Canadian escorts. Nevertheless, Macdonald was provided with the latest statistics, and they should have spoken for themselves: out of seventy-four corvettes, no more than twelve had extended fo'c'sles and improved bridges; just one was fitted with 145X asdic, five had gyroscopic compasses, and sixty-eight were without hedgehog. Only for 271 radar was the situation somewhat satisfactory, as fifty-four corvettes had been fitted with that particular gear.[56]

Although he did not say so for another ten weeks, Macdonald was unhappy with what he considered a quick, almost perfunctory, response that "does not attempt to allocate responsibility for the condition and it does not recommend any definite proposal to rectify a situation which is most alarming."[57] Had the minister expressed his displeasure in August, it would have given the chief of the naval staff a chance to remind him about the Naval Board meeting a few weeks earlier where Macdonald was given a comprehensive brief on their plans to tackle the refit crisis. Without that knowledge, Nelles assumed that Macdonald understood the larger implications of the RCN's modernization problem, which explains why he included a copy of Naval Service Headquarters' latest refit schedule in his response.[58] Nor was Macdonald interested in the staff memos, which, in his view, indicated that "there is fault somewhere in our organization because these matters should

The depth charge, one of the corvette's primary weapons. The towering geyser and dark silt are clear indications that this attack occurred in shallow water. Unlike the contacted-fused hedgehog, the depth charge had settings that determined when it would explode.
DHH 81/520/1000, BOX 141, FILE 23

have engaged my attention before it was necessary for me to call for a report on the basis of information secured from unofficial sources [Strange's Report]."[59] With the exception of the extreme hyperbole contained in that outside source, Macdonald's advisors had once again provided him with everything he needed to know. Moreover, as with the 27 July Naval Board meeting, Nelles would in the not

A gun crew operating a 4-inch gun, the corvette's primary weapon against surfaced submarines. Shortages of these guns reportedly forced some early RCN corvettes to sail with wooden poles that mimicked the barrel of the real thing. DHH 81/520/1000, BOX 141, FILE 16

so distant future turn to Macdonald for assistance after the Naval Staff's plans to combat the refit crisis suffered consecutive setbacks.

The establishment of the Carswell and Rannie surveys into the manpower situation and expansion plans for HMC Dockyard offered a ray of hope to the officers on the Naval Board and Naval Staff. All along they had tried to convince Macdonald

An early difference between British and Canadian corvettes was that the former had the more powerful 2-pound pom-pom gun in the aft gun position, while the latter settled for .50-calibre guns like the one pictured here. DHH 81/520/1000, BOX 141, FILE 16

that there was only so much the navy could do to improve the refit situation without assistance from Munitions and Supply. Indicating that not all his allegations were unfounded, MacLean had even picked up on communication problems between the two departments, rhetorically asking his readers, "won't someone introduce the Department of Munitions and Supply to the Department of Naval Services? They should be interested in what each other is doing."[60] Now, however, while many of those issues remained, the fact that two key officials from Munitions and Supply were going to see the conditions at HMC Dockyard for themselves led to expectations at Naval Service Headquarters that Munitions and Supply would co-operate with their attempts to rectify the refit situation. At the very least, the navy's senior staff hoped that these independent surveys would "shock" the naval minister out of his complacency. Neither happened, as Carswell's and Rannie's findings effectively undercut the navy's position.[61]

The hedgehog projectile was perhaps the most desirable antisubmarine weapon as, unlike the depth charge, its ahead-firing projectiles were contact explosives: they detonated only by hitting a solid object. Another strength over the depth charge was the ship's ability to maintain asdic contact with the target during a hedgehog attack. LAC PA-112918

Much to the Naval Staff's chagrin, both of these men torpedoed the argument that the government needed to expand the facilities at HMC Dockyard as a means to help alleviate the refit situation. In fact, Carswell even went as far as to suggest that the current expansion of HMC Dockyard be stopped, while Rannie argued for a drastic reduction because the navy was not properly utilizing its existing facilities. Both of their final conclusions indicated that, with some minor tinkering, HMC Dockyard could cope with the navy's demands single-handedly. Regarding the manpower situation, Carswell was equally unforgiving, as he accused the navy of exaggeration: "there was no evidence of manpower shortage ... Few major repairs were in process, and the work in hand did not appear [to be] taxing either the workmen or the capacity of the tools already in operation."[62] For a Naval Board that was already experiencing difficulty in getting the minister to understand the importance of the refit situation, these types of observations only made matters worse, all the more so because Carswell's and Rannie's surveys effectively vindicated Macdonald's indifference toward the Naval Board's solutions. Moreover, while it was not their intent to do so, Carswell and Rannie added fuel to Strange's fire, since their surveys arrived on Macdonald's desk only days after he had read the naval information officer's report.[63] Macdonald may never have understood the refit situation, but the suggestion that the Naval Board's interpretation was wrong made it seem more likely that Strange's observations were right.

Naturally, the navy greeted Carswell's and Rannie's surveys with much suspicion. Few doubted both reports contained genuine criticisms, but it was difficult to escape the conclusion drawn by the engineer superintendent, Lieutenant J.G. Knowlton, RCN, who observed that "men engaged in Merchant ship repair and construction have a tendency to be slightly prejudiced against a purely Governmental Yard engaged in Warship repairs." The navy had miscalculated, and Knowlton knew it. In his view, the attempt to involve the Department of Munitions and Supply through the Carswell and Rannie surveys was fundamentally flawed because they, too, were "trying desperately to get men" for the shipyards that were keeping the merchant marine at sea.[64] Knowlton's immediate supervisor, Commodore C.R.H. Taylor, RCN, agreed. Without conclusive proof, Taylor was unwilling to accuse Munitions and Supply of treachery, yet he did find it difficult to overlook the possibility that "Mr. Carswell's report on Naval and civil labour might be influenced by his desire to employ these civil labourers elsewhere."[65] On that score there were grounds for criticism. The navy was asking National Selective Service for 2,445 additional workers for HMC Dockyard, and that put them in direct competition with Carswell's ship repair organization, which needed 5,000 more labourers.[66] In hindsight, Taylor's original recommendation that only top British shipyard officials were capable of conducting a truly unbiased and independent survey of the Dockyard was most likely true.

A letter from Carswell to C.D. Howe in the weeks before the survey suggests that Knowlton's and Taylor's suspicions were well founded. At that time Carswell held an altogether different interpretation, telling Howe that "the refitting of escort vessels for convoy duty has become a serious problem in the Maritimes."[67] Given that he was voicing such views, it is easy to see why the navy had originally asked Munitions and Supply to make Carswell one of the investigators, and why some naval officers thought he had reneged on a pledge to help the RCN with its refit predicament. Perhaps Carswell had simply changed his mind but it seems far more likely that the navy's long-term plan for the refit situation had become a victim of interdepartmental politics and circumstance.

Instead of bridging the gap between the navy and Munitions and Supply, Carswell's report drove the two departments further apart as the Naval Staff realized that other government departments were unlikely to come to the RCN's rescue. This was something Macdonald should have been able to tell his advisors well before it was accentuated by Carswell's survey. The manpower shortage affecting all the essential industries was a serious issue at the highest political level, and it was one in which key ministers were trying to mitigate their responsibility. Certainly, Minister of Labour Humphrey Mitchell had placed Howe firmly in his sights when charging that the ship repair industry would not get its requirement of skilled workers "unless the Department of Munitions and Supply allows us to recruit the required men from other essential industries." Every bit the political marksman, Howe returned fire at Mitchell by observing that the Department of Labour had "performed badly."[68] In private, Macdonald took a shotgun approach, spraying a number of targets in one single blast: "The government ... has suffered chiefly by the stupid way in which Munitions and Supply and Finance have done many things ... and by the administrative incompetence of the Labour Department." The naval minister even went as far as to claim that there should be a "major overhaul of these departments, and the labour angle should be handled much more firmly." Not surprisingly, when King offered him the Labour portfolio on 15 September, Macdonald turned it down.[69]

The navy was not interested in assigning blame when it came to the Canadian ship repair industry. That industry was also in the throes of an unparalleled expansion, which, like the navy, was bound to lead to growing pains and confusion. They nonetheless resented the inference that the RCN's refit problems could be solved without the assistance of Munitions and Supply and the Department of Labour.[70] Macdonald grasped the larger political ramifications of the manpower shortage; nevertheless, his naval advisors began to marshal evidence intended to show the minister not only how the Carswell and Rannie surveys were flawed but also that the labour shortages were indeed linked to the refit situation. Before that task was complete, another pillar of Naval Service Headquarters' plan to combat the refit situation was dealt a crushing blow.

By late June, the Atlantic Command provided Ottawa with a list of forty-one corvettes that still required modernizing. As it did not appear that Canadian refit facilities were going to offer much relief in the near future, Murray was then instructed to make an appeal to the Admiralty to take all these vessels in hand. It was a substantial request, possibly designed to test whether anything had changed since Naval Service Headquarters originally asked for British help in February.[71] On 24 August, the Admiralty finally provided a definitive answer and the news was not good: "Heavy pressure of refitting and other ship work in hand and in prospect in this country, renders remote any likelihood of undertaking even a substantial part of work on remaining [Canadian] ships in question."[72] For some at headquarters, this represented the ultimate betrayal.

Only twelve days earlier, the RCN's representatives at the Canada-UK-US Combined Committee on Ship Repair Problems on the East Coast of Canada and Newfoundland had told their Admiralty counterparts that the situation regarding repair, maintenance, and construction of ships, for both the Naval and Merchant Services was one of the biggest problems of the day, and one of the most important to the war effort ... with regard to merchant ships the present situation was very satisfactory, but with respect to naval ships this was not so, as, due to the shortage of escort vessels in the past, it was not always possible to take ships off escort duty for refits; also, that large alterations and additions to the older corvettes is placing a heavy load on Canadian ports ... The Admiralty have been asked to assist refitting certain of these ... older corvettes. With this assistance, and the completion of present naval repair facilities, and if the manpower situation is overcome, the refitting of Canadian naval vessels will catch up.[73]

Better yet, the foreign members of this board vindicated the Canadian Naval Staff's efforts with the observation that Naval Service Headquarters had taken every reasonable measure to confront the refit crisis. Since the Admiralty representatives seemed to appreciate that the RCN needed assistance, the Naval Staff was surprised to learn the British could not help. That the Admiralty had said so less than a week after Macdonald read Carswell's and Rannie's recommendations to stop or curtail the expansion of the navy's repair facilities (as well as their conclusions that the RCN had exaggerated the manpower shortage) only made matters worse. Naval Service Headquarters' solutions to the refit crisis were evaporating before their eyes.

While just as bothersome, Munitions and Supply's so-called duplicity could be chalked up to interdepartmental politics. The Admiralty's signal, on the other hand, hit particularly hard and smacked of an ungrateful ally who had modernized at the RCN's expense. Perhaps the Admiralty's position, understandable in its own right, would have been easier to take had British authorities not been so easy with their criticism of RCN equipment. Certainly, that was the chief of naval engineering and construction's interpretation, arguing as he did that "it is obvious that, while we have been straining every nerve to keep our ships running and provide escorts, Admiralty have kept their ships at home and modernized them." Likewise, the British-born Johnstone was equally critical of his former countrymen, telling the chief of the naval staff that "unfortunately, the Admiralty do not always live up to their bargains."[74] A product of the RCN's extreme frustration, such views of the Admiralty were not entirely fair. With larger global commitments, they, too, were under considerable strain to keep warships at sea. Moreover, while the Royal Navy had a more established infrastructure to fall back upon, British repair and refit facilities were also finding it difficult to keep up with the demand.

Nor were the Canadians the only Commonwealth navy to ask the Admiralty for assistance. For example, using vocabulary that bore an eerie similarity to that in reports filed in Canada, a senior officer from the Royal Australian Navy wrote on 30 July 1943, "officers and men of HMA [His Majesty's Australian] Ships meet their US equivalents who have just engaged in successful actions against the enemy and they hear how these actions have been fought and won. They see that inferior and older US ships are being kept abreast [of] the times by the fitting of modern radar, 40mm guns, etc. and they know that for lack of similar up to date equipment, they may be denied the chance of meeting the enemy on the same effective terms. This is bad for morale."[75] Another officer sent a similar message when he compared the equipment disparity between Australian and American ships and concluded that it "is too obvious to require further reiteration but its effect on morale cannot be too strongly emphasized."[76]

These reports and others like them indicate that the equipment and refit experience was not nearly as sinister or as confined to the Canadian navy as Strange had implied to the minister. Instead, the situation in Australia suggests that smaller naval powers as a whole had difficulty keeping up with the technological superiority of the United States and Britain. Unlike the Canadians, the Australians did not have a group of influential reservists to turn their equipment woes into a politically charged crusade against their regular force leaders. Overwhelmed by its own requirements, the Admiralty gave the Canadians the same advice it passed on to the Australians – to appeal to the Americans. The Canadian Naval Board was planning to do just that but before getting Macdonald's permission to approach the Americans, the navy first needed a new refit schedule.

The Naval Board went to great lengths to explain the situation to Macdonald at the 16 September meeting. The details provided were impressive. Not only was Macdonald told that forty-one corvettes still required updating but also that the RCN was in a bind because the Admiralty was unable to help. He was further instructed that the "Naval Staff considered it essential that these ships be modernized and, observing that Canadian facilities are overburdened, [it is] recommended ... BAD [British Admiralty Delegation] be approached to ascertain if refits and modernization can be undertaken in the USA." Nor was that all; the minister was provided with an updated financial assessment that indicated it was going to cost an extra $50,000 per corvette to lengthen the fo'c'sles in US ports. In the end, the minister agreed with the argument "that every endeavour should be made to complete modernization of single screw corvettes." As far as the Naval Board was concerned, Macdonald was also willing to wait for the Americans to respond, at which time "the whole question of repair policy will be decided."[77]

The officers on the Naval Board and the minister were on two entirely separate wavelengths. From the navy's perspective, this meeting was like many of the other briefings at which the modernization and refit situations had been discussed with the minister. One solution had suffered a serious setback, and the Board had not only said as much but also offered the minister the alternative of approaching the Americans. In Macdonald's world, the whole issue was something new. Representing ground zero, Strange's report had exploded the modernization question into view. As far as the minister was concerned, the Naval Board's willingness to discuss this issue at the 16 September meeting was the product of his inquiries to Nelles in mid-August, and for Macdonald the sudden interest in modernization was a question of too little, too late. After all, based almost entirely on Strange's report, Macdonald had already agreed to let Connolly travel to St. John's and the United Kingdom to investigate. But that report did more than just affect the minister's mindset, as Strange was also mobilizing the network of informants in Londonderry to pass on interpretations of the RCN's modernization dilemma to the executive assistant. Strange had thus effectively set an unstoppable chain of events in motion that ultimately led to an administrative meltdown at Naval Service Headquarters as well as to Nelles' dismissal.

The more successful informers, like Strange, had many sources of power that were key to their success, such as framing issues in terms the minister could easily understand, important political connections and social influence, and an ability to work outside the navy's chain of command. Another, perhaps more crucial, skill was their ability to network. Capturing the minister's attention was one thing but keeping him interested was another and required a concerted effort from all those involved. For his part, therefore, Strange prepared the ground for Connolly's investigation by acting as the initial contact between the Londonderry officers and the executive assistant.

On the morning of 21 September, Strange met Connolly in order to provide a first-hand account of the events that had led to his report. That allowed Strange to introduce the Londonderry network, which he did by giving the executive assistant "a steer or two about my impressions of these men."[78] Strange then turned to the other side of the Atlantic, dispatching letters to various officers, in order

> to introduce Mr. JJ Connolly. John, besides being a personal friend of mine, is Executive Assistant to the Naval Minister. On my say-so, he has already got a good deal of action underway. Given the information, he can do a lot more: *and I am sure he will.* It is thus up to you sea-going guys to see that he has the dope. Repeat the harangue you delivered to me, and add a bit if you like (making sure of your facts) and you will certainly be helping get results. The point that I want to stress is this. The great difficulty that you fellows have with NSHQ is the remoteness of the men who influence decisions which mean so much to you. In this case, I have overcome that remoteness. Here is your golden opportunity to say what you think, without the slightest fear of consequences, to a man who can quickly get it to the place from which action will certainly come.[79]

Strange's comments cut to the heart of the issue. Perhaps Naval Service Headquarters could have avoided the formation of this particular network had they made an effort to overcome the so-called "remoteness" between themselves and

Vice Admiral Percy W. Nelles, RCN (far left), stands back and watches manoeuvres from the bridge of the fairmile Q 069. Some within the RCN were highly critical of Nelles and other senior officers from Naval Service Headquarters in Ottawa for their "remoteness" from those serving at sea. DHH 2001/11, FILE 1

those at the sharp end of the fighting. This was easier said than done. The Londonderry officers believed that Naval Service Headquarters was not doing anything about their modernization problem, but naval officers in Ottawa had no official link or special authority over this British base – despite the large number of RCN ships there – since it fell within the Royal Navy's jurisdiction. Simpson's decision to deny the Canadians a captain (D) in Londonderry meant that Naval Service Headquarters did not have a formal link to that command. Instead, the Canadian headquarters communicated its concerns with the RCN's equipment situation to its counterparts in the Admiralty. Once in the British chain of command, it was up to the officers in the Admiralty whether they would pass this type of information on to Western Approaches and, ultimately, Londonderry. Those channels no longer mattered, as linking Connolly to the Londonderry officers meant that the Canadian Naval Board had been successfully circumvented. Operating above the chain of command, the Londonderry network was now complete, and as far as the issue of modernization was concerned, these officers would soon become Macdonald's primary source of information.

Partially responsible for further shaking the minister's confidence in his naval advisors, the Londonderry officers were about to reap the benefits of a situation that they themselves had helped sow. The Naval Board had had enough problems trying to keep the minister interested in issues that mattered most to the navy's well-being, and this type of outside interference only made that task more difficult. In addition, however, much of their authority over the equipment and refit situations was effectively being usurped by the commodore (D) Londonderry who, in his future capacity as Connolly's guide during the overseas investigation, temporarily became Macdonald's chief advisor on these issues. Certainly, this was how Strange interpreted Simpson's role for the upcoming inquiry, instructing the commodore (D) that

> the matter was taken up in the manner I indicated, and very definite action is under way ... look out for a Mr. John J Connolly, who is coming over to Derry via service passage. He is wide-awake, intelligent and fearless. He has no axe to grind except the successful prosecution of the war. I think it would be most helpful to the main matter if you spoke as plainly to him as you did to me ... and (to use an Americanism) "give him the works." ... I hope and believe, that the confidence which you gave me will turn out to have started a useful chain of events.[80]

Strange understood that Macdonald was at a crossroads and would want "tangible evidence" before challenging the Naval Board. He was effectively telling Simpson and the Londonderry officers that it was up to them to provide Connolly with that evidence. Meeting with the executive assistant was as close as they could ever get to the minister, and after months of complaining it was an opportunity that the Londonderry officers were not going to waste. And with that, the Londonderry officers began to organize so that they would be able to give Connolly a handguided tour of the RCN's technical backwardness as they had done with Strange some weeks before.

While that marked the end of Strange's involvement, other members of Connolly's personal network of informants continued to play an active role in the planning stages of this investigation. Uncertain of whom he could trust at Naval Service Headquarters, Connolly instead turned to his friends in the RCNVR for help.[81] Although the executive assistant had communicated with old chums like Louis Audette and Barry O'Brien (among others) well before Strange's interference, their letters became more critical during the second half of 1943. These highly educated individuals were creative, and rather than writing in plain language they chose to use poetry or coded messages when discussing problems within the fleet. It was a good idea, particularly since their subject matter was often highly sensitive material that would be governed by the Defence of Canada Regulations. Like the Londonderry officers, they bypassed the chain of command and ran the risk of being charged with insubordination if their activities were ever uncovered. This threat was so real that the executive assistant even went as far as to warn one of his informers that their letters "should be composed with circumspection."[82]

Though much of this poetry is difficult to decipher, it obviously was used as a means of communication. For example, after describing leadership problems at Naval Service Headquarters, Strange wrote the following to Connolly:

> I have written this
> For the few people whom I know
> Who will understand what I am getting at.
> One used to believe in Christmas and the Navy.
> Who knows now in what he believes.[83]

In other cases these poems would criticize the highest-ranking officers within the RCN, providing yet another reason why some were submitted to Connolly anonymously. Reminiscent of MacLean's bitter letters, these submissions indicated that the same type of resentment toward the top brass occasionally prevailed within Connolly's personal network of informants. When compared to MacLean's campaign, such occurrences were the exception rather than the rule.

Complaints on naval leadership were not the only intriguing theme within Connolly's poetry file; equipment was also discussed. In these instances, medical conditions were often used as substitutes for naval terms and secret equipment. A letter from the commanding officer of HMCS *Orillia*, Lieutenant Commander Jim Mitchell, RCNVR, to Connolly, observes, for example, "I saw Louis Audette the other day for a moment only. He is now with us again after a long absence and shall see more of him at our next port of call. It appears that we are now all set for our face lifting so I am looking forward to a spot of leave, when I shall visit all the old haunts." That Mitchell had used this system to tell Connolly his ship was getting its long-awaited refit – the term "face lifting" was one of the network's code words for refit – makes clear that he was one of Connolly's informants. His reference to a key member of that network, Louis Audette, provides further evidence this was a close-knit group, particularly since Mitchell was a fellow lawyer who had worked with the executive assistant at the law firm of Audette and O'Brien Solicitors and Barristers.[84]

A better illustration of how Connolly used this system of communication is revealed in a letter he wrote to lifelong bachelor Audette:

> I am very much concerned about your wife's condition [HMCS *Amherst*]. I would be particularly interested to know the result of her operation [refit]. I should love to be available for the conference of surgeons under Simpson, when you get to that point ... I wish you would let me know what the surgeons [refit facilities] did during the

summer and if you feel she is in as fit condition as the other ladies [corvettes] particularly the English ladies ... I am personally dissatisfied about the treatment which people like yourself have been given for your wives' condition. I need not tell you that Angus [Macdonald] is too.[85]

Clearly, Connolly was asking about *Amherst*'s refit, and replying to this letter, Audette reported that his "wife" (ship) was in a much better state but that the Canadian "doctors" (shipyards) took too long "as they are doing in all similar cases." Appreciative of his friend's interest, Audette then felt compelled to tell Connolly that, "anything you can do for girls [corvettes] in her position will be more than an ordinary good turn. I shall not fail to pass onto other husbands [corvette captains] in my fix that you are helping. It will buck them up no end when they so often feel let down."[86]

While their method of communication may have been creative, these RCNVR officers were obviously passing information directly to Connolly, who, in turn, would then show some of these submissions to Macdonald. Indeed, after reading one of Barry O'Brien's poems the minister scribbled a note to Connolly that "this officer has a gift for writing which he should continue to develop."[87] As indicated by Audette, they were spreading word to other RCNVR officers – most likely the same group of reserve commanding officers that had gained access to Macdonald earlier in the year – that Connolly was sympathetic to their modernization cause. It was exactly what the executive assistant wanted, as from his point of view these old and trusted friends were an invaluable source of information because they were serving where the problems within the navy were most apparent.

Although Connolly had used his informants throughout the year, he did not always listen to their ideas. After receiving Strange's report, Connolly remembered the October 1942 trip to St. John's, when Audette had originally suggested he conduct a similar investigation into the modernization issue. Distracted by MacLean's allegations at the time, Connolly now realized that the failure to follow that advice had been a mistake, and he said as much to Audette: "I guess you have not seen Jim Mitchell, but ... as the original suggestion [for the investigation] came from you ... I feel that you should get some credit."[88] The Strange report had changed everything, and Connolly was able to tell his friend that Macdonald had finally agreed to the proposed investigation. This was exciting news for Audette, who recommended that Connolly join his ship in order to experience a transatlantic sea voyage in a corvette. Unfortunately, the executive assistant could not wait for *Amherst* to finish her annual refit, which left Audette "very disappointed our plans have fallen through, however, it obviously can't be helped."[89] Nevertheless, Audette had provided Connolly with another good idea with important ramifications in that it gave the executive assistant a first-hand perspective of the "terrible conditions" on the corvettes.

Since he could not travel with Audette, Connolly chose to go to sea with Mitchell instead.[90] Indicating the depth of Connolly's connections to the RCNVR, one of Mitchell's officers was Barry O'Brien's younger brother, Gerald, who believed that the executive assistant was on board "checking up" on him at the request of his influential father, John Ambrose O'Brien.[91] With close friends at hand, Connolly sailed with the *Orillia* on 10 October. Although the overseas officers would have the greatest impact on the investigation, Connolly's RCNVR compatriots were a significant factor in its formation and planning stages. It had not always been easy for these officers to get word through to him but they had at last been heard, and in their view that meant their grievances would no longer be ignored. Of course, these officers did not realize that Naval Service Headquarters had listened to their pleas long before this time. Whether these men would still have tried to influence the executive assistant had they known about Naval Service Headquarters' efforts to combat the refit crisis is unknown. It is difficult to escape the conclusion, however, that the reservists' actions only managed to distract the minister further and thus undercut Ottawa's efforts to close the gap that obviously existed between the Naval Board and Macdonald.

Although they did not know the exact reasons why Connolly was going overseas, the Naval Staff was aware of his trip. In fact, it was Naval Service Headquarters that made the arrangements for him to fly to St. John's, where he would spend five days before sailing to Londonderry and then on to London.[92] Perhaps the ultimate irony was that Nelles had helped to organize the investigation that contributed to his downfall. Believing that the Naval Board had finally got their message across to the minister, Nelles actually "welcomed the proposal that Connolly should make this trip," which he interpreted as a sign that Macdonald was finally taking the refit situation seriously.[93] He was. But while Macdonald was using his executive assistant as a conduit, it would be officers in Londonderry rather than those at Naval Service Headquarters who would have the minister's undivided attention.

Before Connolly got the chance to meet the men in Londonderry, he would first get a taste of conditions on the East Coast. Based on Strange's memo, Connolly expected the state of equipment on RCN escorts to dominate his discussions with officers in St. John's. When he began asking questions, he found that the first individuals he encountered were more interested in the discrimination issue. In an unexpected turn of events, some reservists offered criticisms that echoed MacLean's complaints, and it was enough to convince Connolly that "VR [Voluntary Reserve] antagonism is rampant."[94] This view was supported by both Commander Paul Cross, RCNVR, who was the senior ranking reservist at the base and the assistant naval officer in charge, and Lieutenant Commander R.M. Hanbury, RCNVR, the staff signals officer.[95] As far as equipment was concerned, Cross had little to say other than that it had been hard to get Radio Direction Finding gear fitted in the

Rosthern, which he had commanded previously.[96] The topic of reserve discrimination at the hands of the permanent force was a different matter. Hanbury provided Connolly with proof that the initiative to allow reservists a chance to command a group of warships at sea had failed because the regulars apparently did not want "to share seniority with them." As a result, both Cross and Hanbury concluded that the RCNVR would welcome MacLean's suggestion of a reservist appointment to the Naval Board to speak for their interests. So much so that Connolly's diary recorded how Hanbury "says don't put Brocks on the board, promote some good VR's to Capt. – Paul Cross said to be worthy."[97]

Other reserve officers also contributed to the discussion on reserve board representation. Connolly met O'Brien, whose ship, *Snowberry*, was in port and found him greatly concerned with reserve morale issues. So, too, was the staff officer (operations) in St. John's, Lieutenant Commander A.G.S. Griffin, RCNVR. Neither O'Brien nor Griffin intended to imply that there was a serious rift between the RCN and RCNVR, but Connolly may have been oversensitive about this issue due to MacLean's influence. He therefore wrote to Macdonald, "I have had some informative talks with some of the Corvette Captains who are now doing some time ashore ... I find them no complainers. Their views seem fair and objective. They do, however, incline to Diefenback's [sic] suggestion."[98] That was a reference to Diefenbaker's defence of MacLean in June, when it was suggested that Macdonald should consider giving the reserves a seat on the Naval Board. MacLean's original recommendation had taken on a new life as Connolly was finding evidence indicating that board representation might have been a worthwhile suggestion after all.

Some individuals in St. John's were more direct in their advocacy of MacLean's ideas. For example, Connolly had been given a letter from a rating who was deeply upset that the officer selection board was run by the permanent force. This man was trying to become an officer in the RCNVR and was shocked that the selection board consisted exclusively of regulars. "Why should the RCN pick officers for the RCNVR," he asked, continuing with, "this Andrew MacLean has got some-thing!" Connolly sent a copy of this letter to Macdonald, telling him that it was an "indication of a condition which may exist."[99] His uncertainty is understandable. There still was not enough evidence to prove conclusively that a majority of reservists felt that the permanent force had treated them unfairly. But if it can be assumed that a British officer stationed in Canada was capable of drawing an unbiased conclusion, then the comments of Captain Massey Goolden, RN, are significant because he found that there was "a lot of truth in Andy McLean's statements."[100]

Even the possibility that MacLean may have been right was a troubling development, particularly since the complaints circulating around St. John's could easily give MacLean fresh ammunition for a renewed offensive against the minister. The reserve discrimination question was back on Connolly's schedule. Not only did that represent yet another victory for those who were undercutting the Naval

Board's authority but it would further distract the minister from the refit situation. As far as equipment was concerned, things did not appear so bleak, as Connolly would tell Macdonald that "I had gone forewarned that the problem was a serious one and that our ships were in poor fighting shape ... The urgency of the problem was not impressed upon my mind there."[101] This would change once the vice chief of the naval staff turned up in St. John's.

According to Strange, Vice Chief Jones had offered to look into the modernization question by going to the UK on the minister's behalf. Certainly that was the impression Strange had given to Adams, letting him know in September that "very confidentially, the Minister is going strongly into this matter himself, and I understand that VCNS [Vice Chief of the Naval Staff Jones] will, before long, be going over to England to take up these matters with Admiralty. Please keep this information entirely to yourself for obvious reasons ... He [Jones] knows nothing of my part in this. I still haven't met him!"[102] Macdonald was unprepared to send Jones in Connolly's place, but the vice chief still saw an opportunity to renew his whispering campaign against Nelles.[103] As one of the few regulars who understood the significance of what was transpiring in St. John's, Jones needed to get to the port without attracting the suspicions of his fellow officers. He did so by announcing that he was going on an "inspection trip" to the Maritimes.[104] Arriving on 7 October 1943 and leaving on the same day that the executive assistant departed for Londonderry, Jones performed no official functions at the base other than a one-hour tour of the RCN hospital, which he did with Connolly at his side. Nor was Jones' presence in the port a surprise to the executive assistant, who wrote home that "GC Jones arrived and with him I had lunch at Commodore Reid's."[105] In fact, the vice chief of the naval staff's appearance coincided with a significant shift in Connolly's investigation, which, having so far focused on reserve issues, was finally redirected toward modernization.

While this is suggestive, the strongest evidence that the vice chief was participating in the investigation can be found in a letter Connolly wrote to Macdonald, in which he stated that he had "talked to GC Jones" about the difficulties he was encountering in St. John's.[106] Nor was that all. Jones also took the executive assistant to see both Reid and his captain (D), Rowland, whose comments confirmed Connolly's original suspicions on modernization. Unlike the rest of the Naval Board, therefore, Jones understood what was transpiring, and yet apparently said nothing to Nelles when he returned to Naval Service Headquarters. Moreover, Jones' presence legitimized the criticisms that Connolly was about to hear, so the vice chief of naval staff's meddling managed only to further undermine his fellow board member's position with the minister. The more so since Jones neglected to tell Connolly how the refit situation was linked to the modernization issue, as well as how the Naval Board had been trying to enlist Macdonald's support to correct that particular deficiency. Instead, Jones let Reid and Rowland loose on Connolly, and their comments had a profound effect. Reversing his earlier observation to Macdonald, the executive assistant now found that "the general impression which I previously had, namely, that RCN ships were very poorly equipped with the latest mechanical anti-submarine appliances, was confirmed in my necessarily short talk with Captain 'D.'"[107]

With the exception of Rowland and Reid, Connolly's time in St. John's had been disappointing as he had uncovered little evidence that the state of equipment was having an adverse impact on the base's personnel or the morale of the seagoing fleet. Connolly's final conclusion on St. John's was that "generally speaking, I think it is a very happy base and, I think, an efficient one."[108] Once he returned from overseas, he would have a different story to tell. As with Strange's investigation, it would be the officers in Londonderry who would have the greatest impact on Connolly. Thanks to Reid's and Rowland's observations, Connolly had the desired predisposition before he arrived, and that meant the "battle for equipment," as Strange had called it, would soon be in the hands of the Londonderry officers.

Nelles may have been disappointed when Munitions and Supply and the Admiralty handed his refit plans consecutive setbacks, but his real adversaries were the collaborators and informers vying for the minister's attention. Since they operated behind the scenes, Nelles could not compete with the combination of these networks conspiring against him, and that is the key to understanding how Macdonald missed the chief of the naval staff's warnings about the refit situation. Dealing with an overburdened minister had made it difficult for Nelles to keep Macdonald interested in naval affairs, and all these clandestine networks – Jones and his men, MacLean and his followers, Connolly's own network of informers, and the Londonderry officers – only managed to make matters worse. Each of these groups was undermining the chief of the naval staff's authority, and by doing so not only shook Macdonald's confidence in Nelles, but also distorted the minister's perception of the issues that mattered most to the navy.

While MacLean and Jones had certainly contributed to this process, ironically it was the officers who wanted Naval Service Headquarters to focus on the modernization question that caused the most damage. Preying on the minister's vulnerabilities, these men managed to turn an operational deficiency into an artificial political crisis. Without the breadth of vision to place the RCN's modernization into the larger context of the refit situation, Macdonald was led to the faulty assumption that his advisors had never told him about the navy's technical backwardness. Moreover, whether it was reserve discrimination complaints, training, or modernization – all these competing interests left Macdonald confused and uncertain as to what he was to believe. Of course, Connolly's investigation was designed to provide the minister with some clarity, but the executive assistant was going to Londonderry, and as such was turning to the same men whose original interference had begun the process of politicizing the modernization issue.

6
A Loaded Investigation

Connolly's investigation marked a watershed in the RCN's history. This trip not only led to Nelles' replacement but also was directly responsible for "the greatest upheaval" at Naval Service Headquarters during the war because Connolly was convinced that he had unearthed enough evidence to accuse the minister's advisors of negligence and deceit.[1] However, the fact that Connolly had gone to the source of the discontent without any attempt to seek Naval Service Headquarters' perspective suggests that his inquiry was not only biased but prejudicial as well. The Londonderry officers would rely on the same methodology as they had used with Strange, in which hyperbole was the best way to get their point across. It is essential, therefore, to explore the influence that these men had over the executive assistant, as well as the role they played in Nelles' eventual downfall.[2] And that leaves the key question of whether it was Connolly and the Londonderry officers, rather than Macdonald, who were the true masterminds behind the subsequent attack on Nelles and his staff over the RCN's equipment needs.

As the commodore (D) in Londonderry, Simpson had taken particular care to see that Strange received as much information as possible on the RCN's technical backwardness. He would do so again with Connolly, but the advanced warning that the executive assistant was coming to Londonderry allowed him time to make special arrangements. Simpson selected a core team of four individuals who, as the chief architects in making equipment a priority at Naval Service Headquarters, would be responsible for convincing Connolly that their plight was just. Simpson's top engineering officer, Commander Shorto, was a natural selection because he had done such a good job during Strange's trip. The remaining three officers had not participated in that earlier investigation, but each brought a unique perspective to the team. There was the American reservist in charge of the United States Navy (USN) repair base in Londonderry, Lieutenant Commander D. Conklin, USNR, as well as Lieutenant J.J. Pigott, RCNVR, who was the Canadian engineer liaison officer. Simpson's technical experts were well suited for Connolly's investigation, particularly since one Canadian officer observed how "the three top Engineer officers at Londonderry, – RN [Shorto], USN [Conklin], and RCN [Pigott], work not only as an efficient team but as personal friends."[3]

While not an engineer officer like the others, the last member of this group, Simpson's staff officer (administration), Lieutenant Commander C. Copelin, RCNR, nonetheless had the equally important task of co-ordinating Connolly's activities in Londonderry. There was good reason why the commodore had selected Copelin for this assignment. Early on Simpson saw such tremendous potential that when Naval Service Headquarters tried to post Copelin back to Canada, the commodore made a personal request to have this "impressive Canadian officer" stay. Naval Service Headquarters agreed, and with that Simpson made Copelin his unofficial Canadian chief of staff, with responsibility for communicating with RCN ships and therefore the ability to pass their concerns on to the commodore.[4] Such experience made Copelin the ideal tour guide for Connolly.

Other preparations followed. Only days before Connolly arrived, Simpson invited a technical expert from the senior Canadian naval officer's office in London (a title that had replaced the captain commanding Canadian ships) to Londonderry so that he could "discuss the supply of A/S [antisubmarine] and ancillary equipment for RCN ships." This exposed how little the Londonderry officers knew about the RCN's administrative process. In fact, this Canadian officer from London found that "considerable time was spent with the Commodore (D) WA [Western Approaches] who asked many questions concerning the supply of equipment, refitting, etc. of ships under his jurisdiction. It was pointed out that every effort would be made by SCNO(L) [senior Canadian naval officer (London)] to coordinate the supply henceforth."[5] That these observations were made only three days before Connolly arrived suggests that Simpson and his officers had much to learn about Naval Service Headquarters and their efforts to modernize.

Nonetheless, these preparations were impressive, the more so because the presence of James George in Londonderry offered Simpson's team a dry run for Connolly's arrival. It should be remembered that George was the historical officer for London; he was visiting the base for the first time since writing a critical report on modernization. George's account of this encounter provides an excellent illustration of the group's organization and methodology:

> [I had] a lengthy interview in which he [Simpson] discussed frankly the equipment position of Canadian as compared to British Escort Ships, and several other topics relating to Canadian ships operations, administrative and repair problems at Londonderry. The Canadian Engineer Liaison Officer in Staff of Commodore (D), Lt (E) JJ Pigott, RCNVR, and Lt. Cdr. Conklin, USNR, gave me excellent material for a report on the work of the US Naval Repair Base for Canadian ships at Londonderry. The Commodore's Secretarial and Training staffs were again, as on my previous visit, as helpful as they could be, and several documents to back up the points raised by the Commodore were obtained. The Commodore's Staff Officer Administration, Lt. Cdr. Copelin, OBE., RCNR., was of particular assistance.[6]

Between George's earlier interview and Strange's trip, the officers in Londonderry had developed a pattern for dealing with visiting Canadian officers and

While sailing on HMCS *Orillia*, J.J. Connolly learned that operational requirements had led to a doubling of the corvette's original complement. This image from the crew's mess reveals the confined conditions on board as the hammocks slung above crowd sailors who are cleaning up after a meal. DHH 81/520/1000, BOX 141, FILE 27

dignitaries. The fact that George and Strange often used similar phrases and terms, such as referring to Simpson's activities as a part of his command's "battle for equipment," suggests that they were subjected to similar tactics and messages.[7] This strongly implies that Connolly was treated to a well-rehearsed and choreographed routine. Before they got a crack at him, however, the executive assistant first had to endure an eight-day transatlantic crossing with the *Orillia* while it escorted convoy HX 260 from St. John's to Londonderry.[8] For Connolly, it was an agonizing, but enlightening, voyage, as he discovered exactly what it was like to be a sailor in one of Canada's corvettes.

Aside from some pessimism about their ability to deal with the U-boats, the men of *Orillia*'s wardroom offered "no specific complaints." The same was true of the crew who, instead of whining, preferred to follow their Captain's creed of "Bring on the subs."[9] Connolly was puzzled. Equipment was not a big issue to the junior officers he had interviewed in St. John's, and the sailors on *Orillia* had said even less. The only explanation, he reasoned, was that the crew was uncomfortable discussing such an explosive topic with the minister's aide. Perhaps to some degree that was true, but Connolly never considered that those who had complained about

This picture perfectly captures the sea conditions that J.J. Connolly endured on his voyage to Londonderry. The environment appeared to have an undue affect on the chronically seasick executive assistant, who believed that it was "suicide" to send the corvettes across the Atlantic. DHH 84/8

equipment had exaggerated the impact the deficiency was having on the average sailor.[10] Although he had uncovered little evidence to substantiate claims that the fleet was rife with discontent, Connolly nevertheless drew firm conclusions of his own.

Constantly seasick and in a state of terror throughout the voyage, Connolly was "lost in admiration at these young Canadians – giving up so much at home – to do this."[11] He discovered that, carrying double the recommended complement, the corvettes were hopelessly overcrowded and sanitary conditions left much to be desired; disturbed that the ship's officers had to steer by relying on British escorts with gyroscopic compasses, he found that "the equipment carried in 'Orillia' is all quite antiquated."[12] Given what he had experienced, there can be little doubt that Connolly was motivated by a genuine desire to help the common sailor. In his view, the investigation had already developed into something of a crusade to right the wrongs perpetrated by the big-ship regular navy against the little reserve escort force.

Arrogance was mixed with that philanthropy. While observing that some senior officers had not been to sea during the war, Connolly was amused with his achievement: "nothing like a lawyer telling N.S.H.Q. about a sea voyage. An amateur but interested."[13] He was an amateur, and his belief that one transatlantic crossing placed him on an equal footing with experienced naval officers who had fought in the First World War and had commanded warships in the lean interwar period was somewhat naïve. For example, the equipment on RCN escorts had nothing to do with their seaworthiness, yet Connolly confused the two, arguing as he did that "when you see the waves, the rain, and the pitching of the ship you realise that only fair equipment is not enough & they need the best." If Connolly truly wanted to protect sailors from the elements, he should have been a more forceful advocate of the escort destroyers or frigates rather than corvettes.[14] More to the point, such pronouncements were indicative of a man who, having never served in the navy himself, tended to overreact and sensationalized his experiences for political purposes. Connolly was an honest and sincere man, but he was driven by a blinding loyalty to Macdonald that hindered his objectivity. He was looking for trouble, so he had a tendency to see problems where none may have existed. The corvettes were uncomfortable and life at sea in wartime conditions was tough, but extravagant statements that it was "suicide to send ships like Orillia to Derry" distorted the truth. That Connolly was capable of such hyperbole suggests he was susceptible to extreme interpretations. The more so since he had confided to his diary that his experiences on the *Orillia* had led to "a deep emotional reaction," and that made him an easy target for the Londonderry officers and their agenda.[15] Frustrated by what they interpreted as a defunct equipment policy, and forewarned by Strange, they were determined to use Connolly's investigation to ensure that their perspective was heard at the highest levels in Ottawa. With Connolly's own network of informants having laid the groundwork, the executive assistant was already prepared to believe the Londonderry officers. All he needed was the evidence, and it had been marshalled prior to his arrival. By the time the *Orillia* came alongside on the evening of 18 October, Connolly was convinced that Naval Service Headquarters had botched the RCN's modernization; Simpson and his officers would be preaching to the converted.

After a night of much-needed sleep, Connolly was driven by Mitchell to Londonderry to meet Copelin. There were many advantages to starting the investigation in this fashion. Copelin had two years of sea service, including fourteen months as the commanding officer of the corvette HMCS *Halifax*, and according to Connolly that made him an expert on the state of equipment on Canadian warships.[16] Consequently, the first interpretations presented to the executive assistant would not come from foreigners but from a former, as well as a serving, Canadian commanding officer. What Copelin and Mitchell had to say was not flattering, as both explained why so many officers on Simpson's staff wanted the opportunity to speak with Connolly.[17] Nor did Copelin mince words when describing how the Londonderry officers had managed to overcome Ottawa's indecisiveness to get at least some modern equipment to RCN ships.

This initial conversation was exactly what Connolly had expected to hear from seagoing officers in St. John's. After listening to Copelin and Mitchell, the executive assistant drew the conclusion that "it is felt by the sea-going officers in R.C.N. corvettes that it is easier for them to get repairs and equipment in Derry than in Canadian yards."[18] Perhaps that was true, but his only evidence to support such an allegation had come from the fact that Copelin and Mitchell had said so. He did not seem to understand that the information was coming from men who knew little about the tremendous hurdles Naval Service Headquarters faced in its attempt to improve the refit capabilities of the Maritime shipyards. Nor did the officers in Londonderry know that the Admiralty had told their counterparts in Ottawa they were not in a position to provide much help. This important consideration was not presented to Connolly, and without it he was left with the impression that Naval Service Headquarters had done little to improve the situation. This perspective would only be reinforced throughout the course of his investigation.

Copelin then took Connolly to see Simpson. Simpson's opening remarks were equally frank, telling Connolly how the lack of modern equipment meant that the Canadian escort fleet was being deprived of the opportunity to prove itself. Using exercise reports as evidence, Simpson was clearly lost in admiration for the average Canadian sailor whose "intelligence" and "enthusiasm," he believed, was unsurpassed by any other group of seaman, including those of the Royal Navy.[19] He had, of course, said the exact same thing to Strange, but as in that earlier occasion, Simpson did not want any of his comments to be seen as criticism of the Canadians under his command. Instead, his prey rested much higher in the RCN's food chain, and he had little compunction in saying so. Connolly was deeply impressed with his honesty and, like Copelin, the commodore (D) was not afraid to lay the blame for the current fleet's condition squarely on Naval Service Headquarters' doorstep.

Throughout his discussion with Connolly, the commodore (D) left the distinct impression that he did not enjoy being so critical of Naval Service Headquarters. But in the end, he had little choice. To do nothing was unthinkable, particularly when the Canadian commanding officers peppering Simpson with complaints were counting on some type of action. Simpson never provided Connolly with the identities of these men, but it was explained that their resentment was based on the belief that Ottawa did not care about them.

Simpson left it to his officers to make the case against Naval Service Headquarters and its inability to devise an adequate modernization policy. For that they did provide evidence. Shorto was the first officer after Simpson to get a crack at Connolly, and he came out swinging. Shorto explained how his first encounter with Canadian engineering facilities, in 1941, "shocked him." The fact that relatively little had changed since that time only added to his frustration and, as Connolly discovered, "Shorto was very frankly critical of ... N.S.H.Q."[20] In reality, Shorto had not returned to the Canadian East Coast for well over a year, so his observation was not based on any direct empirical evidence, other than his visits to Canadian ships in Londonderry. Such experiences did little to help him understand the Maritime refit crisis. When looking at RCN escorts, Shorto did not realize that the East Coast refit dilemma, rather than any negligence on the part of Naval Service Headquarters, was responsible for what he was witnessing.

Although Connolly was unaware of it at the time, the same was also true for Conklin. Unlike his British and Canadian counterparts at Londonderry, Conklin did not seem to have much contact with the seagoing element because RCN ships rarely used the USN repair yard, suggesting that the American was less likely to have emotional attachments to this issue. Indeed, that was an angle that Conklin played up to the executive assistant when, after handing Connolly a report highly critical of Naval Service Headquarters, he observed, "The attached data is sufficient to get many people in trouble, but it is not intended to do that in the least." Although Conklin's report did just that, there was undoubtedly some truth in his plea to Connolly that "we only want to see better repairs for the ships at sea, and so I trust you will use the information judiciously."[21] Perhaps Conklin would have been disappointed had he learned that the report became one of the bases from which Connolly and Macdonald launched their attack against Nelles. In any case, the notion that Conklin was an impartial advisor was far from true. Although Connolly did not know it at the time of his investigation, Conklin was in contact with Canadian commanding officers, some of whom were members of the executive assistant's own network of reserve informants. In particular, Conklin's correspondence and personal friendship with Louis Audette is highly suspicious and suggests that this American reservist probably collaborated with Audette's plan to get Connolly to Londonderry.[22]

Although claiming he "appreciated that the Canadian dockyards have serious problems with which to cope," Conklin also told Connolly that his report was going to show how these same facilities were failing "to carry their share of the load" in refitting Canadian warships.[23] Without the knowledge that the Canadian Naval Board had taken drastic measures to combat the refit situation, Conklin's report, like the others in Londonderry, left little doubt who was responsible. As with his British and Canadian colleagues, the details of Conklin's account show that his "facts" were not entirely accurate. His illustrations seemed to encompass all that was wrong with the East Coast repair facilities, collectively portraying a story of excessive delay, poor workmanship, and general incompetence. In his report, Conklin provided Connolly with evidence of "four concrete cases where repairs in Canadian ships have been badly bogged down."[24] It is not surprising that Macdonald and Connolly would focus on his example of HMCS *Pictou* when they confronted Nelles and the Naval Board in November, as it was the best illustration of the worst in RCN administration. Appearances, however, were deceiving.

Conklin had distorted the details of *Pictou*'s refit; this case was not as "concrete" as it first appeared. For example, he claimed that between December 1942 and April 1943, *Pictou* was refitted at Liverpool, Nova Scotia, and yet still arrived in Londonderry with a defect list that consisted of sixty-three hull, forty-eight engineering, and thirteen electrical items. "It is difficult to understand why this ship was compelled to remain out of service for five months," Conklin told Connolly, "during which time no work was done that could not have been accomplished in one months time."[25] Had Conklin been more thorough with his research, he would have found his answer.

On 7 November 1942, *Pictou* sailed for Liverpool, England, to be fitted with type 271 radar. On arrival it was discovered that the radar slated for the ship was unavailable, so *Pictou* returned to Halifax empty-handed. Arriving on 10 December, the corvette remained at the jetty for a short repair period, after which time she was reassigned to coastal duties so that she could be taken in hand at the yards in Liverpool, Nova Scotia, for an annual refit. The *Pictou*'s refit, which took place between 23 January and 6 May 1943, was not continuous. Desperate for escorts, *Pictou* was assigned to convoy ON 149, and therefore did not resume her refit until 28 March. Put simply, Conklin's assessment was not accurate; yet Connolly not only accepted it at face value, but also formed the conclusion that Naval Service Headquarters tolerated this type of mismanagement. In fairness, that was not entirely Conklin's fault. He was the first to admit that, having only discussed four specific vessels, his account was "not meant to be a complete report."[26]

Aside from the inaccuracies about the *Pictou*, and exaggerated statements such as Conklin's belief that the defects on HMCS *Drumheller* could "easily cause the loss of the ship," the Naval Staff would not have disagreed with his overall message that the East Coast refit facilities were having difficulties. Certainly, Conklin's characterization of the destroyer HMCS *Skeena*'s problems in Canadian yards was not too far off the mark. After having type 271 radar fitted at the end of November 1942, the *Skeena* began a refit in Halifax that took just over three months to complete.[27] This did not sit well with Simpson, who, according to Conklin, was annoyed that Western Approaches had to do without this valuable assist because the refit took one month longer than the average. Nor was Simpson happy when she eventually rejoined C-3 without hedgehog having been fitted.[28] Likewise, the refitting of *Woodstock* between 25 March and 14 April 1943 appeared to be an even better example of incompetence. After operating on the North Atlantic for the first half of the summer, *Woodstock* was ordered to Liverpool, Nova Scotia, for additional work, and was not ready for operations until 5 October (sailing as part of the convoy that took Connolly to Londonderry). Once she had arrived in Londonderry, some officers were stunned that the commanding officer of the *Woodstock* had "asked for more improvements than all other ships in the group together."[29] Connolly did not realize that Naval Service Headquarters had been equally disappointed with both *Skeena*'s and *Woodstock*'s refits.

It is unlikely that Conklin's report would have had such a profound effect on Connolly except Copelin, Simpson, and Shorto had made similar comments. One by one, each of these officers repeated the message, and this rehearsed redundancy was proving effective. The modernization issue was both serious and common knowledge at Londonderry, and that made Connolly wonder why Macdonald knew nothing about it. A conspiracy of silence perpetrated by Nelles and his officers seemed to be the only reasonable answer.[30] Of course, the truth was not nearly so sinister, and had Connolly explored Naval Service Headquarters' perspective before leaving Ottawa, he would have learned that the navy's top brass was desperately trying to secure Macdonald's support for their efforts to fix the refit situation. All Connolly would have had to do was read Johnstone's July report to get all the answers he needed. Having been approached by men who were not privy to that type of high-level analysis, however, the executive assistant knew nothing about the Naval Staff's perspective. Without that balance, it is unsurprising that he formed the conclusions he did. His interpretation of Naval Service Headquarters only worsened with each day spent at Londonderry since Simpson's team was working to overload him with information.

A report presented to Connolly on 23 October provides a good illustration of how the team's collective efforts were aimed at effecting change at Naval Service Headquarters. "Lieut. Commander Conklin and I have collaborated on a brief memorandum," Pigott boldly admitted to Connolly, which they had done "in the hope that it may help you to make a few constructive suggestions when you return to Canada."[31] Pigott thought that there was no time for subtlety. His experience as the engineer liaison officer in Londonderry had led him to the conclusion that Canadian ships had suffered from long periods of neglect, and that "Engineering conditions on H.M.C.S. Corvettes with regard to efficiency and cleanliness were found to be disgraceful."[32] Cutting down "the red tape" in Halifax was the key to success in Pigott's opinion, as he predicted that Canadian yards would witness a 40 percent increase in efficiency if the administration were reorganized.[33] Of course, after getting Macdonald's permission in July, Naval Service Headquarters had done just that by making G.M. Hibbard the first commodore superintendent in Halifax. The Londonderry officers were unimpressed, as they told Connolly that while Hibbard's appointment was "a great step," it was not nearly enough.[34] Again, Nelles and his officers would have agreed fully with that position, particularly since they were the ones who were disappointed when Macdonald rejected other proposed solutions to the refit situation.

That Connolly did not know about Naval Service Headquarters' efforts to solicit Macdonald's support undoubtedly prejudiced his investigation, but so, too, did the Londonderry officers' tendency to overstate their case. And perhaps the best example of the effect that their hyperbole had on Connolly is when Pigott argued that Naval Service Headquarters was squandering an incredible opportunity to refit Canadian ships at Conklin's yard. According to Pigott, the American yard had 800 men who could "do miraculous things to ships in a short period of time." Conklin went even further, claiming that his yard could "do in six weeks what Canada does in 6 months."[35] Unfortunately for Naval Service Headquarters, Conklin did not stop there. Well-provisioned and filled with highly skilled and experienced workmen, Conklin's yard had been underworked ever since the USN had withdrawn from Londonderry, and he could have taken many RCN ships in hand for modernization. All Ottawa had to do was ask. This hit Connolly like a bombshell, as he now believed that he had done in one visit what Naval Service Headquarters had been unable to do all year: find a solution to the RCN's technical backwardness. Unlike some officers at Londonderry, however, Connolly did not know that Conklin's offer to take RCN ships in hand for refit was premature.

After hearing Conklin claim that his yard could extend the fo'c'sle of a ship in a mere two weeks, even Simpson and Shorto were forced to admit that the American had often been accused of trying to "build a reputation for himself." Nor were they the only ones who thought so, as an engineering rear admiral in the Admiralty politely observed that the capabilities of the USN yard "had been somewhat exaggerated," while yet another officer found that "Conklin was a bluffer."[36] More to the point, when Connolly later came to collect on the promise to modernize RCN corvettes, Conklin was forced to renege because the Admiralty had suddenly sent more ships to his yard. As a result, Conklin came through on only one corvette, HMCS *Morden*, which took over two months to upgrade after she was taken in hand in late November.[37] It is difficult to escape the conclusion that Connolly's "miracle man" was a false prophet. At the time of the investigation, Conklin's "incontrovertible" evidence had convinced Connolly that Naval Service Headquarters had never asked for British or American help, which was of course simply untrue.

No one told Connolly that Conklin was exaggerating. Instead, the assault on the Naval Staff continued as Copelin argued that Naval Service Headquarters needed to develop a definitive refit policy. If such a policy existed, Copelin then explained, it would be possible to use the American yard "up to a point where it will only be necessary in Canada to dry-dock the ship and make major hull alterations." In suggesting this, Copelin was again feeding Connolly misinformation. Naval Service Headquarters had developed a refit policy, and Copelin knew it. For example, in a letter to the executive assistant, Copelin observed, "it is interesting to note that, on the 30th September this year, Naval Service Headquarters stated that, as the whole question of re-modelling R.C.N. Corvettes is at present under review, it is not possible to state at this moment which ships will be taken for these Alterations and Additions."[38] Although Connolly had been told that "the question of remodelling RCN corvettes has never been communicated to the people in Derry," Copelin's letter somehow managed to recite exact segments from Naval Service Headquarters' 30 September refit schedule.[39] Read in isolation, and taken out of context, these extracts were misleading and only managed to strengthen the Londonderry officer's case against Naval Service Headquarters. Had Connolly been presented with the entire document, he would have realized that Copelin was not being entirely forthright with him.

The refit schedule in question was the product of the Admiralty's August message telling Ottawa that they could not spare any British yards for Canadian modernization. As the Admiralty had recommended, the Naval Staff had turned to the Americans, and once yards in the United States had been secured, the new refit schedule was issued. Beginning with HMCS *Dunvegan*, fourteen corvettes had been allocated to shipyards for modernization.[40] While Copelin apparently did not think Connolly should see that part of the memo, he was not the only one concealing information from the executive assistant.

Without providing a copy of the actual refit schedule, Simpson let Connolly read a private letter sent to his boss at Western Approaches in Liverpool, Max Horton, in early October. It was not a flattering account: "So far as I am aware, no Refit Programme affecting C.1 – C.5 Groups has ever been produced at NSHQ, Ottawa, which is sufficiently accurate to be of any value. One reason must be the lack of Canadian control over A/S Equipment. This inability to make forecasts and decisions is a nuisance here and upsetting to the personnel of the ships concerned."[41]

Although Simpson and his officers were only trying to help the Canadians under their command, their tactics with Connolly were somewhat questionable. Certainly, it was significant that the executive assistant was not given a key signal that accompanied the refit schedule. Originating from Naval Service Headquarters, this signal complained that the Admiralty was still too slow in supplying the RCN with certain types of equipment and components for which "the RCN is entirely dependent upon deliveries from the UK."[42]

Although the Admiralty was doing all that it could to accommodate the Canadians, there was resentment at Naval Service Headquarters toward the Royal Navy and in this regard Simpson was not entirely unsympathetic. He realized that

British officials in Ottawa had been too aggressive in acquiring Canadian-built equipment for Royal Navy ships and admitted to Connolly that "better arrangements" were required "because BATM [British Admiralty Technical Mission] have cornered the market on some gear for refits." As Simpson reported to Horton, this hindered the RCN's ability to upgrade, since "little remains for modernization of Canadian ships at present fighting the war."[43] Others in Londonderry agreed, as the antisubmarine officer observed that it was unfair how the RCN had "barriers ... in their way, for DA/SM [director antisubmarine material] over here has stuck his toes in and has not been particularly forthcoming about new gear."[44] Yet Simpson glossed over this problem with Connolly. Instead, his sights remained firmly fixed on Naval Service Headquarters, telling the executive assistant that "to date, HMCS *Edmundston* is the first and only ship modernised with this equipment to cross the Atlantic. Others are on their way, I understand, and when HMCS *Rimouski* arrives, I hope to find her with full equipment. This indicates a general improvement but *Edmundston* took 6½ months to modernise, and in my opinion, this is unacceptable."[45]

Herein lies the major problem with Simpson's analysis: his criticisms of Naval Service Headquarters were at least one year out of date. The real "battle for equipment" had taken place in the fall of 1942, and thanks to the Naval Staff's efforts since that time, things had – as Simpson himself was willing to admit – generally improved. But that was not the message that Simpson's letter conveyed to Connolly. All the executive assistant knew was that one of the most renowned men in Londonderry was slamming the RCN to the highest-ranking officer at Western Approaches, and that spelled trouble for Macdonald. Certainly, it was not difficult to imagine what the official opposition would do if they ever received a copy of a letter like the one Simpson had sent to Horton. The more so since some officers in London would confirm much of what Connolly had been told in Londonderry.[46]

Arriving in London on the morning of 23 October, Connolly first stopped at Commander Fred Price's office. As the major liaison organization between the Admiralty and Naval Service Headquarters, the London office was a key location for Connolly to pick up information, particularly since Price and his staff were responsible for all Canadian personnel serving in the UK. Accordingly, Connolly could use Price as a barometer to confirm whether what Simpson had said about the correlation between equipment and morale among the seagoing fleet was true. Additional perspectives were much needed because Connolly was getting little information from the men at sea. Having been forewarned that convoy conferences often turned into grouch sessions, for example, the executive assistant was puzzled after he attended the conference for convoy HX 260 and did not hear any "outbursts" from Canadian commanding officers at all.[47] As with his visit to St. John's, the executive assistant was once again to be surprised. Modernization may have been a key issue to the Londonderry officers, but the Canadians in London believed that the permanent force's discrimination was having a greater impact on the morale of the reserves.

Price, having had "long talks" with Connolly on the subject of permanent force discrimination, provided various charts and memos showing that the British had long ago given their reserve force the authority to decide which officers would be promoted. These documents also indicated that the Royal Navy had created the position of admiral commanding reserves, who was responsible to the Admiralty for all matters pertaining to the personnel of their naval reserves. Assisted by two commodores from both reserve branches, these officers were "to interpret to ACR [admiral commanding reserves] the feeling of the officers and ratings in the two reserve forces."[48] Clearly, the British had seen the value of giving their reserve forces more autonomy, and according to Price some RCNVRs did not understand why the Canadian navy had not followed suit. This argument had merit, and it echoed the one John Diefenbaker had made to Macdonald in the House of Commons in June. If a morale problem did exist, Price told Connolly, appointing a reservist to the Naval Board would pay huge dividends in easing frustration in the RCNVR and RCNR. Even if this situation had been exaggerated, Price wondered what harm could come from such an appointment.

Price's methodical approach was persuasive. Although Connolly had spent much of 1943 helping the minister battle MacLean on this very issue, he finally conceded defeat by admitting in his diary that "board representation for the VR's is urgently needed – also on promotions + honours boards."[49] The impact that Price's comments had on Connolly was decisive, and it is tempting to claim that he was the key player who eventually made reserve representation on the Naval Board a reality. But it must not be forgotten that without MacLean's interference, Diefenbaker's pressure in the House of Commons, and the observations of the officers in St. John's, it is unlikely that Price's comments would have had the same effect. By extension, it could be reasonably argued that MacLean deserves the lion's share of the credit because he was the one who first turned reserve representation into a political issue. His public campaign had not only led to Diefenbaker's recommendations but also convinced Connolly to explore this issue during the investigation into equipment. In effect, this opened the door for the officers in St. John's and London.

Nor was that the only topic to re-emerge; Price also took an active interest in the question of special service support. According to him, the lack of Canadian recreational, entertainment, and sports facilities at bases in the UK was probably the primary cause of discipline infractions ashore.[50] Originally Connolly had planted Walter Gilhooly into the London organization as the staff officer (special service) in London to gather information on the welfare of Canadian sailors serving in the UK. But Price had been unhappy with Gilhooly's performance and he said as much to Connolly.[51] Little had improved over the year, and as with the equipment situation, Simpson and his officers were also applying much pressure on the senior Canadian naval officer in London to get Naval Service Headquarters to build recreational facilities in Londonderry.[52] Rather than holding an old friend responsible, Connolly conveniently blamed Naval Service Headquarters by observing in his diary that "Walter didn't fail, but Canada did."[53]

The re-emergence of the special service and reserve discrimination issues was intriguing, but by this time Connolly was far more interested in equipment. Pressed on this subject, Price seemed to understand that Macdonald was a weak minister who had neither taken an active interest in his own department nor listened to his military advisors. While not this blunt with the executive assistant, Price still managed to get this point across. "Perhaps the Minister could be more completely in the picture of the Department," Price gently said to his guest, "if each [Board] member knew that at least once a week he would have at least fifteen or twenty minutes on a stated morning with the Minister."[54] This was a good recommendation, but Price soon came to realize that Connolly was fiercely loyal to his political master. Consequently, telling the whole truth was not necessarily in Price's best interest.

While in Londonderry, Connolly had been peppered with comments about the poor state of technical liaison between the RCN and Royal Navy. By virtue of being the senior Canadian naval officer in London this topic fell within Price's bailiwick, and Connolly wanted to know more about it. Before giving Price a chance to talk, however, Connolly repeated Copelin's arguments: the RCN's modernization was being delayed because of the time it was taking to pass British technical advances from London to Ottawa, and Londonderry did not have its own Canadian technical liaison officer. Despite warnings that "too much importance cannot be placed upon the need of good technical men at Derry," pleas from Simpson and his officers had apparently fallen on deaf ears, and Connolly wanted someone to blame.[55]

This put Price in a horrible position. Passing such recommendations on to Naval Service Headquarters was his job, and according to some it was one that he was not doing well. Connolly's observations made him nervous, particularly when the executive assistant had heard that "in some quarters it is felt that a sufficiently strong fight is not put up with Admiralty to get modernising equipment for the corvettes, [and] that this lack of fight was in our Canadian London office."[56] But the fact that Price might be responsible for the breakdown in technical liaison reveals another important weakness in Connolly's investigation. For him, the RCN's equipment deficiency was comparable to a crime and having already identified his suspects at Naval Service Headquarters, he was treating Price as a witness rather than a potential perpetrator.

Price did not immediately finger Naval Service Headquarters, but while defending his liaison set-up he certainly pointed in that direction. There were only two technical liaison officers in London, and, according to Price, that was not nearly enough to cover even a portion of the Royal Navy's research facilities.[57] Simply put, to do the job properly, he needed more experts from Canada. That much was true, but the impression he passed on to Connolly – namely, that Ottawa ignored his pleas for such men – was not. For example, only weeks after Price had asked for a technical officer to help his staff officer (material), Lieutenant Commander W.J. Riddiford, the Naval Staff sent Lieutenant E.G. Law to London. One month later, Price wanted two more experts, which led to the immediate posting of an engineering lieutenant from the manning depot, HMCS *Niobe*, H.H. Wright, as well as another officer who followed soon after that. Perhaps Naval Service Headquarters should have provided these men earlier in the war, but the fact remains that – despite a serious shortage of technical officers in the RCN – Price was getting the help he had requested, and more was on the way. With statements such as "the supply of data has been speeded up" or that "new weapons and methods are being handled not only in greater volume, but also more expeditiously than formerly," Price gave Naval Service Headquarters few hints of trouble or discontent in his reports.[58] Connolly was a different matter. He was obviously on a witch hunt, and Price did not want to be among those tied to the stake after the inquisition was over. Instead, he would help with Nelles' execution by pouring fuel on the kindling that the executive assistant was collecting in the UK.

Although he never explicitly blamed the Naval Staff, Price was clearly covering his tracks while leaving enough crumbs on a trail that led directly to Ottawa. The strongest evidence that he was doing so can be found by comparing the conflicting information he was passing to Naval Service Headquarters on the one hand and Connolly on the other. After Price first met Simpson in May 1943, he reported to Ottawa that "the whole atmosphere of the Londonderry base is one of pleasant co-operation and efficiency and remarks of the Canadian officers seem to indicate that their needs, as far as repairs, etc. are well looked after."[59] It appeared that little had changed over the summer, as Price's latest account, dated 24 September, observed that, "during my stay at Londonderry I had an opportunity of visiting HMC Ships of the C.3 Group and Ships of the EG 10 Group. From my conversation with the Commanding Officers, it appears that the whole tone of the establishment at Londonderry has risen considerably over the last four or five months. These officers had no complaints or criticisms to offer."[60]

The idea that Canadian commanding officers were on the verge of rebelling over equipment was the justification for the Londonderry officers' interference, but Price's comments to Naval Service Headquarters clearly indicate that these same seagoing commanders were more or less content. However, this was not the impression Price passed on to Connolly when he reinforced the Londonderry perspective by remarking that "the sea-going men definitely felt that they were being let down by NSHQ."[61] There was no way that both interpretations could be correct, and given what he would say next, it is difficult to escape the conclusion that Price was saving himself by confirming the Londonderry officers' criticisms of the Naval Staff.

So far the case against Naval Service Headquarters was based almost entirely on circumstantial evidence and hearsay, so corroboration was important. Price went even further, as he was able to give the executive assistant something that the Londonderry officers could not: hard statistical proof that only 15 percent of the RCN's corvettes were modernized. Law and Wright were a little more optimistic, and believed the figure was closer to 20 percent, but such details did not matter once Connolly was told that almost all the Royal Navy's corvettes had been upgraded.[62] He could now give the minister tangible evidence that the RCN was woefully behind the Royal Navy, particularly since Law's records indicated that forty-two out of seventy-one Canadian corvettes were without extended fo'c'sles, and fifty-three did not possess hedgehog.[63] That was supposedly the Naval Staff's terrible secret. However, the Naval Staff would have had little trouble accepting those figures, since they approximated the ones they had passed to Macdonald five weeks earlier.[64] Unaware that they had done so, Connolly saw this evidence in an entirely different light, as it allowed him to tell Macdonald that "everything which Conklin said was endorsed by Comm[ander] Price in London."[65]

Nor did Price stop there. The executive assistant was captivated by his comment that the equipment deficiency was a "matter of common knowledge around NSHQ." This would not have been a problem except that Connolly was already convinced the Naval Staff had conspired to keep the minister in the dark – Price was feeding the paranoia.[66] He encouraged the executive assistant to dig deeper when he returned to Ottawa, going as far as to put him on the trail of the critical reports that had been submitted to Naval Service Headquarters over the previous six months.[67] Armed with this knowledge, Connolly would pore over hundreds of naval documents until he found the memoranda. This was the hard evidence he wanted to support his perception that Nelles and the Naval Staff had known about the discontent over equipment and yet had said nothing to Macdonald.[68] Of course, it is uncertain how Price knew about these reports, since none of the ones Connolly discovered had ever passed through the London office.

Price's motive for attacking Naval Service Headquarters may have been self-serving, but it worked. As far as the London organization was concerned, Connolly was impressed with what he saw. The Canadian personnel there worked hard under heavy personal pressure in order to further the requirements of the RCN. "The man there must be a fighter," he informed Macdonald, and "must have the facilities to apply pressure on lower officials to get stuff from the higher officials."[69] When the minister's axe began to swing in November, Connolly saved Price from the chop because in his opinion, "Commander Price was doing everything he could to make equipment available for the ships which require it when they get to Londonderry."[70] That he had apparently done so without much support from Naval Service Headquarters was even more remarkable, particularly since Ottawa did not always communicate important policy decisions or equipment requirements to him. Not only did this make it difficult, if not impossible, for Price to carry out his duties properly but it also created a perception within the Admiralty that the RCN's top officer in London did not enjoy "the confidence of the Minister, the CNS [chief of the naval staff], and the staff in Ottawa."[71] And that, according to Price, created an adverse working atmosphere whereby he was consistently fighting an uphill battle to gain respect and co-operation from some British officials.[72]

There was some truth to these allegations. Price's predecessor, Captain R.I. Agnew, RCN, found it difficult to fulfil the duties of the London office because of his personal relationship with Nelles. Admirals Murray and Jones' animosity was not the only feud in the permanent force. Nicknamed "the Corsican Brothers" by some, Nelles and Agnew had been friends at one time but according to rumours, that changed in 1934 when Nelles grew jealous over the attention Agnew was getting for having won the Order of the British Empire. How much the feud affected the liaison organization in London is uncertain, but it is clear that Nelles knew the office was having its fair share of problems; he gave Agnew "a very severe rebuke on the subject of his work." Agnew had his own version, of course, which held that Nelles was at fault because he had purposely ignored signals from London. The truth probably rested between these two extremes, and by the time Price took over, one former staff officer was convinced that "the ill-feeling between [Nelles] and [Agnew] may have prevented the establishment of more effective liaison organisation."[73]

Connolly knew little about the feud between Agnew and Nelles, but he nonetheless took the communication gap seriously. Signals should be sent hourly, he believed, so that "Ottawa will know what is going on in the minds of London and London will know what is going on in the minds of Ottawa."[74] This idea was excessive, but like all Connolly's recommendations it can be traced to Londonderry. The commodore (D) and his men were upset because they had been ignored by Canadian officials; it was never to happen again. Levelling his only significant criticism against the London office, Connolly told Price constant communication with Londonderry was to be maintained even if it were "through unofficial channels."[75]

Rightly or wrongly, the executive assistant held Naval Service Headquarters, rather than Price, totally responsible for the communication breakdown between Ottawa and the UK. This too was the product of Connolly's trip to Londonderry, as Shorto and Copelin were deeply disturbed that Naval Service Headquarters rarely responded to signals. In specific, the Londonderry officers were tired of having to first secure financial authority from Ottawa before they could fit equipment on Canadian warships. More often than not, valuable opportunities to acquire this gear were missed because Naval Service Headquarters did not provide its blessing, and due to that frustration, the Londonderry officers were willing to resort to "unorthodox" methods whenever they could get away with it. Connolly found this a sad reflection of Naval Service Headquarters, particularly since Shorto had emphasized that "this is not a satisfactory way to do business but it is the only way that he found workable."[76]

Undoubtedly Naval Service Headquarters was at times either slow to or failed to respond to communications from overseas, and for that should be held accountable. But when it came to condemning the Naval Staff for requiring financial authority for alterations, the Londonderry officers had selected the wrong target. This incident stands as another powerful illustration of how Connolly's investigation based conclusions on questionable methodology and incomplete analysis. It also outlines the dangers sharp-end grousers can pose to the chain of command, no matter how benevolent their motives. The Londonderry officers were maligning Naval Service Headquarters with an outdated criticism.

Connolly was the first to admit that he knew "nothing of the financial transactions" behind the modernization of Canadian corvettes in the UK, but as it turns out neither did Simpson or the Londonderry officers. Largely as a result of Shorto's observations, Connolly left Londonderry with the opinion that Naval Service Headquarters needed to "approach the problem of fitting ships with the latest equipment without much consideration of financial obstacles."[77] Back in Ottawa and having followed up on Price's lead, Connolly found a critical memo that reinforced that conclusion: "There is also the world wide, age old problem of who is going to be responsible for giving the final authority. With the Battle of the Atlantic in its present critical state, questions like these should not be allowed to cause even a moment's delay."[78] Once again, Connolly had discovered a problem through the Londonderry officers, and Price had led him to the corroborating evidence. Had Connolly dug deeper, he would have learned that Price was partially responsible for the criticism.

Naval Service Headquarters' side of the story places this particular criticism in a new light. The issue of financial approval had caused the Naval Staff much concern, and a signal was sent to the London office in late January 1943 instructing Agnew

> to prevent delay in carrying out approved Alterations and Additions [A & A's] in HM Canadian Ships whilst in hand for refit or repairs in the United Kingdom ... It is desired that in addition to Alterations and Additions already approved by NSHQ that such other A & A's as have been approved for RN Ships and are considered by Admiralty necessary for RCN Ships be proceeded with as occasion arises without prior reference for approval to Naval Service Headquarters, Ottawa, Naval Service Headquarters being advised by signal of such intention. It is the general policy at NSHQ to follow the Admiralty lead regarding Alterations and Additions.[79]

Realizing the importance of this signal, Agnew instructed Price, who at this time was the executive officer (personnel) in London, to tell the engineering officer at Londonderry that he could "make good ... any A's and A's authorised by the Admiralty."[80] That was not the message relayed to Londonderry, however, as Price mistakenly informed the port that this new policy only applied to RCN ships on loan to the Royal Navy. It was an unfortunate error, and it was not the only one he would make.

The critical report written by Rowland in May 1943 left some staff officers puzzled as to why the Newfoundland command believed that financial authorization to make alterations was still required. After all, fleet-wide approval for the RCN to receive British modifications had been provided with the publication of Naval Order 2587 in February 1943. As a precaution, Price was given specific instructions in May to personally pass a copy of Naval Order 2587 directly to British authorities and facilities in the UK.[81] Exactly what happened to this request once it reached London is uncertain, but there is evidence that Price had, at the very least, forwarded it to the Admiralty.[82] Given that the Londonderry officers were advocating a change to a policy that had, in fact, already occurred, it is obvious that neither Price nor the Admiralty had forwarded a copy of the order to them. Connolly never knew that, so his conclusion on this matter was incomplete. Moreover, while his investigation may have been born from the mutterings of disgruntled reservists, he did not understand that it had also been fathered by a gigantic communication meltdown involving not only Naval Service Headquarters and the senior Canadian naval officer (London)'s office, but Western Approaches and the Admiralty as well.

The executive assistant never bothered to explore the question of where the breakdown in the chain of command occurred. After all, he had his answer even before leaving Ottawa. While Connolly somewhat conveniently chose to ignore that Macdonald sat at the top of that hierarchy, the military ethos taught commanders to take responsibility for the actions of their subordinates. By virtue of running the navy, Nelles and his most senior officers were accountable for everything that happened on their watch. Regardless, Connolly's interpretation was far too parochial and did not take into account that a crucial breakdown within the British chain of command also contributed to the events that had led him to the UK.

As a British operational command, Western Approaches was not supposed to communicate with the top policy makers at Naval Service Headquarters. That responsibility fell to their superiors at the Admiralty. As a result, from the moment Naval Service Headquarters sent their 15 February signal asking whether British yards could take Canadian ships in hand for upgrading, the Admiralty had a good idea that the RCN was having problems. After the Allied Anti-Submarine Survey Board toured Ottawa, Halifax, and St. John's, that understanding was further refined, particularly since reports to the First Sea Lord noted how the state of the Canadian shipyard repair and refit infrastructure "loomed largely in all discussions." Other encounters, such as the Combined Committee on Ship Repair Problems on the East Coast of Canada, brought the First Sea Lord more "fully in the picture," and it was for that reason, along with the fact that the vast majority of British yards were tied up with RN commitments, that the Admiralty supported Naval Service Headquarters' efforts to reorganize and expand its own facilities.[83] Of course, unless the Admiralty shared this information with Western Approaches, there was no way the Londonderry officers could have known about the East Coast refit situation or, more importantly, what the Canadian headquarters was doing to rectify it. As the senior command, the Admiralty was not obligated to pass the details of its dealings with Naval Service Headquarters on to Western Approaches. The fact that Simpson and his officers lacked this type of crucial background information led to serious trouble for Naval Service Headquarters.

Aside from the therapeutic value of unloading their gripes to Connolly, establishing a direct link with the minister's executive assistant gave the Londonderry officers a chance to recommend changes they believed would make the RCN more efficient. However, more often than not, that advice contradicted the messages that the Admiralty had sent to Naval Service Headquarters. While the Admiralty was telling Ottawa that there were no yards for them in the UK, the Londonderry officers had reported to Connolly that the RCN had squandered chances to have HMC ships modernized in their port. That the executive assistant would hold this against the Canadian Naval Staff was unfair.[84] Londonderry was never mentioned when Naval Service Headquarters asked the British for help, making it clear that the Admiralty was also unaware of Conklin's facilities. Moreover, once it learned that this particular yard was underutilized, the Admiralty immediately sent its own ships to Conklin for refitting. These crossed signals had major repercussions. Thanks to the Londonderry officer's meddling, Conklin's yard became a political issue with Connolly, and it would be Naval Service Headquarters that would pay for a miscommunication that was obviously beyond its control.

Because Simpson and his officers were not privy to the Admiralty's dealings with Naval Service Headquarters, false assumptions were passed on to the executive assistant. Certainly, Connolly was not getting the whole story when Simpson shared a copy of a letter sent to Horton, in which it was observed, "I happen to have obtained a Refit Programme issued by NSHQ, Ottawa, dated 30 September, 1943, and am sending you a copy. Paragraph 2 is typical: – 'As the whole question of extended fo's'cle [sic] and fitting Hedgehog in RCN Corvettes is at present under review, it is not possible to state at this moment which ships will be taken for these Alterations and Additions.' A very remarkable admission in the fifth year of war."[85] This was a noteworthy statement but not for the reasons Simpson gave. He did not know that this revised schedule was the product of the Admiralty's 24

August signal announcing that they could not refit RCN ships in the UK. It left an earlier refit schedule in tatters, but despite this setback officers at Naval Service Headquarters returned to the drawing board to produce a new timetable. Nevertheless, the commodore's letter struck Connolly particularly hard and was one of the major pieces of evidence used against Nelles when the executive assistant returned to Ottawa.

There was more. Simpson also believed that the Naval Staff had mismanaged the RCN's war effort because of its fixation on quantity rather than quality, and his observation had convinced Connolly that "fewer ships with better equipment ... would be more effective, and our final record more impressive." That, however, was a far cry from the Admiralty cautioning Nelles not to cut the RCN's new warship construction program because of fears that there were not enough escorts to deal with the current U-boat threat. Indeed, Simpson's comments to Connolly clearly identify that his command in particular, and Western Approaches as a whole, was asking for more than the Canadian navy could possibly deliver. The commodore wanted Naval Service Headquarters to modernize as quickly as possible, yet according to Connolly the Londonderry officers did not "suggest that ships should come off the Atlantic run to have these installations made. They recommend putting in a little at a time."[86] Due to the pressure that the Admiralty had placed on the RCN to keep its ships at sea, this was exactly what Naval Service Headquarters had tried to do. But modernizing in this fashion took time, and the Londonderry officers clearly did not have much patience. It was totally unrealistic to expect the RCN to maintain its current operational commitments while at the same time quickly modernize; yet that was what Simpson expected from Naval Service Headquarters.

Connolly did not have the slightest idea of the considerable pressure being applied on the RCN to keep its ships at sea. He would have been treated to a different interpretation, however, had he spoken to Murray in Halifax. Ideally, the fastest way to modernize was to take all the ships requiring upgrading off operations and send them to the shipyards. Of course, the refit situation rendered that option moot, so Murray instead believed that "the best that can be done is to organise that a whole group comes out of operation together to have these essential A & A's done."[87] Western Approaches was not impressed. The RCN had to stay on the North Atlantic, and they said as much to Murray. During "conversation with COS [chief of staff] to CinC WA [commander in chief, Western Approaches], he emphasised that strength of C Groups was not to be unduly impaired and 6 effective seagoing [ships] to remain in each group."[88] That the British were placing such demands on his escort forces annoyed Murray, and he was not the only one who felt that way.

At the same time that Connolly was planning his investigation, the Naval Staff was trying to deal with the Admiralty's 24 August signal. News that there were no yards in the UK hit Naval Service Headquarters hard, particularly since "the shortage of labour in Maritime yards still exists, and there is little hope at the present time of any relief." Nor was that the only problem associated with the refit situation that remained unresolved, but to make matters worse, Ottawa received word from the Admiralty indicating that more ships were needed at sea to confront an anticipated U-boat offensive in September.[89] This, in effect, put Naval Service Headquarters' new modernization plans on hold, and the reasons for delay were then fully explained to Macdonald at the 16 September Naval Board meeting:

> Naval Staff was of the opinion that the next three months constitute a critical stage in the Battle of the Atlantic, and therefore considered that no more Corvettes should be taken in hand for prolonged alterations and additions for the time being; however, it was recommended that arrangements to secure the necessary equipment should be proceeded with, and every effort should be made now to secure an agreement with the appropriate authorities for modernisation to be undertaken in USA, when the trend of U-boat warfare is assessed as favourable for this practice to be resumed.[90]

Not everyone at Naval Service Headquarters agreed with that perspective, and some believed that the RCN should finally stand up to the Admiralty and take a large number of ships off operations for modernization. In light of the severity of the refit situation in Canada, and the fact that they had not yet approached the Americans, it is uncertain where these officers expected to find the extra yards for modernization. Nonetheless their frustration with the Royal Navy was understandable, as both the Admiralty and Western Approaches were pressuring the RCN to keep their ships at sea. The difference between these two organizations was that the latter also expected the Canadians to modernize while doing so. Other contradictions followed, and the poor flow of information between the Admiralty and Western Approaches came back to haunt Naval Service Headquarters in a number of cases.

Seeing his surroundings from the perspective of an operational commander, Simpson never considered that his boss at Western Approaches might not be privy to the Admiralty's communiqués with Naval Service Headquarters. Instead he informed Connolly that the fault rested with the Canadian Naval Staff, which needed to foster "better co-operation between Londonderry – Halifax – St. John's."[91] Such a conclusion was not entirely fair, since Simpson was partially responsible for the mess that he was now criticizing. Perhaps realizing that it was a mistake not to allow the RCN their own commander (D) in Londonderry, Simpson believed that it would suffice to make Copelin his *de facto* Canadian chief of staff. He was wrong. Londonderry was the Royal Navy's jurisdiction, and it was unreasonable for the commodore (D) to give Copelin a regular staff position and expect it to carry the same weight as an operational appointment sanctioned by Naval Service Headquarters. This alone denied both Simpson and the Canadians at Londonderry a direct outlet to the Canadian chain of command. Moreover, Simpson's criticism of the Naval Staff is difficult to accept, given that the Naval Staff was trying to improve communications with both the Admiralty and Western Approaches. Earlier in the year Macdonald was asked for two teletype circuits – one that linked the Admiralty directly to Naval Service Headquarters and another that did the same for the Western Approaches and Halifax commands – because, in the words of the navy, "there was an urgent necessity for improving communications between the United Kingdom and Canada."[92] Unfortunately, this took time, and it was not until 8 May 1943 that Macdonald asked Cabinet to approve the money for this network. The Naval Staff was nevertheless on the right track, as shown by Rear Admiral Murray's June 1943 decision to make personal contact with his counterparts in Western Approaches. This gave Horton a much better understanding of the RCN's equipment deficiency.

Prepared to ambush Murray on the question of the RCN's technical backwardness, Horton and his officers were stunned when the Canadian operational commander not only fired back but turned some of the blame onto the British. "I had to tell them," Murray recorded in a postwar interview, "that, it was just because we didn't have any equipment – the equipment was made and tried out in England, and soon as it was found to be useful, put into the British ships, and nobody thought of sending any out to us in Canada to put in our ships."[93] Although outside Horton's bailiwick – the manufacture and distribution of equipment was the Admiralty's responsibility – that observation was not lost on him. For the first time, Horton had to consider the possibility that the Admiralty rather than Naval Service Headquarters was the obstacle blocking the RCN's modernization. The encounter had a considerable impact on Horton, as only six days after Murray had returned to Halifax, a report from the UK observed how "this matter [equipment] again came to a head when Rear Admiral Murray, RCN (C in C CNA) recently visited this country. It is understood that C in C WA [Horton] appreciates the urgency of this matter and approached the Assistant Controller, Bath."[94]

Horton's personally approaching the controller was significant and probably explains the incredible flood of activity regarding the RCN's modernization at the Royal Navy's research laboratories at Bath.[95] In the days that followed, additional pressure was applied to get the controller to send equipment, plans, and prototypes to Canada. To do so, Western Approaches officials even asked Price to go to Bath to "discuss the policy regarding A & A's for HMC Ships in the United Kingdom." Nor was that all. Providing perhaps the strongest evidence that Horton was troubled by the sudden discovery of the apparent indifference of the Admiralty toward the RCN's plight, it was further suggested that Price's staff officer (material) also make a special trip to Bath so he could develop "direct personal contacts with Admiralty officials there with the view to expediting the supply to Canada of technical data."[96]

Horton's efforts with the Admiralty underscore that he was trying to help the RCN. Moreover, unlike his subordinates in Londonderry, he was not nearly so critical of Naval Service Headquarters when meeting Connolly. Having left Liverpool for London to attend First Sea Lord Dudley Pound's funeral on 26 October, Horton was able to give the executive assistant almost two full hours of his time. Connolly was extremely grateful, since talking to the man who was directing the Royal Navy's war against the U-boats represented the pinnacle of his investigation. At first Horton's views were reminiscent of the ones Connolly had heard in Londonderry. Western Approaches appreciated having the RCN as an ally, but there was little doubt the inability of the Canadians to sink U-boats was the product of inadequate equipment.[97] Unlike Simpson, however, Horton knew all too well that modernizing an escort fleet was not easy, telling Connolly that he had had to compete with other Royal Navy fleets and constantly battle the Admiralty for resources. So much so that he had succeeded in upgrading the Royal Navy's escort fleet only by using the "Casablanca statement" to remind the Admiralty that winning the Battle of the Atlantic was a top priority with the prime minister.

Horton offered few complaints about how the Canadian Naval Staff was running their war effort. Probably the product of his encounter with Murray, the only observation that came close to a criticism was his belief that Ottawa was not doing enough to get the Admiralty to release its grip on equipment. Perhaps he was right. Relying on signals as well as Price's London office to persuade the Admiralty to part with equipment was unlikely to have the same impact as a personal visit from high-ranking staff officials. Certainly, Connolly found that the Admiralty was more co-operative after Horton had arranged a meeting for him with British parliamentary undersecretaries as well as the controller at Bath. Eluding Connolly was that Horton and Naval Service Headquarters were on the same side when it came to the "battle for equipment." Unlike Simpson and his officers, Horton neither accused Naval Service Headquarters of incompetence nor was overly critical of their actions, yet somehow the executive assistant still managed to draw the conclusion that the commander in chief Western Approaches' views "coincided exactly with those of Commodore 'D.'"[98] And that further suggests Connolly had a tendency to overlook evidence that contradicted what was by now a firm and unflattering interpretation of the Naval Staff.

Based on the observations from his own network of informants, the executive assistant went over to the UK with the preconceived notion that the navy's top brass had hidden a debilitating equipment deficiency from the minister. The Londonderry officers' confirmation of these suspicions had a remarkable impact; Connolly vented his frustration in his diary, recording that the minister should "fire all the Senior authorities put [Captains] Grant + Mainguy at the top. They only have been through the rough and tumble of this war."[99] While both those officers would get their chance to assume the chief of the naval staff mantle in the postwar period, Connolly's idea was impractical and he knew it. Captain Harold Grant and Rollo Mainguy were far too junior, and the executive assistant was not about to recommend a course of action that would turn the equipment deficiency into a very public affair. When he returned to Ottawa on 4 November, therefore, Connolly kept his anger to himself and instead told Macdonald, "the importance of the problem was urged upon me so often and by so many people that I feel it cannot be ignored. I do not believe I have exaggerated the problem in particular … When our ships lack efficiency, our men lose confidence. The situation is bad for morale. It is also bad advertising for the Service."[100] This last observation cut to the heart of the matter. While Connolly developed a genuine desire to do something about equipment, he was first and foremost a bureaucrat who saw that it would be the navy's senior leadership, rather than Macdonald, who would end up paying for this "bad advertising."

Connolly may not have "exaggerated the problem" but his conclusions to the minister were certainly based on information from men who had done so. Their use of hyperbole was an effective means to get Macdonald's attention, but such tactics only succeeded in turning an operational deficiency into an artificial political crisis. Connolly was worried. The public was not going to be happy when they learned that their fathers, sons, and brothers were being sent to sea in dangerously underequipped ships. As in the early days of the MacLean affair, the executive assistant believed that Macdonald was facing another potential scandal. Based on what Connolly had learned in Londonderry, however, this "equipment crisis" had the potential to cost Macdonald his Cabinet position. The only crisis here was a political one, as the burden of protecting Macdonald's Cabinet position fell on Connolly's shoulders. To help Macdonald, the executive assistant would hold Nelles and his officers responsible for all the problems that had been uncovered in Londonderry and London.

While Nelles and his staff had certainly made mistakes throughout the course of the war, Connolly's charges of incompetence were excessive and biased, consciously formulated on partial information, and even more consciously misleading because they failed to reflect opinions such as those put forward by Horton. Never once did Connolly try to investigate the Naval Staff's position, and all he would have had to do was look at what the top brass had done during the month he was in the UK. Of course, he probably would not have liked what he uncovered, as the Naval Staff's efforts throughout the month of October provide further evidence that it was the minister who was not listening. At the same time Connolly was preparing a briefing on his overseas investigation, the top brass was about to make another appeal to the minister in the hope that Macdonald would finally take an interest in a worsening refit situation.

On 12 October, Commodore G.M. Hibbard submitted a report to headquarters regarding the condition of the RCN's refit facilities when he assumed his newly created appointment as the commodore superintendent in Halifax. Beginning with a self-congratulatory tone, Hibbard noted the progress that had been made since Naval Service Headquarters reaffirmed its decision to further commit to a fleet-wide modernization program in February 1943. Certainly the fact that every RCN corvette had a type 271 or American-built RXU radar set, and that most were equipped with gyroscopic compasses as well as 123D asdic, was encouraging. This was the good news; the other side of his score sheet was not nearly so promising. Out of seventy-two corvettes, only seventeen had had other important modifications, such as the extended fo'c'sles and improved bridge design, which were also required for the fitting of hedgehog. This type of extensive work required considerable time at a shipyard, and for Hibbard that aspect of the RCN's modernization irrevocably led right back to the refit situation.

When it came to the refit situation, Hibbard did not mince his words. He was pleased that another seventeen corvettes were in the process of having extended fo'c'sles and improved bridge modifications completed, and that Naval Service Headquarters had just secured an American promise to immediately do the same for four other corvettes. Having also secured one yard in both the Maritimes and the West Coast meant that Naval Service Headquarters was facing a situation where only twenty-seven corvettes would need to be allotted to the shipyards by the end of the year.[101] Given the state of the RCN's modernization in January 1943, that was a remarkable achievement, but according to Hibbard it was not nearly enough. The problem was that in order to meet its operational commitments the fleet was still expanding, and that was going to further tax a ship repair organization that was already on the brink of collapse. On average, nine ships per month had been taken in hand for various types of refits throughout 1943, but as more ships rolled off the slips, Hibbard was faced with the troubling reality that Canadian yards would now have to handle at least fourteen ships per month. It was a gloomy prediction, and to modernize the remainder of the fleet while at the same time coping with new demands, Hibbard rendered the opinion that "to obtain the increase of from 9 to 14 ships per month, it appears necessary either to increase present facilities, increase production of present facilities, reduce the length of refits or to refit elsewhere, i.e. the UK, USA., Bermuda or on the West Coast."[102]

These were more or less the same ideas that had been presented to the minister three months earlier, but now the Naval Staff was a little wiser. The best it had achieved with foreign yards was an American promise to help where possible. While encouraging, that was not enough, and left Naval Service Headquarters wanting to do what it had recommended in July and was preparing to tell Macdonald yet again, to conduct "a review of the ship repair facilities in Canada ... with a view to expanding yards with all-year facilities."[103] It was frustrating that Macdonald had done so little to fight the RCN's battles with other government departments involved in the refit situation. The Naval Staff watched helplessly as these yards complained how National Selection Service was continually failing to provide the required 10 percent monthly increase in workers, meaning that the manpower situation was "steadily worsening." Nor did the Naval Staff consider it sufficient when the Deputy Minister Gordon Mills tried to make up for Macdonald's apparent lack of interest by going directly to the Department of Labour in the hope that it would understand the navy's predicament.[104] Given the extent of the proposed expansion plan, the Naval Staff still believed that the minister was the only one with the necessary clout to make a difference. This was true. But by this time, Connolly had returned from overseas, and the Naval Staff would have to defend its actions in the face of the executive assistant's charges of negligence and neglect.

No other network had a greater impact on Connolly's perception of the RCN's top brass than the officers in Londonderry. Forewarned of the executive assistant's arrival, Simpson and his hand-picked team of Canadian, American, and British officers were prepared to pass their particular versions of the RCN's technical backwardness directly to the minister's aide. This interpretation did not paint a particularly flattering picture of Naval Service Headquarters, and it was a view Connolly accepted without question. The viewpoint of the sharp-end grouser had now entered the political arena. However, the game of politics had a different set of rules, which suggests that these deficiencies could come back to haunt the minister. Based on the Londonderry officers' meddling, and lacking the balance of the Naval Staff's side of the story, Connolly concluded that the only explanation for why Macdonald did not know about the discontent over equipment was because his advisors had purposely covered it up. Connolly was determined to protect his political master, and therefore he set his sights firmly on Nelles and the Naval Staff.

7
Covering Up the Conspiracy

Connolly returned to Ottawa spoiling for a fight. Based on what he learned in Londonderry, he did not expect the Naval Staff to put up much resistance. He was wrong. When push came to shove, Nelles and the officers loyal to him went on the offensive, counter-charging that it was the minister who was guilty of letting the navy down. This led to a bitter confrontation that almost saw the minister resign. Seeing conspiracy in every corner at Naval Service Headquarters, however, the executive assistant refused to let his chief quit to a bunch of career officers whose so-called "cover up" extended well beyond the battle for equipment. Accordingly, Connolly became the conduit for all the elitist elements that had been undermining Nelles' authority. Animosities that had been brewing below the surface – whether it was MacLean and his followers, the Londonderry officers, Connolly's own reserve network, or even Jones and his men – blew to the surface in a volcanic climax that tore Naval Service Headquarters apart. This confrontation offers final proof that Connolly – and not Macdonald – had the greatest impact on Nelles' fate.[1] Moreover, the chief of the naval staff's dismissal was politically motivated and designed both to protect the minister from any potential public fallout and to appease discontented factions within the navy.

It took Connolly two full days to explain all his findings to Macdonald. The minister was a little overwhelmed. The last word he had received from his executive assistant was an upbeat letter from Newfoundland in early October. Now, he was listening to awful stories of administrative incompetence and inept leadership. At first he did not know what to make of Connolly's analysis and was left asking a troublesome question: "Horton says keep up equipment, why does he have to urge us?"[2] It was not until the third day, 10 November, that Macdonald decided on a course of action. Setting the tone for the rest of the month, he tried to put the Naval Staff on the defensive by giving Nelles a copy of the letter Simpson had sent to Horton. Blasting the Canadian Naval Staff and its mishandling of the RCN's modernization made this a sensational document that was bound to provoke a response.[3] It also served as a warning that Macdonald was suspicious of them, especially as particular care was taken to conceal Simpson and Horton's identities under the veil of "two very responsible officers in the RN."[4] With Connolly now firmly at the helm of the Londonderry officers' modernization cause, this verbal torpedo from overseas hit with such force that it led to a firestorm of activity in the halls of Naval Service Headquarters.

The Naval Staff had finally come in direct contact with the modernization networks that had been circumventing it over the past two years. These complainers had little idea of what Naval Service Headquarters was up against in its collective effort to modernize, and that was evident when Nelles passed Simpson's letter on to his staff officers. They were not amused. With no way of knowing that he was attacking a man of Simpson's rank and stature, one staff officer even went as far as to claim, "the man is mad."[5] Such emotionalism was understandable. Simpson's account was scandalous. The simplicity of his argument makes clear that he was passing judgment on a situation at a headquarters he knew little about. Filled with factual errors as the letter was, the Naval Staff had a hard time swallowing Simpson's conclusion that it was Naval Service Headquarters that did not understand the RCN's modernization problem. Fortunately for the commodore (D) and his network, the Naval Staff assumed that this initial salvo had come from the Admiralty.

After outlining that the Royal Navy was well versed with the Maritime shipyard crisis and its associated modernization deficiency, these staff officers were stunned that the British had attacked them by telling their naval minister that "the modernisation of Canadian Corvettes is an extremely simple matter." Minimizing the extreme complexities of the RCN's refit and repair situation in this fashion was an affront and could not go unanswered. "No one is more grateful than Canada for what they [the British] have done," wrote a confused director of operations, Commander G.F. Griffiths, but "I wonder if this man appreciates what Canada has been trying to do. I wonder whether he knows Canada and some of our problems."[6] Others shared his sense of bewilderment. The RCN had kept its escorts at sea so that the Royal Navy could "complete their own ships first," and it was for that reason the chief of naval engineering and construction, Rear Admiral Stephens, wrote,

> the Admiralty officials who criticise appear to be completely unaware of the difficulties and conditions in this country ... In connection with the quotation obtained from a Refit Programme issued by NSHQ Ottawa dated 30th September, 1943, wherein it is stressed "As the whole question of extended fo'c'sle and fitting Hedgehog in RCN Corvettes is at present under review, it is not possible to state at the moment which ships will be taken for these alterations and additions." To make such a remark ... shows a complete misunderstanding of the situation and the reasons for such a review. This review was entirely due to ... [the] signal from the Admiralty (240128A), which upset all our plans and forced us into establishing a new [refit] policy ... It would appear obvious that if we are to avoid such criticisms we shall have to take a stronger attitude regarding refits and carrying out of modifications, and take our ships off the ocean ... regardless of operational commitments and leave the Admiralty to find the balance of the ships.[7]

At first glance, Stephens had good reason for being a little sore at his Royal Navy counterparts. From his perspective, the Admiralty had upgraded at Canada's expense, and reproaching Naval Service Headquarters for botching the RCN's modernization was an odd way to repay that favour. Of course, without knowing that Simpson and his network were the true accusers, it was impossible for Stephens and the Naval Staff to mount a proper counter-offensive against the charges. Worse still, the Londonderry officers were not the only troublemakers lurking in the shadows and stirring up trouble at Naval Service Headquarters.

After helping Connolly in St. John's, Rear Admiral Jones was aware that this investigation could spell trouble for Nelles, and that was good news for a man who wanted to become the next chief of the naval staff. All he had to do was bide his time until Connolly returned from overseas. It was worth the wait, as the results of that trip turned out better than Jones could have hoped. Perhaps it should not be surprising that his was the lone voice that did not respond with anger when Simpson's letter went the rounds at Naval Service Headquarters. "I ... do not consider it damaging criticism of our whole repair organization," Jones told Nelles on 12 November, "rather, I interpret it as constructive criticism, containing suggestions for improving."[8] Better yet, in a comment that seemed well suited for ministerial consumption, Jones added, "Until our ships are fully modernised, no responsible Officer should be satisfied with the present state of affairs."[9] This was typical of Jones' behaviour throughout the confrontation. Never overtly siding with Macdonald, he kept his distance from the chief of the naval staff while secretly passing documents to Connolly that strengthened the minister's case.[10]

Jones' support was important, since the executive assistant was disappointed that Simpson's letter did not have the desired effect. Instead of falling on its sword as he had expected, the Naval Staff was swinging a blade wildly in all directions, searching to cut the strings that linked the minister to his anonymous puppet masters. Things were quickly getting out of control, and as far as the chief of the naval staff was concerned, it was time to get to the bottom of the charges. The easiest way to do that would have been for Nelles to go to the minister's office and sort these issues out in person. This would have only been possible, however, had Macdonald and Nelles enjoyed the type of open and professional relationship that all ministers and chiefs should share.[11] Whether it was Jones and his men or Connolly's reserve informants, Macdonald had always had a predilection for following advice from outsiders who were undermining Nelles' authority. It is clear that the lines of communication between the navy's top civilian and military leaders were never that strong. Now, thanks to the influence of the Londonderry officers and reserve networks, Connolly had built a wall around Macdonald and become the gatekeeper who controlled all information that crossed into the citadel of the minister's office. By doing so, Connolly further contributed to what was growing into a massive breakdown in the civil-military dialectic as – except for Jones and his men – Naval Service Headquarters was splitting into two fortified camps with the chief of the naval staff and his loyalists on the one side and the minister on the other. But even in these early stages, Nelles came to suspect that it was Connolly who was the true general behind the minister's campaign. What Nelles did not know was that, thanks to the groups undermining his authority, he had been mortally wounded long before this fight with the minister.

The fact that these accusations had surfaced so soon after the executive assistant's return was not lost on Nelles, and in an attempt to get everything out in the open, he invited Connolly to brief the Naval Staff at its 15 November meeting. This put the executive assistant on the spot, but he was confident that the top brass would not be able to counter the information that the Londonderry officers had given him. Once the staff knew that he had "discovered" the RCN's dark secret, Connolly expected them to panic. The frenzy never materialized. Instead, the RCN's chief engineer said out loud what the entire staff was thinking, which was "that the majority of points brought out by Mr. Connolly were known at Naval Service Headquarters and action had been already taken to remedy them."[12] Nothing Connolly reported came as a surprise to the top brass, and the executive assistant was left wondering why they would freely admit that there was a problem, when the minister obviously knew nothing about it.

Blinded by loyalty, Connolly never grasped that his boss might have ignored advice as well as pleas for help from the navy's senior leaders. Nor did he stop to think that the complaints he had heard in Londonderry were outdated and that the Naval Staff had devised various solutions to overcome the Canadian refit and repair situation. Where the top brass offered explanations, Connolly only saw collusion. Building a case to prove a grand "conspiracy" on the part of the Naval Staff to hide the navy's "skeletons" from Macdonald was clearly the best way to stomp out resistance and, thanks to Price, he had a good idea which closets at the headquarters might contain the bones of the RCN's so-called defunct modernization program. Somewhere at Naval Service Headquarters there were critical memos on the equipment situation, and before looking for them, Connolly set the Naval Staff up by advising the minister that "apparently it is a matter of common knowledge at N.S.H.Q. I would think that it might be productive of some results to get a statement in writing as to whether or not reports on the bad situation generally as regards repairs was ever made here."[13] Macdonald did just that, and, somewhat ironically, Naval Service Headquarters lost his request.[14] That, according to Connolly, illustrated his point; but to truly expose the Naval Staff's deceit, he then pored through hundreds of files until he unearthed two of the critical reports. As far as the executive assistant was concerned, these discoveries proved the conspiracy. Indicating that Naval Service Headquarters had known that the fleet was unhappy with its equipment as early as May 1943, Connolly took direct aim at the Naval Staff by sending the following message to the minister: "THESE REPORTS WERE

NOT BROUGHT TO YOUR ATTENTION TO MY KNOWLEDGE. HAD THEY BEEN THOROUGHLY CONSIDERED AND THE GOVERNMENT'S SUPPORT ENLISTED IN JUNE, MANY FURTHER STEPS MIGHT HAVE BEEN TAKEN."[15] With this evidence in hand, Connolly began to plan the minister's next move. His strategy was simple: it was time to pull out the big guns and flatly charge the so-called conspirators with dereliction of duty.

Five days of hard work produced a lengthy fourteen-page indictment, and on 20 November it was ready for presentation to the Naval Staff. With the exception of his signature at the bottom of the page and some minor editorial changes, Macdonald had little to do with this document. The Naval Staff had suspected that there was a puppet master working behind the scenes influencing the minister, and Connolly's rough drafts and personal notes make clear that they were right.[16] On this particular issue, it was the executive assistant who was calling the shots. Of course, he had his own set of strings that led back to Londonderry, and that was also reflected in this new set of allegations.[17]

While he never picked up on the irony, the executive assistant was experiencing some of the same problems that the Naval Board had had over the previous two years in getting Macdonald to understand the nuances of the RCN's modernization. He had to go back and explain the critical reports in greater detail before the minister finally grasped why they were so significant to their case. Lacking a direct means to communicate with his networks, Connolly was also forced to admit that he could not always help the minister with his comprehension "unless I could see Conklin or some other officers in Londonderry, who gave me the information which I supplied to you."[18] And so, while Macdonald's lack of knowledge made it more expedient for the executive assistant to draft the memo to the Naval Staff, Connolly had to do so without his own experts, leading to some creative criticisms of the navy's top brass.

Aside from the "damning evidence" against the Naval Staff, the most important aspect of this letter was the eight concluding criticisms. For the most part, these too, were Connolly's handiwork. Forming the core case against Naval Service Headquarters, these allegations are worth a closer examination. First, the Naval Staff was held responsible for not giving the critical reports the attention they deserved. Next, the minister argued that his August request for information on modernization had not been "dealt with vigorously and promptly"; that rolled into the third and forth points about how the Naval Staff lacked "energy and capacity," explaining why the "failure to secure equipment is to be laid at the doors of NSHQ." Fifth, he conveyed his disappointment that the situation was discovered "from other sources entirely," an obscure reference to both the Londonderry officers and Connolly's own reserve network. His sixth and seventh items found that the Naval Staff was mainly impressed with the size of the navy and that the escort fleet should have been its first priority. And finally, in a comment specifically directed at Nelles,

The war of words in Ottawa was nothing like the real life battles fought at sea. A dramatic photograph taken on 6 March 1944 captures the boarding party from HMCS *Chilliwack* alongside the battle-scarred U-744. The Canadian group C-2 hunted this U-boat for over thirty-two hours, bringing praise from the Commander-in-Chief Western Approaches, Max Horton. DHH, 81/520/1000, BOX 155, FILE 15

it was argued that the greatest failure was that the Naval Staff had not sought a political solution.[19] This seemed like sound logic, and for Connolly it represented the crux of the case against the navy's top brass. But with those criticisms, the skirmishes were over; these allegations triggered the executive assistant's own private little war with the Naval Staff.

Indicating that he was every bit the chair-borne warrior, Connolly did not wait for a response before launching another powerful volley of paperwork. He had finally found the critical report written by Ken Adams – as well as ten other equipment-related documents – and, realizing its potential, he told Macdonald that it "undoubtedly bears out everything that was said by Commodore 'D' and by

Horton." That, of course, should not have come as a surprise, since Adams had been influenced by Strange who, in turn, had just got all his information from Simpson. Nevertheless, it was not only the content that troubled Connolly. He further charged: "In spite of the very strong statements made, apparently memos were passed with abandon, without much action being taken. The situation according to this file at N.S.H.Q. is that nothing can be done."[20] Such ammunition was too powerful to hold in reserve. While the Naval Staff was busy dealing with the main offensive of the minister's eight allegations, Connolly wanted to use the critical memos in a flanking motion to strike at what he considered its soft underbelly. Accordingly, Macdonald sent copies of these documents to Nelles with a covering letter that read, "A perusal of the file will indicate that explanations as to the equipment situation have been made but I see no evidence of any strong action to improve that situation. Again I must point out that after this at least third repetition of the same complaint which I consider to be of a major character, the matter was not referred to me ... I must be furnished immediately with an explanation of this failure."[21]

The barrage clearly hit its mark, as the chief of the naval staff was forced to admit that he had never even heard of Adams' report "until you drew my attention to it this afternoon." This allowed the minister to make yet another request for the Naval Staff to produce "reports made by officials of N.S.H.Q. after visits to the United Kingdom and which bear upon the equipment programme."[22] Nelles promised to do so, but the executive assistant was not optimistic. These requests still served a purpose. Each time the Naval Staff failed to deliver, Connolly's conspiracy theory gained credibility.

Although he had still not scored a direct hit below the waterline, there were signs that Connolly's tactics were chipping away at the armour of the top brass. Certainly, Nelles' sudden decision to make Adams the director of warfare and training – a key position in any future battle for modernization – was encouraging. So, too, was the news that the assistant chief of the naval staff, Captain W.B. Creery, and the commodore superintendent Halifax, Commodore Hibbard, were both going on separate trips to the UK to investigate the modernization question on Nelles' behalf. Such moves, according to the executive assistant, were signs of panic, indicating that the Creery and Hibbard trips were nothing more than "white washing missions."[23]

Believing that the Naval Staff was beating a fast retreat, Connolly took time to thank the men who had first brought the modernization question to his attention. Putting their roles into perspective, he wrote to the most influential member of his reserve informants, Louis Audette, advising him that it could be said "to your friends that if I cannot talk to you, I certainly can and have talked for you."[24] Passing word of what was transpiring in Ottawa on to his reserve network was important. These select few Canadian commanding officers had, in Connolly's view, risked much to orchestrate their grassroots revolt, and it was time to reward them. His motives at this point were purely benevolent, wanting nothing more than to right the wrongs perpetrated on the seagoing element by an uncaring and belligerent headquarters. This also applied to the Londonderry officers, as Connolly scribbled a note to Shorto acknowledging that "the seed with which you planted in my mind, I, in turn, have planted in ground which promises to be fertile."[25] That original acorn of information had sprouted deep roots, and Connolly wanted it to blossom, telling Simpson to "write me as unofficially and as confidentially as you wish."[26] Put another way, the executive assistant was institutionalizing a new and unofficial chain of command whereby he would become the medium between these networks and the minister.

To cement that new relationship, the executive assistant gave Simpson advanced warning that Creery and Hibbard were being dispatched to the UK, and that "they will not know of this letter, but I know they will get the same frank statements as I was given. I hope they can see the necessary people including Conklin and Pigott."[27] Nor did his warnings stop there, as Shorto and Conklin also got letters. And so in the same way that Strange had prepared the Londonderry officers for Connolly's visit, the executive assistant, in turn, tipped them off about Creery and Hibbard. He had good reason to do so. While confident in what he had done since his return, the last thing Connolly needed was for the Londonderry officers to let their "natural service reserve" take over. A sudden case of cold feet could lead to disaster, as it would not help Connolly's case if Creery and Hibbard did not get the same treatment he had received. With the exception of Simpson and Shorto, the remaining men were lieutenants, or at most lieutenant commanders, who might not feel comfortable telling a Canadian commodore and captain the whole truth as they saw it. And it was for that reason Connolly wrote to the more junior officers in an attempt to fortify their courage. "The results of my visit are beginning to make themselves apparent," he told Conklin, which was followed by a veiled plea that "shortly, you will have visits from one perhaps two R.C.N. officers, and I know that you will ... confirm to them the information which you gave me."[28] Once Connolly received copies of Nelles' responses to the minister's allegations, the need for the Londonderry officers to hold their ground became even more critical.

Between 27 November and 5 December, Macdonald travelled to Baltimore, where he inspected the American Naval yard that was refitting HMCS *Dunvegan* and *Antigonish*, and then continued on to Washington, DC.[29] This trip gave him a better understanding of how the Americans were assisting with the RCN's modernization, but it also allowed Nelles and his officers valuable time to plan their own offensive. Just before Macdonald had left, the chief of the naval staff delivered various Board and Staff members' commentaries on the allegations, which were soon followed by his own measured analysis. Immediately on the minister's return from the United States, Nelles hit again with a second broadside consisting of his reply to

Simpson's memo as well as his own set of counter-charges. All these memos packed a powerful punch in a calculated and brilliant barrage that left the minister dazed.

It was obvious to the chief of the naval staff and his officers that the central issue surrounding Macdonald's allegations was the question of blame. He, or more precisely Connolly, wanted the Naval Staff to accept sole responsibility for the state of equipment within the fleet, and that was something Nelles was unprepared to do. No longer willing to mince words, the chief of the naval staff cut through the minister's political double-talk. "My first comment on your paper handed to me on the 20th November," he boldly told Macdonald, "is that it amounts to a very serious charge of *neglect* against almost every Naval Officer at Naval Service Headquarters ... [and] the first part of your paper is an attack on the *efficiency* of the Staff."[30] Nelles was right. The minister was not so much interested in an open dialogue over the causes of the equipment situation, but rather in identifying the naval officers who were responsible for it. But while the chief of the naval staff was willing to name names, the people on his list wore the robes of state instead of uniforms. His goal, therefore, was to re-educate the minister about the RCN's refit and repair problems, and by the end of the lesson there was little doubt it was not the Naval Staff that deserved detention.

History was the first subject on Nelles' curriculum. A chronicle of the fleet's development over a thirty-year period was not just for the minister's edification, although he did manage to explain how modernization was a "continual battle" dating back to the navy's formation. Rather, it was a shrewd tactic that placed the RCN's equipment situation into a larger political perspective. Pre-war governments had not only been tight-fisted with the navy's funding, Nelles argued, but they also failed to build the necessary infrastructure to develop, produce, and then fit new naval equipment on RCN warships. At that time, he had warned various politicians how critical shipyards would be in a time of crisis or war. Nelles, realizing that such infrastructure took time to build, was a chief advocate for a vibrant Canadian shipbuilding industry and technical sector throughout the 1930s, and perhaps because of that he was angry about being charged with the pre-war sins of his short-sighted political masters. Without the ability to fix their own ships, the RCN had little choice but to ask its allies for help; the creation of that infrastructure was the only way the refit and repair crisis could have been avoided. For that reason, Nelles spelled out why he had "with intent, stressed shipbuilding thus far, but only in a very broad way, because it is the thing that has been our initial struggle back to 1910."[31]

Nelles was not going to take the rap for a Liberal government that had been caught off guard by war, nor was he willing to let some anonymous source (Simpson) lecture Naval Service Headquarters on the RCN's modernization. Providing perhaps the best summary of the problems the navy faced in its attempt to modernize, the chief of the naval staff finally responded to Simpson's memo by telling Macdonald,

> The attached paper is a remarkable document from [anonymous] to [anonymous] written [by] [anonymous] ... If there is anything *constructive* to be obtained from the paper it will be used to full advantage. [But] I take very definite issue with the statement "The modernisation of Canadian corvettes is an extremely simple matter." It would be if we had the equipment, dockyards, repair bases, private firms with drawing and technical staffs and experienced shipyard workers such as obtain in a shipbuilding country like the UK. Compared with UK's "simple operation" our modernisation is literally "sweat and tears" with everybody pushing the battle to the utmost.[32]

This represented one of the few times that the chief of the naval staff got a chance to refute his true accusers, and his response identified exactly how weak their case was. As Nelles would once again explain to Macdonald, there were two elements to the fleet's technical backwardness. The first was the question of supply, production, and procurement of the equipment, while the second involved the issue of installation. Simpson and his officers did not understand the latter factor, and that was reflected in their somewhat simplistic criticisms of Naval Service Headquarters. The repair facilities and supporting industry required to keep the RCN up to date had always been too small and could never maintain a service that was in the process of a fifty-fold expansion. But the overseas officers never comprehended the scope of the refit and repair crisis or how it slowed the process of getting newer equipment on Canadian ships. Thanks to their interference and hyperbole, however, modernization had become a political football, and Nelles was facing a hostile minister who was trying to score a victory over a staff that he believed had fumbled the ball.

Given the influence that these informants had had on Connolly, there was little chance of avoiding a confrontation between Macdonald and the Naval Staff. The Londonderry officers' interpretation had made the executive assistant angry, and he in turn had worked the minister into a frenzy with notions of hidden agendas and conspiracies to cover up incompetence. Nelles clearly sensed that the minister was out for blood, but he was not going to let the Naval Staff be circled like prey. Prior to the confrontation, Nelles had maintained that the "repair problem" was an unfortunate product of circumstance. Now that Macdonald was playing the "blame game," he left little doubt that it was the minister's pre-war predecessors who deserved the failing grade for not preparing the navy or country for war. Ironically, under different circumstances the minister probably would have agreed, particularly since – as the former premier of Nova Scotia – he was a powerful champion of the East Coast shipyard industry. Nonetheless, the closer Nelles' history got to the current confrontation, the more attention was paid to Macdonald's performance as naval minister.

Nelles' responses suggested that Macdonald had been a poor and inattentive student of naval affairs. In fact, the chief of the naval staff even handed his boss a tardy slip for not asking questions at an earlier date. Referring to his response to the minister's original request for information, Nelles was unhappy that "at no time from the 1st September to the 20th November, (2 months 20 days) did you intimate that the table given to you on the 1st September did not contain *all* the information you wanted."[33] The criticisms had come late in the day, and Nelles could not understand why Macdonald had not simply sought clarification back in September. The chief of the naval staff could not have known that the minister was dissatisfied as well as suspicious of the entire equipment situation. Moreover, without the knowledge that Macdonald was being swayed by outside influences, Nelles was not in a position to counter any exaggerated claims. As far as Nelles was concerned, Macdonald was involved with Naval Service Headquarters' attempts to combat the refit and repair situation and he therefore could not understand the minister's "hesitancy in asking for further information on Service matters when we meet six days out of seven every week to discuss just such things."[34]

There were a plethora of examples where Macdonald had been told about the RCN's technical backwardness, and that was not lost on the chief of the naval staff, who certainly used them to his advantage. Covering activities ranging from the reorganization at Naval Service Headquarters to the appointment of the commodore superintendent in Halifax, Nelles further reminded the minister how the Naval Board had approved various measures over the past year to deal specifically with the RCN's refit situation and associated modernization shortfall. It was an impressive list, indicating that Nelles was not too far off the mark when he rather bluntly told the minister, "I am completely baffled when I try to fathom why you did not know of the state of affairs practically from the time you took office. It was my particular care to keep you informed of every conceivable thing or happening, even to things that are of no consequence."[35] Nor was he willing to let the minister get away with charging subordinates with neglect, as he further argued,

> I mention the Staff and Repair re-organisations in order to disprove any thought that Naval Staff did not know of and appreciate the serious state of affairs in regard to the modernization of our ships at sea. The Staff have tried and are still trying to cope with the situation. It may be necessary to further extend the scope of the Refitting. From the above you will see that the *organisation* at NSHQ has been under constant revision throughout 1943 in an endeavour to make it work more quickly and more efficiently. The object of this revision is very much tied up with the achievement of complete modernization of ships at sea as well as the maintenance of that condition.[36]

Nelles knew he was right and rammed the point home. Despite sitting in Naval Board meetings at which these issues were discussed, the minister had clearly missed the significance of the refit and repair situation. The chief of the naval staff had to refresh Macdonald's memory on how "our inadequate repair facilities, are the responsible factors for the present state of affairs."

That some members of the Naval Board had asked the minister to approach the Department of Munitions and Supply as well as other government departments for help with the refit situation also weakened Macdonald's charges. The issue of securing outside assistance was an area where Nelles was willing to yield some ground. "It is true," he admitted, "we did not think of recommending that you take the matter up with the First Sea Lord of the Admiralty or that the matter be dealt with by Prime Minister to Prime Minister." Perhaps Nelles did deserve criticism on that score, but the fact that Macdonald was unwilling to explore solutions that involved other Canadian government departments – even after the importance of the refit situation had been explained to him – casts serious doubts on whether this would have been a realistic recommendation. So too does the question of whether the British would have responded to this type of political pressure. After all, the Royal Navy's own requirements had saturated British yards to such an extent that the Admiralty had turned down similar requests from other Commonwealth nations besides Canada.

In the end, Nelles' memos not only stopped the minister's offensive dead in its tracks but also blew his entire argument apart. Nelles was confident, and it showed. Macdonald clearly believed that his own memo had dealt a knockout blow, but the chief of the naval staff had drawn first blood, such that Nelles began to ridicule the minister's position. "I still can not tell you why you were not specifically informed of our modernisation problem which has been going on all about you for a long time," Nelles convincingly crowed. "One of my present worries is what else you don't know."[37] And with that, he certainly got the message across. If Macdonald had missed the significance of the fleet's modernization, he had no one to blame but himself. These memos caught both Macdonald and Connolly off guard. Based on everything the executive assistant had learned in Londonderry, neither Nelles nor his officers were supposed to have any ammunition with which to fight back. As a result, Connolly was worried, particularly since his boss began to crack under the pressure of Nelles' volley.

Macdonald had reached his breaking point. Being part of a government at war had taken its toll on the fifty-three-year-old minister. His trip to the United States saw him check into John Hopkins Hospital, where he was diagnosed with a life-threatening duodenal ulcer. His condition was serious, as doctors went as far as to observe that "if he wants to live he must obey their rules."[38] Put on a strict diet and routine and instructed to reduce his workload, Macdonald was in no condition to take on Nelles and the Naval Staff, and resignation became an attractive option.[39]

Connolly, however, was not happy with Macdonald's thinking. The minister had no fight left in him, and the Herculean task of saving his political career became exclusively the executive assistant's.

Nelles had clearly landed a knock-down blow, but fortunately for Macdonald, his executive assistant refused to let him throw in the towel. Coaching him along, Connolly tried to convince the minister that the confrontation was merely entering a new and more critical stage. "In the first phase I reported to you and then to the Staff on a condition," he told Macdonald, but now Nelles' responses had led to a second phase: "In the second phase, your personal position as Minister came into the picture as regards the service. In this case, I could have stayed out of the picture and let my report speak for itself. However having found influences at work which I felt were tending to obscure the issue I stayed in the picture."[40] By his own admission, Connolly was playing a crucial role in the struggle with the Naval Staff, but this was not the message he wanted to convey to his embattled minister. He had to rebuild the shattered confidence of his boss so that he could come out swinging in the next round. And so, while it was his investigation that had brought the details of this "situation" to light, and he had researched and written most of the memo to Nelles, Connolly still praised Macdonald for discovering "a condition at N.S.H.Q." Nevertheless, the minister had not recovered from Nelles' verbal beating, and that left Connolly little choice but to enter the ring on his behalf.

To some extent, whether or not the fleet possessed modern equipment had become irrelevant. What really mattered was that there was a disgruntled seagoing element that believed the fleet was substandard, and despite Nelles' powerful evidence that the situation was now in hand, Connolly was totally committed to the cause. He had made a promise to the Londonderry officers, and he planned to keep it. Putting the equipment situation into a larger perspective, the executive assistant stressed to Macdonald that the "whole business will get to the men at sea ... What will they say if no effective action is taken? ... Drastic action is *expected* ... If it does not come many ... will be let down."[41] Nor was that the only reason Connolly was unwilling to concede defeat: "I am also prejudiced because I think every devise known to N.S.H.Q. is being used to cover up. I know this from rumours, from direct verbal statements, from documents. As your assistant not only do I resent this treatment which you get, but I am bound to report it. Excuses and explanations in the absence of an energetic overall plan merely add to the fire."[42] A devoted servant, Connolly had to show Macdonald that it was still possible to win the confrontation. The best way, he reasoned, was to take apart the Naval Staff's case systematically and prove that there had been a conspiracy to keep information from the minister.

At no time did the executive assistant believe that Nelles was the ringmaster in the suspected cover-up. Having searched through hundreds of naval files Connolly had seen evidence that, like the minister, Nelles had also been left in the dark. It was something Connolly had long suspected, and he admitted as much to Macdonald. "I don't think he [Nelles] knew the seriousness of the condition of the ships," Connolly observed, and in an extraordinary follow-up remark, he further confided, "I don't think *he* wilfully kept *important* things away from you. But if all this is admitted, the point need not be laboured that his capacity for the job of C.N.S. in war time is not great enough."[43] The importance of this admission cannot be understated, as it conclusively proves – in the early stages of the confrontation, at least – Connolly was not specifically targeting Nelles. Given that Connolly was getting information from Jones, it is equally apparent that the vice chief had escaped the executive assistant's crosshairs.[44] Instead, he condemned the rest of the Naval Staff. This implies another dimension to the confrontation, in which the minister and the chief of the naval staff were merely figureheads for a larger battle raging between a civil mandarin and his naval counterparts.[45]

Just as Connolly was now Macdonald's principal advisor and source of information, Connolly believed that most of the information in the memos to the minister had come from the Naval Staff rather than Nelles. There was some truth to that view, as the chief of the naval staff depended heavily on his officers to help him run the service. As a result, Connolly saw a weakness for the minister to exploit at the tertiary level of the navy's decision-making process, namely the commanders and captains on the Naval Staff. Instead of providing rational answers to what Connolly considered tough questions, the staff seemed determined to deny accountability because "none of the memorandum attached admit fault anywhere. Everything is explained. It seems that better results are practically beyond our control."[46] There was of course good reason why everything was so easily explained, but the executive assistant was unwilling to believe that all the minister's allegations could be wrong. Unlike the Londonderry officers, however, the Naval Staff had avoided any specific facts and figures, and that implied they were hiding things from Macdonald.[47] Nor was Connolly impressed with the contention that the June reorganization of the Naval Staff had led to improvement in the equipment situation. In his view, the minister did not have the experience to provide advice on the reorganization itself; his job was to "judge results." Based on observations from overseas, Connolly tried to bolster the minister's position by observing that "no satisfactory results have been achieved, and no one [on the Naval Staff] has complained that the reports are exaggerated and untrue ... To set up an organisation, however, is not enough."[48] Connolly saved what he considered the strongest point for last, that reorganization had done little to ensure that the critical memos ever made it to the minister's desk.

These critical reports had always represented the strongest evidence supporting the executive assistant's case, and the fact that the Naval Staff refuted their significance only served to reinforce the conspiracy. It was not the content of these memos that Nelles and his officers contested, but rather the way in which they had been interpreted. "In my opinion one cannot and should not just pick out sentences, or even paragraphs from a report and form conclusions therefrom," Nelles informed Macdonald while referring to one report, "because I regret that in this case you appear to have entirely *misread* the intention of the memorandum."[49] Nelles had a point, as the majority of the officers responsible for this particular memo (known to historians as the Bidwell memo) were supporting Naval Service Headquarters' efforts to combat the refit and repair crisis. His comments on a report from the captain (D) in Newfoundland (better known as the Rowland memo) were equally compelling. The Newfoundland captain (D) was just doing his duty in trying to get better equipment for the ships, but the minister failed to appreciate that Rowland's command was not part of the refit and repair structure. Unlike Bidwell and the officers in Halifax, the commanders in Newfoundland did not understand the refit and repair crisis and had "absolutely no idea of the problems involved."[50] This was not good enough for Connolly, who still clung to his conspiracy theory by telling Macdonald that "Capt D. [Rowland] can't be so far wrong when the men in Derry [and] elsewhere support him so strongly."[51] But the chief of the naval staff's criticisms also applied to Londonderry, as they, too, knew little about the East Coast refit and repair organization.

Connolly's conspiracy theory therefore arose from information provided by men who had a limited understanding of the reasons behind the equipment situation. Without fully exploring the Naval Staff's perspective, Connolly was also unaware that Macdonald had given Nelles specific instructions in the spring of 1943 not to bog him down with individual documents. Macdonald wanted more generalized briefings, and as far as the repair and refit situation was concerned, that was exactly what Nelles and the Naval Board had delivered. Moreover, comments from another staff officer make clear that Connolly had jumped to conclusions after returning from overseas. Having assessed the main file in which the executive assistant had found the critical reports, this officer concluded that "what would appear at first sight to be incriminating evidence of the existence of ineffectual administration at Naval Service Headquarters is not the case once the whole story is knitted together." Better yet, tracing the path of the critical memos through the headquarters showed how the trail had led directly to the minister.[52] Connolly did not know, but was soon to find out, that there was a direct correlation between the critical memos and the crucial Naval Board meeting at which Macdonald had been told how the navy planned to deal with the refit and repair crisis. Nor was that all. The executive assistant had placed tremendous faith in the report written by Ken Adams, but a little over a week after adjusting to his new director of warfare and training appointment, Adams' directorate issued a ten-page summary entitled "Inadequacy of Refitting Facilities on East Coast of Canada" making clear that he now understood and supported Naval Service Headquarters' perspective.[53] Adams' defection, however, was not the only sign that Connolly's campaign against the Naval Staff was built on a weak foundation.

Since he did not believe that Nelles was leading the resistance against Macdonald, the executive assistant scrutinized the officers of the Naval Staff and Board in an attempt to identify the top conspirator. After tracing the critical memos, Connolly came to believe (wrongly as it turned out) that they had gone to the assistant chief of the naval staff's office and then no further, making Creery an early frontrunner. Nor was Connolly impressed with his lackadaisical attitude, telling Macdonald that "Creery says that 'it is a fair statement that our R.N. escort ships are better equipped than R.C.N. escort ships.' My comment is 'fair hell!' It is a bad understatement."[54] The problem was that the case against the assistant chief did not extend past his so-called improper handling of the critical memos and was not enough to make him the main conspirator. "In the Navy, in this case, it's hard to put the blame on one man," Connolly told Macdonald, but indicating that he had finally found his mark he suddenly announced, "It might be said to fall on C.N.E.S. if the equipment is bad."[55]

Captain Edmund Johnstone was an odd choice. While the chief of naval equipment and supply (CNES) bore primary responsibility for the modernization of the fleet, Johnstone – who assumed this appointment in October – had not been there long enough to warrant suspicion. Connolly nonetheless remained steadfast in his belief that the true leader of Naval Staff resistance had been unmasked. For instance, after reading one of the memos that Nelles had sent to Macdonald, the executive assistant attributed twelve of its fifty-three points directly to the chief of naval equipment and supply, which, in his view, conclusively proved that the entire document was "obviously Johnstone's work."[56] Comments that Nelles' other responses represented "Johnstone's desire to put you on the spot" or that "he was the bird who tried to clip your wings and give your power to the Board" further suggest that the executive assistant believed Johnstone had a vendetta against the minister.[57] Connolly's personal animosity was so strong that he even tried to build a case against Johnstone, and only stopped gunning for him because "the so called incriminating files did not go to him, according to the record."[58]

Determining why the executive assistant had fingered this particular officer as the minister's main adversary is not easy. Aside from being one of Nelles' most loyal officers, Johnstone's previous appointment as the director of organization seemed to capture Connolly's attention. While serving in that capacity, Johnstone was the chief architect of the Naval Staff's June reorganization, a set-up the executive assistant clearly believed had failed to bring the equipment deficiency to the minister's attention. This in itself does not provide a sufficient explanation as Connolly had charged other staff officers, such as Creery, with a similar offence. Instead, it appears that the following reference from Nelles' second memo to

Macdonald triggered Connolly's suspicion of Johnstone: "It is here pointed out that the study in connection with this new organization commenced *early in June, if not before*, and that Director of Organisation's memorandum on the subject is dated 18 June. This memorandum commences with the sentence, 'The problem of the present unsatisfactory state of affairs, so far as the repairs of HMC Ships is concerned, is so urgent and of such vital importance that time does not permit a full investigation of all the factors contributing to it.'"[59] The minister had no idea what this meant and instructed Connolly to get a copy of Johnstone's 18 June report. The confrontation then took a dramatic twist, in which Connolly's protagonist lost his leading role as the hapless victim.

Johnstone's report – along with its supporting documentation covering other related issues, such as the manpower crisis, the impact of poor technical liaison, and the question of the inadequate supply of equipment and plans from Britain – represented the smoking gun that disproved the executive assistant's conspiracy theory. In effect, these records proved not only that Macdonald had been told the navy had serious problems but also that the Naval Board had asked him to approve their solutions at their 27 July meeting. Johnstone's report should have taught Connolly how the fleet's modernization was linked to the more pressing refit and repair crisis, particularly since it made clear that expanding East Coast repair yards was the best way to expedite the installation of modern equipment. Johnstone represented a tremendous threat to Connolly, as his report had the potential to take the minister down. Whether that explains Connolly's dislike for Johnstone remains a mystery, the more so because there is compelling evidence that Connolly was suffering from denial.

It had been three long and tiresome months since Connolly first took a copy of Strange's report to Macdonald; now his modernization quest had unexpectedly led him full circle, as the evidence left him staring at the minister's office. There was no doubt that the Navy's top brass had made mistakes but so had Macdonald. Flying in the face of everything Connolly had come to believe, he could not accept what Johnstone's report and its associated correspondence so obviously proved. Rather than deal with the fact that the minister should have known about the modernization issue, Connolly desperately grasped at an unrealistic conspiracy theory that conveniently excused his mentor's lack of action. The possibility that Macdonald might have to pay a political price for his previous lack of interest in the navy was too much for his loyal aide to handle, yet it is clear that Johnstone's report had sown a seed of suspicion. Connolly began to have doubts about the veracity of the Londonderry officers' modernization allegations. "I assumed the responsibility for the statements which I made," Connolly wrote to one of his reserve informants, but for the first time he also showed some scepticism in their cause, as he added, "I hope none of them were exaggerated."[60] The minister's entire case was based on the information Connolly had received from his networks, and the fact that he was seeking reaffirmation indicates that the Naval Staff's stubborn defence was having an impact. That marked the beginning of an important transition in the confrontation. What had started out as a crusade to right the wrongs perpetrated against the seagoing element had quickly evolved into a crude political battle for survival, and perhaps more than ever it required a scapegoat.

The real stumbling block in this acrimonious debate between Macdonald and Nelles had always been the issue of blame, and there was good reason why this was so. In Connolly's view, it was only a matter of time before the public learned about the RCN's modernization problems, and their anticipated outrage was bound to produce a scandal that would dwarf Macdonald's experiences with the MacLean affair some six months earlier. From a political perspective, the modernization issue was dynamite, and there is little doubt that Macdonald dreaded the inevitable question of how many sailors and lost ships might have been saved had the RCN possessed up-to-date equipment. Images of discontented sailors, their unhappy relatives, and vengeful voters gave Macdonald good reason for concern. But the public's reaction was not the only threat. Pointing to the explanation for the equipment situation as provided by Nelles and the Naval Staff, Connolly asked Macdonald, "would the House of Commons or the public accept the explanation as good enough? Do the men at sea accept these explanations? The historical fact that our ships have lacked modernization and that we have always had trouble with the problem, at least should prove that if we knew the problem so well from 1910 until now, we should have been better able to meet it."[61] Worse, MacLean was bound to take advantage of a situation that could possibly clear his name and vindicate his charges. This conjured up horrible images of MacLean adding to Parliament's and the public's rage over modernization with a renewed campaign based on his reserve discrimination allegations. How could Macdonald expect to survive such a scenario, Connolly must have wondered, as he would be simultaneously attacked on two fronts?

At the peak of the confrontation, Macdonald's position truly looked unsalvageable. In order to save his boss once the scandal broke, Connolly knew they would need to shift the public's wrath to another target. He believed that a mass confession by the entire Naval Staff would have been enough to grant the minister total absolution, and had these officers done so the confrontation probably would have ended there. While there is no doubt that Connolly would have crucified specific officers, such as Johnstone and Creery, he wanted to avoid moving Nelles and key officers because of the fear that it could lead to public inquiries and the premature uncovering of the equipment situation. But the chief of the naval staff was unwilling to sacrifice any of his officers. Instead Nelles had made a point of praising the entire staff as "the best officers in the Service to N.S.H.Q." Connolly was unimpressed and believed that Nelles was merely following Johnstone's instructions to cover up the staff's negligence.[62] But by defending the

Naval Staff Nelles had effectively put his own head on the chopping block, as the executive assistant told Macdonald:

> In light of your own reasoned memo and of the existing situation in the Navy, it is impossible to read the memo of the C.N.S. [chief of the naval staff] without concluding 1) Either he doesn't appreciate what has gone on. 2) Or, he is determined to resist you on this matter to the end. In either case, I am bound to say that for one, I cannot read it dispassionately. The first thing to note is that he makes no recommendation, he takes no responsibility ... The implication clearly is that you alone must decide of course when the time to take the bows comes.[63]

Connolly had come to the realization that as long as the minister demanded the Naval Staff accept full responsibility for the modernization quagmire, there would be no resolution. Things had gone too far and it was clear that some type of drastic action was required. Punishing "all who are guilty" was clearly not the best way to protect the minister from any potential fallout over public discovery of the RCN's deficiencies, so Connolly finally turned his attention to the chief of the naval staff.[64]

Nelles had played a powerful trump card with his responses to the minister's allegations, and it was clear that Macdonald was not going to emerge unscathed by playing the blame game. With his boss on the verge of resignation, Connolly took total control of the situation. Providing strong evidence that the real crisis was no longer about equipment shortages but had become a political struggle for survival, he gave Macdonald precise instructions on how he was to save his own career:

> IMPLICATIONS OF A POLITICAL (PUBLIC) NATURE
> Some day this story will be out, in whole, or in part. It will be aired in public (parliament, press, platform.) If this happens while you are Minister, and it could begin this session, yours will be the burden of explaining and justifying your position. Unless you have strong action to point to, your lot will not be easy.
>
> ACTION
> The Navy knows one rule well – the captain bears the responsibility for his ship. This of course must be applied with a view to the equalities of a given situation. In this case, looking at the facts, at the men, at the statute, I am unable to escape the conclusion that you must move the C.N.S.[65]

Apparently in Connolly's eyes that responsibility conveniently stopped at Nelles. It is unlikely that Macdonald was nearly so naïve. In his position as the civilian leader of the navy Parliament considered him the captain of the ship, and as such his executive assistant's rationalization represented a total denial of ministerial accountability. Indeed, Connolly's logic was difficult to follow: he argued that the chief should be dismissed because the Naval Staff had let him down but that the minister should keep his job because these same men had kept information from him. That contradiction obviously did not bother Connolly, who encouraged the minister "not [to] give detailed reasons [to the public] for the move ... I think it would be a mistake to tie it up to the modernisation or any other problem specifically."[66] By saying so, the executive assistant was just doing his job. It was his duty after all to guard the minister's career, and he therefore had to find a way to remove Nelles without attracting outside curiosity.

This could be done in a number of ways. The executive assistant offered four options for Nelles: retirement, commanding officer Pacific coast, a Washington appointment, or a position in London. His preference was to transfer Nelles overseas under the guise of supervising the RCN's contribution to the upcoming invasion of Europe. Had the equipment situation became public knowledge, which Connolly clearly believed was inevitable, Macdonald would then have spun the transfer and claimed that Nelles had been fired. It was a clever but dubious plan. An appointment as the senior Canadian flag officer (overseas) offered a legitimate excuse for Nelles' "transfer" while avoiding any hint of the equipment situation. The executive assistant further believed that Macdonald, who never did well with journalists, could even manipulate the press because "London, which has not been publicised could be inflated [and] publicity can be used to help the move in his and in the Service's interests."[67] Ironically, while Connolly had accused the Naval Staff of whitewashing, he was encouraging the minister to do the same with the Canadian public. This contradiction was difficult to overlook, and the deputy minister, Gordon Mills, was nervous about participating in this political façade: "I am not too happy over that 'Flag Officer' title – as hardly embodying what needs to be put over to the public in order to protect the Service. What would you think of bringing in the word 'operations' – such as Chief of Canadian Naval Operations (Overseas) – 'C.C.N.O. (O)'? – more or less meaningless, perhaps, but might sound better."[68]

It is debatable whether Connolly's Machiavellian plan would have fooled anyone but it shows that Nelles' removal was both a smokescreen and a political execution, designed in its entirety to make him the scapegoat in any future scandal. His dismissal also served another purpose, as it was expected that flexing his muscles in this manner would allow Macdonald to regain control over the Naval Staff. And with Naval Service Headquarters in utter chaos and the confrontation reaching a climax, there was good reason for concern about public reaction.

News that Nelles was talking to naval legal experts with the view of taking the entire affair to court martial led to paranoia in the minister's office. For Connolly,

Nelles' possible court martial was just another tactic to "forstall [sic] any effective action on the part of the Minister" because the "C.N.S. will have a story ... he will say he is blameless ... he will say why let Jones, Stephens & Lay and others go free while I take it." The fact that Nelles had vehemently defended his staff made the latter suggestion unlikely, but the threat of a court martial providing Nelles with a public platform from which to scrutinize the actions of the minister's office was very real.[69] This thought troubled Deputy Minister Mills, the more so since he was alarmed when the governor general had warned that "all 'his' Chiefs of Staff were being moved from their positions, and that he hoped that a similar action was not about to occur in the Navy." Clearly, word of the confrontation was spreading beyond the confines of the navy, and Mills tried to convince Macdonald "that no further action is required on this problem. The matter has been thoroughly aired, action has been taken and N.S.H.Q. has had a thorough shaking."[70]

Connolly was not impressed. In his view, Mills was having doubts not because of his fears or his questioning of the minister's case, but because of an ever-widening conspiracy. Mills had been "turned" and could no longer be trusted because "his thinking is affected by Naval Officers talk (Johnstone & Hibbard and perhaps even C.N.S.) ... he may have some remote blame ... I understand that ... the D.M. [Mills] had a hand in the memo prepared by the C.N.S. for you in reply to your charges." Indicating the depths of the executive assistant's obsession with his conspiracy theory, he went even further: "I can't get away from the idea that Johnstone was brought in to make an argument. This he would love to do – if you were on the receiving end of it. If he succeeds he then has established himself with Nelles. He now has the D.M. [Gordon Mills]. He may even have the V.C.N.S."[71] Connolly was not the only one with suspicions, as Nelles was also zeroing in on the outside influences responsible for the current confrontation.

On 3 December, the director of signals, Captain "Sam" Worth, handed Nelles a copy of what became known as the "famous Happy day signal." This was Londonderry's response to Naval Service Headquarters' request that a Canadian corvette have its inferior RXU radar set replaced with Type 271. The signal recorded, "This will be done. The happy day when no more RXU sets will be fitted in Canadian ships is looked forward to in hopeful anticipation." Originally drafted by one of Simpson's officers, the signal was purportedly designed to "give the boys at NSHQ a laugh," but Nelles was not amused and let the commander in chief Western Approaches know as much. "Your attention is drawn to Commodore D WA signal," Nelles blasted at Horton, "there is no time for humour in our struggle to obtain modern equipment for our ships."[72] Given that Nelles was battling the minister on exactly this issue, the timing of the message was impossible to overlook. Nelles had discovered one of the minister's puppet masters and was unwilling to put up with what he interpreted as Simpson's impertinent gloating. It is unlikely that was the author's actual intent but even Connolly had to admit,

Simpson is now of the definite opinion that some people in the RCN seized the opportunity to put him behind the eight-ball principally because they felt he was critical of them to me ... we should not stand by and see Simpson suffer in any way because of his frankness ... I need not add that personally, this fuss which has resulted from the signal is due entirely to the statements which I made on my return ... My own view is that Worth and Nelles together decided to send the [responding] signal as part of the general cover-up scheme which was being worked out.[73]

In reality, Nelles was not going to pass up the chance to tell one of his true accusers that he knew who he was and what he had done. Aside from that moral victory, rebuking Simpson did little. The author of the signal had recently been promoted to the rank of commander, allowing the commodore (D) to respond cheekily with "the officer responsible had been suitably punished."[74] Nonetheless, as far as Connolly was concerned, Nelles was getting a little too close to the mark, and perhaps because of that he started to pressure the minister; the decision to replace the chief of the naval staff "must be made soon."[75]

Macdonald listened, and following his aide's recommendations to the letter sent a memo on 10 December that left no doubt Nelles' days were numbered. Rejecting Nelles' tactics, the minister began his verbal assault by observing that "the intimation here seems to be that if there is anything wrong with the ships, it is my fault as much as anybody else's. This, of course, is an old method of controversy, the method of getting everybody blamed or everybody blameless."[76] Probably in light of Nelles' overwhelming evidence, Macdonald then admitted that he did in fact have a "general understanding" of the equipment situation prior to 20 November. But there the minister's political savvy took over, as he managed to turn the tables on his chief of the naval staff. As a civilian representative, Macdonald explained, these highly technical matters were of a "nature with which a Minister ordinarily is not familiar," and therefore "something beyond mere general statements was necessary if I was to be properly informed."[77] Although the Naval Board had left little doubt that the navy was in trouble at its 27 July meeting, Macdonald had made an interesting observation. If the refit and repair situation were such a grave crisis, the minister wondered why had Nelles not sat down in a one-on-one session and explained it to him in terms that could easily be comprehended? Whether that justified a dismissal given Macdonald's lack of interest in naval affairs is less certain, but it nonetheless allowed the minister to make his most powerful charge yet: "For the above and other reasons, therefore, I repel and repudiate the suggestion that if I did not know certain conditions that it was my own fault. On a question of such importance it was the duty of C.N.S. to bring before me in the most forcible and graphic and explicit way possible the true position of the Canadian Navy."[78] The memo made it clear that Nelles, instead of the entire Naval Staff, was in Macdonald's political crosshairs, and it was obvious by his tone that he was ready to pull the trigger.

Given the growing confidence of his boss and hoping that Nelles' replacement would finally put an end to the confrontation over modernization, Connolly redirected the minister's attention to the issue of permanent force discrimination. He was effectively switching fronts so that Macdonald could also take care of the other disgruntled elite that had battled for his attention over the past two years. To reinforce the conclusion reached after the investigation, Connolly gave Macdonald a letter he had recently received from Commander Horace Read, RCNVR. After touring a number of East Coast ports for his work with the Regulation Revision Committee, Read reported:

> So many reserve officers complained, some bitterly, of what they regard as unfair treatment at the hands of RCN officers, that it was impossible to avoid concluding that, regardless of whether many of the complaints are actually justified, the situation requires immediate remedial action. Two high-ranking reserve officers separately expressed the opinion that the hostility is now so deep-seated as to constitute a serious threat to morale and efficiency ... While many of the individual complaints may well be unjustified or due to unavoidable causes, or even in some cases reflect the shortcomings of those who utter them, we were impressed by their prevalence and the vehemence of their utterance.[79]

Like the officers in Connolly's network, Read was typical of the elitist element within the reserves and had avenues through which to contact the minister. His links were more direct because Read was one of Macdonald's oldest friends; the two men had been fellow law professors and officemates at Dalhousie University in the 1920s.[80] This gave his account instant credibility. Moreover, his observation cut to the heart of the issue. Whether or not a majority of reserve officers actually believed the permanent force discriminated against the RCNVR had become moot. Rather, Connolly was simply unwilling to take the chance that reserve complaints against the permanent force might once again become an issue in the near future, especially since Read's observations were essentially a carbon copy of the letters MacLean had sent Macdonald in July 1942.

Connolly reminded Macdonald that information provided by reserve officers had led to the discovery of both the equipment and the discrimination problems. It had not always been easy for these individuals to gain access to Macdonald, so Connolly wanted to create a new position on the Naval Board called the chief staff officer reserves (CSOR) to represent the "special needs" of the RCNVR and RCNR. This would also institutionalize Macdonald's link to the reserves, as in Connolly's words, the chief staff officer reserves' "principal value is that, for the Reserves, he will have direct access to you."[81] In late December 1943, Connolly began drafting the terms of reference for this position, and they clearly identified that the grouses offered by individuals like MacLean had finally been taken seriously. The new reserve chief was to report directly to Macdonald on all reserve promotions, appointments, honours, and awards as well as on the state of morale within the RCNVR and RCNR.[82] Moreover, indicating the impact that the scholarly reserve elite had had on Connolly, it was further stressed that the minister could make any "sea-going or ex-seagoing Lt. Commander" the chief staff officer reserves, providing the candidate was given double acting rank and had the necessary "education and background."[83]

Following the suggestion that Lieutenant Commander R.M. Hanbury had raised in St. John's, Connolly passed Paul Cross' name on to the minister. With an education from Acadia University, a vice presidency at Hall and Fairweather Limited, and a reputation for always keeping "the interests of the RCNVR at heart," Captain Paul Cross was the ideal choice to become the chief staff officer reserves. To solidify this new link between the minister and the reserves, the executive assistant also wanted to place a member of his personal network into the reserve chief's organization, so it was arranged for Barry O'Brien, who was due for a break from his seagoing command, to assume the duties as Cross' chief of staff.[84] But O'Brien's appointment had a practical purpose as well. Complaints by reserve officers were to be sent to the chief staff officer reserve's office, where O'Brien would filter them. Those considered legitimate would be forwarded to Cross. If he could not devise a solution, the complaint would then be passed on to Connolly, who would decide whether to involve the minister. It was a remarkable process that gave the reserves considerable power. The true significance of this system was that it formalized the informal chain of command initiated by MacLean some seventeen months earlier.

As it turns out, Connolly's plan to place a reserve member on the Naval Board encountered stiff resistance at Naval Service Headquarters, probably because some staff officers felt it an injustice to reward MacLean and other reserve officers for their duplicity. At least one member of the Naval Board later admitted that "from what I know of the matter ... reserve officers had been through various channels attempting to poison the then Minister's mind whereat the Reserves were getting a very raw deal from the permanent force. Pressure got so heavy in fact that I believe the Minister came to the conclusion that the only way to solve the problem was to represent the Reserve officers on the Naval Board."[85] Indeed, the Naval Staff's opposition was so substantial that Connolly reluctantly told Macdonald, "I begin to see what Andy McLean meant. Perhaps you should not have come to the defence of the RCN so magnificently in the House [in February and June]. (For this, I am largely to blame)."[86] The Naval Staff and Board's resistance to reserve representation quickly dissipated once it became apparent that Nelles was about to be replaced, and it was not the only case in which opposition forces on the staff began to crumble because of the realization that the chief of the naval staff was on his way out.

Barry O'Brien's ship, HMCS *Snowberry*, providing close escort for a convoy. O'Brien was a particularly popular and capable commanding officer, but a long overdue shore posting meant that he missed *Snowberry*'s involvement in the sinking of U-536 shortly after he relinquished command. DHH 81/520/8000, BOX 203, FILE 10

For most people at Naval Service Headquarters, the confrontation was a battle between those loyal to either Nelles or Macdonald, but there were individuals who suspected that there was a third group operating within this environment. Captain Eric Brand, the director of trade, was a British officer on loan to the RCN and so had managed to avoid the petty politics that existed among the navy's top brass, but he was troubled that Jones and his supporters were manipulating the confrontation for their own purposes. He went to Nelles with this information, but remarkably the chief of the naval staff did not seem to care. His apathy confused Brand. Unwilling to let his chief fall to someone he considered an unscrupulous officer, Brand took it upon himself to stop Jones before it was too late.[87] Since Nelles had not listened, he reasoned, perhaps the other side would. Brand therefore turned to Connolly. Based on their strong friendship, Brand told the executive assistant that his investigation "was causing strained relations between Percy Nelles + the minister – which were providing Jones + some others with good opportunity to get the skids under Percy – as I had warned him [Nelles] some time before – but he took no notice. I had several talks with Connolly trying to explain to him what was really happening – but to no avail as it turned out."[88] That both Nelles and Connolly had not paid attention to his warnings confused Brand, and in the end he gave up believing that "the pressure against Nelles was too strong."[89] Nor was he the only British officer on loan who was frustrated that Jones was taking advantage of the situation for his own gain.

Currently serving as the naval officer in charge in Esquimalt, British Columbia, Captain Massey Goolden, RN, had been a keen observer of the dramas that were regularly played out between the permanent force's senior officers. After discussing the vice chief's activities with Rear Admiral Victor Brodeur, commanding officer Pacific coast, Goolden confided to his diary that "we [Goolden and Brodeur] discussed Murray and Jones and the intrigues that are apparently going on to get rid of PN [Percy Nelles]. If Jones gets there heaven help the RCN for the next 15 years."[90] That events in Ottawa had reached a climax did not surprise Goolden, who saw such an outcome as the natural though unfortunate by-product of a highly competitive permanent force naval community in which individual careers were guarded with the utmost jealousy. While the Royal Navy was not free of careerism, Goolden was disappointed it was so prevalent in the RCN:

3 No two senior officers trust each other; they are always striving to get ahead of each other, they have less loyalty amongst themselves than they have from us.
4 The Minister (a veritable politician) has too much power and the Board does not really function as such. The "Nelles" episode likewise displays this fact. Everything is done below board and not above ... Leaving Nelles out of it, how can the service function seniority [sic] and efficiently with GC [Jones] – LM [Murray] – RR [Reid] and that despicable creature VB [Brodeur] intriguing and jockeying for their own suds [jobs].[91]

In this case, Jones had just followed his instincts, and his opportunistic nature was about to pay off. The list of candidates to replace Nelles was short. Murray was one option but Connolly did not think he would relinquish his position as commander in chief Canadian North West Atlantic, especially since it was well known he was "doing well."[92] In any event, Murray did not have the personality for what was required, as the executive assistant instructed Macdonald that "firing Nelles won't remedy the repair problems or the N.S.H.Q. problem, but the shake down which his successor must carry out, might go a long way." They needed someone who could maintain control over the Naval Staff once Nelles was gone and at the same time take direction from the minister without question. There was only one officer who fit the description, explaining why Connolly came to the conclusion that "personally I would take Jones."[93]

Both Goolden and Brand were wrong to place Jones at the centre of what Brand had called the "skids under Nelles party" and the "underground movement." Jones' interference simply formed part of a larger tapestry that the reserve elite had started to weave long before the vice chief arrived in Ottawa. Moreover, Brand and Goolden did not comprehend that while Jones' shenanigans may have been annoying, Nelles was too busy dealing with Macdonald's and Connolly's political machinations. In fact, with events overtaking calculated planning, the usually astute Jones was caught totally off guard when it was revealed that he had become chief of the naval staff.[94]

The end came quickly for Nelles once Macdonald decided to implement Connolly's plan. Despite Brand's accusations, Jones' meddling was not an essential factor in the decision to replace Nelles.[95] Instead, comments from one of Brand's subordinates, Commander C.H. Little, RCNVR, suggest that most Canadian staff officers understood what their British colleagues at Naval Service Headquarters did not. As the director of naval intelligence, Little, who was a self-professed Nelles loyalist, had a front row seat for the confrontation and so saw the chief of the naval staff's dismissal as the product of a minister who believed that it was "politically expedient to take this step."[96] And that was exactly what it was. In fact, camouflaging Nelles' removal under the cloak of an overseas "promotion" was such a brilliant example of political expediency that neither the Canadian press nor Parliament saw any reason to seriously challenge Nelles' new appointment as senior Canadian flag officer (overseas) when it was announced on 14 January 1944.[97] Connolly's planning had given Macdonald logical explanations that cleverly screened the real reasons for the move. With the Battle of the Atlantic more or less under control, other Allied navies were getting ready for the invasion of Europe, and it was only natural to expect that the RCN would do the same. Likewise, the fact that the air force and army had recently posted Air Marshal Lloyd Breadner and Lieutenant General Kenneth Steward overseas allowed Macdonald to further sell Nelles' transfer as a tri-service effort to give the military the necessary clout to protect Canadian interests abroad.[98] Keeping the equipment situation and confrontation at Naval Service Headquarters from the press and Parliament was not the only reason why the executive assistant's plan to protect Macdonald's Cabinet post proved so successful.

Getting Nelles out of Ottawa without the prime minister discovering what was truly transpiring at Naval Service Headquarters was perhaps the greatest challenge that faced Macdonald. The politically astute King was not convinced that the new overseas position had to be filled by such a high-ranking officer, and he was also worried that it would give Nelles a chance to "lead us ... to have one Navy for the whole British Empire."[99] Connolly's plan had ensured that no details of either Nelles' removal or the escort fleet's equipment situation ever reached the prime minister's office, and outfoxing the wily King was undoubtedly Connolly's greatest triumph.

Without evidence to support his suspicion, however, the prime minister was forced to admit, albeit grudgingly, that he had no choice but to believe his naval minister was making decisions based on "what is best" for the service. And with that, Connolly had handed Macdonald a resounding victory; he emerged from his two-month confrontation with the Naval Staff relatively unscathed.[100]

With his boss and mentor on the verge of resignation, Connolly had taken control of a difficult situation and played the pivotal role in both the confrontation against the Naval Staff and Nelles' dismissal. In the process, however, Connolly had lost sight of his original motivation. Fighting for the sharp-end grousers and their causes became subordinate to the larger goal of protecting Macdonald from a potential scandal that would probably lead to his removal from Cabinet. Although offered as a sacrifice to those who had complained, Nelles was a victim of a politically expedient plan designed by an executive assistant who wanted to shift the public's anticipated wrath over modernization from his boss to the former chief of the naval staff. It is a testament to Connolly's abilities that he was able to get rid of Nelles without the press, Parliament, or public ever discovering the real reasons for his replacement, not to mention that Macdonald survived such a crisis-filled year.

Afterword: Game's End and the Final Score

After ten years at the helm of the RCN, Nelles' career was effectively over. The victim of a politically expedient plan to save the minister, he was forced into a meaningless post by an artificial crisis caused by the transgressions of officers working outside the confines of normal channels. Whether it was Connolly's informants, various reserve networks, the Londonderry officers, or Jones and his men, the list of those who were involved in Nelles' downfall was extensive. Some had more influence over that process then others, yet it was Connolly who was the hub that brought these spokes together, and that made him the key player with the greatest impact on the Admiral's fate. But while saving Macdonald was undoubtedly the highlight of Connolly's tenure as executive assistant, not all those who had played along were happy with the final score.

The process that led to Nelles' removal began the moment MacLean was given the opportunity in July 1942 to discuss privately with Macdonald his allegations that the regular force discriminated against reserves. His ability to do so made him the first of a number of reservists to seriously challenge the authority of the top brass. Despite being motivated by his own personal ambition, MacLean was relentless in his effort to gain more rights for the reserves, and after two years of fighting, the last of his "major reforms" became a reality when Paul Cross assumed his seat on the Naval Board as the first chief staff officer reserves. The fact that Cross did so the day after Jones had replaced Nelles as the chief of the naval staff was not lost on MacLean. It was a significant and symbolic gesture, and although the renegade informant had long been pushed out of Macdonald's and Connolly's inner circle, he saw no reason to renew his attack against the navy.

Considering that Macdonald and Connolly had finally "accomplished much that we desired," MacLean even tried to make amends by apologizing for not having given the minister enough time to implement his reforms. He had been "so very impatient" because of his deteriorating health. But since their public confrontation, MacLean thought that his constitution had improved to a point where "things are beginning to reappear in their proper perspective."[1] Macdonald was neither interested in reconciliation nor willing to let MacLean enjoy his victory:

> You had done what to me seemed rather a reprehensible thing. You had gone out and attacked the Service to which you had belonged for a good many years ... In such a case it is pertinent to enquire as to the qualifications of a critic. This I did. If you

consider this a personal attack I am sorry that you think so, but when a man takes up the sword he must expect to be met with sword, and the methods I adopted were, it seems to me, fair and well known and long used.[2]

Fresh from decapitating the Naval Staff, the minister's blade was razor sharp, and his verbal jab cut deep into MacLean's ego. Nothing short of total vindication would have satisfied MacLean, including an admission that Macdonald had mistakenly followed the advice of his naval advisors. This was something the minister was not going to do, and MacLean remained bitter toward the navy for the rest of his life. MacLean could not even resist the urge to haunt the navy from his grave. An obituary composed some twenty-seven years after the events fired his parting shot at his former military leaders: "Andrew D. MacLean, 74, former publisher and wartime naval officer ... was buried Saturday ... To many naval veterans, however, he was best known for blasts against the navy published in his magazine Boating [which] ... tore into the Naval Board."[3] In reality, his "verbal torpedoes" had cut through the top brass and detonated much closer to the chief of the naval staff's office than MacLean ever realized.

MacLean's greatest enemy was his own ego. Personal naval ambitions and attempts to avenge his injured pride were too closely linked to the larger crusade to end the permanent force's so-called discrimination against the reserves. MacLean's attitude left the impression that his campaign was being used to cover his own inadequacies as a naval officer, and perhaps he was. While he did have a small core of followers, MacLean offered little tangible evidence to support his allegations. Instead he used powerful political and public connections to intimidate the minister. In the early stages of his campaign, MacLean wielded this power effectively. In doing so he not only forced the minister to take a closer look at the navy but also raised doubts in Macdonald's mind about Nelles' capabilities.

Although he lost his ugly public battle with the minister, MacLean had taught Macdonald a powerful lesson. Whether there was any truth to the allegation that the regulars discriminated against the reserves was less significant than MacLean's ability to draw the public's attention to a perceived problem in the navy. This power made MacLean dangerous, and Macdonald's hypersensitivity to these potential political threats spelled trouble for Nelles. While the reserve discrimination campaign was not enough to damage Macdonald's relationship with the chief of the naval staff irreparably, MacLean's true legacy was in laying the groundwork for the reserve networks that followed by giving them much-needed leverage to influence the minister. Moreover, the fact that Connolly became the lynchpin between these reserve networks and Macdonald was also a product of MacLean's handiwork. MacLean's allegations had led Connolly to St. John's in October 1942, and through investigating whether the reserves were on the verge of rebelling the executive assistant discovered the value of using former legal colleagues and friends in the

RCNVR as informants. This represented a pivotal transformation for Connolly, whose role was evolving from the minister's protector into his watchdog. These new responsibilities led to a well-established pattern: Macdonald would rely on Connolly rather than on normal channels to uncover problems in the fleet, and that gave Connolly influence well beyond the duties usually assigned to an executive assistant. Marking a remarkable progression that was first triggered by MacLean's interference, an additional power structure was inaugurated at Naval Service Headquarters that linked Connolly and Macdonald to the various reserve networks. But while MacLean never came to terms with the impact that he had had on Canadian naval policy, there were others who were content with the pivotal role they had played in Nelles' fate.

Considering all the information that had been fed to Connolly, the Londonderry officers were well aware that there was much more to the chief of the naval staff's replacement than was contained in the official press releases. Certainly, the American reservist David Conklin could not restrain his enthusiasm, writing to the executive assistant only two days after Nelles' removal, "Your stay among us was very short but the effects of it have been lasting. You gained the respect and gratitude of every seagoing Canadian Naval Officer on the North Atlantic by your attitudes and the obvious results of your trip to the United Kingdom. Possibly it caused some of the Navy a little distress but that was for the general good thruout [sic]."[4]

Connolly had promised to act as the Londonderry officers' spokesman, and it was clear that he had kept his word. Although willing to accept their praise, he nonetheless insisted Conklin tell the others that "the action was taken by the Minister."[5] Macdonald was all that mattered, and the executive assistant wanted both the Londonderry officers and the reserve modernization networks to realize that the minister had listened to their grievances. To some degree, therefore, Nelles had been offered up as a sacrifice to all the sharp-end grousers within the seagoing fleet. Certainly, Simpson's special services officer, Lieutenant J.L. Clifford, RCNVR, understood that message, and his reaction was typical of the sense of vindication that these officers felt. "Things have certainly moved quickly since your return to Canada," Clifford told Connolly, "and I must say that it suits all of us here very well."[6]

MacLean's followers, the commanding officers complaining about equipment, Connolly's own group of informants, and even the RCNVR officers on Simpson's team – all those who managed to contact Macdonald – suffered from a perception, albeit to varying degrees, that the RCN's most senior officers did not listen to their advice simply because they were reservists. Personal accounts from members of these networks make it clear that they believed the professionals held too much power. These reservists formed an educated and socially and politically connected clique, and were determined to gain status within the navy's hierarchy. The networks challenged the hegemony of the permanent force's established community because they found it difficult to take orders from men whose schooling was the product of a military infrastructure. By doing so, they turned their struggle with the regulars into a battle of professionalism in which they demanded the same respect that they had been afforded in civilian occupations. The adversarial atmosphere created by the clash of two separate and competing sets of elitist attitudes among small elements within both the reserves and regular forces incubated the conditions that eventually cost Nelles his job.

Although the small group of seagoing commanding officers had not fixated on their lack of status as much as MacLean had done, they certainly wanted their voices to be heard in the halls of Naval Service Headquarters. The most disorganized and individualistic of all the networks, their early efforts to influence the minister had met with disappointing results. Instead, they had better luck with senior operational authorities in Londonderry. By gaining the support of the Londonderry officers, they managed to succeed where MacLean had failed. Originally "Shrimp" Simpson abhorred their efforts to contact the minister, but it did not take long before a small faction of Canadian commanding officers had convinced him there was a direct correlation between poor morale and the equipment situation. In reality, the lack of special service support in Halifax, St. John's, and Londonderry was probably the prime cause of discipline and morale problems among the junior ranks, who tended to get into trouble when there was nothing to do in port. Yet this issue was put on the back burner because the group of reserve commanding officers focusing on equipment had more sway over Simpson and the Londonderry officers.

As the champion of the modernization cause, Simpson and his hand-picked team of British, American, and Canadian officers in Londonderry were willing to employ unorthodox methods to get word through to the highest authority at Naval Service Headquarters. Strong circumstantial evidence suggests that officers in St. John's – most notably Rowland and Houghton – had engineered Strange's trip to Londonderry, and it appears that Simpson was not alone in wanting to get to the bottom of the rumblings within the fleet. It was a fateful decision. As one of the executive assistant's informants, Strange played a pivotal part in linking the Londonderry officers to Connolly. And that represented the conclusion of an extraordinary and intricate domino effect that trickled from MacLean through to the reserve commanding officer's networks, to the operational authorities in St. John's and Londonderry, and finally to the minister via Connolly's web of informants.

Although the chief of the naval staff's removal first and foremost served a political agenda, it is hard to believe that Nelles could have survived much longer with so many groups undermining his authority. Macdonald put this into perspective by observing that Nelles did not have "the power, the personality [or] the respect of his officers."[7] Given that he had been chief of the naval staff for ten years, the statement was perhaps a little excessive, but it was nonetheless obviously time for a change as Nelles' relaxed demeanour and lenient style made him an easy target for disgruntled elements in the navy. Jones was a different matter. Wanting to expedite Nelles' departure, the vice chief of the naval staff was willing to take advantage of the chaos created by the networks to achieve that aim. But once he became chief of the naval staff, he would keep a tight rein on the service, and even though the chief staff officer reserve's position theoretically gave the various reserve networks access to the minister, there were few who would dare repeat this type of behaviour with Jones at the navy's helm. Aside from his political savvy, the new chief of the naval staff's reputation as a shrewd administrator, cutthroat when necessary, made him more than a match for these networks.

Jones' first real challenges, therefore, were to restore Macdonald's confidence in the navy and bring order to a headquarters that had been rocked by two months of intense infighting. To facilitate this, Jones immediately authorized a new administrative body called the Deputy Minister's Advisory Committee. He designed it to streamline the channels of communication between Macdonald and the navy's

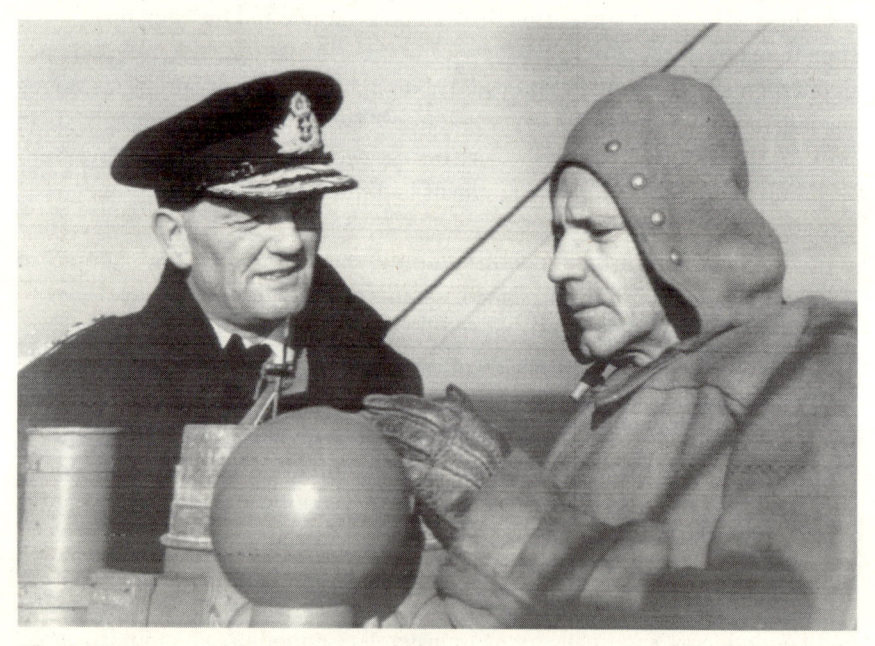

After taking over as chief of the naval staff, Vice Admiral George C. Jones, RCN, proceeds to sea with the naval minister, Angus L. Macdonald, in the destroyer HMCS *Saskatchewan*. While on the bridge, Jones shows Macdonald how to take a bearing from the azimuth. According to numerous sources, Jones spent much time teaching the minister about a great number of the navy's problems with the intention of casting Nelles in a negative light. Some believed that this was the key reason for Nelles' early departure as chief of the naval staff. DHH 81/520/1000, BOX 150, FILE 20 top brass. This organization, which was to consist of every member of the Naval Board except the chief of the naval staff and minister, allowed Jones to avoid one of the key mistakes Nelles had made. Instances where Macdonald had difficulty separating the wheat from the chaff when digesting the vast amounts of information given to him by Nelles were not going to be repeated under Jones. By harvesting staff proposals, the Deputy Minister's Advisory Committee ensured that only vital issues – explained in plain language – would be passed on to Macdonald for consideration.[8]

Jones' political astuteness also helped to alleviate the minister's anxiety over both the modernization situation and the complaints about permanent force discrimination against the reserves. Believing that the latter issue was largely artificial and the product of a small but vocal element, Jones did not agree with Connolly's plan to quell the apparent dissatisfaction by giving the reservists special representation on the Naval Board. Instead of fighting the appointment, the crafty Jones simply arranged that the chief staff officer reserve's "duties were so hazy that he [Cross] could really do not much harm nor too much good."[9] The decision not to resist Macdonald on what Jones considered a valueless board position was undoubtedly the right one. The minister lost interest in the subject once he learned that the voluntary reservists had greeted the post of the chief staff officer reserves with "great satisfaction."[10]

The same was also true for modernization, and it could be argued that Jones was reaping the benefits of what Nelles had sown. The seeds for recovery had already blossomed: by the time of Nelles' dismissal, 70 percent of the single-screw corvettes had either been modernized or were in the process of being upgraded. By May 1944 another 13 percent were allocated to the shipyards, at which time Jones suddenly announced that the corvettes' modernization crisis was over. In reality, the new chief of the naval staff was just telling the minister what he wanted to hear. Fought more than a year after the actual operational crisis, the political battle over modernization – while helping Jones become chief of the naval staff – was an outdated exercise in futility and Jones knew it. With the frigates arriving in large numbers, he gave Macdonald the hard truth: "The fact must be faced that the Corvette, which has given excellent performance in the Battle of Atlantic, must now be regarded as superseded by modern ships." More to the point, Jones' reaction provided the best illustration of how the modernization situation should never have become such a politically charged issue in the first place. Back in July 1942 the minister had been told that the modernization of the corvette fleet would take two years to complete. Through a three-prong plan – which included the short-term solution of asking for British assistance, the mid-term plan of reorganizing Naval Service Headquarters and the existing East Coast refit structure, and the long-term proposal to build more shipyards – Nelles and his staff had produced a minor miracle. By accepting Jones' pronouncement that the fleet was up to date in

May 1944, Macdonald inadvertently confirmed that Nelles' modernization program had actually finished two months ahead of schedule.[11] Nevertheless, Macdonald could rest easy. From his perspective, Jones had exorcised the ghosts of 1943. Even though Connolly's and Macdonald's original fears were largely apparitions in their own right, Jones ensured that the spectre of a parliamentary inquiry into the state of the fleet would no longer haunt the minister.

The fact that his modernization program had turned out better than originally predicted was a small moral victory for Nelles, and it was one that he was willing to hold over his accusers. Certainly the news that the senior Canadian flag officer (overseas) had taken advantage of a spring 1944 trip to Londonderry troubled Connolly, particularly since Nelles had gone to such lengths to clarify for these officers "how the modernization programme ... is the result of [his] own planning and that he must get whatever credit is due."[12] Nor was that the only chance Nelles got to confront some of those who had participated in his downfall. On his arrival in London, Nelles had some tough questions for Captain Frank Houghton, who had taken over the senior Canadian naval officer position in London from Fred Price in early November 1943. At first, the two straight stripers squabbled over the repetitive nature of their terms of reference. This was neither man's fault, as Connolly had simply mimicked a copy of the Air Force's terms for Air Marshal Breadner without realizing that they replicated the functions already assigned to the senior Canadian naval officer in London.[13] "Unworkable" arrangements in London, however, were something that Nelles would take up with the minister. Nelles was still not impressed with the current senior Canadian naval officer in London who he charged with being "disloyal." Perhaps that was a bit harsh, though Nelles' accusation was not entirely baseless. After all, it was Houghton – serving in the capacity of the chief of staff in Newfoundland – who had received a full briefing from Strange on the results of his overseas trip. Despite Strange's revelation that he was going directly to the minister, Houghton never said a word to Nelles. Now Nelles was in the UK and that decision was going to cost Houghton, who claimed that he was being passed over in "the matter of periodic recommendations for honours and awards."[14]

Nelles' case against the administrative staff officer at London, Commander R.A. Pennington, RCNVR, was much stronger. As the former secretary to the Naval Board, Pennington knew Nelles well. But as Pennington told one of the navy's serving historians in May 1945,

> the Admiral dwelt with Athanasian fervour on the topic of the loyalty due from all ranks to their commanding officer. If the junior officers were perplexed, their seniors were decidedly uncomfortable and embarrassed. It was soon clear that the Admiral questioned the loyalty of Captain Houghton and Commander Pennington. On one occasion some two months after his arrival, Commander Pennington felt compelled

to ask the Admiral the reason for his unusually harsh and critical bearing towards him. The reply was that Pennington had openly said that he was "out to get" the Admiral. The Admiral was fully convinced of the truth of this charge which had been made by a "completely reliable" informant. The time and place of Pennington's alleged threat were stated as November 1943, and Ottawa, a circumstance which enabled him to disprove the story, for he had been in London at that time.[15]

Despite his claims of innocence, Pennington had been a member of Connolly's personal reserve network and he fit the mould perfectly. Having left a top civil service position in the British Columbia provincial government to join the navy, Pennington was a man who possessed "intellectual powers" that, it was observed, he "uses to great advantage." Moreover, like so many of Connolly's informants, he had difficulty taking direction from permanent force officers and was "inclined to be sensitive to criticism."[16] And perhaps that was what drew him to the executive assistant. But no matter what his motivations, there is no doubt that Pennington was a full participant in the modernization campaign. Connolly praised him for his assistance during the investigation because "had it not been for the industry which Fred [Price] and yourself displayed, I could not have accomplished anything like the work I got through." But it was Pennington himself who vindicated Nelles' suspicion by replying to Connolly that he was impressed with "the speed with which our recommendations ... have been cracking over."[17]

Such skirmishes were as close as Nelles would get to Connolly's reserve network. Instead, he continued to do battle with Macdonald throughout March and April 1944 over his ambiguous terms of reference.[18] Even though Nelles won some minor concessions – like heading the newly formed Canadian Naval Mission Overseas on 15 May – the difficulties between him and Macdonald continued throughout the year, and Nelles was ultimately fired for a second time in January 1945. In trouble with the prime minister over the RCN's Pacific theatre policy, Macdonald once again used Nelles as a convenient scapegoat. Keeping his mouth shut for the good of the service, Nelles had had enough of the navy's politics and agreed to retire early.

Perhaps wanting to get as far away from Ottawa as possible, Nelles left for British Columbia, where he remained until his death in 1951.[19] Copying the same tactics they had used on MacLean, Nelles was given the rank of full Admiral to ease the pain of his forced retirement from the navy. But at the time of Nelles' retirement, the minister's days were also numbered: a worsening relationship with Prime Minister King would lead to his early departure from Cabinet in April 1945. Nor was he the only one whose final days in the navy were marred by acrimony. Rear Admiral Murray was held responsible for the public relations disaster of the VE day riots in Halifax and had to leave the navy immediately. Murray was unconvinced that this was the only reason behind his early retirement and made an impassioned plea to Jones, saying that he wanted "to finish up this war cleanly at sea, [and] I am not gunning for your job, now or later."[20] Having usurped the commander in chief Canadian North West Atlantic's appointment on 12 May 1945, Jones brought his longstanding feud with Murray to an end as he was now both the navy's senior chief and its top operational commander.

True to form, Jones then consolidated his power from potential competitors by abolishing the position of vice chief of the naval staff. Though such actions were typical of his ambitious nature, it is important to provide some balance to a portrait of this complex and enigmatic officer. Jones was a product of his environment. The compassionate, gentler side he had displayed as a young man was largely snuffed out by a highly competitive officer corps that encouraged career manipulation. Reports that Jones had refused to rank two promising RCN officers for fear of creating a new rivalry suggest that he did not want the next generation to go through what he had experienced.[21] Jones may have mastered the art of staying ahead of rivals but these activities cost him more than just the innocence of youth. His last day in the navy on 8 February 1946 was undoubtedly the most tragic. He died of a massive heart attack at the age of fifty, caused by chronic hypertension. His health could no longer compete with his personal ambition.[22]

Of course, not everyone involved in Nelles' removal was so cursed. Most of those who belonged to the reserve networks returned to their respective professions after demobilization. A number rose to prominent positions in the civil service, and others would get a chance to mould the postwar navy. For example, Louis Audette's appointment as one of three commissioners responsible for the Mainguy Report – a response to the infamous mutinies in 1949 – allowed him to stamp his Second World War experiences and social reengineering onto the future development of the RCN.[23] Others, like William Strange, chose not only to remain in the navy but also became members of the regular force. In fact, having built his own "empire within the navy," Strange rose to the rank of captain while serving as the director of naval information and did not retire until 27 February 1959.[24] Simpson, on the other hand, left the Royal Navy and settled in New Zealand, where he took over as that nation's chief of the naval staff.

As for Connolly, he was offered an opportunity to continue as the executive assistant for the new naval minister, Douglas Abbott, but he saw no reason to stay. Humble to the very end, Connolly's parting thoughts to Macdonald reflect a man lost in admiration for his boss and mentor:

> You have ignored so many of my shortcomings ... I want you to know how grateful I am to you. It was an honour to have been associated with you. That is compensation enough. But through that opportunity I was able to do some war work, to see a Navy both from behind a desk and from the bridge of a ship – to know what it was to be

afraid ... I had an inside to government, saw the heartbreak of politics but through it all I had the privilege of a delightful and inspiring association [with Macdonald].[25]

Of course it was Connolly who ignored Macdonald's shortcomings. Running one of the three services was by no means an easy task, but Macdonald was nonetheless a weak naval minister. While Nelles certainly had made mistakes as chief of the naval staff, Macdonald's reaction in November and December 1943 represented nothing short of a total denial of the principle of ministerial responsibility. Blinded by loyalty, Connolly could never accept the fact that his mentor's experience in federal politics was less than stellar, explaining why he saw Macdonald as a victim when the prime minister more or less forced him out of Cabinet. With his boss back in Nova Scotia, Connolly's future lay in a law firm and eventually a life in politics with a seat in the Canadian Senate. He did well in the Upper Chamber; his experience as Macdonald's executive assistant illustrated that he had a gift for politics.

While a blessing for Macdonald, the executive assistant's political intuition and acumen was a curse for Nelles. Heavily influenced by various networks, Connolly was convinced that the RCN's modernization shortfall represented a tremendous threat to the minister's federal career. Unfortunately, that interpretation was the result of being too easily swayed by sharp-end grousers who knew nothing about the tremendous effort Naval Service Headquarters had been making to combat the refit situation and close the equipment gap. And that was the problem. The political insecurity created by the MacLean affair had left Macdonald vulnerable, and that in turn gave the modernization network instant credibility with Connolly. Besides bestowing a remarkable amount of power upon them, Connolly's trust of the reserve networks and the Londonderry officers was a dangerous breach in civil-military relations because it resulted in a biased investigation. But while all those who had bypassed normal channels had a significant impact in creating the circumstances that led to Nelles' downfall, it was Connolly himself who ultimately pulled the trigger.

With Macdonald on the verge of collapse and resignation, the executive assistant took charge of a situation that he had helped to create and that was rapidly growing out of control. After coming back from Londonderry, Connolly was confident in his position that the Naval Staff had duped the minister. Nelles put up an effective defence – including the knock-down punch of Johnstone's report – which clearly indicated that the Naval Staff had in fact told Macdonald about the equipment deficiencies. This gave Macdonald reason to pause. After all, had the confrontation been purely about equipment, Macdonald should have had little difficulty making the decision to fire Nelles as soon as Connolly had come back from overseas with his allegedly incontrovertible evidence. Instead, Connolly's recommendation to oust Nelles was made three weeks into the crisis. It was a response to the chief of the naval staff's refusal to let his staff officers take the blame for the minister's ignorance. Ironically, had Nelles simply caved in and protected the minister, he probably would have weathered the immediate political storm. His determined defence sent a powerful message that the minister was not going to escape any future political scandal unscathed. Tragically, Nelles' integrity sealed his fate. It guaranteed that he would be offered as the sacrificial lamb to protect Macdonald's reputation. Nelles, like all senior leaders before and after him, had made his fair share of mistakes but his politically motivated removal cannot be easily justified.

Appendices

Abbreviations

ACNS	Assistant chief of the naval staff
Capt. (D)	Captain (destroyers)
CCCS	Commodore/captain commanding Canadian ships
CCHF	Commodore/captain Halifax force
CCNF	Commodore commanding Newfoundland force
CinC CNA	Commander in chief, Canadian North-West Atlantic
CNEC	Chief of naval engineering and construction
CNES	Chief of naval equipment and supply
CNMO	Canadian naval mission overseas
CNP	Chief of naval personnel
CNS	Chief of the naval staff
CO	Commanding officer
COAC	Commanding officer Atlantic coast
Commodore (D)	Commodore (destroyers)
COPC	Commanding officer Pacific coast
CSOR	Chief staff officer reserves
DCNS	Deputy chief of the naval staff
DM	Deputy minister
DMAC	Deputy minister's advisory committee
DNAD	Director of naval air divisions
DNI	Director of naval intelligence
DOD	Director of operations division
DOR	Director of operational research
DPD	Director of plans division
DSD	Director of signals division
DTD	Director of trade division / Director of technical division
DWT	Director of warfare and training
FONF	Flag officer Newfoundland force
MND	Minister of National Defence
NSHQ	Naval Service Headquarters
OIC	Operational intelligence centre
SCFO (O)	Senior Canadian flag officer (Overseas)
SCNO (L)	Senior Canadian naval officer (London)
Sec NB	Secretary, Naval Board
SOE	Senior officer escorts
USN	United States Navy
VCNS	Vice chief of the naval staff

Appendix A:
Senior Appointments, Royal Canadian Navy, 1939-45

Naval Service Headquarters (NSHQ), Ottawa

MINISTER OF NATIONAL DEFENCE FOR NAVAL SERVICES
A.L. Macdonald, 12 July 1940-18 April 1945
D.C. Abbott, 18 April 1945-12 December 1946

DEPUTY MINISTER OF NATIONAL DEFENCE FOR NAVAL SERVICES (DM)
W.G. Mills, dates unavailable

CHIEF OF THE NAVAL STAFF (CNS)
Vice Admiral P.W. Nelles, 1 January 1934–15 January 1944
Vice Admiral G.C. Jones, 15 January 1944–8 February 1946

DEPUTY CHIEF OF THE NAVAL STAFF (DCNS), VICE CHIEF OF THE NAVAL STAFF (VCNS)
Captain L.W. Murray, 30 August 1939–15 October 1940
Commodore H.E. Reid, 15 October 1940–9 October 1942
Rear Admiral G.C. Jones, 9 October 1942–15 January 1944

The title changed from DCNS to VCNS in January 1942. When Jones assumed the duties of CNS, the position of VCNS was left vacant for the duration of the war.

ASSISTANT CHIEF OF THE NAVAL STAFF (ACNS)
Captain W. Creery, 1 June 1943–1 December 1944
Captain H.G. DeWolf, 1 December 1944-?

This position was created during the 1 June 1943 reorganization.

CHIEF OF NAVAL PERSONNEL (CNP)
Captain C.R.H. Taylor, 15 December 1938–2 September 1940
Captain H.T.W. Grant, 2 September 1940–23 September 1942
Captain E.R. Mainguy, 15 November 1942–15 August 1944
Captain H. McMaster, 15 August 1944–1 April 1945
Captain A.M. Hope, 1 April 1945–?

DIRECTOR TECHNICAL DIVISION (DTD), CHIEF OF NAVAL EQUIPMENT AND SUPPLY (CNES)
Commander J.F. Bell, 15 July 1940–18 February 1941
Captain G. Hibbard, 18 February 1941–15 October 1943
Captain E. Johnstone, 29 December 1943–1 November 1944
Captain G.B. Hope, 1 November 1944–?

The title changed from DTD to CNES in January 1942. There was no listing prior to July 1940.

ENGINEER IN CHIEF (NAVAL ENGINEERING BRANCH),
CHIEF OF NAVAL ENGINEERING AND CONSTRUCTION (CNEC)
Captain A.D.M. Curry, 1 May 1935-10 February 1941
Rear Admiral G.L. Stephens, 10 February 1941-?

The title engineer in chief was abolished on 24 October 1942 and replaced by CNEC.

CHIEF STAFF OFFICER RESERVES (CSOR)
Captain P. Cross, 15 January 1944-21 May 1945
Captain P.W. Earl, 21 May 1945-?

NAVAL SECRETARY, SECRETARY NAVAL BOARD (SEC NB)
Paymaster Captain M.J.R.O. Cossette, 1 May 1934-9 February 1942
Paymaster Captain R.A. Pennington, 9 February 1942-26 June 1943
Captain J. Jeffrey, 26 June 1943-?

DIRECTOR OPERATIONS DIVISION (DOD)
Commander J.W.R. Roy, 20 December 1937-10 June 1940
Captain R.E.S. Bidwell, 10 June 1940-1 June 1941
Captain H.N. Lay, 30 June 1941-24 April 1943
Captain W.B. Creery, 24 April 1943-1 June 1943
Captain G.H. Griffiths, 1 June 1943-9 October 1944
Captain D.K. Laidlaw, 9 October 1944-7 July 1945

DIRECTOR OF TRADE (DTD)
Captain E.S. Brand, 29 July 1939-?

DIRECTOR OF NAVAL INTELLIGENCE (DNI)
Captain E.S. Brand, 29 July 1939-1 July 1942
Commander C.H. Little, 1 July 1942-12 June 1945

Prior to 7 January 1942, intelligence was incorporated with trade (director of naval intelligence and trade) under Brand. DTD and DNI were recombined into one directorate on 12 June 1945.

DIRECTOR OF PLANS DIVISION (DPD)
Captain F.L. Houghton, 8 July 1939-25 May 1942
Captain H.G. DeWolf, 25 May 1942-1 July 1943
Lieutenant Commander G.F. Todd, 17 July 1943-6 December 1943
Captain G.R. Miles, 6 December 1943-30 September 1944
Captain H.S. Rayner, 30 September 1944-?

DIRECTOR SIGNALS DIVISION (DSD)
Captain G.A. Worth, 16 February 1942-?

Prior to the January 1942 reorganization, signals was incorporated with plans (Plans and Signals Division) under Houghton.

DIRECTOR OF WARFARE AND TRAINING (DWT)
Captain H. McMaster, 7 June 1943-6 December 1943
Captain K.F. Adams, 6 December 1943-1 August 1944
Captain D.L. Raymond, 1 August 1944-?

This position was created during the June 1943 reorganization. Although created in June, it was not filled until Adams assumed the post in December 1943 – McMaster was actually the deputy DWT.

Halifax

COMMANDING OFFICER ATLANTIC COAST (COAC),
COMMANDER IN CHIEF CANADIAN NORTH WEST ATLANTIC (CinC CNA)

COAC
Commodore H.E. Reid, 1 October 1938-28 September 1940
Rear Admiral G.C. Jones, 28 September 1940-18 September 1942

COAC/CinC CNA
Rear Admiral L.W. Murray, 18 September 1942-12 May 1945

CinC CNA
Vice Admiral G.C. Jones, 12 May 1945-?

The title COAC was replaced by CinC CNA in April 1943.

CHIEF OF STAFF (OPERATIONS) TO COAC/CINC CNA
Lieutenant Commander H.N. Lay, 27 August 1939-1 December 1939
Captain H.T.W. Grant, 2 December 1939-26 August 1940
Captain H.G. DeWolf, 1 October 1941-28 April 1942
Captain W.B. Creery, 28 April 1942-24 April 1943
Captain R.E.S. Bidwell, 24 April 1943-1 April 1944
Captain D.K. Laidlaw, 1 April 1944-20 October 1944
Captain G.R. Miles, 2 October 1944-?

COMMODORE/CAPTAIN HALIFAX FORCE (CCHF), CAPTAIN (D) HALIFAX

CCHF
Commodore G.C. Jones, 7 June 1940-24 September 1940
Commodore L.W. Murray, 24 October 1940-12 February 1941

Captain (D)
Captain E.R. Mainguy, 27 August 1941-1 November 1941
Captain G.R. Miles, 1 November 1941-7 December 1942
Captain J.D. Prentice, 7 December 1942-15 April 1944
Captain W. Puxley, 15 April 1944-4 May 1945
Captain J.C. Hibbard, 4 May 1945-?

St. John's, Newfoundland

COMMODORE COMMANDING NEWFOUNDLAND FORCE (CCNF),
FLAG OFFICER NEWFOUNDLAND FORCE (FONF)
Commodore L.W. Murray, 10 June 1941-28 August 1942
Captain E.R. Mainguy, 28 August 1942-24 October 1942
Commodore H.E. Reid, 24 October 1942-1 November 1943
Commodore C.R.H. Taylor, 1 November 1943-?

The title CCNF was replaced by FONF in September 1941.

CHIEF OF STAFF
Captain R.E.S. Bidwell, 3 July 1941-22 March 1943
Captain F.L. Houghton, 22 March 1943-15 September 1943
Captain G.A.M.V. Harrison, 15 September 1943-16 October 1944
Captain G. Griffiths, 16 October 1944-?

CAPTAIN (D) NEWFOUNDLAND
Captain E.B.K. Stevens, June 1941-8 November 1941
Captain E.R. Mainguy, 8 November 1941-23 September 1942
Captain H.T.W. Grant, 23 September 1942-10 March 1943
Captain J. Rowland, 10 March 1943-26 June 1944
Captain E. Gibbs, 26 June 1944-?

Esquimalt/Vancouver

COMMANDING OFFICER PACIFIC COAST (COPC)
Captain V.G. Brodeur, 14 October 1938-4 September 1940
Commodore W.J.R. Beech, 4 September 1940-1 September 1943
Rear Admiral V.G. Brodeur, 1 September 1943-?

London, UK

HEAD OF THE CANADIAN NAVAL MISSION OVERSEAS (CNMO),
SENIOR CANADIAN FLAG OFFICER OVERSEAS [SCFO (O)]
Vice Admiral P.W. Nelles, 15 January 1944-6 January 1945
Captain F.L. Houghton, 6 January 1945-?

The CNMO was established on 15 May 1945. The SCNO (L) was abolished while the title of SCFO (O) was not only retained but also became head of the mission.

COMMODORE/CAPTAIN COMMANDING CANADIAN SHIPS (CCCS), SENIOR CANADIAN NAVAL OFFICER (LONDON) [SCNO (L)], DEPUTY HEAD OF THE CANADIAN NAVAL MISSION OVERSEAS

CCCS/SCNO (L)
Captain C.R.H. Taylor, January 1941-12 February 1941
Commodore L.W. Murray, 12 February 1941-1 June 1941
Captain C.R.H. Taylor, 1 June 1941-1 February 1942
Captain R.I. Agnew, 1 February 1942-20 April 1943
Commander F. Price, 20 April 1943-23 October 1943
Captain F.L. Houghton, 23 October 1943-6 January 1945

The title CCCS was replaced by SCNO (L) on 15 June 1943.

Deputy Head CNMO
Houghton assumed this position on 15 May 1944.

Appendix B:
Naval Service Headquarters Organizational Charts

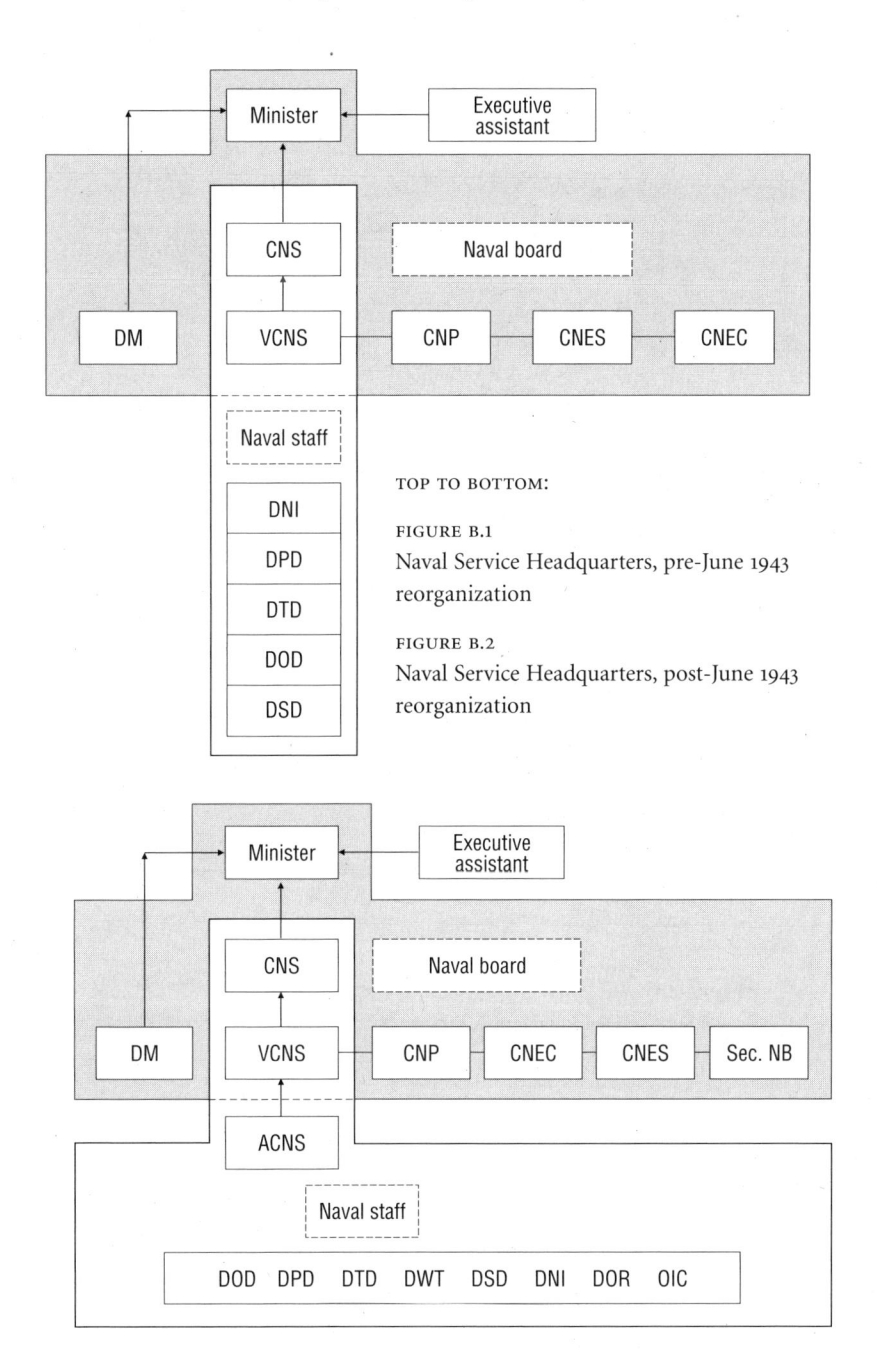

TOP TO BOTTOM:

FIGURE B.1
Naval Service Headquarters, pre-June 1943 reorganization

FIGURE B.2
Naval Service Headquarters, post-June 1943 reorganization

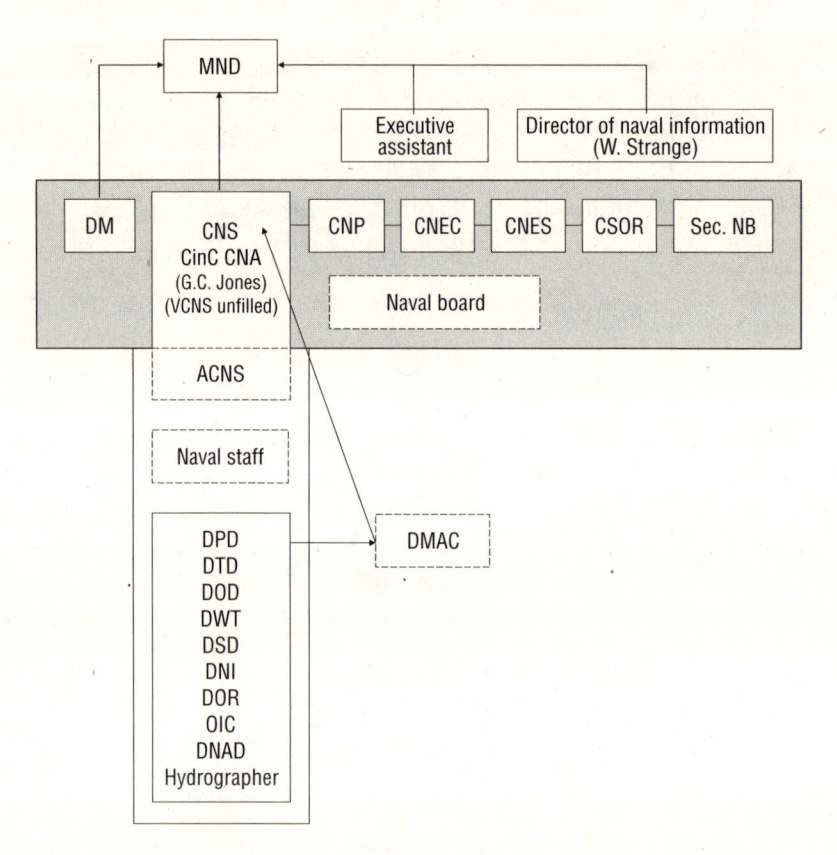

FIGURE B.3
Naval Service Headquarters, May 1945

Appendix C:
Official and Unofficial Command Arrangements, 1942-43

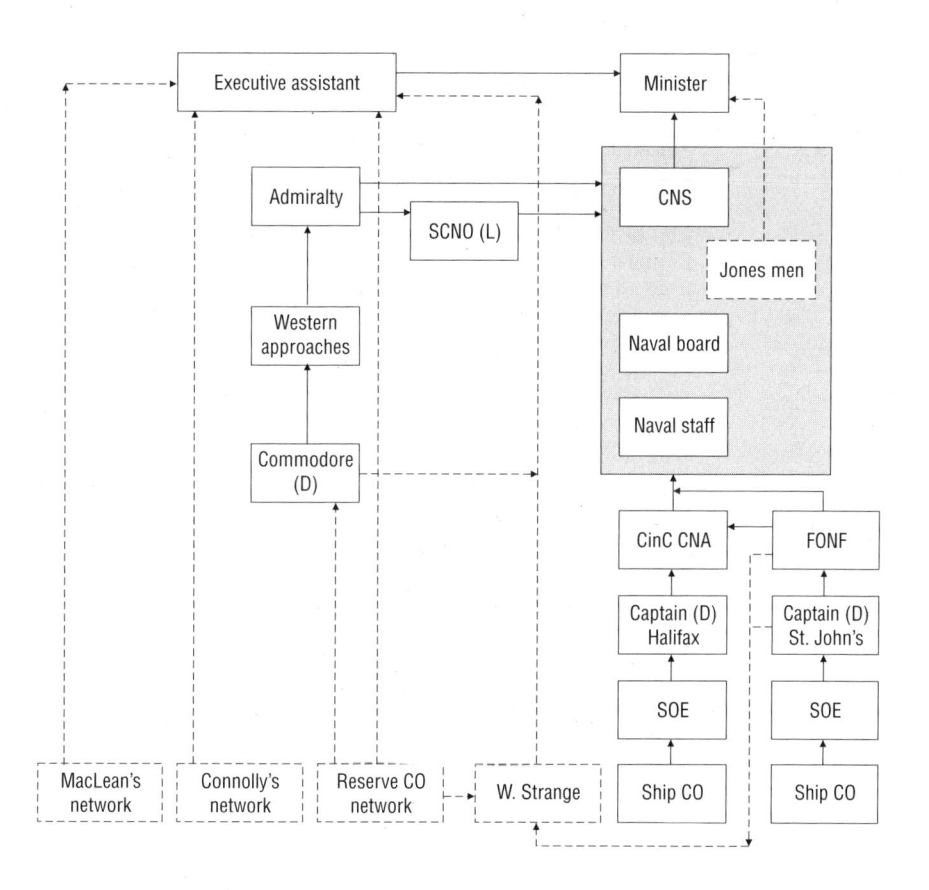

NOTE: Solid lines indicate the formal chain of command and dashed lines indicate unofficial connections.

Notes

Abbreviations
A & A's	Alterations and additions
A/S	Antisubmarine
AASSB	Allied Anti-Submarine Survey Board
CCCS	Commodore/captain commanding Canadian ships
CEF	Canadian Expeditionary Force
CinC CNA	Commander in chief, Canadian North West Atlantic
CinC WA	Commander in chief, Western Approaches
CNP	Chief of naval personnel
COAC	Commanding officer Atlantic coast
CTF	Commander task force
CTG	Commander task group
DHH	Directorate of History and Heritage
DMS	Department of Munitions and Supply
DOD	Date of death
DSD	Director of signals division
DSS	Director of special services
DWT	Director of warfare and training
FONF	Flag officer, Newfoundland
HMC	His Majesty's Canadian
HMCS	His Majesty's Canadian Ship
HRO	Historical records officer
LAC	Library and Archives Canada
NMM	National Maritime Museum
NOIC	Naval officer in charge
NSHQ	Naval Service Headquarters
PANS	Public Archives of Nova Scotia
PRO	Public Records Office
RDFO	Radio direction finding officer
RofP (or ROP)	Report of proceedings
SCFO (O)	Senior Canadian flag officer (overseas)
SCNO (L)	Senior Canadian naval officer (London)
Sec NB	Secretary, Naval Board
USN	United States Navy
USNA	United States National Archives
VCNS	Vice chief of the naval staff

Introduction: The Game and Its Players

1 W.A.B. Douglas, Roger Sarty, and Michael Whitby, *A Blue Water Navy: The Official Operational History of the Royal Canadian Navy in the Second World War, 1943-1945.* Vol. 2, part 2 (St. Catharines, ON: Vanwell Publishing, 2006); Tony German, *The Sea Is at Our Gates: The History of the Royal Canadian Navy* (Toronto: McClelland and Stewart, 1990), 148; David

Bercuson, *Maple Leaf against the Axis: Canada's Second World War* (Toronto: Stoddart, 1995), 144. For more information on other trends within Canadian naval history see Marc Milner, "The Historiography of the Canadian Navy: The State of the Art," in *A Nation's Navy: In Quest of Canadian Naval Identity*, ed. Michael Hadley, Rob Huebert, and Fred Crickard (Montreal and Kingston: McGill-Queen's University Press, 1996), 23-34; and David Zimmerman, "New Dimensions in Canadian Naval History," *The American Neptune* 60, 3 (2001): 263-75.

2 E.C. Russell to director, 27 September 1965, Directorate of History and Heritage (hereafter cited as DHH), Nelles Papers, folder A. In this letter, Russell also observed that there was evidence that Nelles had destroyed documents to protect his actions as CNS in the past. C.P. Stacey to E.C. Russell, 27 September 1965, DHH, Nelles Papers, folder A; C.P. Stacey, *Arms, Men and Governments: The War Policies of Canada, 1939-1945* (Ottawa: Queen's Printer, 1970), 318-19.

3 Roger Sarty, "Admiral Percy W. Nelles: Diligent Guardian of the Vision," in *The Admirals: Canada's Senior Leadership in the Twentieth Century*, ed. Michael Whitby, Richard Gimblett, and Peter Haydon (Toronto: Dundurn Press, 2006), 69-77.

4 GN Tucker, *The Naval Service of Canada* (Ottawa: King's Printer, 1952), 21; and C.P. Stacey, *Arms, Men and Governments* (Ottawa: Queen's Printer, 1970), 315. Also see Dan van der Vat, *The Atlantic Campaign: World War II's Great Struggle at Sea* (London: Harper and Row, 1988), 135. A comparison with other allied navies gives a sense of the level at which the RCN expanded during the Second World War. By 1945, the US navy grew some twenty times its original size, the Royal Navy eight times, and the Royal Australian Navy fourteen times.

5 "Rear Admiral L.W. Murray Recollections of his Naval Career recorded at Dhist, May 1970," DHH, BIOG M.

6 Captain Eric Brand, RN, interview by E.C. Russell, 22 February 1967, Ottawa, tape recording transcript, DHH, Brand Papers, 84/145, vol. 7, 28.

7 Rear Admiral Victor G. Brodeur, interview by anonymous official historian, c. 1950, Halifax, tape recording transcript, DHH, BIOG B, 26.

8 Two excellent accounts of the RCN's operational deficiencies are Marc Milner, *North Atlantic Run: The Royal Canadian Navy and the Battle for the Convoys* (Toronto: University of Toronto Press, 1985); and David Zimmerman, *The Great Naval Battle of Ottawa* (Toronto: University of Toronto Press, 1989). Also see Marc Milner, *The U-Boat Hunters: The Royal Canadian Navy and the Offensive against Germany's Submarines* (Toronto: University of Toronto Press, 1994), 96. The most recent, and undoubtedly most comprehensive, study of the RCN's trials and tribulations at sea is W.A.B. Douglas, Roger Sarty, and Michael Whitby, *No Higher Purpose: The Official Operational History of the Royal Canadian Navy in the Second World War, 1939-1943*, vol. 2, part 1 (St. Catharines, ON: Vanwell Publishing, 2002).

9 Milner, "The Historiography of the Canadian Navy," 33. While the secondary level of naval leadership has not been thoroughly documented, various chiefs of the naval staff and theatre commanders have been covered. For the best illustrations of this trend in the literature, see Michael Whitby, Richard H. Gimblett, and Peter Haydon, *The Admirals: Canada's Senior Naval Leadership in the Twentieth Century* (Toronto: Dundurn Press, 2006). For earlier interpretations, see James Eayrs, *In Defence of Canada*, vol. 3, *From the Great War to the Great Depression* (Toronto: University of Toronto Press, 1964); 23-8, 106-107, 261-65; Michael Hadley and Roger Sarty, *Tin-Pots and Pirate Ships: Canadian Naval Forces and German Sea Raiders, 1880-1918* (Montreal and Kingston: McGill-Queen's University Press, 1991), 295-97; John Armstrong, *The Halifax Explosion and the Royal Canadian Navy: Inquiry and Intrigue* (Vancouver: UBC Press, 2002); Richard H. Gimblett, "Gunboat Diplomacy, Mutiny and National Identity in the Postwar Royal Canadian Navy: The Cruise of HMC *Crescent* to China" (PhD diss., Laval University, 2000); Roger Sarty, "Rear Admiral L.W. Murray and the Battle of the Atlantic: The Professional Who Led Canada's Citizen Sailors," in *Warrior Chiefs: Perspectives*

on *Senior Canadian Military Leaders*, ed. Bernd Horn and Stephen Harris (Toronto: Dundurn Press, 2001), 165-91; Wilfred Lund, "Vice-Admiral Harold Grant: Father of the Post-War Royal Canadian Navy," in Horn and Harris, *Warrior Chiefs*, 193-217.

10 Stacey, *Arms, Men and Governments*; W.A.B. Douglas and Brereton Greenhous, *Out of the Shadows: Canada in the Second World War* (Toronto: Oxford University Press, 1977); Milner, *North Atlantic Run*; Michael Hadley, *U-Boats against Canada: German Submarines in Canadian Waters* (Montreal and Kingston: McGill-Queen's University Press, 1985); Zimmerman, *The Great Naval Battle of Ottawa*; Derek G. Law, "The Historiography of the Battle of the Atlantic," in *The Battle of the Atlantic 1939-1945: The 50th Anniversary International Naval Conference*, ed. Stephen Howarth (London: Greenhill Books, 1994), 600. According to Law, "a curious feature of the Battle of Atlantic history writing is that it took Canadians some 35 years to begin seriously to address their contribution." Law's observation was an accurate depiction of the state of Canadian naval historical writing during the first three decades following the war. Between Tucker and Schull's official histories and Marc Milner's publication of *North Atlantic Run*, W.A.B. Douglas was one of the few military historians who actively tried to drum up interest throughout the late 1970s and early 1980s in the history of the RCN.

11 This book's methodology was influenced by the "new naval history" as defined by John Sumida and David Rosenberg. Believing that too much emphasis is placed on senior leadership, these two American scholars have argued that naval historians can learn more about the decision-making process in complex organizations like the navy through the study of its bureaucracy. This approach suggests that key governmental and military figures depend on a large supporting bureaucracy that both informs and shapes their decisions. By reversing the direction of previous approaches, the goal of the new naval history is to convince historians that they should begin their research with junior bureaucrats and follow the decision-making process up to the senior levels. The standard approach to the process has tended to be the "rational actor" model, which was first explored in Graham Allison, *The Essence of Decision: Explaining the Cuban Missile Crisis* (Boston: Little Brown, 1971), 18, 36, 48. For a discussion on the new naval history, see John T. Sumida and David Rosenberg, "Machines, Men, Manufacturing and Money: The Study of Navies as Complex Organizations and the Transformation of Twentieth Century Naval History," in *Doing Naval History*, ed. John Hattendorf (Newport: Naval War College Press, 1995), 25-40.

12 Captain Eric Brand, RN, interview by E.C. Russell, 22 February 1967, Ottawa, tape recording transcript, DHH, Brand Papers, 84/145, vol. 7, 27.

13 Commander F.E. Grubb, RCN (Ret.), "Problems of Leadership in the RCN during and after World War 2," DHH, 82/532.

14 Stacey, *Arms, Men and Governments*, 316; Milner, *North Atlantic Run*, 256; Zimmerman, *The Great Naval Battle of Ottawa*, 137-38. Zimmerman was the first to emphasize that there were possible political motives behind Nelles' dismissal.

15 Perhaps the most important of these new sources is the J.J. Connolly Papers at Library and Archives Canada (MG 32, C 71), which remained closed to researchers until the mid-1990s. Without these papers, it would have been impossible to piece the full story of the reserve networks together.

16 See various correspondence and research notes on file, DHH, HMCS *Bytown*, 8000, vol. 1, as well as "Personal Correspondence with Dr. Tucker," c. 1944-45, DHH, Historical Records Office, 1700/100/78A.

17 Stacey, *Arms, Men and Governments*, 230-31. This type of foreign interference was not unique in the Canadian military experience. For example, Stacey describes how British officers played a role in convincing the minister of national defence, J.L. Ralston, to replace General A.G.L. McNaughton. Although the part these RN officers played in Nelles' dismissal was more

extreme, the McNaughton case shows that the Canadian Army was also subjected to British interference.
18 Andrew D. MacLean, "Fairmiles and Foul," *Boating Magazine*, January-February 1943, DHH, 94/127.

Chapter 1: Confused Seas

1 The brothers handled their publishing empires independently from each other. Hugh C. MacLean Publishing was eventually absorbed by Southam Press, whereas John Maclean's company merged with those of Horace Hunter to form Maclean-Hunter Ltd.
2 *The Canadian Who's Who*, vol. 5 (Toronto: Trans-Canada Press, 1949-51), 631-32.
3 Lieutenant Joseph Clark, interview by Hal Lawrence, 19 May 1983, Toronto, tape recording transcript, Directorate of History and Heritage (hereafter cited as DHH), 90/86, vol. 1; *Canadian Naval List*, June 1928, DHH Library.
4 Lieutenant Commander Charles Burk, interview by Hal Lawrence, 28 May 1987, Baie d'Urfe, Quebec, tape recording transcript, DHH, BIOG B; Rear Admiral Charles Joseph Dillon, interview by Hal Lawrence, 10 February 1983, tape recording transcript, DHH, BIOG D; Lieutenant Commander James Goad, interview by Hal Lawrence, n.d., Halifax, tape recording transcript, DHH, BIOG G; Sub-Lieutenant Donald Harrison, interview by Hal Lawrence, 28 October 1986, Toronto, tape recording transcript, DHH, BIOG H; Lieutenant Commander Alex Joy, interview by Hal Lawrence, 24 September 1986, Toronto, tape recording transcript, DHH, BIOG J; Lieutenant Daniel Lang, interview by Hal Lawrence, 15 November 1986, Toronto, tape recording transcript, DHH, BIOG L; Lieutenant Allan Watson, interview by Hal Lawrence, 1 April 1986, Halifax, tape recording transcript, DHH, BIOG W.
5 Tony German, *The Sea Is at Our Gates: The History of the Royal Canadian Navy* (Toronto: McClelland and Stewart, 1990), 59-60.
6 Rear Admiral Michael Grote-Sterling, interview by Hal Lawrence, tape recording transcript, in Victoria, BC, 8 January 1985, DHH, 85/476.
7 For one of the best accounts on naval officer training during the war see: William R. Glover, "Officer Training and the Quest for Operational Efficiency in the RCN, 1939-1945" (PhD diss., University of London, 1998).
8 Jeffry V. Brock, *The Dark Broad Seas* (Toronto: McClelland and Steward, 1981), 18.
9 Louis Audette, "Naval Recollections," DHH, 80/256, folder 9, 2.
10 Ibid., 4.
11 Lieutenant Commander R.M. Hanbury, RCNVR, interview by Hal Lawrence, 18 May 1983, Toronto, tape recording transcript, DHH, BIOG H.
12 Memo notes written on MacLean to the Naval Secretary, 16 July 1940, Library and Archives Canada (hereafter cited as LAC), MacLean personnel file (O-45050, date of death (hereafter DOD), January 1971); Cossette to MacLean, 13 July 1940, and MacLean to Cossette, 16 July 1940, Public Archives of Nova Scotia (hereafter cited as PANS), Macdonald Papers, MG 2, F 818/6, F 818/5.
13 Hugh MacLean to W.P. Mulock, 16 July 1940, PANS, Macdonald Papers, MG 2, F 818/4.
14 Nelles to CNP, minute note on naval secretary to Miss Phyllis Axford, 12 November 1940, LAC, MacLean personnel file.
14 Hugh MacLean to W.P. Mulock, 16 July 1940, PANS, Macdonald Papers, MG 2, F 818/4.
15 Quotation from Hugh MacLean to Macdonald, 22 August 1940, PANS, Macdonald Papers, MG 2, F 818/8, F 818/9; see also 6 September 1940, ibid.
16 Also known as motor launches, the fairmiles were 112 feet long, carried a mixed armament of depth charges and small calibre guns, and had a top speed of 18 knots. For more information see John Burgess and Ken Macpherson, *The Ships of Canada's Naval Forces, 1910-1993*

(St. Catharines, ON: Vanwell Publishing, 1994), 142; and Motor Launches (General), DHH, 8000, vol. 1.
17 MacLean summary, January 1943, PANS, Macdonald Papers, MG 2, F 818/80.
18 Mainguy to MacLean, 25 September 1941, LAC, MacLean personnel file.
19 *Toronto Star*, 29 September 1941.
20 Brand to Hibbard and Grant, minute note, "Inadvisable Press Release," 3 October 1941, 103-M-11, LAC, MacLean personnel file.
21 Naval Service memo, "Subject: Lieutenant Commander AD MacLean, RCNVR, Senior Officer of Fairmiles," n.d. [fall 1941], LAC, MacLean personnel file.
22 Hibbard to Grant and Mainguy, 3 October 1941, 103-M-11, LAC, MacLean personnel file; Cossette to MacLean, 17 December 1941, LAC, MacLean personnel file.
23 Andrew Dyas MacLean, "Fairmiles and Foul," *Boating Magazine*, January-February 1943, DHH, 94/127, 8.
24 NSHQ to COAC, naval message, 23 November 1941, DHH, 8000, Motor Launches (General) vol. 1; Roger Sarty, *Canada and the Battle of the Atlantic* (Montreal: Art Global, 1998), 76.
25 "Chiefs of Staff Committee, Appendix A: Participation by RCN Instructed to Work in Closest Co-operation with HM Forces," 17 September 1939, Queen's Archives, Power Papers, 2150, box 1, vol. 1, 5.
26 MacLean, "Fairmiles and Foul," 8.
27 A good example of MacLean's disdain of administration can be found in a speech he made to a public gathering, in which he warned, "the bureaucracy is ... the curse of Canada." As cited in John Swettenham and David Kealy, *Serving the State: A History of the Professional Institute of the Public Service of Canada, 1920-1970* (Ottawa: Le Droit, 1970), 35-36.
28 House of Commons, *Debates*, 23, 25 February 1942, 761, 810-11; Naval Board Meeting, 12 February 1942, DHH.
29 "Fairmile Fuddle," *Boating Magazine*, January-February 1942; "Asks about Fairmile Fuddle," *Boating Magazine*, January-February 1942. It is likely that MacLean was the author because he used the same journal to attack the navy publicly in January 1943. In that edition he made reference to "Fairmile Fuddle," which he observed had "created such a furore that questions were asked in parliament." Moreover, the terms used in, and style of, the two articles are almost identical. Quotation in text from A.D. MacLean, *R.B. Bennett, Prime Minister of Canada* (Toronto: Excelsior Publishing, 1934), 51.
30 Nelles to Macdonald, weekly naval reports, 7 May 1942, DHH, 1000-5-7, vol. 2. For comments on the operational performance of the fairmiles, see Sydney monthly reports, May-September 1942, DHH, 1000-5-21, vol. 1.
31 MacLean to Miles, 10 June 1942, LAC, MacLean personnel file; MacLean, "Fairmiles and Foul," 9.
32 Miles to Jones, 19 May 1942, LAC, Connolly Papers, MG 32, C 71, vol. 3, file 8; MacLean to Miles, 11 May 1942, LAC, Connolly Papers, MG 32, C 71, vol. 3, file 8; History of HMCS *Lynx*, Armed Yacht, DHH, HMCS *Lynx*, 8000.
33 Jones to Pennington, 27 May 1942, LAC, Connolly Papers, MG 32, C 71, vol. 3, file 8.
34 MacLean to Miles, 15 July 1942, 10 June 1942, LAC, MacLean personnel file.
35 MacLean summary, January 1943, PANS, Macdonald Papers, MG 2, F 818/80; A.G.S. Griffin, letter to author, 17 May 2000.
36 Extract from MacLean personnel file, 11 July 1942, LAC, Connolly Papers, MG 32, C71, vol. 3, file 8.
37 *The Canadian Who's Who*, vol. 8 (Toronto: Trans-Canada Press, 1960), 693; J. MacKay to Macdonald, 3 July 1942, PANS, MG 2, Macdonald Papers, F 818/30.
38 MacLean summary, n.d. [spring 1943], LAC, Connolly Papers, MG 32, C 71, vol. 3, file 8.
39 Various anonymous reports, n.d. [July 1942], LAC, Connolly Papers, MG 32, C 71, vol. 3, file 8.

40 MacLean, "Fairmiles and Foul." Operationally speaking, MacLean's timing was perfect, as Macdonald was dealing with the political ramifications of the spring 1942 Canadian inshore campaign in which U-boats had sunk vessels in the St. Lawrence. For more information on this campaign, see Michael Hadley, *U-Boats against Canada: German Submarines in Canadian Waters* (Montreal and Kingston: McGill-Queen's University Press, 1985), particularly ch. 3.
41 "Comments on the Confidential Report on Efficiency of RCN (Atlantic Seaboard)," n.d. [July 1942], LAC, Connolly Papers, MG 32, C 71, vol. 3, file 8; "Confidential Report on Efficiency of RCN (Atlantic Seaboard)," n.d. [July 1942], LAC, Connolly Papers, MG 32, C 71, vol. 3, file 8.
42 Anonymous cover letter, n.d. [July 1942], LAC, Connolly Papers, MG 32, C 71, vol. 3, file 8.
43 A.D. MacLean, "Reply to Navy Minister," *Boating Magazine*, 19, 2 (March-April 1943): 5-10. Both the terms "people's navy" and "citizen sailor" were used throughout this issue to demonstrate the changing nature of the RCN.
44 MacLean to Connolly, 15 July 1942, LAC, Connolly Papers, MG 32, C 71, vol. 3, file 8; Connolly to Macdonald, 7 July 1942, PANS, Macdonald Papers, MG 2, F 818/31; and Hugh MacLean to Macdonald, 8 July 1942, PANS, Macdonald Papers, MG 2, F 818/32.
45 Anonymous cover letter, n.d. [July 1942], LAC, Connolly Papers, MG 32, C 71, vol. 3, file 8.
46 "Comments on the Confidential Report on Efficiency of RCN (Atlantic Seaboard)," n.d. [July 1942], LAC, Connolly Papers, MG 32, C 71, vol. 3, file 8.
47 "Confidential Report on Efficiency of RCN (Atlantic Seaboard)," n.d. [July 1942], LAC, Connolly Papers, MG 32, C 71, vol. 3, file 8; Connolly to Macdonald, 18 July 1942, LAC, Connolly Papers, MG 32, C 71, vol. 3, file 8; House of Commons, *Debates*, 22 July 1942, 4,772.
48 Connolly to Macdonald, 18 July 1942, LAC, Connolly Papers, MG 32, C 71, vol. 3, file 8; House of Commons, *Debates*, 20 April 1942, 1,724-25.
49 *The Canadian Who's Who*, vol. 8 (Toronto: Trans-Canada Press, 1960), 693; House of Commons, *Debates*, 9 June 1943, 3,482-83.
50 Macdonald personal service notes, 16 June 1943, PANS, Macdonald Papers, MG 2, F 305; MacLean summary, spring 1943 (13 May 1941 entry), LAC, Connolly Papers, MG 32, C 71, vol. 3, file 8; MacLean summary, January 1943, PANS, Macdonald Papers, MG 2, F 818/80.
51 "Lieutenant Commander Rowland Bourke, Press Release," LAC, Bourke personnel file, (O-7860, DOD, 29 August 1958). It is likely that Bourke and MacLean knew each other from the First World War, as they both served on the RN's motor launches at the same time.
52 Connolly to Macdonald, 18 July 1942, LAC, Connolly Papers, MG 32, C 71, vol. 3, file 8; MacLean to Connolly, 29 July 1942, LAC, Connolly Papers, MG 32, C 71, vol. 3, file 8.
53 MacLean, *R.B. Bennett Prime Minister*, 33.
54 MacLean to Connolly, 29 July 1942, LAC, Connolly Papers, MG 32, C 71, vol. 3, file 8.
55 MacLean to Connolly, 5 August 1942, PANS, Macdonald Papers, MG 2, F 818/42; Connolly to MacLean, 13 August 1942, PANS, Macdonald Papers, MG 2, F 818/33; MacLean to Connolly, 3 September 1942, PANS, Macdonald Papers, MG 2, F 818/35; MacLean to Macdonald, 18 September 1942, PANS, Macdonald Papers, MG 2, F 818/36.
56 Lieutenant Commander James B. Goad, RCNVR, interview by Hal Lawrence, n.d., Halifax, tape recording transcript, DHH, BIOG G, 5.
57 MacLean to Macdonald, 8 September 1942, PANS, Macdonald Papers, MG 2, F 818/36.
58 MacLean summary, January 1943, PANS, Macdonald Papers, MG 2, F 818/80; Macdonald personal service notes, 16 June 1943, PANS, Macdonald Papers, MG 2, F 305.
60 MacLean to Connolly, 15 July 1942, LAC, Connolly Papers, MG 32, C 71, vol. 3, file 8.
61 Johnstone to Nelles and Macdonald, Lieutenant Commander Andrew D. MacLean RCNVR, 20 August 1942, LAC, MacLean personnel file.
62 MacLean to Connolly, 13 October 1942, PANS, Macdonald Papers, MG 2, F 818/41.

63 Johnstone to Nelles, 19 October 1942, LAC, MacLean personnel file.
64 Connolly to Audette, 20 October 1942, LAC, Audette Papers, MG 31, E 18, vol. 1, file 5.
65 Macdonald to Stanley Clark, 31 December 1941, PANS, Macdonald Papers, MG 2, F 589/3.
66 "The Captain and the Capital," n.d. [late 1942], LAC, Joseph Schull Papers, MG 31, D 5, vol. 76, file 15.
67 Connolly diary, February 1942, LAC, Connolly Papers, MG 32, C 71, vol. 2, file 4.
68 Brand diary, October 1942, DHH, Brand Papers, 81/45, 57-60; FONF report of proceedings, October 1942, DHH, 1000-5-20, vol. 2.
69 Macdonald to Jones, 4 June 1942, PANS, Macdonald Papers, MG 2, F 883/1.
70 Irwin to Macdonald, Canadian National telegram, 6 June 1942, PANS, Macdonald Papers, MG 2, F 883/3.
71 Jones to Macdonald, 8 June 1942, PANS, Macdonald Papers, MG 2, F 883/3; Macdonald to Jones, 4 June 1942, PANS, Macdonald Papers, MG 2, F 883/1.
72 "Memo for File Enquiry into Naval Incidents," 25 October 1949, LAC, Audette Papers, MG 31, E 18, vol. 12, file 16. Audette attributed these remarks to Rear Admiral H.T.W. Grant who – while attending a dinner at Audette's house – was himself apparently intoxicated.
73 Macdonald to Gillis, 14 July 1942, PANS, Macdonald Papers, MG 2, F 883/16.
74 Connolly diary, October 1942, LAC, Connolly Papers, MG 32, C 71, vol. 2, file 4; Scott Young, *O'Brien: From Water Boy to One Million a Year* (Burnstown, ON: The General Store Publishing House, 1967), 180-82. I am also grateful to Mrs. Frances O'Brien for information on Connolly's association with O'Brien.
75 Mac Johnston, *Corvettes Canada: Convoy Veterans of WW II Tell Their True Stories* (Toronto: McGraw-Hill Ryerson, 1994), 270, 272.
76 *Canadian Who's Who*, vol. 9 (Toronto: Trans Canada Press, 1963), 509; W.A.B. Douglas, "Conflict and Innovation in the Royal Canadian Navy, 1939-1945," in *Naval Warfare in the Twentieth Century*, ed. Gerald Jordan (New York: Crane Russak, 1977), 216-17; Various Naval Council, Staff, and Board Meetings, 1941-42, DHH.
77 Hodgson to Connolly, 22 November 1942, LAC, Connolly Papers, MG 32, C 71, vol. 2, file 15; *Canadian Naval Lists*, September 1942, DHH Library.
78 Louis Audette, interview by Salty Dips Association, in *Salty Dips*, vol. 2, ed. Mac Lynch (Ottawa: Privately printed, 1985), 64.
79 Louis Audette, "Naval Recollections," DHH, 80/256, folder 9, 51; Louis Audette, interview by Salty Dips Association; Connolly to Mary Audette, 2 November 1942, LAC, Connolly Papers, MG 32, C 71, vol. 2, file 15; Connolly to Audette, 25 November 1943, LAC, Connolly Papers, MG 32, C 71, vol. 2, file 17.
80 Marc Milner, *Canada's Navy: The First Century* (Toronto: University of Toronto Press, 1999), 113; Sarty, *Canada and the Battle of the Atlantic*, 124-26.
81 W.A.B. Douglas, Roger Sarty, and Michael Whitby, *No Higher Purpose: The Official Operational History of the Royal Canadian Navy in the Second World War, 1939-1943*, vol. 2, part 1 (St. Catharines, ON: Vanwell Publishing, 2002), 524-27; Marc Milner, "Royal Canadian Navy Participation in the Battle of the Atlantic Crisis of 1943," in *The RCN in Retrospect, 1910-1968*, ed. James Boutilier (Vancouver: University of British Columbia Press, 1982), 167.
82 "Confidential Report on Efficiency of RCN (Atlantic Seaboard)," n.d. [July 1942], MG 32, C 71, vol. 3, file 8.
83 "Comments on the Confidential Report on Efficiency of RCN (Atlantic Seaboard)," n.d. [July 1942], LAC, Connolly Papers, MG 32, C 71, vol. 3, file 8.
84 James Lamb, *The Corvette Navy: True Stories from Canada's Atlantic War* (Toronto: Macmillan, 1977), 8, 126, 177.
85 Audette to Marc Milner, 16 November 1978, LAC, Audette Papers, MG 31, E 18, vol. 15, file 1.
86 Murray to Pennington, 20 October 1942, LAC, Murray personnel file (O-54510, DOD 25 November 1971).

87 Sec NB to COAC, 2 October 1942, LAC, Murray personnel file
88 Reid to Nelles, 12 September 1942, LAC, Murray personnel file.
89 "Confidential Report on Efficiency of RCN (Atlantic Seaboard)," n.d. [July 1942], LAC, Connolly Papers, MG 32, C 71, vol. 3, file 8.
90 A.G.S. Griffin to St. Clair Balfour, 10 May 2000. I am grateful to Tony Griffin for providing me with a copy of this letter.
91 *Salty Dips*, 2:200.
92 O'Brien to Connolly, "Chase me Charlie," October 1942, LAC, Connolly Papers, MG 32, C 71, vol. 4, file 14. The three corvettes were the *Lunenburg*, *Weyburn*, and *Nasturtium*, which sailed with SC 100 but then were reassigned so that they could participate in the landings in North Africa (Operation Torch) scheduled for November 1942. For more information on Operation Torch, see Sean Cafferky, "'A Use Lot, These Canadian Ships': The Royal Canadian Navy and Operation Torch, 1942-1943," *The Northern Mariner* 3, 4 (October 1993): 1-17.
93 Connolly to Macdonald, 18 July 1942, LAC, Connolly Papers, MG 32, C 71, vol. 3, file 8.
94 Connolly diary, n.d., LAC, Connolly Papers, MG 32, C 71, vol. 3. I am grateful to Mr. J.M. Connolly for telling me about his father's friendship with Gilhooly.
95 Connolly to Reid, 3 November 1942, LAC, Connolly Papers, MG 32, C 71, vol. 2, file 15.
96 John Connolly to Ida Connolly, 9 October 1943, LAC, Connolly Papers, MG 32, C 71, vol. 1, file 1.
97 Rear Admiral Michael Grote Sterling, interview by Hal Lawrence, 8 January 1985, Victoria, BC, tape recording transcript, DHH, 85/476.
98 Audette to Brooke Claxton, 11 October 1949, LAC, Audette Papers, MG 31, E 18, vol. 12, file 16.

Chapter 2: Equal Privileges for Greater Sacrifices

1 Hugh MacLean to Macdonald, 2 November 1942, Public Archives of Nova Scotia (hereafter cited as PANS), Macdonald Papers, MG 2, F 818/43; Andrew MacLean to Macdonald, 3 November 1942, PANS, Macdonald Papers, MG 2, F 818/56.
2 MacLean to Connolly, PANS, Macdonald Papers, MG 2, F 818/52.
3 Connolly's notes, n.d. [July 1942], Library and Archives Canada (hereafter cited as LAC), Connolly Papers, MG 32, C 71, vol. 3, file 8; Connolly to Macdonald, Notes on anonymous memo, n.d. [July 1942], LAC, Connolly Papers, MG 32, C 71, vol. 3, file 8.
4 Power to King, 17 November 1942, and Macdonald to King, 24 February 1943, Queen's Archives, Power Papers, 2150, box 1, vol. 1. In part, this can be linked to Chubby Power's efforts in November 1942 to convince the prime minister that the War Cabinet committee needed to be reorganized because, as Macdonald observed, it "is too large."
5 Connolly to Macdonald, 18 July 1942, LAC, Connolly Papers, MG 32, C 71, vol. 3, file 8.
6 Connolly to MacLean, 2 December 1943, PANS, Macdonald Papers, MG 2, F 818/46; MacLean to Connolly, n.d. [December 1942], PANS, Macdonald Papers, MG 2, F 1818/5; J.J. Connolly to J.P. Connolly, 11 December 1942, PANS, Macdonald Papers, MG 2, F 818/53; MacLean to Macdonald, 14 December 1942, PANS, Macdonald Papers, MG 2, F 818/55.
7 MacLean to Connolly, 1 December 1943, PANS, Macdonald Papers, MG 2, F 818/47.
8 Connolly to MacLean, 2 December 1943, PANS, Macdonald Papers, MG 2, F 818/47 and F 818/46; Connolly to MacLean, 11 December 1942, PANS, Macdonald Papers, MG 2, F 818/50.
9 Anonymous cover letter, n.d. [July 1942], LAC, Connolly Papers, MG 32, C 71, vol. 3, file 8. Naval Board meeting, 9 November 1942, Directorate of History and Heritage (hereafter cited as DHH).
10 Naval Board meeting, 9 November 1942, DHH; Connolly diary, October 1943, LAC, Connolly Papers, MG 32, C 71, vol. 2, file 7.
11 Naval Board meeting, 24 December 1942, DHH.
12 Confidential naval orders, January 1944, DHH Library; Naval Board meeting, 10 December 1942, DHH; Naval Order 2508, 16 January 1943, DHH Library.

13 Naval Board meeting, 26 November 1942, DHH; MacLean to Macdonald, 28 December 1942, PANS, Macdonald Papers, MG 2, F 818/57.
14 Naval Board meeting, 26 November 1942, DHH; Toronto telephone book, 1942, National Library; MacLean to Macdonald, 28 December 1942, PANS, Macdonald Papers, MG 2, F 818/57.
15 Naval Board meeting, 18 January 1943, DHH; also see various correspondence on LAC, RG 24, vol. 11,957, file 16-29-1.
16 "Committee on Motor Launches (Fairmile)," 10 February 1943, DHH, 8000, Motor Launches Fairmile General, vol. 1.
17 W.A.B. Douglas, Roger Sarty, and Michael Whitby, *No Higher Purpose: The Official Operational History of the Royal Canadian Navy in the Second World War, 1939-1943*, vol. 2, part 1 (St. Catharines, ON: Vanwell Publishing, 2002), 528.
18 House of Commons, *Debates*, 20 April 1942, 1,724-25. These statistics were prepared for Macdonald so that he could answer a question from Conservative MP George R. Boucher, who wanted to know what percentage of RCN, RCNR, and RCNVR officers were serving at sea. That he also asked how many reservists had been granted commissions in the naval service as lieutenants or lieutenant commanders suggests that Boucher was another MP that MacLean had approached. Nelles to Macdonald, Naval weekly reports, 7 May 1942, DHH, 1000-5-7, vol. 2. This report indicated that the 33,727 personnel in the navy at the time consisted of 3,885 RCN, 5,110 RCNR, and 24,732 RCNVR.
19 "Notes on the Charges made by MacLean in General," n.d. [February 1943], LAC, Connolly Papers, MG 32, C 71, vol. 3, file 10.
20 Commander R.L. Roome to Connolly, 19 February 1943, LAC, Connolly Papers, MG 32, C 71, vol. 3, file 11.
21 Macdonald to MacLean, 23 December 1942, PANS, Macdonald Papers, MG 2, F 818/54.
22 Sub-Lieutenant William Pugsley, n.d., LAC, Connolly Papers, MG 32, C 71, vol. 3, file 11.
23 Connolly's notes, n.d. [July 1942], LAC, Connolly Papers, MG 32, C 71, vol. 3, file 8; "Notes on the Charges made by MacLean in General," n.d. [February 1943], LAC, Connolly Papers, MG 32, C 71, vol. 3, file 10; Lieutenant Commander William Pugsley to Nelles, n.d. [February 1943], LAC, Connolly Papers, MG 32, C71, vol. 3, file 8.
24 Naval Board minutes, 9 November 1942, DHH. Also see the minutes for 26 November and 7 December 1942.
25 Prentice to Murray, and Murray to Jeffrey, "Promotion RCNVR Officers," 16 July 1943, LAC, RG 24, vol. 3,811, 1012-5-35, vol. 1.
26 2nd Sea Lord's office to Brand, 22 March 1943, LAC, RG 24, vol. 3,811, 1012-5-35, vol. 1.
27 Macdonald to MacLean, 23 December 1942, PANS, Macdonald Papers, MG 2, F 818/54.
28 MacLean to Connolly, n.d. [December 1942]; Connolly to MacLean, 11 December 1942; J.J. Connolly to J.P. Connolly, 11 December 1942; and MacLean to Macdonald, 14 December 1942, PANS, Macdonald Papers, MG 2, F 818/51, F 818/50, F 818/53, and F 818/55.
29 MacLean to Macdonald, 4 January 1943, PANS, Macdonald Papers, MG 2, F 818/60; MacLean to Macdonald, 8 January 1943, PANS, Macdonald Papers, MG 2, F 818/62.
30 "Wants Representative Naval Board," article galley, n.d., PANS, Macdonald Papers, MG 2, F 818/57.
31 Macdonald to MacLean, 13 January 1943, PANS, Macdonald Papers, MG 2, F 818/61; MacLean to Macdonald, 14 January 1943, PANS, Macdonald Papers, MG 2, F 818/63; MacLean to Macdonald, 25 January 1943, PANS, Macdonald Papers, MG 2, F 818/64.
32 MacLean to Macdonald, 13 January 1943, LAC, Connolly Papers, MG 32, C 71, vol. 3, file 10; MacLean to Macdonald, 14 January 1943, PANS, Macdonald Papers, MG 2, F 818/63.
33 MacLean to Macdonald, 25 January 1943, PANS, Macdonald Papers, MG 2, F 818/64.
34 Jones minute note, 26 January 1943, LAC, Connolly Papers, MG 32, C 71, vol. 3, file 10.

35 Quotations from MacTavish to DeWolf, 22 January 1943, LAC, Connolly Papers, MG 32, C 71, vol. 3, file 10; Defence of Canada Regulations, 1942, DHH, 81/520/1540-12.
36 "Temporary Memorandum No. 69 Minister's Itinerary," 23 January 1943; Macdonald to Crooke, 29 January 1943, PANS, Macdonald Papers, MG 2, F 876/48 and F 876/37.
37 NSHQ to COAC, 10 July 1942; and COAC to NSHQ, 28 July 1942, LAC, RG 24, vol. 6,742, 8000-496/13; History of HMCS *Lynx*, 22 June 1955, DHH, 81/520/8000, box 60, file 2. The error was caught when COAC responded to NSHQ's message and asked, "How is ship to be destroyed?"
38 Lieutenant Commander James Goad, interview by Hal Lawrence, n.d., Halifax, tape recording transcript, DHH, BIOG G.
39 *Globe and Mail*, 2 February 1943; *Globe and Mail*, 3 February 1943.
40 Andrew Dyas MacLean, "Fairmiles and Foul," *Boating Magazine,* January-February 1943, DHH, 94/127.
41 "General Allegations Made by MacLean and upon which an Answer Must Be Prepared," n.d. [February 1943], LAC, Connolly Papers, MG 32, C 71, vol. 3, file 10.
42 *Globe and Mail*, 3 February 1943.
43 House of Commons, *Debates*, 3 February 1943, 105; House of Commons, *Debates*, 5 February 1943, 176-177.
44 For further examples of the press reaction to MacLean's article, see the following newspapers for the period of 3-15 February 1943: *Montreal Gazette*, *Ottawa Citizen*, *Globe and Mail*, *Vancouver Sun*, and *Winnipeg Free Press*.
45 House of Commons, *Debates*, 5 February 1943, 177.
46 *Globe and Mail*, 6 February 1943; *Vancouver Sun*, 6 February 1943.
47 Lay to Nelles, 3 February 1943, LAC, Connolly Papers, MG 32, C 71, vol. 3, file 10.
48 H.C. Howard to Nelles, "Report of Activities, January and February 1943," 17 March 1943, LAC, RG 24, vol. 8,165. In fact, the only distinction that separated the "special article requested by *Boating Magazine*" from all the rest was a small pencil mark on Nelles' copy of the report.
49 Macdonald to MacLean, 20 February 1943, PANS, Macdonald Papers, MG 2, F 818/71; A.D. MacLean, *Boating Magazine*, January-February 1943, DHH, 94/127.
50 Roome to Connolly, 19 February 1943, LAC, Connolly Papers, MG 32, C 71, vol. 3, file 11.
51 "Andy MacLean," n.d., PANS, Macdonald Papers, MG 2, F 818/9.
52 Powell to Lay, and Lay to Nelles, 3 February 1943, LAC, Connolly Papers, MG 32, C 71, vol. 3, file 10.
53 Powell to Lay, 3 February 1943, LAC, Connolly Papers, MG 32, C 71, vol. 3, file 10; Lay to Nelles, 3 February 1943, LAC, Connolly Papers, MG 32, C 71, vol. 3, file 10; Defence of Canada Regulations, 1942, DHH, 81/520/1540-12; MacTavish to DeWolf, 22 January 1943, LAC, Connolly Papers, MG 32, C 71, vol. 3, file 10; Jones minute note, 26 January 1943, LAC, Connolly Papers, MG 32, C 71, vol. 3, file 10.
54 Nelles to Macdonald, "Proposed Speech," n.d. [February 1943], LAC, Connolly Papers, MG 32, C 71, vol. 3, file 11; "Notes on the Charges Made by MacLean in General," n.d. [February 1943], LAC, Connolly Papers, MG 32, C 71, vol. 3, file 10.
55 Nelles to Macdonald, "Proposed Speech," n.d. [February 1943], LAC, Connolly Papers, MG 32, C 71, vol. 3, file 11.
56 Pugsley to Nelles, n.d. [February 1943], LAC, Connolly Papers, MG 32, C 71, vol. 3, file 11.
57 Nelles to Macdonald, "Proposed Speech," n.d. [February 1943], LAC, Connolly Papers, MG 32, C 71, vol. 3, file 11.
58 DeWolf to MacTavish, minute note, n.d. [February 1943], LAC, Connolly Papers, MG 32, C 71, vol. 3, file 11.
59 Quotations from Pugsley to Nelles, n.d. [February 1943] and Pugsley to Nelles, "Candidate," n.d., LAC, Connolly Papers, MG 32, C 71, vol. 3, file 11.

60 Macdonald to MacLean, 20 February 1943, LAC, Connolly Papers, MG 32, C 71, vol. 3, file 11; Roome to Connolly, 19 February 1943, LAC, Connolly Papers, MG 32, C 71, vol. 3, file 11.
61 Marc Milner, "The Royal Canadian Navy and 1943: A Year Best Forgotten?" in *1943: The Beginning of the End*, ed. Paul D. Dickson (Waterloo: Canadian Committee for the History of the Second World War, 1995), 126.
62 MacLean to Pennington, 12 April 1943, 20 April 1943; PANS, Macdonald Papers, MG 2, F 818/73, F 818/74; also see MacLean personnel file, LAC.
63 For more information on the conscription crisis and King's attitude toward the Liberal Party, see J.L. Granatstein and J.M. Hitsman, *Broken Promises: A History of Conscription in Canada* (Toronto: Oxford University Press, 1977); André Laurendeau, *La Crise de la Conscription 1942* (Montreal: Editions du Jour, 1962); Reginald Hardy, *Mackenzie King of Canada: A Biography* (Toronto: Oxford University Press, 1949); and Robert Bothwell, Ian Drummond, and John English, *Canada 1900-1945* (Toronto: University of Toronto Press, 1987).
64 House of Commons, *Debates*, 17 February 1943, 493.
65 "Notes on the Charges Made by MacLean in General," n.d. [February 1943], LAC, Connolly Papers, MG 32, C 71, vol. 3, file 10; Connolly's notes, n.d. [July 1942], LAC, Connolly Papers, MG 32, C 71, vol. 3, file 8.
66 King diary, 17 February 1943, DHH, 83/530, 121-22.
67 Roome to Connolly, 19 February 1943, LAC, Connolly Papers, MG 32, C 71, vol. 3, file 11.
68 Hugh MacLean to Macdonald, 18 February 1943; and Macdonald to Hugh MacLean, 20 February 1943, PANS, Macdonald Papers, MG 2, F 818/71, F 818/72.
69 "Reply to Navy Minister," *Boating Magazine*, 19, 2 (March-April 1943): 42.
70 Ibid.
71 MacLean to Pennington, 12 and 20 April 1943, PANS, Macdonald Papers, MG 2, F 818/73, F 818/74; also see MacLean personnel file, LAC.
72 Various minute notes, MacLean personnel file, LAC.
73 Naval Board meetings, February 1942-April 1945, DHH. The raw figures are as follows: from 9 February 1942 to 15 April 1943 Macdonald missed 57 out of 112 Naval Board meetings, while from 19 April 1943 to 16 April 1945 he was absent from only 4 out of 53 meetings.
74 H. Nelson Lay, *Memoirs of a Mariner* (Stittsville, ON: Canada's Wings, 1982), 148.
75 MacTavish to DeWolf, 22 January 1943, LAC, Connolly Papers, MG 32, C 71, vol. 3, file 10; House of Commons, *Debates*, 10 February 1943.
76 Roome to Connolly, 19 February 1943, LAC, Connolly Papers, MG 32, C 71, vol. 3, file 11.
77 Connolly diary notes, 8 April 1943, LAC, Connolly Papers, MG 32, C 71, vol. 2, file 6.
78 MacLean to Connolly, 12 April 1943, PANS, Macdonald Papers, MG 2, F 818/76.
79 "Bytown," n.d. [late 1942], LAC, Joseph Schull Papers, MG 31, D5, vol. 76, file 15; Lieutenant Commander E.J. Downton, RCNVR, interview by Hal Lawrence, 20 November 1982, Vancouver, tape recording transcript, DHH, BIOG D.
80 MacLean to King, 3 May 1943, PANS, MG 2, Macdonald Papers, F 818/82; Heeney to Macdonald, 12 May 1943, PANS, Macdonald Papers, MG 2, F 818/83.
81 *Quebec Chronicle-Telegraph*, 8 May 1943.
82 House of Commons, *Debates*, 9 June 1943, 3,482-83.
83 House of Commons, *Debates*, 9-11 June 1943, 3,564-65.
84 House of Commons, *Debates*, 11 June 1943, 3,565.
85 MacLean to Connolly, 12 April 1943, PANS, Macdonald Papers, MG 2, F 818/77.
86 *Boating Magazine*, 19, 2 (March-April 1943): 37.
87 Connolly to Macdonald, n.d., LAC, Connolly Papers, MG 32, C 71, vol. 4.

Chapter 3: The Strange Interpretation

1 Simpson to Audette, 21 June 1950, Library and Archives Canada (hereafter cited as LAC), Audette Papers, MG 31, E 18, vol. 13, file 2.

2 "Canada's New Navy: An Outline Sketch," n.d. [c. 1947], Directorate of History and Heritage (hereafter cited as DHH), 1700, Organization General.
3 Rowland to Reid, 1 May 1943, "Proposed Alterations and Additions – Ships of the Mid-Ocean Escort Force"; and Reid to Pennington, 13 May 1943, cover letter, PANS, Macdonald Papers, MG 2, F 276/9, F 276/10.
4 HMCS *Restigouche*, ship's movement cards, DHH; Piers to Rowland, 1 June 1943, "Comments on the Operation and Performance of HMC Ships, Establishment and Personnel in the Battle of the Atlantic," LAC, RG 24, vol. 3,997, 1057-3-24, vol. 1. I am grateful to Rear Admiral Piers for the information regarding his discussion on equipment with Simpson prior to sailing for St. John's. Rear Admiral Debby Piers, telephone conversation with author, 21 September 2000. Piers wrote this report only three days after escorting his last convoy, ONS 8, from Londonderry to St. John's.
5 George to Price, "Summarizing RCN Wardroom Technical Grouses," n.d. [mid-June 1943], DHH, 77/467, M-11. It is possible to date this report because of George's reference to the sinking of two U-boats by HMS *Broadway* and *Lagan* as occurring "last month." This action took place on 14 May 1943, indicating that George's report was written in mid-June. Fraser McKee and R. Darlington, *The Canadian Naval Chronicle, 1939-1945* (St. Catharines, ON: Vanwell Publishing, 1996), 180-81.
6 "Canada's New Navy: An Outline Sketch," n.d. [c. 1947], DHH, 1700, Organization General.
7 C.P. Stacey, *Arms, Men and Governments: The War Policies of Canada, 1939-1945* (Ottawa: Queen's Printer, 1970), 315-19; W.A.B. Douglas and Brereton Greenhous, *Out of the Shadows: Canada in the Second World War* (Toronto: Oxford University Press, 1977), 79-82; Marc Milner, *North Atlantic Run: The Royal Canadian Navy and the Battle for the Convoys* (Toronto: University of Toronto Press, 1985), 242-68; David Zimmerman, *The Great Naval Battle of Ottawa* (Toronto: University of Toronto Press, 1989), particularly Chapter 11; Tony German, *The Sea Is at Our Gates: The History of the Royal Canadian Navy* (Toronto: McClelland and Stewart, 1990), 146-48; R.C. Fisher, "The Impact of German Technology on the Royal Canadian Navy in the Battle of the Atlantic, 1942-1943," *The Northern Marnier* 7, 4 (October 1997): 1-13; Roger Sarty, *Canada and the Battle of the Atlantic* (Montreal: Art Global, 1998), 139-40.
8 James George, interview by historical records officer, 15 November 1943, Ottawa, written notes, DHH, BIOG G; Piers to Rowland, 1 June 1943, "Comments on the Operation and Performance of HMC Ships, Establishment and Personnel in the Battle of the Atlantic," LAC, RG 24, vol. 3,997, 1057-3-24, vol. 1.
9 I read hundreds of reports of proceedings from January through June 1943 before reaching this conclusion. Too numerous to list here, these reports can be found at DHH in the 8000 ship files or at Library and Archives Canada in RG 24. Likewise, postwar interviews with seagoing officers can be found in the Hal Lawrence collection at DHH. Other sources include the *Salty Dips* series and Mac Johnston, *Corvettes Canada: Convoy Veterans of WW II Tell Their True Stories* (Toronto: McGraw-Hill Ryerson, 1994), particularly Chapter 15.
10 Secretary NB to FONF, 18 July 1943, DHH, Nelles Papers, folder B, file 15.
11 David Groos to Audette, 15 April 1949; and Audette to Marc Milner, 16 November 1983, LAC, Audette Papers, MG 31, E 18, vol. 15, file 1.
12 LCdr K. Johnson to Audette, 19 December 1942, LAC, Audette Papers, MG 31, E 18, vol. 14, file 7.
13 Piers to Rowland, "Comments on the Operation and Performance of HMC Ships," 1 June 1943, LAC, RG 24, 3,997, 1057-3-24, vol. 1.
14 Captain Eric Brand, RN, interview by E.C. Russell, 22 February 1967, Ottawa, tape recording transcript, DHH, Brand Papers, 84/145, vol. 7, 25.
15 House of Commons, *Debates*, 11 June 1943, 3,564.
16 Briggs to Agnew, "Personal Appreciation of Situation for RCN Ships in United Kingdom," LAC, RG 24, 3,997, 1057-3-24, vol. 1.

17 German, *The Sea Is at Our Gates*, Appendix C.
18 Donald Macintyre, *U-boat Killer* (London: Weidenfeld and Nicholson, 1956), 88-89.
19 LCdr F.O. Gerity, interview by historical records officer, n.d. [c. 1944], written notes, DHH, 1650-239/15.
20 Brand to Sir Peter Gretton, 21 November 1981, DHH, Brand Papers, 81/145, vol. 7.
21 Captain H.C. Fitz, USN to CTG 24, 12 October 1942, United States National Archives (hereafter cited as USNA), RG 313, box 8701.
22 Bill Glover, "Royal Colonial or Royal Canadian Navy?" in *A Nation's Navy: In Quest of Canadian Naval Identity*, ed. Michael Hadley, Rob Huebert, and Fred Crickard (Montreal and Kingston: McGill-Queen's University Press, 1996), 77-80.
23 Ibid., 89-90. Although Andrew MacLean and his followers first coined the phrase "people's navy," some historians have begun to investigate the impact that the influx of RCNVR had in changing the social fabric and culture of the RCN. For an illustration of this new trend, see R.H. Caldwell, "The VE Day Riots in Halifax, 7-8 May 1945," *The Northern Mariner* 10, 1 (January 2000): 3-20.
24 CinC WA to Sec Admiralty, 3 April 1943, Public Records Office (hereafter cited as PRO), ADM 1/13150; Allied Anti-Submarine Survey Board meeting minutes, 11 April 1943, PRO, ADM 1/13756; "Report of Washington Convoy Conference (1-12 Mar. 1943)," 19 March 1943, PRO, ADM 205/27; Price to Sec NB, 28 May 1943, LAC, RG 24, vol. 11,721, file 34.
25 Piers to Rowland, "Comments on the Operation and Performance of HMC Ships, Establishment and Personnel in the Battle of the Atlantic," 1 June 1943, LAC, RG 24, vol. 3,997, 1057-3-24, vol. 1.
26 M.A. McMullen, 27 July 1943, PRO, ADM 1/13756, 68354.
27 Price to Jeffrey, 28 May 1943, DHH, HMCS *Niobe* 1939-1945, 8000, vol. 1.
28 M.A. McMullen, 27 July 1943, PRO, ADM 1/13756, 68354.
29 Price to Sec NB, 28 May 1943, DHH, HMCS *Niobe* 1939-1945, 8000, vol. 1.
30 Ross to Horton, 27 August 1942, PRO, ADM 205/22A, 112924.
31 Price to Sec NB, 28 May 1943, DHH, HMCS *Niobe* 1939-1945, 8000, vol. 1.
32 "Interview with Captain R.I. Agnew, OBE, RCN, Captain Commanding Canadian Ships and Checked by Him" n.d. [c. 1945]; and interviews with R.A. Pennington entitled "Canadian Naval Liaison in the United Kingdom" and "The Feud (or The Corsican Brothers)," interview by Historical Records Officer, 5 May 1946, Ottawa, written notes, DHH, 1700 193/96B. According to Price, NSHQ ignored the captain commanding Canadian ships because of a personal feud between Nelles and Agnew. This dispute was rumoured to have been the product of Nelles' longstanding resentment of Agnew's award of the Order of the British Empire.
33 G.N. Tucker, *The Naval Service of Canada: Its Official History* (Ottawa: King's Printer, 1952), 453.
34 Price to Sec NB, 28 May 1943, DHH, HMCS *Niobe* 1939-1945, 8000, vol. 1; Piers to Rowland, "Comments on the Operation and Performance of HMC Ships, Establishment and Personnel in the Battle of the Atlantic," 1 June 1943, LAC, RG 24, vol. 3,997, 1057-3-24, vol. 1.
35 Price to Sec NB, 28 May 1943, DHH, HMCS *Niobe* 1939-1945, 8000, vol. 1.
36 Strange to Connolly, 13-15 July 1943, LAC, Connolly Papers, MG 32, C 71, vol. 3; William Strange, "The Canadian Naval Equipment Crisis – 1943: A Personal Memoir," December 1968, DHH, E.C. Russell Papers, 91/298, vol. 4; Louis Audette, "Naval Recollections," DHH, Audette Papers, 80/256, folder 9, 184-85.
37 G.W.G. Simpson, *Periscope View* (London: Macmillan, 1972), 285.
38 J. Pickford, "Recollections of a Young Corvette Captain," in *Salty Dips*, vol. 2, ed. Mac Lynch (Ottawa: Privately printed, 1985), 106.
39 Simpson to Audette, 21 June 1950, LAC, Audette Papers, MG 31, E 18, vol. 13, file 2.

40 Simpson to Audette, 21 June 1950, LAC, Audette Papers, MG 31, E 18, vol. 13, file 2.
41 Ibid.
42 Lieutenant Commander R.M. Hanbury, interview by Hal Lawrence, 18 May 1983, Toronto, tape recording transcript, DHH, BIOG H.
43 Rowland to Reid, "Proposed Alterations and Additions – Ships of the Mid-Ocean Escort Force," 1 May 1943, and Reid to Pennington, cover letter, 13 May 1943, PANS, Macdonald Papers, MG 2, F 276/9, F 276/10.
44 Rowland to Simpson, 9 July 1943, LAC, RG 24, vol. 11,948.
45 Connolly to Macdonald, 9 November 1943, LAC, Connolly Papers, MG 32, C 71, vol. 3.
46 Piers to Rowland, "Comments on the Operation and Performance of HMC Ships, Establishment and Personnel in the Battle of the Atlantic," 1 June 1943, LAC, RG 24, vol. 3,997, 1057-3-24, vol. 1. After mentioning Simpson and other officers at Western Approaches, Piers observed that "from these conversations, and many other interesting service contacts the following facts emerge ... "
47 Milner, *Canada's Navy: The First Century* (Toronto: University of Toronto Press, 1999), 121; Itinerary of Allied Anti-Submarine Survey Board, 1943, PRO, ADM 1/13756, 68354.
48 Allied Anti-Submarine Survey Board (hereafter AASSB), Meeting at Londonderry, 17 April 1943, PRO, ADM 1/13756, 68354.
49 AASSB, Meeting at Liverpool, 11 April 1943, PRO, ADM 1/13756, 68354; Halifax War Diary, May 1943, DHH, 1000-5-13, vol. 18.
50 AASSB, Meeting at Liverpool, 11 April 1943; AASSB, Meeting at Londonderry, 17 April 1943, PRO, ADM 1/13756, 68354.
51 HMCS *Niobe* War Diary, June 1943, DHH, SCNO (L) War Diary, 1000-5-35, vol. 1; Murray Memoir, LAC, Murray Papers, M 30, E 207, vol. 4, 51.
52 Murray Memoir, LAC, Murray Papers, M 30, E 207, vol. 4, 51.
53 M.A. McMullen, 27 July 1943, PRO, ADM 1/13756, 68354.
54 Piers to Captain (D) Nfld, 1 June 1943, LAC, RG 24, vol. 3997, file 1057-3-24.
55 Price to Sec NB, 9 June 1943, Price to Simpson, 28 May 1943, LAC, RG 24, vol. 11,721, file 34; Price to Lt F.G.G. Carr, RN, 27 May 1943, LAC, RG 24, vol. 11,705, N-1-8-4; Piers to Rowland, "Comments on the Operation and Performance of HMC Ships, Establishment and Personnel in the Battle of the Atlantic," 1 June 1943, LAC, RG 24, vol. 3,997, 1057-3-24, vol. 1; Angus to Audette, 9 November 1950, LAC, Audette Papers, MG 31, E 18, vol. 12, file 16; Various clippings from *The Derry Standard*, DHH, Personnel A-Z (Prior 1950), 4000-100/14.
56 Caldwell, "The VE Day Riots in Halifax, 7-8 May 1945," 15.
57 Angus to Audette, 9 November 1950, LAC, Audette Papers, MG 31, E 18, vol. 12, file 16.
58 Strange to E.C. Russell, 9 December 1968, DHH, E.C. Russell Papers, 91/298, vol. 4; Strange, "Canadian Naval Equipment Crisis," 2.
59 Reid to Jeffrey, 18 June 1943, LAC, RG 24, vol. 3,997, 1057-3-24.
60 Murray to Jeffery, 24 June 1943, LAC, RG 24, vol. 3,997, 1057-3-24.
61 Murray to Admiralty, 5 July 1943, LAC, RG 24, vol. 11,718, NRC 144229; SCNO (L) War Diary, July 1943, DHH, 1000-5-35, vol. 1; Bidwell to Houghton, 21 July 1943, LAC, RG 24, vol. 11,987, F 1292; Horton to Price, 3 July 1943, LAC, RG 24, vol. 11,718, NRC 14229.
62 LCdr Eric J. Downton, interview by Hal Lawrence, 20 November 1982, Vancouver, tape recording transcript, DHH, BIOG D; Strange to Simpson, 22 September 1943, DHH, E.C. Russell Papers, 91/298, vol. 4.
63 Strange to Connolly, n.d. [August 1943], LAC, MG 32, C 71, vol. 3, part 1 n.d. 1943.
64 Strange to Simpson, 2 September 1943, DHH, E.C. Russell Papers, 91/298, vol. 4.
65 Strange, "Canadian Naval Equipment Crisis," 4.
66 FONF to NSHQ, 241303, 24 June 1943, LAC, Strange personnel file (O-70680, DOD, 30 April 1983); FONF to Sec NB, 24 June 1943, LAC, RG 24, vol. 8,196, 1880-2-37/3; Strange to Connolly,

"Strange Report," 15 July 1943, LAC, Connolly Papers, MG 32, C 71, vol. 3, part 1; Strange, "Canadian Naval Equipment Crisis," 3.
67 FONF to NSHQ, 27 September 1943, LAC, RG 24, vol. 3,997, 1057-3-24, vol. 1. For example, when NSHQ asked for opinions on their staff summary of Piers' report, the CinC CNA's response took six weeks to complete while the FONF's did not arrive in Ottawa until two months after its initial receipt in St. John's. Moreover, Rowland's original submission sat on Reid's desk for almost a full two weeks before being sent to NSHQ on 13 May 1943.
68 Peter Gretton to Marc Milner, 5 August 1982, National Maritime Museum (hereafter cited as NMM) – Greenwich, Gretton Papers; Strange to Simpson, 22 September 1943, DHH, E.C. Russell Papers, 91/298, vol. 4; Strange, "Canadian Naval Equipment Crisis," 1; Reid to Murray, Convoy schedules, 18 June 1943, LAC, RG 24, vol. 11,928, 220-1-2.
69 Strange, "Canadian Naval Equipment Crisis," 1-2.
70 A.G.S. Griffin, letter to author, 24 May 2000.
71 HMCS *Skeena*, Ship's movement cards, DHH; quotations from Strange, "Canadian Naval Equipment Crisis," 3.
72 Strange to Connolly, 13-15 July 1943, LAC, Connolly Papers, MG 32, C 71, vol. 3; Strange, "Canadian Naval Equipment Crisis," 2.
73 Strange, "Canadian Naval Equipment Crisis," 3. Strange to Connolly, 13-15 July 1943, LAC, Connolly Papers, MG 32, C 71, vol. 3.
74 Strange to Simpson, 22 September 1943, DHH, E.C. Russell Papers, 91/298, vol. 4.
75 Simpson to NSHQ, Naval message 141825, 15 July 1943, LAC, Strange personnel file (O-70680, DOD 30 April 1983); Arnold Hague, *The Allied Convoy System, 1939-1945* (St. Catharines, ON: Vanwell Publishing, 2000), 159.
76 Strange to Connolly, 13-15 July 1943, LAC, Connolly Papers, MG 32, C 71, vol. 3; *Royal Navy List*, February 1943, DHH Library, 1585.
77 Lee to Strange, 4 October 1943, LAC, Connolly Papers, MG 32, C 71, vol. 3.
78 Strange, "Canadian Naval Equipment Crisis," 4.
79 Ibid.
80 Strange to Connolly, 21 September 1943, LAC, Connolly Papers, MG 32, C 71, vol. 3; Strange to Connolly, 13-15 July 1943, LAC, Connolly Papers, MG 32, C 71, vol. 3; Strange, "Canadian Naval Equipment Crisis," 4-5.
81 Strange, "Canadian Naval Equipment Crisis," 5.
82 Simpson to Adams, 241145B, 25 July 1943, LAC, Strange personnel file (O-70680, DOD 30 April 1983); Reid to Murray, Convoy schedules, 18 June 1943, LAC, RG 24, vol. 11,928, 220-1-2; HMCS *Assiniboine*, DHH, Ship movement cards.
83 Rear Admiral Kenneth F. Adams, interview by Hal Lawrence, n.d., Sydney, BC, tape recording transcript, DHH, BIOG A, 38.
84 Strange, "Canadian Naval Equipment Crisis," 5. I am grateful to Marc Milner for drawing my attention to the fact that Adams' observation echoed ones offered by the British in 1941.
85 "HMCS *Assiniboine* (I) (1931-48), A Brief History," DHH, 8000, 31; Rear Admiral Kenneth F. Adams, interview by Hal Lawrence, n.d., Sydney, BC, tape recording transcript, DHH, BIOG A, 38.
86 James Lamb, *The Corvette Navy: True Stories from Canada's Atlantic War* (Toronto: Macmillan, 1977), 134.
87 Strange to LCdr F.O. Gerity, 21 September 1943, DHH, E.C. Russell Papers, 91/298.
88 Strange, "Canadian Naval Equipment Crisis," 7.
89 Mr. J.J. Connolly, interview by LCdr T.R. Daly, 26 January 1945, Ottawa, written notes, DHH, 1700-193/96D.
90 Strange, "Canadian Naval Equipment Crisis," 6, emphasis in original; Strange to Russell, 9 December 1943, DHH, E.C. Russell Papers, 91/298, vol. 4.

91 Strange to Connolly, 12 December 1943, LAC, Connolly Papers, MG 32, C 71, vol. 2, file 18.
92 Simpson, *Periscope View*, 21; LAC, Strange personnel file (O-70680, DOD 30 April 1983); Strange to E.C. Russell, 9 December 1968, DHH, E.C. Russell Papers, 91/298, vol. 4; Strange to Connolly, 13-15 July 1943, LAC, Connolly Papers, MG 32, C 71, vol. 3; Strange to E.C. Russell, 9 December 1968, DHH, E.C. Russell Papers, 91/298, vol. 4; *British Naval Lists*, DHH Library, 1915.
93 Strange to E.C. Russell, 9 December 1968, DHH, E.C. Russell Papers, 91/298, vol. 4; Strange, "Canadian Naval Equipment Crisis," 2.
94 Simpson to Audette, 21 June 1950, LAC, Audette Papers, MG 31, E 18, vol. 13, file 2.
95 Audette to Simpson, 25 September 1950, LAC, Audette Papers, MG 31, E 18, vol. 13, file 2.
96 Strange to E.C. Russell, 9 December 1968, DHH, E.C. Russell Papers, 91/298, vol. 4, 2.
97 W.A.B. Douglas, Roger Sarty, and Michael Whitby, *No Higher Purpose: The Official Operational History of the Royal Canadian Navy in the Second World War, 1939-1943*, vol. 2, part 1 (St. Catharines, ON: Vanwell Publishing, 2002). The concept that the equipment situation represented more of a "gap" than a "crisis" comes from the authors of the official history.

Chapter 4: Trying to Keep Afloat

1 Quotation from Marc Milner, *Canada's Navy: The First Century* (Toronto: University of Toronto Press, 1999), 113. Michael Gannon, *Black May: The Epic Story of the Allies' Defeat of German U-boats in May 1943* (New York: Dell Books, 1989), 410-24; Peter Padfield, *War beneath the Sea: Submarine Conflict 1939-1945* (London: Random House, 1995), 308-36.
2 Marc Milner, *The U-Boat Hunters: The Royal Canadian Navy and the Offensive against Germany's Submarines* (Toronto: University of Toronto Press, 1994), 274.
3 Michael Hadley, *U-Boats against Canada: German Submarines in Canadian Waters* (Montreal and Kingston: McGill-Queen's University Press, 1985), 302, 304.
4 David Zimmerman, *The Great Naval Battle of Ottawa* (Toronto: University of Toronto Press, 1989), 100.
5 British Admiralty Technical Mission, 6 March 1942, Library and Archives Canada (hereafter cited as LAC), RG 24, Accession 1983-84/167, vol. 2,585, 6101-1, part 1; "Notes on Interviews with Commanding Officers of HMC Ships *Haida* and *Iroquois*" (DeWolf and Hibbard), 18 February 1944, Directorate of History and Heritage (hereafter cited as DHH), 1650-239/15; Naval Staff meeting, DHH, 13 July 1942.
6 Naval Staff meetings, 26 May and 22 July 1942, DHH.
7 Naval Board meeting, 30 April 1942, DHH.
8 Naval Board meetings, 13 July 1942, 31 August 1942, and 17 September 1942, DHH; Naval Staff meetings, 30 April, 14 May, 18 May, 26 May, 28 May, 1 June, 9 June, 15 June, 29 June, 6 July, 9 July, 13 July, 22 July, 20 August, 31 August, 8 September, and 17 September 1942, DHH.
9 Naval Board meeting, 1 October 1942, DHH; Anonymous narrative, "Alterations and Additions," c. mid-1945, DHH, 8060, 15. Editorial comments by Gilbert Tucker clearly indicate that one of his staff, possibly Lieutenant Commander James George, wrote this narrative.
10 Naval Staff meeting, 26 November 1942, DHH; Naval Board meeting, 30 November 1942, DHH.
11 For more information see W.A.B. Douglas, Roger Sarty, and Michael Whitby, *No Higher Purpose: The Official Operational History of the Royal Canadian Navy in the Second World War, 1939-1943*, vol. 2, part 1 (St. Catharines, ON: Vanwell Publishing, 2002); Marc Milner, *North Atlantic Run: The Royal Canadian Navy and the Battle for the Convoys* (Toronto: University of Toronto Press, 1985); and Roger Sarty, *Canada and the Battle of the Atlantic* (Montreal: Art Global, 1998).
12 Marc Milner was the first historian to fully explore the transfer and its implications in his article, "Royal Canadian Navy Participation in the Battle of the Atlantic Crisis of 1943," in

The RCN in Retrospect, 1910-1968, ed. James Boutilier (Vancouver: University of British Columbia Press, 1982), 158-74.
13 DeWolf to Nelles, 21 December 1942, DHH 77/467, M-11.
14 Douglas, Sarty, and Whitby, *No Higher Purpose*, 576; Milner, "Royal Canadian Navy Participation in the Battle of the Atlantic," 168-69.
15 Milner, *North Atlantic Run*, 210.
16 Tony German, *The Sea Is at Our Gates: The History of the Royal Canadian Navy* (Toronto: McClelland and Stewart, 1990), 148.
17 Captain Eric Brand diary, January 1943, DHH, Brand Papers, 81/145.
18 Nelles to Macdonald, "Disposition of Escort Ships of the RCN," 5 January 1943, LAC, RG 24, vol. 6,796, 8375/4; Nelles to Macdonald, "Reference – Dispatches 264 and 265," n.d. [5 January 1943], LAC, RG 24, vol. 6,796, 8375/4.
19 "Report of Conference on Fuel Supply to UK and Africa," 4 January 1943, LAC, RG 24, vol. 6,796, 8375/4, emphasis in original.
20 Nelles to Macdonald, "Disposition of Escort Ships of the RCN," 5 January 1943, LAC, RG 24, vol. 6,796, 8375/4.
21 Nelles to Macdonald, "Disposition of Escort Ships of the RCN," 5 January 1943, LAC, RG 24, vol. 6,796, 8375/4; Nelles to Macdonald, "Reference – Dispatches 264 and 265," n.d. [5 January 1943], LAC, RG 24, vol. 6,796, 8375/4.
22 War Cabinet Committee, 6 January 1943, DHH, 83/345.
23 Nelles to Macdonald, "Disposition of Escort Ships of the RCN," 5 January 1943, LAC, RG 24, vol. 6,796, 8375-4.
24 Macdonald's personal notes, 2 January 1943, PANS, Macdonald Papers, MG 2, F 305.
25 Nelles to Macdonald, n.d. [5 January 1943], LAC, RG 24, vol. 6,796, 8375/4.
26 "Confidential Report on Efficiency of RCN (Atlantic Seaboard)," n.d. [July 1942], LAC, Connolly Papers, MG 32, C 71, vol. 3, file 8.
27 "Equipment Division A/S – Naval Board 8-6-5," 5 March 1942, DHH, Nelles Papers, folder B, file 1, 1078-8-1.
28 Naval Board meetings, 15 June and 8 September 1942, DHH.
29 Nelles to Macdonald, n.d. [5 January 1943], LAC, RG 24, vol. 6,796, 8375/4.
30 Anonymous narrative, "Alterations and Additions," n.d. [c. 1945], DHH, 8060, 15; Stephens to Nelles, 26 November 1943, PANS, Macdonald Papers, MG 2, F 276/37.
31 "Development of Canadian Naval Policy," 21 December 1943, LAC, RG 24, vol. 11,963. This report, and others like it, claim that while the RCN was transferred to RN control "the ships never actually proceeded to undertake these duties [UK to Gibraltar convoys] as the arrangements were superseded by others before they could come into effect." Recently, some modern historians have also accepted the view that the transfer was not carried out as the British had intended it. See Sarty, *Canada and the Battle of the Atlantic*, 131; and Douglas, Sarty, and Whitby, *No Higher Purpose*, 612.
32 "Canada's New Navy: An Outline Sketch," n.d. [c. 1947], DHH, 1700, Organization General.
33 For example, Nelles was told that "the Admiralty has, only very recently, started conversion of their own equipments to Mark IV [a variant of the 271 radar] and verbal assurance was given to RDFO [radio direction finding officer] while in the UK that RCN ships would be taken in hand along with RN units whenever equipments and facilities were available." Extracts from various memoranda, DHH, Nelles Papers, folder B, file 5. Also see Douglas, Sarty, and Whitby, *No Higher Purpose*, particularly Chapters 10 and 11.
34 Nelles to Macdonald, 27 November 1943, PANS, Macdonald Papers, MG 2, F 276/34.
35 Lay to Jones, 27 January 1943, DHH, 8780.
36 Naval Staff meeting, 15 February 1943, DHH.
37 NSHQ to Admiralty, 15 February 1943, DHH, Nelles Papers, folder B, file 4.

38 Admiralty to NSHQ, 20 February 1943, DHH, Nelles Papers, folder B, file 4.
39 Canadian Naval Orders 2587, 27 February 1943, DHH Library, nos. 2477-3283, vol. 3.
40 Naval weekly reports to the minister, 25 February 43, DHH, 1000-5-7, vol. 2.
41 Annual Departmental Reports, 31 March 1943, LAC; Stephens to Nelles, 26 November 1943, PANS, Macdonald Papers, MG 2, F 276/37.
42 Macdonald to King, 24 February 1943, Queen's Archives, Power Papers, 2150, box 1, vol. 1.
43 King diary, 9 March 1943, DHH, 83/530, 184-185.
44 Naval Board meeting, 15 March 1943, DHH.
45 Sec NB to COAC and FONF, 6 August 1942, LAC, RG 24, vol. 11,568, 27-C-0; NSHQ to all HMC Ships, 4 November 1942, LAC, RG 24, vol. 3,995, 1057-1-20; COAC Secretary to Secretary Capt (D) Halifax, "Enquiry for Report Overdue," 20 February 1943, LAC, RG 24, vol. 11,568, 27-C-0.
46 Prentice to Murray, 3 March 1943, LAC, RG 24, vol. 11,568, 27-C-0.
47 For example, in December 1942 one officer had estimated that 45 percent of corvettes possessed 271 radar at this time. While the 271 situation was improving for the Mid-Ocean Escort Fleet, the figures from the Western Local Escort Fleet and Halifax Fleet clearly indicate that the overall percentage was wrong. See Brown to Nelles, 24 December 1942, DHH, 77/467, M-11; Nelles to Macdonald, 24 December 1942, DHH, Weekly reports to the minister, 1000-5-7, vol. 4.
48 Murray to BAMR, 9 March 1943, LAC, RG 24, vol. 3,996, 1057-1-35, vol. 2.
49 Murray to Pennington, 27 March 1943, LAC, RG 24, vol. 3,996, 1057-1-35, vol. 1.
50 Ibid.
51 Bidwell to Lay, March 1943, LAC, RG 24, vol. 11,987, F 1292.
52 Lay to Jones and Nelles, 22 March 1943, DHH, 8780; Lay to Jones and Nelles, 22 March 1943, DHH, 81/520, 1000-973, vol. 4; Lay to Jones, Minute sheet, 22 March 1943, LAC, RG 24, vol. 3,996, 1057-1-35, vol. 1.
53 Naval Board meeting, 1 February 1943, DHH; and Director of Organization to VCNS, "East Coast Outports Development," 1 February 1943, attached as appendix to Naval Board meeting, 1 February 1943, DHH.
54 Naval Board meeting, 8 February 1943, DHH.
55 Captain J.G. Knowlton to Chief Engineer HMC Dockyard, 1 March 1943, and Jefferson to Murray, "Drafting of Civilian Skilled Labour into Armed Forces – Effect on Repair of HMC Ships," 14 April 1943, LAC, RG 24, vol. 3,996, 1057-1-35, vol. 1.
56 Jefferson to Murray, "Proposed Refitting Programme for Destroyers, Corvette, Minesweepers, etc – Western Local and Mid-Ocean Escort Force," 24 March 1943, LAC, RG 24, vol. 3,996, 1057-1-35, vol. 1.
57 Mills (Deputy Minister) to DMS, 31 March 1943, LAC, RG 24, vol. 3,996, 1057-1-35, vol. 3.
58 Mills to Carswell, 13 April 1943, LAC, RG 24, vol. 3,996, 1057-1-35, vol. 1; Stephens to Mills, 12 May 1943, and Stephens to Director of Operations Division, 25 May 1943, LAC, RG 24, vol. 3,996, 1057-1-35, vol. 1.
59 Naval Board meeting, 18 March 1943, DHH.
60 Naval Board meetings, 8 February, 8 March, 15 March, and 29 March 1943, DHH.
61 Heeney to W.C. Ronson (Sec. Treasury Board, Dept of Finance), 19 April 1943, LAC, RG 2, vol. 18, file 24, C-10-3-C; Cabinet War Committee, Schedule of Decision, 16 April 1943, LAC, RG 2, vol. 35, C-10-3-F.
62 Naval Board meeting, 8 March 1943, DHH.
63 Nelles to Macdonald, 25 March 1943, DHH, 1000-5-7.
64 Malcolm MacDonald to Norman Robertson, 12 April 1943, DHH, 8780, Repairs and Refits.
65 C.J. Burchell to Scott Macdonald, 16 April 1943, LAC, RG 24, vol. 3,996, 1057-1-35, vol. 1; Naval Board meeting, 19 April 1943, DHH; Letter to Mansfield, 5 May 1943, PRO, ADM 1/13756,

68354; "Minutes of Combined Canadian, United Kingdom and United States Committee to Examine Repair Problem for Warships and Merchant Vessels on the East Coast of Canada," 12 August 1943, DHH, Repair and Refits, 8780.
66 AASSB Canadian itinerary, May 1943, DHH, 77/467, M-11; Itinerary of Allied Anti-Submarine Survey Board, PRO, ADM 1/13756.
67 Meeting with A/S Survey Board, 8 May 1943, DHH, 77/467, M-11; Naval Staff meeting, 3 June 1943, DHH.
68 Meeting with A/S Survey Board, 8 May 1943, DHH, 77/467, M-11.
69 AASSB to Nelles, 18 May 1943, DHH, 77/467, M-11.
70 Nelles to Macdonald, 27 November 1943, PANS, Macdonald Papers, MG 2, F 276/34; AASSB to Nelles, 18 May 1943, DHH, 77/467, M-11.
71 G.N. Tucker, *The Naval Service of Canada: Its Official History* (Ottawa: King's Printer, 1952), 160.
72 Pennington's comments were recorded in the dairy of Captain Massey Goolden. Goolden diary, 28 October 1942, DHH, BIOG G.
73 Jeffrey to Tucker, 1 December 1947, DHH, 8000, HMCS *Bytown*, vol. 1; Johnstone to Youle, 20 January 1948, DHH, 8000, HMCS *Bytown*, vol. 1.
74 Jones minute note on Johnstone to Jones, 28 January 1943, DHH, 8000, HMCS *Bytown*, vol. 2.
75 Pennington, Naval Staff Branch Reorganization, 1 June 1943, DHH, 1700, Organization and Administration.
76 Nelles to Macdonald, 27 November 1943, PANS, Macdonald Papers, MG 2, F 276/34.
77 Johnstone to Youle, 20 January 1948, DHH, 8000, HMCS *Bytown*, vol. 1; Naval Staff meeting, 3 June 1943, DHH.
78 As cited in Roger Sarty, "Admiral Percy W. Nelles: Diligent Guardian of the Vision" (paper presented at the 6th MARCOM Conference, Halifax, September 2002).
79 Naval Board meeting, 21 June 1943, DHH; Stephens to Assistant Chief of the Naval Staff, 7 June 1943, LAC, RG 24, vol. 3,997, 1057-1-39, vol. 1; Nelles to Macdonald, 4 December 1943, PANS, Macdonald Papers, MG 2, F 276/39.
80 Stephens to Creery, 9 June 1943, LAC, RG 24, vol. 3,997, 1057-1-39, vol. 1.
81 Naval Board meeting, 21 June 1943, DHH.
82 Stephens to Nelles, Mills, and Macdonald, 24 June 1943, Macdonald to Howe, 28 June 1943, and Howe to Macdonald, 5 July 1943, LAC, RG 24, vol. 3,997, 1057-1-39, vol. 1, emphasis added.
83 Itinerary of AASSB visit to Canada, May 1943, DHH, 77/467, M-11.
84 Macdonald to Howe, 13 July 1943, Mills to Stephens, 8 July 1943, Carswell to Macdonald, 6 July 1943, and Rannie to Macdonald, 21 July 1943, LAC, RG 24, vol. 3,997, 1057-1-39, vol. 1; Nelles' decision for Johnstone to look into this matter can be found in his handwritten comments on Stephens' memo.
85 DeWolf to Creery, 3 July 1943, Appendix A to Naval Board meeting, 5 July 1943, DHH.
86 Stephens to Creery, 9 June 1943, LAC, RG 24, vol. 3,997, 1057-1-39, vol. 1.
87 Johnstone to Jones, "East Coast Outports Development," 1 February 1943, attached as appendix A to Naval Board meeting, 1 February 1943, DHH.
88 Stephens to Nelles, 17 July 1943, LAC, RG 24, vol. 3,996, 1057-1-35, vol. 2.
89 Johnstone, "Repairs and Refitting, East Coast," 18 June 1943, DHH, 8780.
90 Naval Staff meeting, 21 June 1943, DHH.
91 Johnstone, "Repairs and Refitting, East Coast," 18 June 1943, DHH, 8780.
92 Murray to NSHQ, 27 June 1943, Hibbard to Creery, 28 June 1943, and Stephens to Creery, 21 June 1943, LAC, RG 24, vol. 3,997, 1057-1-39, vol. 1.
93 Creery to Nelles, 5 July 1943, DHH, 8780.
94 Creery to Nelles, 8 July 1943, DHH, 8780.
95 Creery to Nelles, 5 July 1943, DHH, 8780.
96 Naval Board meeting, 27 July 1943, DHH.

97   Murray to NSHQ, 27 June 1943, LAC, RG 24, vol. 3,997, 1057-1-39, vol. 1.
98   Nelles to Macdonald, 27 November 1943, PANS, Macdonald Papers, MG 2, F 276/34.
99   Johnstone to Captain A. Youle, 20 January 1948, DHH, HMCS *Bytown* (Base) 8000, vol. 1.
100 Johnstone, "Repairs and Refitting, East Coast," 18 June 1943, DHH, 8780.
101 Lieutenant Commander Todd, interview by Lieutenant T.R. Dale (historical records officer), September 1945, written notes, DHH, 1700-193/96.
102 SCNO (L) War Diary, November 1943, DHH, 81/520/1000-5-35; Sec NB to SCNO (L), 15 June 1943, LAC, RG 24, vol. 11,714, file 1-1-1; Zimmerman, *The Great Naval Battle of Ottawa*, 131; Tucker, *The Naval Service of Canada*, 427.
103 Nelles to Macdonald, 27 November 1943, PANS, Macdonald Papers, MG 2, F 276/34.
104 Naval Board meeting, 15 June 1942, DHH.
105 Naval Board meeting, 13 July 1943, DHH.
106 Naval Board meetings, 1 May and 23 June 1944, DHH.

Chapter 5: Informers, Collaborators, and Promise Breakers

1   Andrew Dyas MacLean, "Fairmiles and Foul," *Boating Magazine*, January-February 1943, Directorate of History and Heritage (hereafter cited as DHH), 94/127.
2   Quotation from Macdonald to King, 24 February 1943, Queen's University Archives, 2150, box 1, vol. 1; Naval Board meetings for late 1942 and early 1943, DHH.
3   Power to King, 17 November 1942, A.L. Macdonald, 24 February 1943, Queen's Archives, Power Papers, 2150, box 1, vol. 1; Frederick W. Gibson and Barbara Robertson, eds., *Ottawa at War: The Grant Dexter Memoranda, 1939-1945* (Winnipeg: The Manitoba Record Society, 1994).
4   King diary, 11 February 1943, DHH, 83/530, 110-111.
5   Lieutenant Victor Brodeur, "Present RCN Naval Organization," n.d. [c. 1922], DHH, Brodeur Papers, 79/19, folder 2.
6   Marc Milner, *North Atlantic Run: The Royal Canadian Navy and the Battle for the Convoys* (Toronto: University of Toronto Press, 1985), 93; Wilfred Lund, "The Rise and Fall of the Royal Canadian Navy, 1945-1964: A Critical Study of the Senior Leadership, Policy and Manpower Management" (PhD diss., University of Victoria, 1999), 33-37.
7   Hose to minister, n.d. [August 1924], Library and Archives Canada (hereafter cited as LAC), Jones personnel file (O-37330, DOD 08 February 1946); *Sea Breezes* 2, 3 (June 1921): 1-2, DHH Library; John Burgess and Ken Macpherson, *The Ships of Canada's Naval Forces, 1910-1993* (St. Catharines, ON: Vanwell Publishing, 1994), 190-203; Royal Naval College of Canada (1911-1922) Class List, 1 March 1968, DHH.
8   *Sea Breezes* 1, 1 (December 1914), 6; *Sea Breezes* 2, 3 (June 1921), 1-2; Commodore Walter Hose to H. Steele, 15 April 1921, LAC, Jones personnel file (LAC, 0-37330, DOD 08 February 1946); J.D. Gow, *Alongside the Navy, 1910-1950: An Intimate Account* (Ottawa: JDG Press, 1999), 19.
9   One of the only published academic accounts on Canada's naval defence in the interwar era remains Roger Sarty's *The Maritime Defence of Canada* (Toronto: Canadian Institute of Strategic Studies, 1996). For an excellent summary of relations between officers in this period, see Lund, "The Rise and Fall of the Royal Canadian Navy," particularly Chapter 1; Tony German, *The Sea Is at Our Gates: The History of the Royal Canadian Navy* (Toronto: McClelland and Stewart, 1990), 59-61; Office of Director of Public Information, 17 July 1941, DHH, Jones file, BIOG J. Jean Donald Gow, *Alongside the Navy*, 19; Katherine Roberts to Roger Sarty, 19 December 1991, DHH, Jones file, BIOG J.
10 Office of Director of Public Information, Commodore George C. Jones (career summary), 17 July 1941, DHH, BIOG J; Lieutenant Commander D.A.J. Higgs, interview by Hal Lawrence, n.d., Victoria, BC, tape recording transcript, DHH, BIOG H.
11 Massey Goolden diary, 24 October 1943, DHH, BIOG G; Gow, *Alongside the Navy*, 19, 50. K.F. Adams Memoir, DHH, 89/19, 42; "Narrative Summary of Interviews by Hal Lawrence," Entry for Lieutenant Commander A.A. Beveridge interview, DHH, 90/86; Lieutenant

MacFayden, interview by William Glover, n.d., tape recording transcript; John Wade, interview by William Glover, 4 February 1992, Victoria, BC, tape recording transcript, DHH, Glover Papers, 97/8; Angus G. Boulton, interview by Hal Lawrence, n.d., Victoria, BC, tape recording transcript, DHH, BIOG B; Katherine Roberts to Roger Sarty, 19 December 1991, DHH, BIOG J.

12 Lay to Marc Milner, 8 October 1981, LAC, Lay Papers, MG 30, E 420, vol. 1, file 16; Marc Milner, *North Atlantic Run*, 93; Captain Eric S. Brand, interview by E.C. Russell, 22 February 1967, Ottawa, tape recording transcript, DHH, Brand Papers, 84/145, vol. 7, 6. Lund, "The Rise and Fall of the Royal Canadian Navy," 36. Lund cites an interview with Harry DeWolf, who indicated that Jones had "managed to persuade Rear Admiral Nelles, then CNS, to grant him one day of seniority over Murray because he had completed the Imperial Defence course and Murray had not."

13 Walter Gilhooly (Director of Naval Information) to DSS, 22 December 1941, and NSHQ fleet signal, 22 December 1941, LAC, Jones personnel file (O-37330, DOD 8 February 1946); Rear Admiral H.N. Lay, interview by Hal Lawrence, 25 January 1986, Victoria, BC, tape recording transcript, DHH, BIOG L.

14 William Slater to R.C. Hayden, 14 October 1959, DHH, BIOG J, Jones file.

15 Lay to Milner, 8 October 1981, LAC, Lay Papers, MG 30, E 420, vol. 1.

16 Halifax telephone directory, 1925-1933, National Library of Canada; Vice Admiral David Allan Collins, interview by Hal Lawrence, June 1984, Victoria, BC, tape recording transcript, DHH, BIOG C, 36. H.N. Lay, interview by Hal Lawrence, 25 January 1986, Victoria, BC, tape recording transcript, DHH, BIOG L.

17 "Angus L. Macdonald," in *The Canadian Who's Who*, 1955-57, vol. 7 (Toronto: Trans Canada Press, 1957), 902; J.P. Connolly personnel file, LAC (O-15160, DOD 31 January 1955); Macdonald to J.P. Connolly, 16 July 1938, PANS, Macdonald Papers, MG 2, F 396/75; Macdonald to R.H. Winters, 24 April 1950, PANS, Macdonald Papers, MG 2, F 312/29; Connolly, Joseph Patrick, Lieutenant (CEF), LAC, RG 150, Accession 1992-93/166, box 1966-55; Macdonald, Angus Lewis, Lieutenant (CEF), LAC, RG 150, Accession 1992-93/166, box 6702-23.

18 J.J. Connolly to Edward Connolly, 15 January 1944, LAC, Connolly Papers, MG 32, C 71, vol. 1.

19 Massey Golden, RN, diary, 24 October 1943, DHH, BIOG G.

20 Captain Eric S. Brand, interview by E.C. Russell, 22 February 1967, Ottawa, tape recording transcript, DHH, Brand Papers, 84/145, vol. 7, 23, 27, 35-36.

21 Massey Golden, RN, diary, 11 December 1943, DHH, BIOG G.

22 Diary notes, 22 March and 1 April 1943, LAC, Connolly Papers, MG 32, C 71, vol. 2, file 5; H. Nelson Lay, interview by Hal Lawrence, 25 January 1986, Victoria, BC, tape recording transcript, DHH, BIOG L.

23 H. Nelson Lay, *Memoirs of a Mariner* (Stittsville, ON: Canada's Wings, 1982), 148.

24 H. Nelson Lay, interview by Hal Lawrence, 25 January 1986, Victoria, BC, tape recording transcript, DHH, BIOG L, 13.

25 King diary, 5 April 1943, DHH, 83/530, 185, 255.

26 King diary, 29 March 1943 and 5 April 1943, DHH, 83/530, 185, 231.

27 King diary, 14 September and 19 October 1940, DHH, 83/530. I would like to thank Roger Sarty for drawing my attention to the October entry.

28 Lund, "The Rise and Fall of the Royal Canadian Navy," 36; Jones to Nelles, on Lay to Jones, 22 March 1943, LAC, RG 24, vol. 3,996, 1057-1-35, vol. 1.

29 As quoted in Michael Whitby, "Matelots, Martinets, and Mutineers: The Mutiny in HMCS *Iroquois*, 19 July 1943," *The Journal of Military History*, 65, 1 (January 2001): 89.

30 Jones to Nelles, on Lay to Jones, 22 March 1943, LAC, RG 24, vol. 3,996, 1057-1-35, vol. 1.

31 Anonymous memo to Macdonald, n.d. [July 1942], LAC, Connolly Papers, MG 32, C 71, vol. 3, file 8.

32 R.H. Angus to Audette, 9 November 1950, LAC, Audette Papers, MG 31, E 18, vol. 12, file 16.
33 William Strange, "The Canadian Naval Equipment Crisis – 1943: A Personal Memoir," December 1968, E.C. Russell Papers, DHH, 91/298, vol. 4, 7; Strange to Connolly, 13-15 July 1943, LAC, Connolly Papers, MG 32, C 71, vol. 3.
34 Strange, "Canadian Naval Equipment Crisis," 7.
35 Quotation from ibid.
36 Ibid.
37 Macdonald to Nelles, n.d. [20 November 1943], PANS, Macdonald Papers, MG 2, F 276/3.
38 Naval Board meeting, 19 April 1943, DHH.
39 Strange to Simpson, 21 September 1943, and Strange, "Canadian Naval Equipment Crisis," 5-6, both DHH, E.C. Russell Papers, 91/298, vol. 4; Reid to Murray, 18 June 1943, LAC, RG 24, vol. 11,928, 220-1-2.
40 Bidwell to Houghton, 20 May 1943, Houghton to Bidwell, 29 May 1943, and Bidwell to Houghton, 2 June 1943, LAC, RG 24, vol. 11,987, F 1292.
41 Rear Admiral K.F. Adams, interview by Hal Lawrence, n.d., Sydney, BC, tape recording transcript, DHH, BIOG A; Strange, "Canadian Naval Equipment Crisis."
42 Strange to Connolly, 4 December 1942, LAC, Connolly Papers, MG 32, C 71, vol. 3, file 18.
43 "Adams Memoir," DHH, BIOG A.
44 Strange to Adams, 21 September 1943, DHH, Russell Papers, 91/298, vol. 4.
45 Adams to Rowland, "Equipment on RCN ships," 9 August 1943, DHH, Nelles Papers, folder B, file 10.
46 "Report of Interview with Rear Admiral Kenneth F. Adams," DHH, BIOG A, 39; "Adams Memoir," DHH, BIOG A, 72-73. Nelles received a copy of Adam's report from Macdonald after Connolly had found it in a backlog of messages at NSHQ. Nelles' response, while embarrassing for the chief of the naval staff, was, "I never knew of this report until you drew my attention to it this afternoon" (Nelles to Macdonald, 25 November 1943, LAC, Connolly Papers, MG 32, C 71, vol. 3).
47 Details on Macdonald's service in the Canadian Expeditionary Force can be found in Macdonald, Angus Lewis, Lieutenant, LAC, RG 150, Accession 1992-93/166, box 6702-23.
48 Macdonald notes, "Talk with Lt Cdr Brown," 8 December 1942, PANS, Macdonald Papers, MG 2, vol. 1501, F 305; Nelles to Macdonald, n.d. [5 January 1943], LAC, RG 24, vol. 6,796, 8375/4.
49 Nelles to Macdonald, 27 November 1943, PANS, Macdonald Papers, MG 2, F 276/34.
50 Ibid.
51 Minister's note on Nelles to Macdonald, 4 December 1943, PANS, Macdonald Papers, MG 2, F 276/39.
52 Strange, "Canadian Naval Equipment Crisis," 7.
53 Milner, *North Atlantic Run*, 253.
54 J.W. Pickersgill, *The Mackenzie King Record* (Toronto: University of Toronto Press, 1960), 587-88. King's own nephew, Dr. William Lyon Mackenzie King, was one of those lost when HMCS *St. Croix* was torpedoed in mid-September. Influenced by that personal tragedy, King reminded his ministers "to keep in mind, first and foremost, until the war was over, the men who are giving their lives at sea, on land and in the air ... and to do all in their [Cabinet's] power to shorten the war by concentrated effort of all that would help to win the war" (Pickersgill, *Mackenzie King Record*, pp. 582, 587). That was something Strange's memo claimed the navy was not doing. For more on the loss of the *St. Croix*, see David Bercuson and Holger H. Herwig, *Deadly Seas: The Duel between the St. Croix and the U-305 in the Battle of the Atlantic* (Toronto: Vintage Canada, 1997).
55 Macdonald to Nelles, 21 August 1943, DHH, 77/467, M-11; Nelles to Macdonald, 1 September 1943, DSD (Sam Worth) to DWT, 27 August 1943, LAC, vol. 3995, 1057-1-27, vol. 1.

56 "Comparison of Equipment Fitted in Escort Destroyers and Corvettes, RN and RCN as of August 1st 1943," Chart attached to D/DWT to A/CNS, 30 August 1943, LAC, RG 24, vol. 3,995, 1057-1-27, vol. 1.
57 Macdonald to Nelles, n.d. [20 November 1943], PANS, Macdonald Papers, MG 2, F 276/3.
58 "Summary as of 18th August 1943," PANS, Macdonald Papers, MG 2, F 276/18.
59 Macdonald to Nelles, n.d. [20 November 1943], PANS, Macdonald Papers, MG 2, F 276/3.
60 Andrew Dyas MacLean, "Fairmiles and Foul," *Boating Magazine,* January-February 1943, DHH, 94/127, 6.
61 Carswell to Macdonald, 5 August 1943, LAC, RG 24, vol. 3,997, 1057-1-39, vol. 1.
62 Carswell to Macdonald, "Survey of HMC Dockyard Ship Maintenance Operation. July and August 1943," 5 August 1943, and Rannie to Macdonald, "Report on Survey of HMC Dockyard, Halifax NS – July 24 to July 28 1943," n.d., PANS, Macdonald Papers, MG 2, F 276/15, F 276/14.
63 Macdonald to Treasury Board, 23 August 1943, LAC, RG 24, vol. 3,997, 1057-1-39, vol. 2.
64 Knowlton to C.R.H. Taylor, 24 August 1943, LAC, RG 24, vol. 3,997, 1057-1-39, vol. 1.
65 Taylor to Murray, 27 August 1943, LAC, RG 24, vol. 3,997, 1057-1-39, vol. 1.
66 Mills to Carswell, 30 June 1943, LAC, RG 24, vol. 3,997, 1057-1-39, vol. 1.
67 D.B. Carswell to C.D. Howe, 8 May 1943, Cabinet War Committee Document 511, LAC, RG 2.
68 Mitchell to Howe, 2 September 1943, LAC, Howe Papers, MG 27, III, B 20, vol. 42, file 5-9-25; Howe to Beaverbrook, 10 August 1943, LAC, Howe Papers, MG 27, III, B 20, vol. 170, file 90.
69 Gibson and Robertson, *Ottawa at War,* 430-31; King diary, 15 September 1943, DHH, 83/530, vol. 192,798.
70 Jefferson to Murray, 18 August 1943, LAC, RG 24, vol. 3997, 1057-1-39, vol. 2.
71 Naval Staff meeting, 10 June 1943, DHH. Indicating that NSHQ was suspicious about the prospects of Admiralty assistance, the chief of naval engineering and construction had observed three weeks prior to Murray's request that RCN "escort vessels in UK Ports now have as much work carried out both in the form of repairs and alterations as the Admiralty will undertake."
72 Admiralty to Murray, message 240128A, 24 August 1943, PANS, Macdonald Papers, MG 2, F 276/24.
73 "Combined Canadian, United Kingdom and United States Committee to Examine Repair Problems for Warships and Merchant Vessels on the East Coast of Canada and Newfoundland," 12 August 1943, DHH, Repairs and Refits, 8780.
74 Stephens to Nelles, 26 November 1943, PANS, MG 2, Macdonald Papers, F 276/37; Johnstone to Nelles, 13 November 1943, PANS, MG 2, Macdonald Papers, F 276/25.
75 Rear Admiral V. Crutchley, "HMA Ships – Requirements for Improved Fighting Efficiency," 30 July 1943, PRO, ADM 1/13045.
76 Director of Gunnery and Anti-Aircraft Warfare, 6 October 1943, PRO, ADM 1/13045.
77 Naval Board meeting, 16 September 1943, DHH.
78 Strange to Connolly, "Confidential Memorandum," 21 September 1943, LAC, Connolly Papers, MG 32, C 71, vol. 3.
79 Strange to Gerity, 21 September 1943, DHH, Russell Papers, 91/298, vol. 4, emphasis in original.
80 Strange to Simpson, 22 September 1943, DHH, Russell Papers, 91/298, vol. 4.
81 Mr. J.J. Connolly, interview by HRO LCdr T.R. Daly, 26 January 1945, Ottawa, written notes, DHH, 1700-193/96D.
82 Untitled poem, n.d., LAC, Connolly Papers, MG 32, C 71, vol. 4, file 23.
83 Strange to Connolly, "Thoughts on an Afternoon before Christmas," n.d., LAC, Connolly Papers, MG 32, C 71, vol. 4, file 23.
84 Mitchell to Connolly, 29 December 1943, LAC, Connolly Papers, MG 32, C 71, vol. 2, file 18.

85 Connolly to Audette, 25 November 1943, LAC, Connolly Papers, MG 32, C 71, vol. 2, file 17. I am indebted to Bob Caldwell for drawing my attention to this letter and for his realization that these medical terms were in fact being substituted for their ship's equipment.
86 Audette to Connolly, 5 December 1943, LAC, Connolly Papers, MG 32, C 71, vol. 2, file 17.
87 O'Brien to Connolly, "Chase Me Charlie," October 1943, LAC, Connolly Papers, MG 32, C 71, vol. 4, file 14.
88 Connolly to Audette, 25 November 1943, LAC, Connolly Papers, MG 32, C 71, vol. 2, file 17.
89 Audette to Connolly, 22 and 29 September 1943, LAC, Connolly Papers, MG 32, C 71, vol. 2, file 16.
90 Connolly to Mitchell, 16 November 1943, LAC, Connolly Papers, MG 32, C 71, vol. 2, file 17.
91 I am grateful to Mr. Gerald O'Brien for this information.
92 FONF to NSHQ, Ref Signal 212204, 29 September 1943, and NSHQ to FONF, 29 September 1943, LAC, RG 24, vol. 11,749.
93 Nelles to Macdonald, 26 November 1943, and Nelles to Macdonald, 4 December 1943, PANS, Macdonald Papers, MG 2, F 276/33, F 276/39.
94 Connolly diary, 6 October 1943, LAC, Connolly Papers, MG 32, C 71, vol. 2, file 6.
95 RCN Naval List, October 1943, DHH.
96 Connolly diary, 7 October 1943, LAC, Connolly Papers, MG 32, C 71, vol. 2, file 6; Burgess and MacPherson, *The Ships of Canada's Naval Forces, 1910-1993*, 200.
97 Connolly diary, 6-7 October 1943, LAC, Connolly Papers, MG 32, C 71, vol. 2, file 6.
98 Connolly to Macdonald, 9 October 1943, PANS, Macdonald Papers, MG 2, F 297.
99 Copy letter ("Bob to Unc"), 8 October 1943, PANS, Macdonald Papers, MG 2, F 297; Connolly to Macdonald, 9 October 1943, PANS, Macdonald Papers, MG 2, F 297.
100 Goolden diary, 25 September 1943, BIOG G, DHH.
101 Connolly to Macdonald, 8 November 1943, LAC, Connolly Papers, MG 32, C 71, vol. 3.
102 Strange to Adams, 21 September 1943, DHH, E.C. Russell Papers, 91/298.
103 David Zimmerman, *The Great Naval Battle of Ottawa* (Toronto: University of Toronto Press, 1989), 110.
104 NOIC St. John's War Diary, FONF Monthly ROP, October 1943, DHH, 1000-5-20, vol. 4; Sydney Monthly Reports, DHH, 1000-5-21, vol. 2; *Stadaconna* War Diary, DHH, 1000-5-13, vol. 20; Jones personnel file, LAC; Connolly diary, 8 October 1943, LAC, Connolly Papers, MG 32, C 71, vol. 2, file 6; Nelles to Macdonald, 26 November 1943, PANS, Macdonald Papers, MG 2, F 276/39.
105 Connolly to Ida Connolly, 9 October 1943, LAC, Connolly Papers, MG 32, C 71, vol. 1.
106 Connolly diary, 7 October 1943, LAC, Connolly Papers, MG 32, C 71, vol. 3; Connolly to Macdonald, 8 November 1943, LAC, Connolly Papers, MG 32, C 71, vol. 3; Connolly to Ida Connolly, 9 October 1943, LAC, Connolly Papers, MG 32, C 71, vol. 1. Connolly to Macdonald, 9 October 1943, PANS, Macdonald Papers, MG 2, F 297.
107 Connolly to Macdonald, 8 November 1943, LAC, Connolly Papers, MG 32, C 71, vol. 3; Connolly diary, 8-9 October 1943, LAC, Connolly Papers, MG 32, C 71, vol. 2, file 6.
108 Connolly to Macdonald, 9 October 1943, PANS, Macdonald Papers, MG 2, F 297.

Chapter 6: A Loaded Investigation

1 Mr. J.J. Connolly, interview by LCdr T.R. Daly, 26 January 1945, Ottawa, written notes, Directorate of History and Heritage (hereafter cited as DHH), 1700-193/96D.
2 Richard Oliver Mayne, "A Covert Naval Investigation: Overseas Officers, John J. Connolly, and the Equipment Crisis of 1943," *The Northern Mariner* 10, 1 (January 2000): 37-52. The ideas in this chapter were first developed in this article.
3 Price to Shorto, 28 May 1943, and Price to Jeffery, 23 September 1943, Library and Archives Canada (hereafter cited as LAC), RG 24, vol. 11,721, file 34; George to Price, "US Naval Repair Base," 21 December 1943, LAC, RG 24, vol. 11,695, 1003-2-13.

4 Horton to NSHQ, 30 July 1943, and NSHQ to Niobe, 30 July 1943, LAC, RG 24, vols. 12,117 and 12,122.
5 SCNO (L) War Diary, "Activities of A/S Technical Liaison Officer," October 1943, DHH, 1000-5-35, vol. 1.
6 George to Price, "HRO's Third Report of Activities," 16 October 1943, DHH, SCNO(L) War Diaries, 1000-5-35, vol. 1.
7 George to Price, "US Naval Repair Base," 21 December 1943, LAC, RG 24, vol. 11,695, 1003-2-13.
8 "Report of Mr. J.J. Connolly's trip to the U.K. in one of H.M.C.S. Corvettes," 15 November 1943, DHH, Nelles Papers, folder B, file 14, 1.
9 Connolly diary, 16 October 1943, LAC, Connolly Papers, MG 32, C 71, vol. 2, file 16.
10 Connolly to Macdonald, 8 November 1943, LAC, Connolly Papers, MG 32, C 71, vol. 3. Connolly diary, 13 October 1943, LAC, Connolly Papers, MG 32, C 71, vol. 2, file 16.
11 Connolly diary, 12 October 1943, LAC, Connolly Papers, MG 32, C 71, vol. 2, file 6.
12 Connolly to Macdonald, 8 November 1943, LAC, Connolly Papers, MG 32, C 71, vol. 3. The *Orillia* was a microcosm of the problems faced by the entire escort fleet. One of these problems included the poor accommodations that were common on corvettes. Originally built to accommodate approximately forty-five sailors, the complement of *Orillia* during this passage was eighty-nine officers and men. As for equipment, Connolly found it disturbing that the officer of the watch on *Orillia* often had to steer and depend on the ships with gyroscopic compasses, which incidentally were mostly the British vessels of C.4, because their own magnetic compass was so unreliable.
13 Connolly diary, n.d., LAC, Connolly Papers, MG 32, C 71, vol. 2, file 4.
14 Connolly diary, "Diary Notes March-April 1943," n.d., LAC, Connolly Papers, MG 32, C 71, vol. 2, file 5. Within his diary, Connolly admitted that the RCN probably would have been better off had it built more escort destroyers rather than corvettes.
15 Connolly diary, "General Conclusions," n.d., LAC, Connolly Papers, MG 32, C 71, vol. 2, file 7.
16 Connolly diary, 19 October 1943, LAC, Connolly Papers, MG 32, C 71, vol. 2, file 6.
17 Connolly to Macdonald, 8 November 1943, LAC, Connolly Papers, MG 32, C 71, vol. 3.
18 Ibid.
19 Connolly to Macdonald, 8 November 1943, LAC, Connolly Papers, MG 32, C 71, vol. 2, file 6.
20 Connolly diary, October 1943, LAC, Connolly Papers, MG 32, C 71, vol. 2, file 6.
21 Conklin to Connolly, 23 August [October] 1943, LAC, Connolly Papers, MG 32, C 71, vol. 3. As Connolly later noted to Macdonald, the letter from Conklin was incorrectly dated 23 August, although it was actually written on 23 October. Furthermore, on the actual report Conklin mistakenly identifies Connolly as the deputy minister rather than executive assistant.
22 Postwar correspondence between Audette and Conklin clearly identifies the level of their friendship. For example, Conklin once wrote to Audette, "Golly Louis, I think so many times and yarn for our L'derry days. We realize we had a good thing at that time, but not to the extent we should." Conklin to Audette, June 1947, LAC, Audette Papers, MG 31, E 18, vol. 14, file 6.
23 Conklin to Connolly, 23 August [October] 1943, LAC, Connolly Papers, MG 32, C 71, vol. 3.
24 Connolly to Macdonald, 8 November 1943, LAC, Connolly Papers, MG 32, C 71, vol. 3.
25 Conklin to Connolly, "Deficiencies in Canadian Ship Repairs," 23 October 1943, LAC, Connolly Papers, MG 32, C 71, vol. 3, "Equipment on RCN ships part 1 nd 1943."
26 Ibid.
27 "HMCS *Skeena*, A Brief History," 4 May 1960, DHH, 8000; HMCS *Skeena*, Ship's movement cards, DHH.

28 Connolly personal minute note, n.d. [October 1943], LAC, Connolly Papers, MG 32, C 71, vol. 3.
29 HMCS *Woodstock* Signals, DHH, 8000; "HMCS *Woodstock* – A Brief History," DHH, 8000; HMCS *Woodstock*, Ship's movement cards, DHH; "Report of Mr. JJ Connolly's Trip to UK in one of HMC Corvette," DHH, Nelles Papers, folder B, file 14.
30 Mr. John Connolly, interview by LCdr T.R. Daly, 26 January 1945, Ottawa, written notes, DHH, 1700-193/96D.
31 Lt J.J. Pigott to Connolly, 23 October 1943, LAC, Connolly Papers, MG 32, C 71, vol. 3.
32 Ibid.
33 Connolly to Macdonald, 9 November 1943, LAC, Connolly Papers, MG 32, C 71, vol. 3.
34 Connolly diary, n.d. [October 1943], "Conclusions," LAC, Connolly Papers, MG 32, C 71, vol. 2, file 6.
35 Connolly diary, n.d., LAC, Connolly Papers, MG 32, C 71, vol. 2, file 6.
36 Quotations from, respectively, anonymous author, c. 1940s, "Modernization of Armament and Equipment," DHH, 8060; Connolly to Macdonald, 8 November 1943, LAC, Connolly Papers, MG 32, C 71, vol. 3.
37 John Burgess and Ken Macpherson, *The Ships of Canada's Naval Forces, 1910-1993* (St. Catharines, ON: Vanwell Publishing, 1994), 81; Mr. John Connolly, interview by LCdr T.R. Dale, 26 January 1945, Ottawa, written notes, DHH, SCNO (L), 1700-193/96D.
38 Copelin to Connolly, 23 October 1943, LAC, Connolly Papers, MG 32, C 71, vol. 3.
39 Connolly to Macdonald, 8 November 1943, LAC, Connolly Papers, MG 32, C 71, vol. 3.
40 Fighting efficiency/DWT to D/DWT, 12 October 1943, and Hibbard to NSHQ, "Refitting of HMC Ships and HM Ships under RCN Authorities in the Maritime Area," 12 October 1943, LAC, RG 24, vol. 3,996, 1057-1-35, vol. 3; NSHQ to SCNO (L), "A&A's to RCN Corvettes," 30 September 1943, PANS, Macdonald Papers, MG 2, F 276/38.
41 Simpson to Horton, n.d. [October 1943], LAC, Connolly Papers, MG 32, C 71, vol. 3.
42 Ibid.
43 Connolly diary, October 1943, LAC, Connolly Papers, MG 32, C 71, vol. 2, file 6; Simpson to Horton, n.d. [October 1943], LAC, Connolly Papers, MG 32, C 71, vol. 3.
44 Lee to Strange, 4 October 1943, LAC, Connolly Papers, MG 32, C 71, vol. 3, file 12.
45 Simpson to Horton, n.d. [October 1943], LAC, Connolly Papers, MG 32, C 71, vol. 3.
46 Connolly diary, n.d. [October 1943], LAC, Connolly Papers, MG 32, C 71, vol. 2, file 6.
47 "Report of Mr. JJ Connolly's Trip to UK in one of HMC Corvette," 15 November 1943, DHH, Nelles Papers, folder B, file 14.
48 SCNO (L) to Sec NB, Functions of admiral commanding reserves, 21 July 1943, LAC, RG 24, vol. 11,705, N-1-8-4.
49 Connolly diary, 23 October 1943, LAC, Connolly Papers, MG 32, C 71, vol. 2, file 6; Connolly to Macdonald, 9 November 1943, LAC, Connolly Papers, MG 32, C 71, vol. 3.
50 War Diary of the SCNO (L) for the month of October 1943, October 1943, DHH, 1000-5-35, vol. 1, 2: Connolly diary, n.d. [October 1943], LAC, Connolly Papers, MG 32, C 71, vol. 2, file 7. For two of the best interpretations of the causes for various mutinies in the Canadian Navy, see Richard Gimblett, "Too Many Chiefs and Not Enough Seamen: The Lower-Deck Complement of a Postwar Canadian Navy Destroyer – The Case of HMCS *Crescent*, March 1949," *The Northern Mariner* 9, 3 (July 1999): 1-22; and Michael Whitby, "Matelots, Martinets, and Mutineers: The Mutiny in HMCS *Iroquois*, 19 July 1943," *The Journal of Military History* 65, 1 (January 2001): 77-103.
51 Gilhooly to CCCS, "Memorandum – Special services," 8 April 1943, LAC, RG 24, vol. 11,705.
52 Connolly to Macdonald, 9 November 1943, LAC, Connolly Papers, MG 32, C 71, vol. 3; Clifford to Price, 2 September 1943, LAC, RG 24, vol. 11,721, file 34; Price to Jeffery, 24 September 1943, DHH, 24/8200, 1920/102 98/1; other reports can be found at the LAC, RG 24, vol. 11,705.

53 Connolly diary, n.d. [October 1943], LAC, Connolly Papers, MG 32, C 71, vol. 2, file 7.
54 Connolly to Macdonald, "Memorandum to the Minister," 9 November 1943, LAC, Connolly Papers, MG 32, C 71, vol. 3.
55 Connolly to Macdonald, "General Observations on the Royal Canadian Navy," 9 November 1943, LAC, Connolly Papers, MG 32, C 71, vol. 3.
56 Connolly to Macdonald, 11 November 1943, LAC, Connolly Papers, MG 32, C 71, vol. 3.
57 Connolly diary, 22 October 1943, LAC, Connolly Papers, MG 32, C 71, vol. 2, file 7, 28; Connolly to Macdonald, 8 November 1943, LAC, Connolly Papers, MG 32, C 71, vol. 3.
58 SCNO (L) War Diary, July 1943, DHH, 1000-5-35, vol. 1; SCNO (L) War Diary, August 1943, DHH, 1000-5-35, vol. 1; Price to NSHQ, "Organization of Material Division," 20 July 1943, LAC, RG 24, vol. 4,060, 1081-1-2.
59 F. Price, "Londonderry naval base," n.d. [spring 1943], LAC, RG 24, vol. 11,721, file 34.
60 SCNO(L) to Sec NB, 24 September 1943, DHH, 8200, 1920/102.
61 Connolly to Macdonald, 8 November 1943, LAC, Connolly Papers, MG 32, C 71, vol. 3.
62 SCNO (L), October 1943, War Diary, "Monthly Report of Activities of A/S Technical Liaison Officer," DHH, 1000-5-35, vol. 1.
63 Connolly to Macdonald, 8 November 1943, LAC, Connolly Papers, MG 32, C 71, vol. 3.
64 Naval Board meeting, 13 September 1943, DHH; GM Hibbard, "Refitting Position of HMC Ships and HM Ships under RCN Authorities in Maritime Area, 1942-45," 12 October 1943, LAC, RG 24, vol. 3,996, 1057-1-35, vol. 3.
65 Connolly to Macdonald, 8 November 1943, LAC, Connolly Papers, MG 32, C 71, vol. 3.
66 Ibid.
67 Minute note, n.d. [October 1943], LAC, Connolly Papers, MG 32, C 71, vol. 3.
68 Connolly to Macdonald, 13 November 1943, LAC, Connolly Papers, MG 32, C 71, vol. 3. After discovering the Adams report on 23 November, Connolly remarked to Macdonald that "the Adams report undoubtedly bears out everything that was said by Commodore "D" [Simpson] and by Horton. Inspite [sic] of the very strong statements made [in Adams' report], apparently memos were passed with abandon, without much action being taken. The situation according to this file at N.S.H.Q. is that nothing can be done" (Connolly to Macdonald, 23 November 1943, LAC, Connolly Papers, MG 32, C 71, vol. 3).
69 Connolly to Macdonald, 9 November 1943, LAC, Connolly Papers, MG 32, C 71, vol. 3.
70 Connolly to Macdonald, 8 November 1943, LAC, Connolly Papers, MG 32, C 71, vol. 3.
71 Connolly to Macdonald, 15 November 1943, LAC, Connolly Papers, MG 32, C 71, vol. 3.
72 Connolly to Macdonald, 10 November 1943, LAC, Connolly Papers, MG 32, C 71, vol. 3.
73 R.A. Pennington, interview by historical records officer, 5 May 1946, Ottawa, DHH, 1700-193/96D.
74 "Notes Taken at Staff Meeting of Report Given by J.J. Connolly, Executive Asst. to the Minister," 11 November 1943, LAC, Connolly Papers, MG 32, C 71, vol. 3.
75 Connolly to Macdonald, 8 November 1943, LAC, Connolly Papers, MG 32, C 71, vol. 3.
76 Connolly diary, October 1943, LAC, Connolly Papers, MG 32, C 71, vol. 2, file 6; Connolly to Macdonald, 8 November 1943, LAC, Connolly Papers, MG 32, C 71, vol. 3.
77 Connolly to Macdonald, 8 November 1943, LAC, Connolly Papers, MG 32, C 71, vol. 3.
78 Rowland to Reid, 1 May 1943, PANS, Macdonald Papers, MG 2, F 276/10.
79 Pennington to Agnew, "A's & A's – Canadian Ships in UK," 31 January 1943, DHH, Nelles Papers, folder B, file 3.
80 Agnew to Price, 12 March 1943, LAC, vol. 11,714, 384/5.
81 CCCS to Lev, 18 May 1943, DHH, Nelles Papers, folder B, file 6.
82 "A & A Procedure re HMC Ships refitting in UK," Draft Admiralty Fleet Order, 23 June 1943, DHH, Nelles Papers, folder B, file 9.
83 Mansfield to Pound, n.d. [May 1943], and Mansfield, "Notes for the First Sea Lord," 19 May 1943, PRO, ADM 1/13756, 68354.

84 All Naval Service Headquarters heard about the base were signals suggesting that "this gear is not available in Londonderry," or that "it is not always possible to ... effect the necessary repairs due to the fact that special items required are not immediately available at Londonderry." Simpson to Admiralty, 1031A/19/3/43, DHH, Nelles Papers, folder B, file 4; CTG 24.7 to CTF 24, 1621/2/12/42, DHH, Nelles Papers, folder B, file 2; SCNO (L), 29 December 1943, LAC, RG 24, vol. 11,721, file 34.
85 Simpson to Horton, n.d. [October 1943], LAC, Connolly Papers, MG 32, C 71, vol. 3.
86 Quotations from Connolly to Macdonald, 8 November 1943, LAC, Connolly Papers, MG 32, C 71, vol. 3.
87 Murray to BAMR, 9 March 1943, LAC, RG 24, vol. 3,996, 1057-1-35, vol. 2.
88 Murray to Reid, 23 August 1943, LAC, RG 24, vol. 11,987, F 1292.
89 Stephens to Staff, 9 September 1943, LAC, RG 24, vol. 3,996, 1057-1-35, vol. 3; DeWolf, "Review of RCN Ship Requirements 1944-45 Shipbuilding Programme," 18 August 1943, DHH, 1650-1.
90 Naval Board meeting, 16 September 1943, DHH.
91 Connolly to Macdonald, 8 November 1943, LAC, Connolly Papers, MG 32, C 71, vol. 3.
92 Macdonald to Cabinet, "Memorandum to: War Committee of the Cabinet," 8 May 1943, LAC, RG 2, Document 510.
93 Murray Memoir, LAC, Murray Papers, M 30, E 207, vol. 4, 51.
94 SCNO (L) War diaries, July 1943, DHH, 1000-5-35, vol. 1.
95 "Modernization of HMC Flower Class Corvettes," n.d., DHH, Nelles Papers, folder B, file 4.
96 HMCS *Niobe* War Diary, June 1943, DHH, SCNO (L) War Diary, 1000-5-35, vol. 1.
97 "Notes taken at Staff Meeting of Report Given by Mr. J.J. Connolly, Executive Asst. to Minister," 11 November 1943, LAC, Connolly Papers, MG 32, C 71, vol. 3.
98 SCNO (L) War diaries, "Monthly Report of Activities A/S Technical Liaison Officers," DHH, 1000-5-35, vol. 1; War Diary of the SCNO (L) for the month of October 1943, October 1943, DHH, 1000-5-35, vol. 1, 3; Report of Mr J.J. Connolly's Trip, DHH, Nelles Papers, folder B, file 14; Connolly to Macdonald, 8 November 1943, LAC, Connolly Papers, MG 32, C 71, vol. 3.
99 Connolly diary, 23 October 1943, LAC, Connolly Papers, MG 32, C 71, vol. 2, file 7.
100 Connolly to Macdonald, 8 November 1943, LAC, Connolly Papers, MG 32, C 71, vol. 3.
101 G.M. Hibbard, "Refitting Position of HMC Ships and HM Ships under RCN Authorities in Maritime Area, 1942-45," 12 October 1943, LAC, RG 24, vol. 3,996, 1057-1-35, vol. 3.
102 Ibid.
103 Naval Staff meeting, 18 October 1943, DHH.
104 H.A. Wilson (Director Civilian Personnel) to A.B. Coulter (Assistant Deputy Minister for Naval Services), "Progress in Securing Additional Manpower," 22 October 1943, J.G. Fargo (Associate Coordinator of Controls) to Carswell, Ship Repair Manpower, 4 October 1943, Carswell to Department of Labour, Canadian National Telegraphs, 5 October 1943, and Carswell to various ships yards, Copy – Canadian Pacific Telegraphs, October 1943, LAC, RG 24, vol. 3,997, 1057-1-39, vol. 2.

Chapter 7: Covering Up the Conspiracy

1 Richard Oliver Mayne, "A Political Execution: Expediency and the Firing of Vice Admiral Percy W. Nelles," *The American Review of Canadian Studies*, 29, 4 (1999): 557-92.
2 Macdonald diary, November 1943, PANS, Macdonald Papers, MG 2, vol. 1501, F 305.
3 David Zimmerman, *The Great Naval Battle of Ottawa* (Toronto: University of Toronto Press, 1989), 138. Zimmerman calls this memorandum a "damning indictment of Naval Service Headquarters' handling of equipment," which was exactly what it was.
4 Simpson to Horton, "Extract of Letter from Commodore 'D' Western Approaches, to C in C, Western Approaches," n.d., Library and Archives Canada (hereafter cited as LAC), Connolly Papers, MG 32, C 71, vol. 3; Connolly to Nelles, cover letter, 10 November 1943, PANS, Macdonald Papers, MG 2, F 276/44.

5 Griffiths to Nelles, 16 November 1943, PANS, Macdonald Papers, MG 2, F 276/26; Johnston to Nelles, 13 November 1943, PANS, Macdonald Papers, MG 2, F 276/25.
6 Griffiths to Nelles, 16 November 1943, PANS, Macdonald Papers, MG 2, F 276/26.
7 Stephens to Nelles, 11 November 1943, PANS, Macdonald Papers, MG 2, F 276/23.
8 Jones to Nelles, 12 November 1943, PANS, Macdonald Papers, MG 2, F 276/22.
9 Jones to Nelles, 12 November 1943, PANS, Macdonald Papers, MG 2, F 276/25.
10 Simpson to Horton, n.d., LAC, Connolly Papers, MG 32, C 71, vol. 3; Jones to Nelles, 12 November 1943, PANS, Macdonald Papers, MG 2, F 276/22; Griffiths to Nelles, 16 November 1943, PANS, Macdonald Papers, MG 2, F 276/26; Johnstone to Nelles, 13 November 1943, PANS, Macdonald Papers, MG 2, F 276/25; Mr. John Connolly, interview by LCdr T.R. Daly, 26 January 1945, Ottawa, written notes, Directorate of History and Heritage (hereafter cited as DHH), 1700-196/96D; Connolly to Nelles, 10 November 1943, PANS, Macdonald Papers, MG 2, F 276/44; Simpson to Horton, n.d., LAC, Connolly Papers, MG 32, C 71, vol. 3; Minute note, Jones to Connolly, on SCNO (L) to Sec NB, 29 October 1943, DHH, 1000-5-35, vol. 1.
11 Marc Milner, *North Atlantic Run: The Royal Canadian Navy and the Battle for the Convoys* (Toronto: University of Toronto Press, 1985), 263-64.
12 "Report of Mr. J.J. Connolly's Trip to U.K. in One of H.M.C. Corvettes," 15 November 1943, DHH, Nelles Papers, folder B, file 14.
13 Connolly to Macdonald, 8 November 1943, LAC, Connolly Papers, MG 32, C 71, vol. 3.
14 Zimmerman, *The Great Naval Battle of Ottawa*, 140.
15 Connolly to Macdonald, 13 November 1943, LAC, Connolly Papers, MG 32, C 71, vol. 3.
16 Draft copy of memorandum to CNS, 16 November 1943, LAC, Connolly Papers, MG 32, C 71, vol. 3; Connolly to Macdonald, 13 November 1943, LAC, Connolly Papers, MG 32, C 71, vol. 3. In a number of locations, Macdonald altered the text so that it would read as if he was responsible for the entire document.
17 Macdonald to Nelles, "Memorandum on the State of Equipment on R.C.N. ships," n.d. [20 November 1943], PANS, Macdonald Papers, MG 2, F 276/3; "Draft Copy of Memorandum to CNS," 16 November 1943, LAC, Connolly Papers, MG 32, C 71, vol. 3; Connolly to Macdonald, 8 November 1943, LAC, Connolly Papers, MG 32, C 71, vol. 3. Although too numerous to list completely here, one example of the Londonderry officers' influence can be found in the fact that the cases of poor equipment on *Skeena*, *St. Laurent*, *Pictou*, *Restigouche*, and *Drumheller* were all used within this memorandum to Nelles. These were the ships that Conklin used in his report to Connolly to illustrate his concern with the state of equipment within the RCN.
18 Connolly to Macdonald, "JJC Rough Notes on Nelles Memo," n.d. [5 December 1943], LAC, Connolly Papers, MG 32, C 71, vol. 3.
19 Macdonald to Nelles, "Memorandum on the State of Equipment on R.C.N. Ships," n.d. [November 1943], PANS, Macdonald Papers, MG 2, F 276/3, 14.
20 Connolly to Macdonald, 23 November 1943, LAC, Connolly Papers, MG 32, C 71, vol. 3; "Personal Memorandum Notes," n.d. [October 1943], LAC, Connolly Papers, MG 32, C 71, vol. 3.
21 Macdonald to Nelles, 25 November 1943, PANS, Macdonald Papers, MG 2, F 276/28.
22 Macdonald to Nelles, 25 November 1943, LAC, Connolly Papers, MG 32, C 71, vol. 3.
23 Mr. John Connolly, interview by LCdr T.R. Daly, 26 January 1945, Ottawa, written notes, DHH, 1700-196/96D.
24 Connolly to Audette, 25 November 1943, LAC, Connolly Papers, MG 32, C 71, vol. 2, file 17.
25 Connolly to Shorto, 18 November 1943, LAC, Connolly Papers, MG 32, C 71, vol. 2, file 17.
26 Connolly to Simpson, 18 November 1943, LAC, Connolly Papers, MG 32, C 71, vol. 2, file 17.
27 Ibid.
28 Connolly to Conklin, 18 November 1943, LAC, Connolly Papers, MG 32, C 71, vol. 2, file 17.
29 See Macdonald diary, 29 November-5 December 1943, PANS, Macdonald Papers, MG 2, F 391.

30 Nelles to Macdonald, 4 December 1943, PANS, Macdonald Papers, MG 2, F 276/39, emphasis in original.
31 Nelles to Macdonald, 27 November 1943, PANS, Macdonald Papers, MG 2, F 276/34.
32 Nelles to Macdonald, 29 November, PANS, Macdonald Papers, MG 2, F 276/43, emphasis in original.
33 Nelles to Macdonald, 4 December 1943, PANS, Macdonald Paper, MG 2, F 276/39, emphasis in the original.
34 Ibid.
35 Nelles to Macdonald, 27 November 1943, PANS, Macdonald Papers, MG 2, F 276/34.
36 Nelles to Macdonald, 4 December 1943, PANS, Macdonald Paper, MG 2, F 276/39, emphasis in the original.
37 Ibid.
38 Frederick W. Gibson and Barbara Robertson, eds., *Ottawa at War: The Grant Dexter Memoranda, 1939-1945* (Winnipeg: The Manitoba Record Society, 1994), 452.
39 Mr. John Connolly, interview by LCdr T.R. Daly, 26 January 1945, Ottawa, written notes, DHH, 1700-196/96D.
40 Connolly to Macdonald, unsigned memorandum for the minister, 30 November 1943, LAC, Connolly Papers, MG 32, C 71, vol. 3.
41 Naval Board meeting, 27 July 1943, DHH; Nelles to Macdonald, 26 November 1943, PANS, Macdonald Papers, MG 2, F 276, emphasis in original.
42 Connolly to Macdonald, unsigned memorandum for the minister, 30 November 1943, LAC, Connolly Papers, MG 32, C 71, vol. 3.
43 Connolly to Macdonald, unsigned memorandum for the minister, 30 November 1943, LAC, Connolly Papers, MG 32, C 71, vol. 3, emphasis in original.
44 J.J. Connolly to Edward Connolly, 15 January 1944, LAC, MG 32, C 71, vol. 1. Halifax telephone directory, 1925-33, National Library of Canada; Vice Admiral David Allan Collins, interview by Hal Lawrence, June 1984, Victoria, BC, tape recording transcript, DHH, BIOG C; H.N. Lay, interview by Hal Lawrence, 25 January 1986, Victoria, BC, tape recording transcript, DHH, BIOG L.
45 For more information on the power of the civil service, see Jack Granatstein, *The Ottawa Men: The Civil Service Mandarins, 1935-1957* (Toronto: Oxford University Press, 1982).
46 Connolly to Macdonald, 13 November 1943, LAC, Connolly Papers, MG 32, C 71, vol. 3; Connolly to Macdonald, n.d. [28 November 1943], LAC, Connolly Papers, MG 32, C 71, vol. 3.
47 Connolly to Macdonald, n.d. [28 November 1943], LAC, Connolly Papers, MG 32, C 71, vol. 3.
48 Ibid.
49 Nelles to Macdonald, 4 December 1943, PANS, Macdonald Papers, MG 2, F 276/39, emphasis in the original.
50 Ibid.
51 Connolly to Macdonald, "JJC Rough Notes on Nelles Memo," n.d. [5 December 1943], LAC, Connolly Papers, MG 32, C 71, vol. 3.
52 Pressey to Nelles, 2 December 1943, DHH, Nelles Papers, folder B, file 17.
53 Adams to Creery, 7 December 1943, LAC, RG 24, vol. 3,996, 1057-1-35, vol. 2.
54 Connolly to Macdonald, unsigned memorandum for the minister, 30 November 1943, LAC, Connolly Papers, MG 32, C 71, vol. 3.
55 Connolly to Macdonald, unsigned memorandum for the minister, 30 November 1943, LAC, Connolly Papers, MG 32, C 71, vol. 3; G.N. Tucker, *The Naval Service of Canada: Its Official History* (Ottawa: King's Printer, 1952), 431.
56 Connolly to Macdonald, "JJC Rough Notes on Nelles' Memo," n.d. [5 December 1943], LAC, Connolly Papers, MG 32, C 71, vol. 3.

57 Connolly to Macdonald, unsigned memorandum for the minister, 30 November 1943, LAC, Connolly Papers, MG 32, C 71, vol. 3; Connolly to Macdonald, "JJC Rough Notes on Nelles' Memo," n.d. [5 December 1943], LAC, Connolly Papers, MG 32, C 71, vol. 3.
58 Connolly to Macdonald, unsigned memorandum for the minister, 30 November 1943, LAC, Connolly Papers, MG 32, C 71, vol. 3.
59 Nelles to Macdonald, 4 December 1943, PANS, Macdonald Papers, MG 2, F 276/39, emphasis in original.
60 Connolly to Pennington, 7 December 1943, LAC, Connolly Papers, MG 32, C 71, vol. 2, file 18.
61 Connolly to Macdonald, n.d. [28 November], LAC, Connolly Papers, MG 32, C 71, vol. 3.
62 Quotation from Nelles to Macdonald, 27 November 1943, PANS, Macdonald Papers, MG 2, F 276/34; Connolly to Macdonald, "JJC Rough Notes on Nelles Memo," n.d. [5 December 1943], LAC, Connolly Papers, MG 32, C 71, vol. 3; Connolly to Macdonald, unsigned memorandum for the minister, 30 November 1943, LAC, Connolly Papers, MG 32, C 71, vol. 3.
63 Connolly to Macdonald, n.d. [December 1943], LAC, Connolly Papers, MG 32, C 71, vol. 4.
64 Connolly to Macdonald, unsigned memorandum for the minister, 30 November 1943, LAC, Connolly Papers, MG 32, C 71, vol. 3.
65 Ibid.
66 Ibid.
67 Interview with Senator Gordon B. Isnor, 15 August 1967, in John Hawkins, *The Life and Times of Angus L* (Windsor, NS: Lancelot Press, 1969), 224; Connolly to Macdonald, 30 November 1943, LAC, Connolly Papers, MG 32, C 71, vol. 3.
68 Mills to Macdonald, 11 January 1944, PANS, Macdonald Papers, MG 2, F 736/4.
69 Connolly to Macdonald, "The Governor General," 30 November 1943, LAC, Connolly Papers, MG 32, C 71, vol. 3.
70 Ibid.
71 Connolly to Macdonald, unsigned memorandum for the minister, 30 November 1943, LAC, Connolly Papers, MG 32, C 71, vol. 3; Connolly to Macdonald, "JJC Rough Notes on Nelles' Memo," n.d. [5 December 1943], LAC, Connolly Papers, MG 32, C 71, vol. 3.
72 Copies of signal NSHQ to CinC WA, 3 December 1943, contained in Macdonald to Horton, 19 April 1944, PANS, Macdonald Papers, MG 2, F 1067/4.
73 Connolly to Macdonald, 15 March 1944, PANS, Macdonald Papers, MG 2, F 1067/2.
74 "To Make the Punishment Fit the Crime," *Salty Dips*, vol. 2, ed. Mac Lynch (Ottawa: Privately printed, 1985), 76.
75 Connolly to Macdonald, 30 November 1943, LAC, Connolly Papers, MG 32, C 71, vol. 3.
76 Macdonald to Nelles, 10 December 1943, PANS, Macdonald Papers, MG 2, F 276/47.
77 Ibid.
78 Ibid.
79 Read to Connolly, 23 December 1943, LAC, Connolly Papers, MG 32, C 71, vol. 2, file 18.
80 "Horace Read," *Canada's Who's Who* (Toronto: Trans Canada Press, 1951), 837; Read to Macdonald, 13 July 1943, PANS, Macdonald Papers, MG 2, F 1029/1; Read to Macdonald, 12 February 1950, PANS, Macdonald Papers, MG 2, F 243/5; Horace Read, DHH BIOG R; Hawkins, *The Life and Times of Angus L*, 39.
81 Connolly to Macdonald, n.d. [December 1943], LAC, Connolly Papers, MG 32, C 71, vol. 4.
82 Chief Staff Officer Reserves, n.d. [January 1944], Organization and Administration, DHH, 1700.
83 Connolly to Macdonald, n.d. [December 1943], LAC, Connolly Papers, MG 32, C 71, vol. 4.
84 Connolly to Macdonald, January 1944, LAC, Connolly Papers, MG 32, C 71, vol. 3, file 17.
85 Youle to Jeffrey, 9 December 1947, DHH, 8000, HMCS *Bytown*, vol. 2.
86 Connolly to Macdonald, n.d. [December 1943], LAC, Connolly Papers, MG 32, C 71, vol. 4.
87 Brand diary, November 1943, DHH, Brand Papers, 81/145.

88 Ibid.
89 Eric Brand, interview by E.C. Russell, 22 February 1967, Ottawa, tape recording transcript, DHH, Brand Papers, 84/145.
90 Massey Goolden, RN, diary, 11 December 1943, DHH, BIOG G.
91 Bill Glover, "Royal Colonial or Royal Canadian Navy?" in *A Nation's Navy: In Quest of Canadian Naval Identity*, ed. Michael Hadley, Rob Huebert, and Fred Crickard (Montreal and Kingston: McGill-Queen's University Press, 1996), 271; Massey Goolden, diary, 26 May 1944, DHH, BIOG G.
92 Ibid.
93 Connolly to Macdonald, 30 November 1943, LAC, Connolly Papers, MG 32, C 71, vol. 3.
94 "Nelles Named Canadian Overseas Head," *Montreal Gazette*, 15 January 1944, 3.
95 Ibid.
96 C.H. Little, interview with Salty Dips project, in *Salty Dips*, vol. 2, ed. Mac Lynch (Ottawa: Privately printed, 1985), 225-26.
97 RCN press release, 14 January 1944, Maritime Command Museum, Nelles Collection; House of Commons, *Debates*, 24 February 1944, 814; "Canadian Navy Prepares for Invasion," *Ottawa Journal*, 14 January 1944, 4; "Canadian Trends," *Canada Newsweek*, 31 January 1944, 14.
98 Royal Canadian Navy press release, 14 January 1944, Maritime Command Museum, Nelles Collection.
99 King diary, 5 January 1944, DHH, 83/530, vol. 196-10; King diary, 7 January 1944, DHH, 83/530, vol. 197-17.
100 Macdonald diary, 12 January 1944, PANS, Macdonald Papers, MG 2, F 391; King diary, 15 January 1944, DHH, 83/530, vol. 197-44; Macdonald diary, 5 January 1944, PANS, Macdonald Papers, MG 2, F 391.

Afterword: Game's End and the Final Score
1 MacLean to Macdonald, 3 March 1944, PANS, Macdonald Papers, MG 2, F 818/85.
2 Macdonald to MacLean, 21 March 1944, PANS, Macdonald Papers, MG 2, F 818/84.
3 "Publisher, Naval Critic A. MacLean Is Dead," *Montreal Gazette*, 26 January 1971, Directorate of History and Heritage (hereafter cited as DHH), 4000-100/14 G-M "M."
4 Conklin to Connolly, 16 January 1944, Library and Archives Canada (hereafter cited as LAC), Connolly Papers, MG 32, C 71, vol. 2, file 19.
5 Connolly to Conklin, 3 February 1944, LAC, Connolly Papers, MG 32, C 71, vol. 2, file 19.
6 Jack Clifford to Connolly, 21 January 1944, LAC, Connolly Papers, MG 32, C 71, vol. 2, file 19.
7 Connolly diary, 5 February 1945, LAC, Connolly Papers, MG 32, C 71, vol. 2, file 8.
8 Nelles to Macdonald, 27 November 1943, PANS, Macdonald Papers, MG 2, F 276/39; Naval Board meeting, 24 January 1944, DHH; Deputy Minister Advisory Committee, 28, 31 January, 1944, 3, 4, 23 February 1944, DHH; "Miscellaneous Papers on the History of the RCN," Naval Historical Section, August 1960, DHH, 75/496; Connolly diary, 12 September 1944, LAC, Connolly Papers, MG 32, C 71, vol. 2, file 8.
9 Jeffrey to Captain G.A. Youle, 9 December 1947, DHH, 8000, HMCS *Bytown*, vol. 2.
10 As quoted in Connolly to Macdonald, 14 July 1944, LAC, Connolly Papers, MG 32, C 71, vol. 4, file 12; Jeffrey to G.A. Youle (naval historical section), 9 December 1947, DHH, 8000, HMCS *Bytown*, vol. 2.
11 Naval Board meetings, 14 February, 1 May, and 23 June 1944, DHH, quotation from 1 May; Command of the Honourable Minister, Appointment sheet, 9 May 1944, LAC, Jones personnel file; "The Modernisation of Armament and Equipment," DHH, 8060. At the 1 May 1944 Naval Board meeting, Jones declared that "the present situation concerning equipment now seems improved."
12 Connolly to Macdonald, 15 March 1944, PANS, Macdonald Papers, MG 2, vol. 1522.

13 Macdonald to Robertson, 19 January 1944, PANS, Macdonald Papers, MG 2, F 736/26; Macdonald to Robertson, 19 January 1944, PANS, Macdonald Papers, MG 2, F 736/33; Chubby Power to Breadner, terms of reference, 9 December 1943, PANS, Macdonald Papers, MG 2, F 736/23; "First Draft of Terms of Reference for Nelles," n.d., PANS, Macdonald Papers, F 736/27; Macdonald to Nelles, "SCFO(O) Terms of Reference," 19 January 1944, PANS, Macdonald Papers, MG 2, F 736/30.
14 Nelles to Macdonald, 15 March 1944, DHH, Nelles Papers, folder E, file 11; "Wickedness in High Places," interview with Captain R.A. Pennington, 5 May 1946, DHH, 1700-193/96D.
15 "Wickedness in High Places," interview with Captain R.A. Pennington, 5 May 1946, DHH, 1700-193/96D.
16 Various S. 206s and "Occupational History Form," Pennington personnel file (O-58480, DOD, 5 March 1962), LAC.
17 Connolly to Pennington, 7 December 1943, and Pennington to Connolly, 7 January 1944, LAC, Connolly Papers, MG 32, C 71, vol. 2, files 18, 19.
18 Frank L. Houghton, "A Sailor's Life for Me," LAC, Houghton Papers, MG 30, E 444, 165; Nelles to Macdonald, 30 March 1944, PANS, Macdonald Papers, MG 2, F 737/7.
19 Nelles personnel file, LAC (O-54990, DOD, 13 June 1951).
20 Wilfred Lund, "The Rise and Fall of the Royal Canadian Navy, 1945-1964: A Critical Study of the Senior Leadership, Policy and Manpower Management" (PhD diss., University of Victoria, 1999), 76.
21 Michael Whitby, "Vice-Admiral Harry G. DeWolf: Pragmatic Navalist," in *The Admirals: Canada's Senior Naval Leadership in the Twentieth Century*, edited by Michael Whitby, Richard H. Gimblett, and Peter Haydon (Toronto: Dundurn Press, 2006), 241. The officers in question, Harry DeWolf and Nelson Lay, were both "Jones men." As Whitby observes, they were good friends and it appears that Jones did not want to see career advancement come between two of his favourites. As events would prove, his instincts were correct. DeWolf would get promoted ahead of Lay and their friendship was never the same.
22 Jones death certificate, 27 February 1946, LAC, Jones personnel file (O-37330, 08 February 1946); Naval Board meetings, February to July 1946, DHH; Wilfred Lund, "Vice-Admiral Harold Grant: Father of the Post-War Royal Canadian Navy," in *Warrior Chiefs: Perspectives on Senior Canadian Military Leaders*, ed. Bernd Horn and Stephen Harris (Toronto: Dundurn Press, 2001), 193. I would like to thank Mike Whitby for pointing out that Murray was not the only Canadian theatre commander, as Jones also shared that distinction when he took over the commander in chief Canadian North West Atlantic position.
23 L.C. Audette, "The Lower Deck and the Mainguy Report of 1949," in *The RCN in Retrospect, 1910-1968*, ed. James Boutilier (Vancouver: University of British Columbia Press, 1982), 244-45; for an excellent account of the incidents and the impact they had on the navy, see Richard Gimblett, "Too Many Chiefs and Not Enough Seamen: The Lower-Deck Complement of a Postwar Canadian Navy Destroyer – The Case of HMCS *Crescent*, March 1949," *The Northern Mariner*, 9, 3 (July 1999), 23-22; and Richard Gimblett, "What the Mainguy Report Never Told Us: The Tradition of Mutiny in the Royal Canadian Navy Before 1949," *Canadian Military Journal* 1, 2 (Summer 2000): 87-94.
24 "Founder of 'The Crowsnest' Retires," March 1959, DHH, 4000-100/14.
25 Connolly to Macdonald, 15 April 1945, LAC, Connolly Papers, MG 32, C 71, vol. 4, file 15.

Bibliography

Archival Sources

LIBRARY AND ARCHIVES CANADA, OTTAWA
Atlantic Command, RG 24, D 10
Audette, L. de C., Papers, MG 31, E 18
Canadian Expeditionary Force files, RG 150
Connolly, J.J., Papers, MG 32, C 71
Houghton, F.L., Papers, MG 30, E 444
Howe, C.D., Papers, MG 27, III B 20
Lay, H.N., Papers, MG 30, E 420
Murray, L.W., Papers, MG 30, E 207
Naval messages, Naval personnel files, RG 24, D 20
Newfoundland Command, RG 24, D 12
NSHQ Central Registry Files, RG 24, D 1
Privy Council Office, RG 2
Pugsley, W.H., Papers, MG 30, E 422
Schull, J., Papers, MG 31, D 5
Senior Canadian Naval Officer (London) files, RG 24, D 13
Ships' Logs, RG 24, D 2

DIRECTORATE OF HISTORY AND HERITAGE, NATIONAL DEFENCE HEADQUARTERS
Audette, L. de C. (Lieutenant-Commander), Papers, 80/256
Biography files, BIOG
Brand, E.S. (Captain), Papers, 81/145
Brodeur, V.G. (Rear Admiral), Papers, 79/19
Canadian Naval Mission Overseas files, 75/197
M-11 Criticisms, 77/467
Mackenzie King Diary, 83/530
Naval Historian Files, 81/520
Nelles, P.W. (Admiral), Papers
Russell, E.C., Papers, 91/298
Ship's Movement Cards
War Cabinet Committee Minutes, 83/345

DHH LIBRARY PRIMARY SOURCES
Admiralty Fleet Orders
Confidential Admiralty Fleet Orders
King's Regulations and Administrative Orders
RCN Naval Lists
RCN Naval Orders
RCN Confidential Naval Orders
RN Naval Lists
Royal Naval College of Canada, *Sea Breeze*

PUBLIC ARCHIVES OF NOVA SCOTIA
Macdonald, Angus L., Papers, MG 2

QUEEN'S UNIVERSITY ARCHIVES, KINGSTON
Power, Charles G., Papers, 2150

MARITIME COMMAND MUSEUM, HALIFAX
Nelles, P.W. (Vice-Admiral), Collection

UNITED STATES NATIONAL ARCHIVES, WASHINGTON
Commander Task Group, RG 313 CTG 24 Files
Office of the Chief of Naval Operations, RG 38

PUBLIC RECORDS OFFICE, KEW
First Sea Lord's Papers, ADM 205
General Files, ADM 1
Western Approaches Command Files, ADM 217

NATIONAL MARITIME MUSEUM, GREENWICH ENGLAND
Gretton, Peter, Papers

Other Sources
Allison, Graham. *The Essence of Decision: Explaining the Cuban Missile Crisis*. Boston: Little Brown, 1971.
Anonymous. "Public Opinion Polls." *Public Opinion Quarterly* 7 (winter 1943): 40-45.
Armstrong, John. *The Halifax Explosion and the Royal Canadian Navy: Inquiry and Intrigue*. Vancouver: UBC Press, 2002.
Bercuson, David J. *Maple Leaf against the Axis: Canada's Second World War*. Toronto: Stoddart, 1995.
Bercuson, David J., and Holger H. Herwig. *Deadly Seas: The Duel between the St. Croix and the U-305 in the Battle of the Atlantic*. Toronto: Vintage Canada, 1997.
Bothwell, Robert, Ian Drummond, and John English. *Canada 1900-1945*. Toronto: University of Toronto Press, 1987.
Boutilier, James A., ed. *The RCN in Retrospect, 1910-1968*. Vancouver: University of British Columbia Press, 1982.
Brock, J.V. *The Dark and Broad Sea*. Toronto: McClelland and Stewart, 1981.
Burgess, John, and Ken Macpherson. *The Ships of Canada's Naval Forces 1910-1993*. St. Catharines, ON: Vanwell Publishing, 1994.
Cafferky, S. "'A Useful Lot, These Canadian Ships': The Royal Canadian Navy and Operation Torch, 1942-1943." *The Northern Mariner* 3, 4 (October 1993): 1-17.
Caldwell, R.H. "The VE Day Riots in Halifax, 7-8 May 1945." *The Northern Mariner* 10, 1 (January 2000): 3-20.
Cameron, James M. *Murray: The Martyred Admiral*. Hantsport, NS: Lancelot Press, 1980.
Canada. *Annual Department Reports: Report of the Chief Electoral Officer for the Fiscal Year Ending March 31, 1942*. Ottawa: Edmond Cloutier, 1943.
–. *Annual Departmental Reports: Report of the Department of National Defence for the Fiscal Year Ending March 31, 1943*. Ottawa: Edmond Cloutier, 1944.
–. *Annual Departmental Reports: Report of the Department of National Defence for the Fiscal Year Ending March 31, 1944*. Ottawa: Edmond Cloutier, 1945.
–. *House of Commons. Debates*.

Chalmers, William. *Max Horton and the Western Approaches: A Biography of Admiral Sir Max Horton*. London: Hodder and Stoughton, 1954.

Darlington, Robert A., and Fraser M. McKee. *The Canadian Naval Chronicle*. St. Catharines, ON: Vanwell Publishing, 1996.

Douglas, W.A.B. "Conflict and Innovation in the Royal Canadian Navy, 1939-1945." In *Naval Warfare in the Twentieth Century*, edited by Gerald Jordan, 210-32. New York: Crane Russak, 1977.

–, ed. *The RCN in Transition, 1910-1985*. Vancouver: UBC Press, 1988.

Douglas, W.A.B., and Brereton Greenhous. *Out of the Shadows: Canada in the Second World War*. Toronto: Oxford University Press, 1977.

Douglas, W.A.B., Roger Sarty, and Michael Whitby. *No Higher Purpose: The Official Operational History of the Royal Canadian Navy in the Second World War, 1939-1943*. Vol. 2, part 1. St. Catharines, ON: Vanwell Publishing, 2002.

–. *A Blue Water Navy: The Official Operational History of the Royal Canadian Navy in the Second World War, 1943-1945*. Vol. 2, part 2. St. Catharines, ON: Vanwell Publishing, 2006.

Easton, Allan. *50 North: An Atlantic Battleground*. Toronto: Ryerson Press, 1963.

Eayrs, James. *In Defence of Canada*. Vol. 1, *From the Great War to the Great Depression*. Toronto: University of Toronto Press, 1964.

English, John, and J.O. Stubbs. *Mackenzie King: Widening the Debate*. Toronto: Macmillan, 1977.

Fisher, R.C. "The Impact of German Technology on the Royal Canadian Navy in the Battle of the Atlantic, 1942-1943." *The Northern Mariner* 7, 4 (October 1997): 1-13.

–. "Tactics, Training and Technology: The RCN's Summer of Success, July-September 1942." *Canadian Military History* 6, 2 (1997): 9-12.

–. "'We'll Get Our Own': Canada and the Oil Shipping Crisis of 1942." *The Northern Mariner* 3, 2 (April 1993): 33-39.

Freidman, N. *Naval Radar*. Annapolis: Naval Institute Press, 1981.

Gannon, Michael. *Black May: The Epic Story of the Allies' Defeat of German U-boats in May 1943*. New York: Dell Books, 1989.

German, Tony. *The Sea Is at Our Gates: The History of the Royal Canadian Navy*. Toronto: McClelland and Stewart, 1990.

Gibson, Frederick W., and Barbara Robertson, eds. *Ottawa at War: The Grant Dexter Memoranda, 1939-1945*. Winnipeg: The Manitoba Record Society, 1994.

Gimblett, Richard H. "A Century of Canadian Naval Force Development: A Reinterpretation." In *Canadian Military History Since the 17th Century*, edited by Yves Tremblay, 277-86. Ottawa: Department of National Defence, 2000.

–. "Gunboat Diplomacy, Mutiny and National Identity in the Postwar Royal Canadian Navy: The Cruise of HMC *Crescent* to China." PhD diss., Laval University, 2000.

–. "Too Many Chiefs and Not Enough Seamen: The Lower-Deck Complement of a Postwar Canadian Navy Destroyer – The Case of HMCS *Crescent*, March 1949." *The Northern Mariner* 9, 3 (July 1999): 1-22.

–. "What the Mainguy Report Never Told Us: The Tradition of Mutiny in the Royal Canadian Navy Before 1949." *Canadian Military Journal* 1, 2 (Summer 2000): 87-94.

Glover, W.R. "Officer Training and the Quest for Operational Efficiency in the RCN, 1939-1945." PhD diss., University of London, 1998.

Goldrick, James. "The Problems of Modern Naval History." In *Doing Naval History: Essays Toward Improvement*, edited by John B. Hattendorf, 11-24. Newport: Naval War College Press, 1995.

Gow, J.D. *Alongside the Navy, 1910-1950: An Intimate Account*. Ottawa: JDG Press, 1999.

Granatstein, J.L. *Canada's War: The Politics of the Mackenzie King Government, 1939-1945.* Toronto: Oxford University Press, 1975.
–. *A Man of Influence: Norman A. Robertson and Canadian Statecraft, 1929-68.* Toronto: Deneau, 1980.
–. *The Ottawa Men: The Civil Service Mandarins, 1935-1957.* Toronto: Oxford University Press, 1982.
Granatstein, J.L., and J.M. Hitsman. *Broken Promises: A History of Conscription in Canada.* Toronto: Oxford University Press, 1977.
Granatstein, J.L., and Desmond Morton. *A Nation Forged in Fire: Canadians and the Second World War 1939-1945.* Toronto: Lester and Orpen Dennys, 1989.
Gretton, Peter. *Crisis Convoy: The Story of HX 231.* London: P. Davis, 1974.
Griffin, A. "A Naval Officer's War: Episode One." *Starshell* 7 (spring 1999): 10-12.
Hadley, Michael L. *U-Boats against Canada: German Submarines in Canadian Waters.* Montreal and Kingston: McGill-Queen's University Press, 1985.
Hadley, Michael L., Rob Huebert, and Fred W. Crickard, eds. *A Nation's Navy: In Quest of Canadian Naval Identity.* Montreal and Kingston: McGill-Queen's University Press, 1996.
Hadley, Michael, and Roger Sarty. *Tin-Pots and Pirate Ships: Canadian Naval Forces and German Sea Raiders, 1880-1918.* Montreal and Kingston: McGill-Queen's University Press, 1991.
Hague, Arnold. *The Allied Convoy System, 1939-1945.* St. Catharines, ON: Vanwell Publishing, 2000.
Harbron, John D. *The Longest Battle: The Royal Canadian Navy in the Atlantic 1939-1945.* St. Catharines, ON: Vanwell Publishing, 1993.
Hardy, Reginald. *Mackenzie King of Canada: A Biography.* Toronto: Oxford University Press, 1949.
Harris, Stephen J. *Canadian Brass: The Making of a Professional Army, 1860-1939.* Toronto: University of Toronto Press, 1988.
Hawkins, John. *The Life and Times of Angus L.* Windsor, NS: Lancelot Press, 1969.
Henderson, T.S. "Angus L. Macdonald and the Conscription Crisis of 1944." *Acadiensis* 27, 1 (1997): 85-104.
Horn, Bernd, and Stephen Harris. *Warrior Chiefs: Perspectives on Senior Canadian Military Leaders.* Toronto: Dundurn Press, 2001.
Howarth, Stephen, ed. *The Battle of the Atlantic 1939-1945: The 50th Anniversary International Naval Conference.* London: Greenhill Books, 1994.
Howse, D. *Radar at Sea: The Royal Navy in World War II.* Annapolis: Naval Institute Press, 1993.
Johnston, Mac. *Corvettes Canada: Convoy Veterans of WW II Tell Their True Stories.* Toronto: McGraw-Hill Ryerson, 1994.
Kealy, J.D.F., and E.C. Russell. *A History of Canadian Naval Aviation 1918-1962.* Ottawa: Queen's Printer, 1965.
Kennedy, J. de N. *History of the Department of Munitions and Supply.* Vols. 1-2. Ottawa: King's Printer, 1950.
Lamb, James B. *The Corvette Navy: True Stories from Canada's Atlantic War.* Toronto: Macmillan, 1977.
–. *On the Triangle Run.* Toronto: Macmillan, 1986.
Lambert, J. *The Fairmile "D" Type Motor Torpedo Boat.* London: Conway, 1985.
Laurendeau, Andre. *La Crise de la Conscription 1942.* Montreal: Editions du Jour, 1962.
Law, C.A. *White Plumes Astern: The Short, Daring Life of Canada's MTB Flotilla.* Halifax: Nimbus, 1989.

Lawrence, Hal. *A Bloody War: One Man's Memories of the Canadian Navy, 1939-1945*. Toronto: Macmillan, 1979.
Lay, H. Nelson. *Memoirs of a Mariner*. Stittsville, ON: Canada's Wings, 1982.
Lund, Wilfred. "The Rise and Fall of the Royal Canadian Navy, 1945-1964: A Critical Study of the Senior Leadership, Policy and Manpower Management." PhD diss., University of Victoria, 1999.
Lynch, Mac, ed. *Salty Dips*. 6 vols. Ottawa: Privately printed, 1983-85.
Macintyre, Donald. *U-Boat Killer*. London: Weidenfeld and Nicholson, 1956.
McKee, Fraser. *The Armed Yachts of Canada*. Erin, ON: Boston Mills, 1983.
McKee, Fraser, and R. Darlington. *The Canadian Naval Chronicle*. St. Catharines, ON: Vanwell Publishing, 1996.
MacLean, Andrew Dyas. *R.B. Bennett Prime Minister of Canada*. Toronto: Excelsior Publishing, 1934.
MacLean, Doug. "The Last Cruel Winter: RCN Support Groups and the U-Boat Offensive." MA thesis, Royal Military College, 1992.
Macpherson, K.R. *Frigates of the Royal Canadian Navy, 1943-1974*. St. Catharines, ON: Vanwell Publishing, 1989.
Macpherson, K.R., and Marc Milner. *Corvettes of the Royal Canadian Navy, 1939-1945*. St. Catharines, ON: Vanwell Publishing, 1993.
Mayne, R.O. "Behind the Scenes at Naval Service Headquarters: Bureaucratic Politics and the Dismissal of Vice-Admiral Percy W. Nelles." MA thesis, Wilfrid Laurier University, 1998.
–. "Bypassing the Chain of Command: The Political Origins of the Equipment Crisis of 1943." *Canadian Military History* 9, 3 (Summer 2000): 7-22.
–. "A Covert Naval Investigation: Overseas Officers, John J. Connolly, and the Equipment Crisis of 1943." *The Northern Mariner* 10, 1 (January 2000): 37-49.
–. "A Political Execution: Expediency and the Firing of Vice Admiral Percy W. Nelles." *The American Review of Canadian Studies* 29, 4 (winter 1999): 557-84.
Milner, Marc. "Canada's Naval War." *Acadiensis* 12, 2 (spring 1983): 162-71.
–. *Canada's Navy: The First Century*. Toronto: University of Toronto Press, 1999.
–. "The Implications of Technological Backwardness: The Royal Canadian Navy 1939-1945." *Canadian Defence Quarterly* 19, 3 (winter 1989): 46-52.
–. *North Atlantic Run: The Royal Canadian Navy and the Battle for the Convoys*. Toronto: University of Toronto Press, 1985.
–. "The Royal Canadian Navy and 1943: A Year Best Forgotten?" In *1943: The Beginning of the End*, edited by Paul D. Dickson, 123-36. Waterloo, ON: Canadian Committee for the History of the Second World War, 1995.
–. "Squaring Some of the Corners: The Royal Canadian Navy and the Pattern of the Atlantic War." In *To Die Gallantly: The Battle of the Atlantic*, edited by Tim Runyan and Jan M. Copes, 121-36. Boulder, CO: Westview Press, 1994.
–. *The U-Boat Hunters: The Royal Canadian Navy and the Offensive against Germany's Submarines*. Toronto: University of Toronto Press, 1994.
Morton, Desmond. *Ministers and Generals: Politics and the Canadian Militia*. Toronto: University of Toronto Press, 1970.
Padfield, Peter. *War beneath the Sea: Submarine Conflict 1939-1945*. London: Random House, 1995.
Pickersgill, J.W. *The Mackenzie King Record*. Toronto: University of Toronto Press, 1960.
Pope, M.A. *Soldiers and Politicians: The Memoirs of Lt-Gen Maurice A. Pope*. Toronto: University of Toronto Press, 1962.

Power, Chubby. *A Party Politician.* Toronto: Macmillan, 1966.
Rawling, Bill. "The Challenge of Modernization: The Royal Canadian Navy and Antisubmarine Weapons, 1944-1945." *The Journal of Military History* 63 (April 1999): 355-78.
–. "Only a Foolish Escapade by Young Ratings?" *Northern Mariner* 10, 2 (April 2000): 59-69.
Sarty, Roger. *Canada and the Battle of the Atlantic.* Montreal: Art Global, 1998.
–. "The Ghost of Fisher and Jellicoe: The Royal Canadian Navy and the Quebec Conferences." In *The Second Quebec Conference Revised. Waging War, Formulating Peace: Canada Great Britain, and the United States in 1944-1945*, edited by David B. Woolner, 143-70. New York: St. Martin's Press, 1998.
–. *The Maritime Defence of Canada.* Toronto: Canadian Institute of Strategic Studies, 1996.
–. "Silent Sentry: A Military and Political History of Canadian Coast Defence, 1860-1945." PhD diss., University of Toronto, 1982.
Schull, Joseph. *The Far Distant Ships: An Official Account of Canadian Naval Operations in the Second World War.* Ottawa: King's Printer, 1950.
Simpson, G.W.G. *Periscope View.* London: Macmillan, 1972.
Soward, Steward. *Hands to Flying Stations: A Recollective History of Canadian Naval Aviation.* Victoria, BC: Neptune Developments, 1993.
Stacey, C.P. *Arms, Men and Governments: The War Policies of Canada, 1939-1945.* Ottawa: Queen's Printer, 1970.
–. *Canada and the Age of Conflict: A History of Canadian External Policies.* Toronto: University of Toronto Press, 1981.
Stephen, M. *The Fighting Admirals.* Annapolis, MD: Naval Institute Press, 1991.
Sumida, John T., and David A. Rosenberg. "Machines, Men, Manufacturing and Money: The Study of Navies as Complex Organizations and the Transformation of Twentieth Century Naval History." In *Doing Naval History: Essays Toward Improvement*, edited by John B. Hattendorf, 25-40. Newport, RI: Naval War College Press, 1995.
Swettenham, John, and David Kealy. *Serving the State: A History of the Professional Institute of the Public Service of Canada, 1920-1970.* Ottawa: Le Droit, 1970.
Tennyson, B., and R. Sarty. *Guardian of the Gulf: Sydney, Cape Breton, and the Atlantic Wars.* Toronto: University of Toronto Press, 2000.
Tucker, Gilbert Norman. *The Naval Service of Canada: Its Official History.* Ottawa: King's Printer, 1952.
van der Vat, Dan. *The Atlantic Campaign: World War II's Great Struggle at Sea.* London: Harper and Row, 1988.
Whitby, Michael. "Instruments of Security: The Royal Canadian Navy's Procurement of the Tribal-Class Destroyers." *The Northern Mariner* 2, 3 (July 1992): 1-15.
–. "Matelots, Martinets, and Mutineers: The Mutiny in HMCS *Iroquois*, 1943." *Journal of Military History* 1 (January 2001): 77-103.
–. "The 'Other' Navy at War: The RCN's Tribal Class Destroyers 1939-44." MA thesis, Carleton University, 1988.
Whitby, Michael, Richard H. Gimblett, and Peter Haydon, eds. *The Admirals: Canada's Senior Naval Leadership in the Twentieth Century.* Toronto: Dundurn Press, 2006.
Young, Scott. *O'Brien: From Water Boy to One Million a Year.* Burnstown, ON: The General Store Publishing House, 1967.
Zimmerman, David. *The Great Naval Battle of Ottawa.* Toronto: University of Toronto Press, 1989.
–. "New Dimensions in Canadian Naval History." *The American Neptune* 60, 3 (2001): 263-75.

Index

Abbott, Douglas, 216
Adams, K.L., 88-89, 132-33, 151, 185-86, 194-95
Admiralty, 9; attitude toward RCN, 72; Australian Navy and, 142-43; Brand's reports to, 31; on Canadian repair facilities, 107; and Conklin's facilities, 172; and Connolly, 176; and equipment issue, 95, 100, 163, 176; First Sea Lord, 172, 191; and Londonderry base, 96; Londonderry network and, 145; and modernization issue, 141-42, 174, 175; and Naval Order 2587, 171; Nelles and, 96-97, 118; NSHQ and, 76, 79, 99, 117, 141, 171-72; on RCN use of British yards, 172; and refit issue, 99, 142, 143, 163; technical liaison with, 117, 118; and transfer of ships to British, 98; and Western Approaches, 174
Agnew, R.I., 169, 170-71
Allied Anti-Submarine Survey Board, 80-81, 108-9, 111, 112, 171-72
Amherst (HMCS), 31, 32-34, 147, 148
Antigonish (HMCS), 187
Army, 5, 6, 43
asdic, 95, 104; type 123D, 68, 69(f), 178; type 144, 95, 100; type 145X, 135
Assiniboine (HMCS), 88, 132
Athlone, Earl of, 200
Atlantic Command, 18, 104, 105, 141; and equipment crisis, 70
Audette, J. de G. "Gap," 32
Audette, Louis, 16, 31-35, 36, 39-40, 91, 146-48, 159, 216

Bath: Assistant Controller, 175, 176
Battle of the Atlantic, 72, 93, 94, 115, 170, 176, 206
Bennett, Richard, 13, 15
Bidwell, Roger E.S., 83, 104, 131, 194
A Blue Water Navy, 3
Boating Magazine, 22, 51, 54, 55, 56, 60, 61, 64-66, 209

Botwood, fairmiles based at, 22
Boulton, Angus G., 123
Bourke, Roland, 27
Bowater's, 107
Brand, Eric, 19-20, 31, 32-33, 34(f), 125, 204, 206
Breadner, Lloyd, 206, 214
bridges, improvements to, 135, 178
Briggs, W.E.S., 71-72, 79, 80, 87, 88
British Admiralty Technical Mission (BATM), 164
Britton, J.C., 32
Brock, Eustace, 47
Brodeur, Victor, 125, 205

Cabinet, reorganization of, 121
Caldwell, Bob, 82
Canada-UK-US Combined Committee on Ship Repair Problems on the East Coast of Canada and Newfoundland. *See* Combined Committee on Ship Repair Problems
Canadian Naval Mission Overseas, 215
careerism, 10, 122, 133, 205, 216
Carswell, D.B., 106, 108, 112-13, 137-40, 141, 142
chains of command, 7, 10; Adams and, 89; Audette and, 146-47; British, 145, 171-72; complaints through, 77, 130; critical memos regarding equipment and, 129; and chief staff officer reserves (CSOR) position, 203; discipline and, 9, 130; downward flow of information and, 70; and equipment situation, 76; gaps in, 74; grievances filtered through, 11; Londonderry network and, 145, 170; Macdonald and, 10, 40, 67; MacLean and, 18, 21; Naval Board and, 40; Naval Order 2587 and, 171; networks and, 9, 11; O'Brien and, 146-47; overseas accessing of, 80; permanent force officers and, 90; Price

and, 79; reserve officers and, 77; service discipline and, 77; sharp-end grousers and, 170; Simpson and, 67, 79, 82, 90-91, 92; Strange and, 84, 89, 90-91
Chilliwack (HMCS), 185(f)
Clifford, J.L., 210
CNES (Chief Naval Equipment and Supply), 117, 118
Coldwell, M.J., 54
Combined Committee on Ship Repair Problems 107-8, 141-42, 172
commanding officer Atlantic Coast (COAC), 47, 50, 70, 77, 101, 117-18
commanding officer Pacific Coast (COPC), 47
Conklin, David, 153, 154, 159-61, 162, 168, 172, 187, 210
Connolly, John Joseph, 7, 34(f); Adams and, 132, 185-86, 194-95; Admiralty and, 176; and Audette, 31-32, 146-48, 186; and blame for equipment crisis, 188; Brand and, 204-5; career of, 30, 216-18; and chief staff officer reserves (CSOR), 202-3; as conduit for networks, 9; Conklin and, 159-60, 172; conspiracy theory of, 186, 189, 192, 193-94, 195, 200; consultation of reserve officers, 38-39; Copelin and, 154, 157-58, 163, 166; and Creery, 195; and Creery's and Hibbard's trips to UK, 187; and critical memos to NSHQ on modernization, 129, 193-94; and equipment issue, 89, 99, 152, 177; as executive assistant, 216-18; and financial authority for equipment, 170; on frequency of signals, 169; as gatekeeper to Macdonald, 182; Gilhooly and, 165, 166; Horton and, 176; hyperbole of, 157; influence of, 30, 210; insider information for, 39; investigative trip to East Coast (1942), 29, 30-35, 99, 148; investigative trip to St. John's and UK (1943), 7, 89, 144, 149-52, 153, 164; Johnstone and, 195; and Jones, 125, 151, 182, 193, 205; and King, 206-7; Londonderry network and, 144, 145, 146, 152, 157, 163, 172, 179, 187, 192, 210, 211; Macdonald and, 124-25, 151, 152, 216-17; as Macdonald's protector, 7, 30, 179, 182, 192, 198-99, 210; as Macdonald's watchdog, 30, 210; and MacLean, 26, 27-29, 30, 45-46, 49-50, 56-57, 62, 64, 128, 134, 148, 150; Mitchell and, 147, 149, 158; and modernization issue, 34, 35, 148; and morale of reservists, 26, 39; and Naval Board, 43-44, 46, 145; Naval Order 2587 and, 171; Naval Staff and, 183, 185, 192, 193; and Nelles, 59, 62, 149, 180, 183, 191-93, 198-200, 208, 217-18; network of informants, 132, 144, 189, 209-10; network of personal informants, 12, 39, 67, 89, 146, 147-48, 176, 203, 215; networks and, 7, 9, 10, 27, 180, 184, 186-87, 196-97, 208, 210, 211, 217; NSHQ and, 161, 192; on Orillia, 155-57; Pennington and, 215; personality of, 30; and Pictou refit, 160; power of, 30; preconceived notions of, 176; and Price, 164, 165-70; as puppet master, 184; and refits in USN yard, 162; and reserve discrimination question, 150-51; Roome and, 59-60; Shorto and, 159; Simpson and, 92, 146, 153-54, 158-59, 164, 173, 187, 200-1; and St. John's network, 40; Strange and, 86-87, 89, 132, 134, 144, 146, 147, 211; and technical liaison, 166
Connolly, J.P., 124, 125, 127-28
conscription crisis, 58
Conservative Party of Canada, 13, 27, 63-64. See also official opposition and MacLean issue
convoys: British arrangement of, 96; corvette captains' discussions following, 70-71; cycles of, 73-74, 97; escort conferences, 74; HX 260, 155, 164; losses from, 96; manning policies, 35; merchant ships in, 93-94; ON 127, 35; ON 137, 33; ON 149, 160; ON 195, 88; OS 154, 96; protection of, 99; RN and, 93-94; SC 100, 38; SC 107, 35; SC 135, 84; stress of, 71
Co-operative Commonwealth Federation (CCF), 54
Copelin, C., 153-54, 157-58, 161, 162-63, 166, 169, 174
corvettes, 8, 20, 34-35; British view of, 88; conditions on, 65, 148; equipment on, 86; frigates vs, 94, 95; modern equipment for, 67; modernization of, 100, 103, 213; as superseded, 213; upgrading of RN, 168
Creery, W.B., 110, 186, 187, 195
critical memos, 67-68, 129-30, 131, 183-84, 186, 193-94
Cross, Paul, 149-50, 203, 208, 213

CSOR (chief staff officer reserves), 202-3, 208

decision making, bottom-up approach to, 5
Defence of Canada Regulations, 22, 52, 56, 146
demobilization, 6
Department of Finance, 103
Department of Labour, 105, 108, 111, 115, 141, 179
Department of Munitions and Supply: and Carswell's committee, 106; and Combined Committee on Ship Repair Problems, 107-8; communication with naval service, 111; equipment acquisitions and, 102, 103; and HMC Dockyard, 111, 115; and interdepartmental approach to refit crisis, 116; and labour for expansion of facilities, 105, 106; and private shipyards, 108, 113; refit crisis and, 111, 113, 138, 140, 141, 142, 191. *See also* Howe, C.D.
depth charges, 136(f)
Deputy Minister's Advisory Committee, 212-13
The Derry Standard, 82
destroyers, 35, 36, 48, 157
DeWolf, Harry G., 47, 57
Diefenbaker, John, 64, 150, 165
Directorate of Naval Information, 39, 83
Directorate of Organization, 109, 113
Directorate of Warfare and Training, 110
discipline: and chains of command, 9, 77, 130; equipment issue and, 82; in Halifax, 82; infractions, 81, 82-83, 211; in Londonderry, 82-83; in St. John's, 82
discontent, 10-11; causes of, 36, 39; and chains of command, 77; and equipment, 36, 69, 78, 86-87, 179, 192; exaggeration of, 70, 92; Macdonald and, 135; morale as cause, 40; Naval Staff and, 168; Nelles and, 168; and official opposition, 42; and press, 42; recreational facilities and, 81-82; reserve officers and, 42; size of, 78
discrimination, 16; modernization issue, 35; by permanent force against reservists, 54, 197, 202, 213; RCNVR vs RCNR officers, 50; reserve and permanent force officers, 39, 42, 121, 149, 150-51; against reserves, 45, 165; "reverse," 49

dockyards. *See* Halifax: HMC Dockyard; shipyards
Donaldson, Charlie, 32
Drumheller (HMCS), 72, 160
Duncan (HMS), 84
Dunvegan (HMCS), 163, 187

East Coast: Connolly on, 29, 30-35, 99, 148; refit and repair facilities, 105, 160, 172, 194; shipyards, 100, 101, 104, 105-6, 190. *See also* Combined Committee on Ship Repair Problems; Halifax
Edmundston (HMCS), 99, 101, 164
elitism, 10, 15-17, 211
equipment: acquisitions of, 102-3; Admiralty release of, 163, 176; battle for, 164, 176; costs of, 102; Cross on, 149-50; and discipline problems, 82; discontent over, 67, 69, 78, 86-87, 179, 192; and efficiency of RCN, 84; financial authority from NSHQ, 169-70; gap between RCN and RN, 69-70, 100, 129, 168; inadequacy of, 33-35; inferior, 34; installation of, 100, 102, 103, 189, 195; lists of, 103-4; in Londonderry, 79-80, 85; Macdonald and, 135, 179; and Naval Staff reorganization, 193, 195; Nelles' report on, 135; NSHQ and, 79, 85; *Orillia* and, 155-56; rebellion over, 67, 167; seaworthiness and, 157; Simpson on, 164; sources of, 94-95; as substandard, 67; supplies of, 95, 101, 175. *See also* modernization; refits
equipment issue: blame for, 188; chains of command and, 76; Connolly and, 89, 99; cover-up of, 152; as crisis, 68, 70, 73-74, 100, 129, 131, 177, 188; critical memos on, 183-84; as gap vs crisis, 92; in historical/political perspective, 188; lack of communication and, 73-74; Macdonald and, 74, 89, 201; and MacLean network, 98-99; and morale, 67, 70, 85-86, 92, 152, 211; Naval Staff and, 129; Nelles and, 73, 93, 188; NSHQ and, 70, 73, 86, 91, 93, 129, 131; politicization of, 134-35; Strange and, 83-84, 85-88; welfare question and, 85-86
escort ships, 93-94; building of, 34-35, 93-94 (*see also* shipbuilding); in Londonderry, 67; manned by reservists, 7; quantity vs quality of, 173. *See also* corvettes; fairmiles; minesweepers

fairmiles, 18, 19(f), 20, 21(f), 22, 27-28, 36, 47, 50, 52, 54, 64-65; captain (motor launches) position, 47; Q 052, 19(f), 23(f); Q 117, 21(f)
"Fairmiles and Foul" (MacLean), 53-54
flag officers, 9, 48, 68, 70, 77, 199
fo'c'sles (forecastles), extension of, 100, 104, 135, 143, 162, 168, 178
frigates, 94, 95, 109, 157, 213

Gaspé, 105; fairmiles based at, 22
George, James, 68, 71, 79, 154, 155
Gerity, F.O., 72, 88
Gilhooly, Walter, 39, 165-66
Globe and Mail, 54
Goolden, Massey, 150, 205, 206
governor general, 200
Grant, Harold T.W., 19-20, 20, 176-77
Graydon, G., 54, 55
Gretton, Peter, 84-85
Griffin, A.G.S., 23, 150
Griffiths, G.F., 181
guns, 137(f), 138(f)
gyroscopic compasses, 85, 86, 95, 100, 104, 135, 178

Halifax: Allied Anti-Submarine Survey Board visit to, 108, 109; commodore superintendent at, 117, 162; and director of dockyards, 114; discipline problems in, 82; discontent at, 31; fairmiles based at, 22; Force, 104; HMC Dockyard, 105, 111, 113, 115, 137, 138, 139, 140; reorganization in, 161-62; rowdiness in, 31; VE day riots in, 215
Halifax (HMCS), 157
Hanbury, R.M., 149-50, 203
Hanson, R.B., 27, 63
hedgehog, 85, 86, 95, 99, 100, 135, 139(f), 161, 168, 178
Hibbard, G.M., 19-20, 27, 117, 162, 178, 186, 187
Hodgson, J.S., 32
Horton, Max, 81, 82, 163, 164, 172-73, 175-76, 177, 180-81, 186, 200
Hose, Walter, 3, 122
Houghton, Frank L., 83, 85, 130-31, 132, 211, 214
Howard, H.C., 55
Howe, C.D., 102, 108, 111, 112, 116, 140, 141

Hugh C. MacLean Publishing, 13, 41
hyperbole: of Conklin, 162; of Connolly, 157; of Londonderry officers, 153, 162, 189; and Macdonald, 177; of networks, 10; of Simpson, 87; of Strange, 134, 136

information, flow of, 9, 40, 70, 130, 174

Johnstone, Edmund: on Admiralty, 142; Connolly and, 195-96, 197-98, 200; and decentralization of Naval Staff, 110; and Directorate of Organization, 109, 113; Nelles and, 217; refit crisis and, 113; report of, 114-15, 117, 134, 161
Jones, George C., 212(f); abolition of vice chief of naval staff position, 216; on Adams, 132; as administrator, 126; Boulton on, 123; Brand and, 125, 204-5; Brodeur on, 125; careerism and, 216; as chief of naval staff, 206, 212-13; as commander in chief North West Atlantic, 216; death of, 216; and discrimination against reserves, 213; Goolden on, 205; heart attack of, 124; Hose on, 122; inspection trip to Maritimes, 151; and J.J. Connolly, 125, 151, 193; "Jones men," 124, 125; and J.P. Connolly, 124, 125, 127-28; and King, 126, 127; and Macdonald, 124, 125, 127, 151, 212; MacLean and, 18, 21, 22, 23, 24, 127-28, 208; Miles and, 22, 24; and modernization issue, 213; and Murray, 122, 124, 169, 216; Naval Information Department on, 123; and Nelles, 10, 109-10, 120, 123-24, 125, 126-27, 151, 182, 204-5; and networks' access to minister, 212; and NSHQ, 212-13; on officer promotions, 46; personality of, 122-23, 126; on problems in Halifax, 31; promotion of, 124; at Royal Naval College of Canada, 122; temper of, 122-23; trip to investigate modernization question, 151; as vice chief of naval staff, 109-10, 124

Kauffman, J.L., 80, 81
Keith, Bob, 32
King, William Lyon Mackenzie: and expenditure restraints, 103; and interdepartmental approach to refit crisis, 191; Jones and, 125, 126, 127; Lay and, 125, 126; and Macdonald, 58, 59, 103, 121, 141,

207, 215; and MacLean's charges, 54, 58, 59; on Nelles' London posting, 206-7; on reorganization of Cabinet, 121; and training issue, 98
Knights of Columbus, 82
Knowlton, J.G., 140
Kyle, J.H., 32

Lamb, James, 36
Laurier, Wilfrid, 3
Law, E.G., 167, 168
Lay, Horatio Nelson, 55, 56, 62, 100-1, 104-5, 114, 124, 125-26
Lee, A.M., 87
Lethbridge (HMCS), 34(f)
Liberal Party of Canada, 13, 54, 61, 135
Little, C.H., 206
London office: and Admiralty, 176; Connolly in, 164-65; and equipment issue, 176; and Londonderry base, 74, 75-76, 169; Nelles in, 214; technical liaison officers in, 167. *See also* Price, Fred
Londonderry base, 67; and Admiralty, 96; behaviour of sailors in, 81-82; captain (D) in, 145; discipline problems in, 82-83; and equipment issue, 79-80, 85; George in, 154; Lion and Eagle club, 82; and London office, 74, 75-76, 169; and modernization issue, 96, 161; and Naval Order 2587, 171; Nelles in, 214; NSHQ communication with, 169-70; Price and, 76, 167; RCN at, 73-74; recreational facilities in, 166; and refit situation, 80, 131; seagoing officers and, 211; Simpson's role in, 76; special services officer in, 82; Strange in, 85-86, 130-31; technical liaison officer in, 166; USN withdrawal from, 74, 162. *See also* Simpson, G.W.G. "Shrimp"
Londonderry network: and Admiralty, 145; and chains of command, 145, 170; changes recommended by, 172; and Connolly, 144, 145, 146, 152, 153, 157, 163, 172, 187, 192, 196-97, 210; and financial authority from NSHQ for equipment, 169-70; hyperbole of, 162; impact of, 179; and Macdonald, 145-46, 149, 210; and Nelles, 153, 210; NSHQ and, 144-45, 183; Strange and, 144, 153, 157; and visitors to Londonderry, 154-55

Luftwaffe, 98
Lynx (HMCS), 22, 52-53

Macdonald, Angus L., 13(f), 212(f); accountability of, 198-99; and Adams report, 185-86; and A.D. MacLean (*see* Macdonald, Angus L., and MacLean); and Allied Anti-Submarine Survey Board, 112; and anonymous memos from reserve officers, 29; in Baltimore, 187; and Bidwell memo, 194; blame game of, 188, 189, 198; Cabinet and, 106-7; and Carswell-Rannie investigation, 112; and chain of command, 9, 10; chief staff officer reserves (CSOR) position and, 203, 213; and Combined Committee on Ship Repair Problems, 107-8; Connolly and, 7, 124-25, 151, 152, 179, 182, 184, 192, 198-99, 210, 216-17; Conservative attack on, 63-64; and critical memos, 129-30, 184, 194; death of mother, 53, 54; Deputy Minister's Advisory Committee, 213; Diefenbaker and, 64, 150; and discontent in navy, 135; and equipment issue, 74, 89, 177, 201; and fairmiles, 21-22; flow of information to, 130; and H.C. MacLean, 18; health of, 191; and Howe, 108, 111, 112, 116; hyperbole and, 177; influences on, 5, 190; informants of, 48-49; information hidden from, 40, 103, 176, 179; insecurities of, 40, 134; instructions for more generalized briefings, 194; and interdepartmental approach to refit crisis, 116-17, 140-41, 178-79, 191; interest in naval affairs, 63; Johnstone and, 114-15, 134, 195; Jones and, 124, 125, 127, 151, 182; journalists and, 199; and King, 58, 59, 103, 121, 141, 207, 215; and Labour portfolio, 141; Lay and, 125; and Londonderry network, 145-46, 210; Mansfield and, 98; and ministerial responsibility, 217; and modernization issue, 92, 98-99, 102, 103, 118, 120-21, 129, 130, 133, 143-44, 191, 196; and Munitions and Supply, 137-38, 191; and Naval Board (*see* Macdonald, Angus L., and Naval Board); and Naval Staff, 52, 92, 168, 180, 183, 193, 217; and Nelles (*see* Macdonald, Angus L., and Nelles); networks and, 10, 40-41, 152, 210; and NSHQ, 93, 161, 162; Pennington and,

130; and perceived vs real problems, 65-66; performance of, 190; and *Pictou* refit, 160; Price on, 166; priorities of, 121; Read and, 202; and refit issue, 100, 105, 106-7, 119, 120-21, 133, 139-40, 149, 151, 161, 177, 190, 191; reputation of, 218; resignation threat, 191-92, 198, 207, 217; and Rowland memo, 194; scandal facing, 11, 197, 207, 218; shortcomings of, 217; Simpson and, 67, 77, 128, 146, 164; speech in House of Commons, 60; in St. John's, 52; Strange and, 86, 89, 91, 92, 118, 128-29, 131, 134, 135-36, 143-44; survival of, 198-99, 207; training and, 98; understanding of naval service, 133; vulnerability of, 42, 66, 152, 217-18

Macdonald, Angus L., and MacLean: anonymous memos and, 28-29, 202; *Boating Magazine* and, 51-52, 60; danger to political career, 63; defence against in House of Commons, 56; discrediting of, 58; discrimination against reservists and, 24; fairmiles and, 21-22, 27-28, 51; fear of, 28, 58, 64; and ignoring of criticism, 128; MacLean network and, 16-17; MacLean's apologies to Macdonald, 208-9; MacLean's personal connections and, 26-27, 58, 128-29; opinion of, 58-59, 208-9; and political pressure, 55; private interview between, 24; promotions and, 49-50, 50; refit crisis and, 120-21; and reforms based on MacLean's charges, 47-48, 208-9; and relationship with Nelles, 127; reserve discrimination issue and, 150; sensitivity to naval problems, 65, 128, 209; and shift in Macdonald's attitude toward navy, 61-62

Macdonald, Angus L., and Naval Board: communication with, 130, 146, 149; confidence in, 66; Connolly's reforms and, 46; interdepartmental approach and, 108; at meetings, 62, 107, 113, 121, 133, 134, 135, 143, 144, 174, 191, 194, 195, 201; modernization issue and, 99, 103, 143-44; and Munitions and Supply, 112-13; refit issue and, 139-40; reliance on, 63; reservists on Board and, 43-44

Macdonald, Angus L., and Nelles: communication with, 11, 27, 30, 118-19, 120, 168, 190, 201; critical memos and, 129-30;

equipment issue and, 98-99; firing of, 3, 4; Jones and, 127, 128, 182; link between repairs and modernization, 134; and MacLean issue, 30, 59, 61-62, 127, 128; and modernization issue, 103, 111; Nelles' defence and, 187-88, 189-90, 215; networks and, 40, 152; opinion of, 211; refit issue and, 102, 111, 118-19, 149; relationship with, 66; report on equipment, 135-36; and shortage of repair facilities, 107; Strange and, 92, 93; and technical liaison, 118; and transfer to UK, 97-98

Macdonald, Veronica, 53, 54

MacLean, Andrew Dyas, 23(f); background of, 12-13; bitterness toward navy, 209; and *Boating Magazine*, 22, 51, 54, 55; and Brock, 47; bullying by, 27; career of, 13-14; and chain of command, 18, 21; character of, 28, 29, 64; command of HMCS *Lynx*, 22; Connolly and, 26, 27-29, 45-46, 56-57, 62, 64, 128, 134, 148, 150; Diefenbaker and, 64, 150, 165; discrediting of, 58-59; disregard for orders, 18, 27; ego of, 209; elitism of, 39; and fairmiles, 21, 22, 27-28; "Fairmiles and Foul," 53-54; followers of, 23-24, 57, 60, 64; Hibbard on, 19-20; as informant, 24, 27; on interdepartmental communication, 138; Jones and, 18, 21, 127-28; and J.P. Connolly, 127-28; legacy of, 65; and Macdonald (*see* MacLean, Andrew Dyas, and Macdonald); and Miles, 22, 23; motivations of, 41, 57; Murray and, 36-37; and Naval Board, 43, 44-45, 55, 57, 66; and Naval Information office, 55; Naval Staff and, 61; Nelles and, 17, 28, 42-43, 52, 56, 57, 61, 208, 209; network of, 12, 26, 40, 71-72, 98-99; NSHQ and, 55-56, 57; official opposition and, 60-61; opinions regarding, 52, 57; on "people's navy," 73; performance report, 24; on permanent force discrimination, 23; persecution by navy, 54; personal connections of, 26-27; personality of, 28, 29; personnel file, 51; plan for Sydney fairmile command, 22; political connections of, 28-29, 58; political pressure by, 26, 66; political understanding of, 134; position in navy, 17-18; Powell on, 56; Power and, 54-55; and press, 63; promotion to commander, 29; on promotions,

49-50, 61; prosecution of, 56; public opinion and, 62, 66; in RCAF, 17; reappearances of, 62, 64; reform proposals, 43, 47-48; reforms resulting from charges of, 56, 59, 64; reserve officers' support for, 60; retirement of commission, 29; return to Hugh C. MacLean Publishing, 41; revenge of, 42; Roome on, 59-60; and Royal Navy, 13, 18, 20, 28, 52, 58-59; second attack by, 60, 61; as senior officer fairmiles, 18, 20, 22, 23, 24; stylistic tactics of, 133, 134; threats to go public, 45; *Toronto Star* article about, 19; use of media for own purposes, 19-20; on *York,* 14-15

MacLean, Andrew Dyas, and Macdonald, 29; anonymous memos and, 29; apology to, 208-9; *Boating Magazine* and, 51-52, 60; communication between, 51; and counterattack by Macdonald, 59; Diefenbaker and, 64, 150; fairmiles and, 27-28, 50-51; Macdonald's fear of, 28, 51, 134; Macdonald's opinion of, 58-59; and Macdonald's speech in House of Commons, 60; modernization issue and, 120-21; and Nelles, 127; personal connections and, 26-27; political pressure and, 55; private interview with, 24; reconciliation attempt, 208-9; reserve discrimination issue and, 150; and shift in Macdonald's attitude toward navy, 61-62; speeches in House of Commons, 64; Strange and, 128-29; and truth of MacLean's allegations, 65

MacLean, Hugh C., 12, 17, 18, 43, 47, 60
Maclean, John Bayne, 12
MacTavish, Duncan, 52, 56, 57
Mainguy, E.R. (Rollo), 18-19, 22, 176-77, 216
manpower shortages, 105, 106, 109, 115, 137, 139, 141, 179
Mansfield, J.M., 97, 98
McMullen, M.A., 81
memos, critical. *See* critical memos
merchant marine, 5, 25, 93, 140; losses of ships, 35; protection of, 34; repairs to ships, 100, 111, 142
Mid-Ocean Escort Force, 103-4
Miles, G.R., 22, 23, 24
Mills, Gordon, 106, 179, 199, 200
minesweepers, 20, 34-35; conditions on, 65; modern equipment for, 67; modernization of, 103
Mitchell, Humphrey, 141
Mitchell, Jim, 147, 148, 149, 158
modernization, 9, 67; Admiralty and, 141-42; and Admiralty pressure for more ships, 95; Canadian industry and, 94-95, 100; and chains of command, 80; CNES and, 195-96; and commitment on North Atlantic run, 94; as continual battle, 188; of corvettes, 100; costs, 103, 104; crisis of, 118; critical memos to NSHQ on, 129; frigate building vs, 95; gap between RCN and RN, 71-72, 78, 92, 100, 129, 217; Jones and, 151, 213; Macdonald and, 130, 191; and morale, 78, 82, 143; Naval Board and, 190; Naval Staff and, 104; Nelles and, 33, 111, 120, 189; NSHQ and, 80, 81, 93, 94, 131, 152, 157, 190; political aspects, 128, 189; program of, 95; RCN policy, 79-80; refit issue and, 100-1, 117, 130, 151, 152, 173, 174, 178-79, 195; and RN, 94, 142; and September (1943) U-boat offensive, 174; shipyards and, 95, 178-79; Simpson and, 78-79; and sinking of U-boats, 176; timing of, 173; United States and, 162, 187; Western Approaches command and, 81; withdrawal of ships for, 81, 101. *See also* equipment; refits
modernization issue: Admiralty and, 175; and Assistant Controller, Bath, 175; Connolly and, 148; as crisis, 120-21, 143-44, 213; at Londonderry, 161; Macdonald and, 92, 98-99, 102, 103, 118, 120-21, 129, 133, 143-44, 196; Naval Board and, 94, 96; Naval Staff and, 190; Nelles and, 98-99, 102, 103, 128; NSHQ and, 37, 87, 91, 92, 96, 99, 103-4, 213-14; public knowledge of, 197; RN and, 87; Simpson and, 211; Strange and, 88; training vs, 96
modernization network, 9-10, 12, 78
morale, 31, 211; among reserves, 62; as cause for discontent, 40; and discrimination against reservists, 24, 150; equipment and, 67, 69, 70, 85-86, 92, 152; modernization and, 78, 82, 143; modernization network and, 12; permanent force discrimination and, 165; as political crisis, 67; of regulars, 50; representation

on Naval Board and, 64, 165; of reserve officers, 26, 39; and RN attitude toward Canadians, 10; special service support and, 82, 85-86
Morden (HMCS), 162
Mulock, W.P., 17
Murray, Leonard W.: and Admiralty, 141; and discipline problems, 83; equipment issue and, 82, 175; Horton and, 175, 176; and Jones, 122, 124, 169, 215-16; and modernization issue, 81, 104, 173; and Nelles, 205; and NSHQ, 36-37; on promotions, 36-37; and refits, 114, 115, 116; retirement of, 215-16; and theatre command, 127; and VE day riots in Halifax, 215; and Western Approaches, 175
mutiny, 10, 87

National Selective Service, 108, 140, 179
Naval Board, 9, 40; and British equipment for ships, 96; chief staff officer reserves (CSOR), 202-3, 208; composition of, 59; and Deputy Minister's Advisory Committee, 213; fairmiles and, 47; frigate program, 94; functions of, 43-44; and Johnstone report, 115-17; and Macdonald (*see* Naval Board, and Macdonald); MacLean and, 55, 57, 66; meetings, 111, 113-14, 174; micromanagement by, 110; and modernization issue, 94, 96, 190; and Munitions and Supply, 112; and naval budget, 102-3; and officer promotions, 50; and refits, 105, 139-40, 160, 190; reservists on, 43-45, 47, 51, 54, 59, 64, 150, 165, 203, 208, 213; seagoing reserve officers' bypassing of, 71
Naval Board, and Macdonald, 109; communication between, 130, 146, 149; flow of information between, 40, 130; interdepartmental approach and, 108; Macdonald's confidence in, 66; Macdonald's reliance on, 63; at meetings, 62, 107, 113, 121, 133, 134, 135, 143, 144, 174, 191, 194, 195, 201; modernization issue and, 99, 103, 143-44; and Munitions and Supply, 112-13; refit issue and, 139-40
Naval Council. *See* Naval Board
Naval Order 2587, 102-3, 171
Naval Service Headquarters (NSHQ), 9; administrative meltdown at, 144; and Admiralty, 76, 79, 99, 117, 141, 171-72; allegations against, 184-85; and Allied Anti-Submarine Survey Board report, 109; attitudes toward, 37-38; and British equipment for ships, 96; and captain superintendent of dockyards, 113; and chief staff officer reserves (CSOR) position and, 203, 213; collaborators in, 120; communication with Londonderry, 169-70; complaints handling at, 77, 130; and conditions on escort ships, 65; Conklin and, 159, 172; Connolly and, 89, 161; conspiracies in, 161, 180; cover-ups by, 180, 192; critical memos to, 129-30, 168, 183-84; position, 203; and director of dockyards, 114; and discrimination against reservists, 26; division of loyalties in, 183; and equipment issue, 68, 70, 73, 79, 85, 86, 91, 93, 129, 131, 169-71; and expansion of navy, 109; factionalism at, 121; Horton and, 176; Houghton and, 131; interest in outside advice, 36; Jones and, 212-13; Jones men at, 124; and Londonderry network, 144-45; and *Lynx*, 52-53; Macdonald and, 93, 161, 162; and MacLean, 55-56, 57; and modernization issue, 37, 80, 81, 87, 91, 92, 93, 94, 96, 99, 103-4, 131, 152, 157, 213-14; networks and, 40, 180; Prentice and, 37; Price and, 166, 167-68; and recreational facilities in Londonderry, 166; refits and, 99, 100-1, 104-5, 114, 130, 131, 142, 149, 161, 162-63, 190; remoteness of, 144-45; reorganization of, 109-10, 113, 117-18, 190, 213; reprimand of Murray, 36; reservist representation in, 64; and RN, 163-64; seagoing officers, 211; Simpson and, 76, 79, 158-59, 164, 173; and *Skeena* refit, 161; special committee to co-ordinate refits, 104-5; special services and, 82; strain at, 109; Strange and, 88, 89; training and, 100; vice chief of naval staff position at, 216; visits to, 37-38; Western Approaches and, 171-72; and *Woodstock* refit, 161
Naval Staff, 9, 10, 11, 39; blame for equipment crisis, 188; Connolly and, 184-85, 192, 193; conspiracies of, 186, 189; decentralization of, 110; defence by Nelles, 218; directorates, 110; and discontent, 168; and equipment crisis, 70,

129; Macdonald and, 52, 92, 168, 180, 183, 193, 217; and MacLean, 52, 61; meetings, 101, 183; micromanagement by, 110; and modernization issue, 104, 190; Nelles' praise for, 197-98; and networks, 181; and refit crisis, 183; reorganization of, 195; resistance to charges, 180; restructuring of, 117; and Simpson's letter to Horton, 181-82

Nelles, Percy Walker, 14(f); accused of incompetence, 11; accusers of, 200-1; and Adams, 186; and Admiralty, 96-97, 118; adversaries of, 152; Agnew and, 169; and Allied Anti-Submarine Survey Board, 108, 109; appearance of, 4; and blame for equipment crisis, 188; Brand and, 125, 204-5; in British Columbia, 215; and British request for control of mid-ocean groups, 96-98; Brodeur on movement against, 125; on building warships in Canada, 111; campaign against, 4; Connolly and, 30, 59, 62, 89, 149, 180, 183, 198-99, 208, 217-18; counter-charges by, 187-88; and court martial, 199-200; and Creery, 186; and critical memos, 186, 194; death of, 215; defence of staff, 197-98, 200, 218; and discontent, 168; dismissal of, 3, 4, 9, 118, 119, 129, 144, 180, 199, 206, 208, 215, 217-18; and equipment issue, 73, 93, 177, 188; as flag officer, 199; and Happy day signal, 200; and Hibbard, 186; historians on, 3; Houghton and, 131, 214; integrity of, 218; and Johnstone, 113, 115; Jones and, 109-10, 120, 123-24, 125, 126-27, 151, 182; Lay and, 104, 125; leadership style, 4, 20; in London, 214; in Londonderry, 214; Londonderry network and, 153, 210; and Macdonald (*see* Nelles, Percy Walker, and Macdonald); and MacLean, 12, 17, 28, 29, 42-43, 52, 56, 57, 61, 208, 209; and modernization issue, 33, 98-99, 102, 103, 111, 120, 128, 189; naval career of, 3-4; networks and, 152, 214-15; options for, 199; and Pennington, 214-15; personality, 212; praise for Naval Staff, 197-98; Price and, 167; and refit crisis, 113, 118, 120, 130; regular force officers' network and, 10; regulars vs reservists and, 15; removal as political solution, 11, 207, 211-12, 218; and reorganization of NSHQ, 109-10; on repairs as part of modernization, 133-34; replacement of, 201, 202, 203; reserve networks and, 6; as scapegoat, 199, 215; seagoing reserve officers' bypassing of, 71; self-defence, 180, 187-91, 217; as senior flag officer (O), 206; sharp-end grousers and, 210; on shipyards and shipbuilding, 188; and signals from London, 169; and Simpson, 173, 181-82, 187-88, 189, 200-1; Strange and, 67, 93, 118; on technical liaison with RN, 118; on training, 97, 98; transfer overseas of, 199; "underground movement" against, 5

Nelles, Percy Walker, and Macdonald: communication with, 11, 27, 30, 118-19, 120, 133, 168, 190, 201; critical memos and, 129-30; equipment issue and, 98-99; Jones and, 127, 128, 182; link between repairs and modernization, 134; Macdonald's opinion of, 40, 211; MacLean issue and, 30, 59, 61-62, 127, 128; and modernization issue, 103, 111; and naval transfer to UK, 97-98; networks and, 40, 152, 182, 211, 215; refit issue and, 102, 111, 118-19, 149; relationship with, 66; report on equipment and, 135-36; self-defence, 187-88, 189-90, 215; shortage of repair facilities and, 107; Strange and, 92, 93; and technical liaison, 118

networks, 6-7, 9-11; and chain of command, 9, 11; and Connolly, 7, 9, 180, 184, 186-87, 210, 217; hyperbole of, 10; Jones and, 212; legitimacy of grievances, 40; and Macdonald, 9, 11, 40-41, 152, 210; manipulation of political process, 11; Naval Staff and, 181; and Nelles, 9, 152, 214-15; and NSHQ, 40, 180; permanent force professionals vs, 210-11; personal connections of, 10; power of, 9, 144; Simpson and, 77; and social elite, 10. *See also names of individual networks*

New Liskeard (HMCS), 65(f)

Newfoundland: COAC and, 117-18. *See also* Combined Committee on Ship Repair Problems; St. John's

Niobe (HMCS), 167

No Higher Purpose, 3

Noble, Percy, 106

North Africa: invasion of, 38; landings, 97; routes, 98

O'Brien, Barry, 32, 34, 38, 146-47, 148, 149, 150, 203, 204(f)
O'Brien, Gerald, 149
O'Brien, John Ambrose, 32, 149
official opposition and MacLean issue, 26, 42, 54, 59, 60-61. *See also* Conservative Party of Canada
oil crisis, 96, 97, 98
Operation Torch, 97
Orillia (HMCS), 147, 149, 155-57
outports, 108, 109, 113, 118

Paterson, John, 105-6
Pennington, R.A., 110, 130, 214-15
permanent force, 5, 6; adaptation to needs of citizen sailors, 25; animosities among, 121-22; attitude toward reservists, 12, 15-16, 24; attitude toward volunteers, 26; careerism by, 10; and chains of command, 90; challenge by elitist elements within reserves, 40-41; discrimination against reservists, 10, 23, 28, 29, 39, 42, 54, 121, 149, 150-51, 165, 197, 202, 213; elitism of, 15-16; leadership abilities, 16; and merchant navy, 25; morale of, 50; network, 10; numbers of officers, 48, 49; numbers of promotions vs reserves, 48; and officer selection board, 150; power of, 26; reserve networks vs, 5-6, 16, 210-11; use of seniority by, 16
Pictou (HMCS), 160
Piers, Desmond "Debby," 68, 70, 71, 75, 79, 80
Pigott, J.J., 153, 154, 161, 162, 187
Pound, Dudley, 176
Powell, R.M., 56, 57
Power, Charles Gavin "Chubby," 54-55, 121
Prentice, J.D., 37
Price, Fred, 214; and Admiralty, 76; and channels of communication, 79; Connolly and, 164, 165-70, 183, 215; and discrimination against reservists, 165, 166; and equipment issue, 168-69; and Gilhooly, 165; and Londonderry base, 76, 167, 168; and Macdonald, 166; and modernization issue, 175; and NSHQ, 166-68; responsibilities of, 76; Simpson and, 76, 79, 82; and special services, 82, 165; and technical liaison, 166-67
professionalism, 6, 7, 211

promotion(s): acceleration of, 46-47; automatic, 50; based on merit vs seniority, 49; MacLean and, 29, 61; Price on, 165; of RCNVR vs RCNR officers, 50; of regulars vs reservists, 48-49; reorganization of board, 47; reserve force and, 165; of reserve officers, 24-25, 43, 45, 46-47; and sea vs shore issue, 36
Pugsley, William, 49, 57

Quebec Chronicle-Telegraph, 63

radar, 34-35, 95; RXU, 178, 200; SW2C, 33; type 271, 33, 68, 86, 95, 100, 104, 135, 160, 178, 200
Ralston, J.L., 58
Rannie, John, 112-13, 137-40, 141, 142
RCN (Royal Canadian Navy): Admiralty attitude toward, 72; as amateurs, 67; budget for, 102-3; communication with Munitions and Supply, 111-12; efficiency of, 53, 56, 84, 96, 98; equipment gap with RN, 69-70, 78, 92, 94, 95, 100, 129, 168, 175; equity among three branches, 25, 41, 43, 46-47, 48; expansion of, 4, 34-35, 92, 110, 178, 189; and interwar years, 15; kill ratio of, 72, 84, 94; leadership of, 121-22; life at sea, 35-36; at Londonderry, 73-74; MacLean's article and, 62; modernization of, 33, 71-72 (*see also* modernization); numbers of officers, 48; as outdated, 68; Pacific theatre policy, 215; refits of, 108, 131 (*see also* refits); reforms, 42, 46; relations with RN, 72-73, 74, 80, 87-89, 96; secondary figures in history of, 4-5; shore-orientated organization of, 36; stripes of, 7, 25; technical liaison with RN, 166; three branches of, 5-6, 24
RCNR (Royal Canadian Naval Reserve), 5; numbers of officers from, 48; on promotion of RCNVR officers, 50
RCNVR (Royal Canadian Naval Volunteer Reserve), 5, 73; and MacLean's allegations, 57; numbers of officers from, 48; promotions and, 46; RCNR reaction to promotions, 50
Read, Horace, 202
recreational facilities, 39, 81-82
refits, 100; Admiralty and, 99, 101, 142, 143, 163; Allied Anti-Submarine Survey

Board visits to facilities, 111; Cabinet authorization for, 106-7; Carswell on, 140; code words for, 147; under commodore superintendent, 117; as crisis, 109, 110-11, 113-14, 127, 191; of *Drumheller*, 160; on East Coast, 101, 172, 194; emergency repairs and, 100; to escort vs merchant ships, 111; facilities for, 99, 101-2; Hibbard on, 178; HMC Dockyard and, 113, 139; impact on RCN, 131; infrastructure for, 188; interdepartmental approach to, 115-16, 140, 179, 191; interdepartmental committee, 115-16; interdepartmental politics and, 140; labour shortage for, 115, 141; Macdonald and, 100, 105, 106-7, 119, 120-21, 133, 139-40, 149, 151, 161, 177, 190, 191; modernization and, 117, 130, 151, 152, 173, 174, 178-79, 195; Munitions and Supply and, 113, 115, 138; Murray and, 116; Naval Board and, 105, 139-40, 160, 190; Nelles and, 120, 130, 190; new schedule for, 143, 172-73; NSHQ and, 99, 100-1, 104-5, 114, 130, 131, 142, 149, 161, 190; opportunities in Londonderry, 79-80, 85; payment for, 80, 102; of *Pictou*, 160; policy for, 162-63; RN and, 101-2, 191; schedules, 172-73; shipbuilding and, 111; and shipyards, 108, 188; and shortage of escort vessels, 142; "situation," 100-3; of *Skeena*, 160-61; in UK, 101-2, 106; in United States, 106; and US Navy, 143, 162, 163, 178; of *Woodstock*, 161. *See also* equipment; modernization
regular force. *See* permanent force
Regulation Revision Committee, 202
Reid, H.E., 32, 68, 83, 151-52, 205
repairs, 178; emergency, 100; to merchant ships, 100, 111, 142; and modernization, 133-34; at St. John's, 106
Reports of Proceedings, 69
reserve force: disbandment of branches, 43; as "people's navy," 73; reorganization of divisions, 47
reserve networks: and Connolly, 7, 9, 27; demand for professional respect, 5-6; social status and, 16
reservists, 6; adjustment to RCN, 40-41; anonymous letters re treatment by regulars, 24-26, 27, 29; appointment to promotion and honours boards, 43; attitude of regulars toward, 15-16, 24, 26; backgrounds of, 7, 10; behaviour of, 31; and breakdowns in chains of command, 77; direct contact with Macdonald by, 73; discontent among, 10-11, 42, 78; discrimination against, 23, 24-25, 28, 29, 39, 42, 45, 54, 121, 149, 150-51, 165, 197, 202, 213; equality with regulars, 11, 12; grouses of, 25-26; influx into RCN, 5; later careers of, 216; MacLean and, 60, 65; manning of escort ships, 7; modernization and, 12; morale of, 24, 26, 39, 62; on Naval Board, 43-45, 47, 51, 59, 64, 165; in NSHQ, 64; opinions regarding, 6; performance of same tasks as regulars, 6; performance reports on, 28; personal perceptions/experiences of, 63; political connections of, 74, 87; professionalism of, 7; promotions of, 24-25, 43, 45, 46-47, 50, 165; ranks and positions of, 16; reverse discrimination for, 49; and RN, 43, 73; segregation of, 7; Simpson on, 78; from social elite, 10; as special class, 44; stripes of, 7; *Toronto Star* article about, 19; training of, 16; and US Navy, 73-74
Restigouche (HMCS), 68
Riddiford, W.J., 167
Rimouski (HMCS), 164
Robertson, Norman, 107
Roome, G.L., 59-60
Rosthern (HMCS), 150
Rowland, J.M.: and channels of communication, 71; and Connolly, 151-52; critical memo from, 67-68, 70, 71, 171, 194; and equipment issue, 67-68, 70; and Gretton, 84; and recreation facilities, 83; and refit issue, 80; and Simpson, 80; and Strange, 85, 211
Royal Australian Navy (RAN), 142-43
Royal Canadian Air Force (RCAF), 17, 43, 214
Royal Navy (RN): admiral commanding reserves, 165; attitude toward Canadians, 10, 72, 80, 87-88; Canadian equipment for, 164; control of mid-ocean groups by, 96; and convoys, 93-94; destruction of U-boats, 72; efficiency of, 84; equipment data in, 135; equipment gap with RCN, 68, 69-70, 78, 92, 94, 95, 100, 129, 168, 175; during First World War, 13, 18; and

Londonderry base, 145; MacLean and, 13, 18, 20, 28, 52, 58-59; modernization and, 71-72, 87, 94, 142; new equipment in, 117; NSHQ attitude toward, 163-64; refits by, 101-2, 181-82, 191; relations with RCN, 72-73, 74, 87-89, 96, 166; reserve officers in, 43; retired captains in NSHQ, 48; Strange in, 90; technical liaison, 166, 167; training by, 73, 96, 100; upgrading of corvettes, 168; and US jurisdiction over RCN in Londonderry, 74

Royal Naval College of Canada, 15, 16, 122

Saskatchewan (HMCS), 212(f)
Saskatoon (HMCS), 99
seagoing officers: attitudes of, 68; contacting Macdonald directly, 70; Londonderry and, 211; and NSHQ, 211; political connections of, 92; rebellion over equipment, 67, 167; taking concerns to Macdonald, 71
seniority, 16, 45; experience vs, 43
sharp-end grousers, 48, 63, 129, 131, 145, 170, 179, 207, 210
Shedden, W.G., 38-39
Shelburne, 31, 105, 114
shipbuilding, 173; Nelles on, 188; program, 20, 173; and refit crisis, 111
shipyards: Allied Anti-Submarine Survey Board report on, 109; American, 101-2; British, 101-2, 172, 173-74, 191; captain superintendent of, 113-14; director of, 114; dry docks, 108; East Coast, 100, 101, 104, 105-6, 190; expansion of, 104, 105, 109, 141, 172, 178-79, 195; inefficiency of, 109; labour shortages in, 115, 140, 173-74; modernization and, 178-79; Nelles on, 188; private, 107, 108, 110-11, 113; refits and, 100, 101, 108; reorganization of, 114; survey of, 105-6
shore personnel, seagoing vs, 35-36, 37
Shorto, R.R., 86-87, 89, 153, 159, 161, 162, 169, 170, 187
signals, regularity of, 169
Simpson, G.W.G. "Shrimp," 67, 76, 94, 95; accessibility of, 77-78; and Audette, 91; and British equipment in Londonderry, 96; and captain (D) in Londonderry, 145; and chains of command, 67, 77, 79, 82, 90-91, 92, 211; and Conklin, 162; and Connolly, 67, 91, 92, 146, 153-54, 158-59, 164, 185-86, 187; and Copelin, 153-54, 174-75; on equipment, 164; George and, 154; and Horton, 164, 172-73, 180-81; hyperbole of, 87; later career of, 216; and Macdonald, 67, 77, 146, 164, 211; and modernization issue, 78-79, 92; on morale, 92; on Naval Staff, 173; Nelles and, 90, 189, 200-1; and networks, 77, 128; and NSHQ, 79, 158-59, 164, 173; and Piers, 80; on political interference, 67, 91, 92; politically connected reserve officers and, 87; Price and, 79, 167; qualities of, 74-75, 76-77; on RCN sailors, 67, 82, 158; on refits, 163-64; reorganization of Londonderry base, 74; on reservists, 78; and Rowland, 80; and *Skeena* refit, 160-61; Strange and, 83, 85-86, 87, 88, 90-91, 92, 146, 153, 158. *See also* Londonderry base

Skeena (HMCS), 160-61
Snowberry (HMCS), 150, 204(f)
sonar. *See* asdic
special service support, 82, 130-31, 211; equipment issue and, 85-86; morale and, 85-86; Price and, 165-66
St. John's: Allied Anti-Submarine Survey Board visit to, 108, 109; Connolly in, 148, 149-52; discipline problems in, 82-83; expansion of base at, 106-7; fairmiles based at, 22; network in, 32, 39, 40; and refit situation, 131; reserve informants in, 31; running repairs at, 106; Strange and, 84; welfare grouses in, 82-83. *See also* Newfoundland; Rowland, J.M.
St. Lawrence River, 22
Stephens, G.L., 101, 103, 106, 111, 113, 114, 117, 181-82
Steward, Kenneth, 206
Strange, A.B., 23(f)
Strange, William: and Adams, 88, 132-33, 151, 186; as assistant naval information officer, 83; career of, 83; and Carswell and Rannie reports, 140; and chains of command, 84, 89, 90-91; and Connolly, 86-87, 89, 132, 134, 144, 146, 147, 187, 211; and equipment issue, 83-88; George and, 155; and Gretton, 84-85; Houghton and, 83, 85, 130-31, 132, 214; later career of, 216; on Londonderry, 131; and Londonderry

network, 144, 157, 211; and Macdonald, 86, 89, 91, 92, 128-29, 134, 135-36; modernization issue and, 88; Nelles and, 67, 89-90, 93; NSHQ and, 88, 89; personal ambition of, 89; political interference by, 91-92; political understanding of, 134; and politically connected reserve officers, 87; report of, 93, 118, 134, 135-36, 143-44; and RN, 90; and Shorto, 86-87; Simpson and, 67, 83, 85-86, 87, 88, 90-91, 92, 146, 153, 158; and special service support in Londonderry, 83; stylistic tactics of, 133, 134; and welfare question, 130-31

submarines. *See* U-boats

Summerside (HMCS), 72

Survey Board. *See* Allied Anti-Submarine Survey Board

Sydney, 22, 105, 114

Taylor, C.R.H., 140

technical officers, 118

theatre command, 127

training, 6, 35, 62, 127; British facilities for, 97; education vs, 16, 39-40; and efficiency of RCN, 84, 98; Macdonald and, 98; modernization issue vs, 96; Nelles on, 97, 98; NSHQ and, 100; of reserve officers, 16; RN and, 73, 96, 100

Trillium (HMCS), 32

Tucker, Gilbert Norman, 9, 68

U-boats: asdic and, 69(f); destruction of, 34; escort vessels and, 93, 173, 174; hunting/sinking of, 35, 72, 84-85, 93, 94, 176; merchant vessels and, 93; refits and, 102; reservists and, 25; Type IXC, 21(f); U-456, 72; U-536, 204(f); U-744, 185(f); U-889, 21(f)

United Shipyards, 112

United States Navy: Atlantic obligations of, 94; Australian Navy and, 143; commander of task group (CTG) 24.7, 73-74; in Londonderry, 162, 163; in Pacific theatre, 94; refits and, 106, 143, 163, 178, 187; repair yards, 159; reservists and, 73-74; U-boats and, 99

welfare question. *See* special service support

Western Approaches Command, 9, 94; Headquarters, Liverpool, 72; and Naval Order 2587, 171; and RCN, 98, 173, 174

Western Local Escort Force, 97, 104

Woodstock (HMCS), 161

Worth, "Sam," 200, 201

Wright, H.H., 167, 168

YMCA, 82

York (HMCS), 14-15, 39

Printed and bound in Canada by Friesens

Set in Minion and Helvetica Condensed by Artegraphica Design Co. Ltd.

Copy editor: Andy Carroll

Proofreader: Gail Copeland

Indexer: Noeline Bridge